THE SLAUGHTERHOUSE CASES

The Crescent City Company's abattoir and stockyard as depicted in an 1875 report to the board of health. (John P. Ische Library, LSU Health Sciences Center, New Orleans.)

THE
SLAUGHTERHOUSE
CASES

Regulation, Reconstruction, and the Fourteenth Amendment

Ronald M. Labbé
Jonathan Lurie

University Press of Kansas

Published by the University Press of Kansas (Lawrence, Kansas 66049),
which was organized by the Kansas Board of Regents and is operated and
funded by Emporia State University, Fort Hays State University,
Kansas State University, Pittsburg State University, the University of Kansas,
and Wichita State University

Library of Congress Cataloging-in-Publication Data
Labbé, Ronald M., 1933–
The slaughterhouse cases : regulation, reconstruction, and the
Fourteenth Amendment / Ronald M. Labbé, Jonathan Lurie.
    p.   cm.
Includes bibliographical references and index.
ISBN 0-7006-1290-4 (cloth : alk. paper)
1. Slaughtering and slaughter-houses—Law and
legislation—Louisiana—History—19th century. 2. Civil rights—United
States—History—19th century. 3. Monopolies—United
States—History—19th century. I. Lurie, Jonathan, 1939– II. Title.
KF228.S545L33 2003
342.73'042—dc22 2003015864

British Library Cataloguing-in-Publication Data is available.
Printed in the United States of America

10 9 8 7 6 5 4 3 2 1

The paper used in this publication meets the minimum requirements
of the American National Standard for Permanence of Paper
for Printed Library Materials z39.48-1984.

For Dolores and Mac—

Whose toleration was unending,
Whose perception was appreciated, and
Whose encouragement was vital.

The Law . . . cannot be dealt with as
if it contained only the axioms
and corollaries of a book of
mathematics. In order to know what
it is, we must know what it has
been, and what it tends to become.

—Holmes, "The Common Law"

It is carrying fiction too far to say that the
Courts must always know how the law will be.

—Lord Abbinger

CONTENTS

ILLUSTRATIONS

ACKNOWLEDGMENTS

This book on the *Slaughterhouse Cases* was suggested to one of us by Professor David Fellman during a summer seminar sponsored by the National Endowment for the Humanities at the University of Wisconsin in 1975. By coincidence, that same year, Professor Harold Hyman suggested the identical project to the other one. Scholars and gentlemen both, these two professors and their enthusiasm for the study served as a source of motivation for what follows.

In the years since, quite a few debts have been accumulated. This research could not have been accomplished without the aid of several grants from the National Endowment for the Humanities, a grant from the American Philosophical Society, several research awards from the University of Louisiana at Lafayette, and grants from the Rutgers University Research Council. Special thanks are due to the donors and administrators of the Bernard and Kaye L. Crocker Professorship of Political Science at the University of Louisiana at Lafayette.

We are particularly grateful to a number of individuals, among them Jean Kiesel and Alvin Bethard, directors of the Louisiana and Microform Collections, respectively, at the Dupré Library at the University of Louisiana at Lafayette, and Susan Daigle and her staff at the university's Department of Printing Services; Leon C. Miller, Joan G. Caldwell, Kenneth Owen, and other members of the staff in the Special Collections Division of Tulane's Howard-Tilton Memorial Library; David Combe, director of Tulane's law library; Patsy Copeland, the very helpful gatekeeper of the historical collection at Tulane's Rudolph Matas Medical Library; Collin B. Hamer Jr. and Wayne Everard in the research gold mine that is the Louisiana Division of the New Orleans Public Library; Sally S. Stassi at the Williams Research Center of the Historic New Orleans Collection; Wilba Swearingen and Pauline Fulda at the library of the Louisiana State University Health Sciences Center in New Orleans; Sally K. Reeves and Ann Wakefield at the New Orleans Notarial Archives; Kathryn Page, curator at the Louisiana State Museum library; and the incomparable and ever-encouraging Marie Windell at the Supreme Court's archives at the Earl K. Long Library at the University of New Orleans. We also acknowledge the kind cooperation of the U.S. Supreme Court Historical Society.

The late Judge Albert Tate Jr. of the U.S. Court of Appeals for the Fifth Circuit was a scholar in his own right and a warm friend to this project in its early stages. We have enjoyed the open-door policies of all the libraries just mentioned and of several others, including the library at the Paul M. Hebert Law Center and the Louisiana Collection of the Middleton Library at Louisiana State University in Baton Rouge; the Louisiana Supreme Court's Law Library of Louisiana; both the main library and the Moritz Law Library at the Ohio State University; the Library of Congress and its legal division; the Southern Historical Collection at the University of North Carolina library; and the Barker Texas History Center, University of Texas.

Special mention needs to be made of the assistance given by friends and colleagues at the University of Louisiana. Mathé Allain in the Department of Modern Languages never failed to provide encouragement during all the years it took to complete this book. And whether as department heads or friends, Donn M. Kurtz II, Janet E. Frantz, and Thomas Ferrell in the Department of Political Science provided support by every means available to them. We are deeply indebted to Michael Briggs, editor in chief of the University Press of Kansas, for his persistent inquiries about the state of our manuscript and for his very bright idea of bringing the two of us together. We are also grateful to Paul Kens and Phillip Paludan for their careful examination of our manuscript.

Again, we thank our wives, Dolores Egger Labbé and Maxine N. Lurie. Scholars in their own right, they deserve more credit than can be stated here. Finally, we would like to acknowledge our debt to each other. This work is the result of a close collaboration that took place over six years, with never a quibble. "What, *never?*"

"Well, hardly ever."

1

Beef from the Pork Barrel?
Introduction and Overview

Y ou never know. Historical events intended for one purpose sometimes
result in the unintended, and American history is not immune from
this tendency. Thus the Civil War—first considered by Lincoln as nothing
more than an attempt to prevent Southern secession—ultimately went far
beyond an effort to preserve the Union, far beyond ending American Negro
slavery, far beyond even ensuring continued western expansion. By 1866,
the war had wrought changes in the relationship between the federal government and the states, the federal government and its people, as well as the
states and their citizenry. Although they may well have been unintended
and their extent unclear, these transformations doomed continuance of the
Union as it had been—producing instead a new connection between the
American people and their legal order that is still evolving.[1] One manifesta-
tion of such change was the Fourteenth Amendment, adopted by Congress
in 1866 and ratified by the states as part of the Constitution in 1868. Five
years later, the Supreme Court first considered its meaning and scope; and
there lies a story rich in irony.

INTENDED TO FACILITATE a changed relationship between the ex-slave and
white America, the new amendment was first presented to the Court on
behalf of some white butchers arguing with other white butchers and livestock dealers over a Louisiana statute enacted in 1869. Their lawyer—a
former Supreme Court justice who had resigned his seat when his state
(Alabama) seceded—now called for a new level of federal supremacy and

---

1. "I claim not to have controlled events," wrote Lincoln in 1864, "but confess plainly
that events have controlled me." In 1864, "the nation's condition is not what either party,
or any man, devised or expected." *Collected Works*, ed. Roy P. Basler, vol. 5 (New Brunswick, N.J.: Rutgers University Press, 1953–1955), 338. See also Jonathan Lurie, *Law and the
Nation* (New York: Alfred A. Knopf, 1983), 3.

state subordination diametrically opposed to both his own long-held views and past American history. Finally, the high court, whose function was and remains the reconciliation of law with ongoing change, could not agree on the extent of constitutional alteration mandated by the amendment.

In this the justices were not alone. Uncertainty as to what the new provision meant, its application and scope, characterized both congressional debates and contemporary commentary. In April 1873, by a five-to-four vote, the Court first interpreted the Fourteenth Amendment and offered its own assessment—one that remains a landmark in American legal history. Speaking for a five-member majority, Justice Samuel F. Miller sustained the Louisiana statute regulating slaughterhouses and held that with the exception of the ex-slave, the new addition to the Constitution had not altered in any significant fashion the traditional pattern of federalism. Although at least two later members of his Court endorsed this analysis, more frequently Miller's opinion has been rebutted, denounced, and condemned, almost from its announcement.

Indeed, a cacophony of criticism has enveloped his decision for more than a century. A recent comment by the late Yale law professor Charles Black is typical. Miller's opinion, he wrote, "is probably the worst holding, in its effect on human rights, ever uttered by the Supreme Court."[2] According to Lawrence Tribe, "there is considerable consensus among constitutional thinkers that the Supreme Court made a scandalously wrong decision in this case."[3] Yet Miller's decision has not been overruled. Moreover, it did not prevent his Court, sometimes with his concurrence, from finding awesome breadth and depth in the amendment—a process that accelerated after his death and especially during the mid and late twentieth century.

Given such criticism for so long, why has the Court retained *Slaughterhouse?* Why this veneration for stare decisis in the face of sustained denunciation? We know that when it so desires, the Court can overrule itself, sometimes within a brief span of years. The *Legal Tender Cases, Betts v. Brady,* or *Brown v. Board of Education* immediately come to mind, and more recent examples can readily be cited. Perhaps one answer is simply that the justices, for whatever reason, do not wish to overrule the 1873 holding. And here again, we may ask, why? A possible answer may be found in careful reexamination of (1) the background of the case, (2) the context in which it

2. Quoted by Lawrence Tribe in "Pursuing the Pursuit of Happiness," review of *A New Birth of Freedom: Human Rights, Named and Unnamed,* by Charles Black, *New York Review of Books,* September 24, 1998, 34.
3. Ibid., 30.

arose, (3) exactly what Miller's majority believed it had decided, and (4) what the dissenters insisted were the real issues involved in the litigation.

In trying to explain what the litigation meant to the Court in 1872–1873, some legal scholars have focused on several alleged flaws in Miller's opinion. Writing in the context of the Fourteenth Amendment that they now know, and with what they consider clear evidence of its intent, it is viewed as a virile source of what seems to be almost unlimited federal authority. Seen in the light of this seemingly filiopietistic veneration of the Fourteenth Amendment, of course Miller's narrow holding would appear misguided, if not malevolent. Further, when one places the case in the context of a Reconstruction history that emphasizes the negative aspects of that era, it becomes easy to dismiss the statute involved in the litigation as a product of a corrupt, reconstructed Louisiana legislature. Finally, when we add an interpretation that focuses on the intentions of the amendment's framers— one that emphasizes the clarity and breadth of their vision—besides these other flaws, Miller's opinion appears to defy the clear mandate of the national legislature.

Here, in short, is a modern Whiggish historical interpretation of *Slaughterhouse*, seen—as with most Whig history—through the eyes of the present rather than of the applicable era.[4] Does it represent an adequate and accurate evaluation of the case? Some recent scholarship indicates that it does not, and although in any five-to-four decision debate and disagreement are inevitable, it may be appropriate to reexamine the case, especially Miller's opinion.[5] Too often it has been cited rather than studied. For reasons

4. See Herbert Butterfield's classic study *The Whig Interpretation of History* (London: G. Bell and Sons, 1951). Real historical understanding, he notes, "is not achieved by the subordination of the past to the present, but rather by our making the past our present and attempting to see life with the eyes of another century other than our own." Ibid., 16.

5. See in particular the work of Patrick Ballard, whose unpublished paper for Professor William Ross's History of Constitutional Law Seminar (Samford University Law School, 1995) "Strangled in the Crib? Or Proper Limitations? Another Look at the Slaughterhouse Cases" was made available to us by Professor Ross; Herbert Hovenkamp, *Enterprise and American Law 1836–1937* (Cambridge: Harvard University Press, 1991); Ronald M. Labbé, "New Light on the Slaughterhouse Monopoly Act of 1869," in *Louisiana's Legal Heritage*, ed. Edward F. Haas (New Orleans: Louisiana State Museum, 1983), 143–61; William J. Novak, *The People's Welfare: Law and Regulation in Nineteenth Century America* (Chapel Hill: University of North Carolina Press, 1996); Wendy E. Parmet, "From Slaughterhouse to Lochner: The Rise and Fall of the Constitutionalization of Public Health," *American Journal of Legal History* 40 (1996): 476–505; Michael A. Ross, "Justice Miller's Reconstruction: The Slaughterhouse Cases, Health Codes, and Civil Rights in New Orleans, 1861–1873," *Journal of Southern History* 64 (1998): 649–76.

that follow, this study looks anew at *Slaughterhouse,* including what seems to have become the standard negative interpretation. The purpose of our book, however, is one of reinterpretation rather than refutation. Given the varied ways in which the Fourteenth Amendment was perceived, the lack of certainty as to its intent, the existing tradition of federalism, the potency of the police power as a constitutional doctrine, and the unusual background of sanitation reform efforts in New Orleans, it is far from clear that in 1873 Miller's opinion was "scandalously wrong."

TURNING FIRST to the question of legislative intent and the Fourteenth Amendment, its adoption *must* be seen in the context of federalism and the police power as understood during the mid-nineteenth century. Moreover, the conservative nature of the new enactment—specifically Section 1— should be noted. The terms *equality, freedom,* and *civil rights* do not appear; nor is there any hint of suffrage for the ex-slave. Scholarly emphasis on its conservative character is not new. More than twenty-five years ago, Michael Les Benedict pointed out that the amendment's framers intentionally left most Southern rebels with the vote and Southern blacks without it.[6] He argues that the amendment "in no way challenged the tradition that states had primary jurisdiction over citizens in matters of police regulation, the regulation of conduct for the protection of the community."[7]

More recently, William Nelson concluded that "confusion and contradiction abound" concerning the Fourteenth Amendment's adoption.[8] He infers, however, that the new enactment had meaning for its proponents. Nelson may well be correct, but we would caution that it had a number of meanings. Various senators and congressmen could support the same amendment, but for different reasons and with different expectations. Nel-

6. Michael Les Benedict, *A Compromise of Principle: Congressional Republicans and Reconstruction* (New York: W.W. Norton, 1974), 170, 186. The Republican party in 1866 has been accurately described as "radical in sentiments but exceedingly conservative in actions." Ibid., 48.

7. Ibid., 170. Facing important elections in 1866, the Republicans "had eschewed ideology in favor of practicality." Ibid., 182. But what was practical also had to be practicable.

8. William Nelson, *The Fourteenth Amendment: From Political Principle to Judicial Doctrine* (Cambridge: Harvard University Press, 1988), 4. Nelson sees its enactment as an effort to resolve the tension between equality and individualism, as well as between federalism and majoritarianism. The method was to employ vague language, leaving the precise accommodation between these principles to be resolved at a later time and by different participants. The framers, Nelson implies, dealt with conflict not by resolving it but by bequeathing it to the future.

son notes further that the Republicans remained committed both to completing the unfinished wartime work of emancipation and to retaining the "traditional values of federalism." The new provision may well be seen as satisfying both commitments. He writes that its framers sought to reaffirm a long-standing "commitment to general principles of equality, individual rights, and local self rule."[9]

Nelson insists that the amendment "simply fails to specify the particular rights to which it applies." Also, any implied distinction between absolute rights and equality of rights remains unclear, as is the difference between an absolute right and its regulation. "Every lawyer," according to the conservative Republican senator George Edmunds, knows that "it is one thing to have a right which is absolute and unalienable, and it is quite another thing for the body of the community to regulate . . . the exercise of that right."[10]

Finally, Nelson emphasizes how quick the Republicans were to reject the claim that their amendment "would give Congress power to legislate about matters previously reserved to the states and thereby result in a consolidation of power and the destruction of the federal system as America had known it." John Bingham, the primary author of Section 1 and a speaker not always distinguished for his clearness of thought, had no difficulty making this point. His wording, he insisted, "took from no State any right that ever pertained to it."[11]

A search of the congressional debates for insights concerning the scope of Section 1 leaves us with ambiguity and uncertainty. A variety of views concerning its intended coverage were offered, but the words employed "made so many promises to so many persons."[12] Contrary to the positions taken by Michael Curtis and Akhil Reed Amar, it can be argued that in the absence of more specific wording in the amendment, a measure of diffidence is in order when drawing conclusions concerning its scope.[13] For our purposes, the most important point is that when the Court interpreted the new amendment, Miller could have reasonably concluded that the congressional debates furnished no

9. Ibid., 7–8. One can argue that such is exactly what Miller attempted to do in *Slaughterhouse*. His decision emphasized not only that all who wished to butcher could do so but also that legislative authority (home rule and the police power) remained inviolate.

10. Ibid., 120. Edmunds's point has relevance for Miller's opinion in *Slaughterhouse*.

11. Ibid., 115.

12. Mark DeWolfe Howe, "Federalism and Civil Rights" (pamphlet of lecture delivered November 19, 1965, Massachusetts Historical Society), 26.

13. See, e.g., Akhil Reed Amar, *The Bill of Rights: Creation and Reconstruction* (New Haven, Conn.: Yale University Press, 1998); Michael K. Curtis, *No State Shall Abridge: The Fourteenth Amendment and the Bill of Rights* (Durham, N.C.: Duke University Press, 1986).

clear guidance as to intent in general and certainly no specific mandate that federalism was to undergo a major transformation. Leonard Levy reminds us that "whatever the [amendment's] framers . . . intended, they did not possess ultimate wisdom as to the precise meaning of their words."[14]

BESIDES THE INTENTIONS of the Fourteenth Amendment's framers, attention must also be focused on the historical and political context in which the 1869 Louisiana statute was adopted. There can be no doubt that for New Orleans in particular, the slaughtering of cattle and hogs represented a long-standing health problem of impressive dimensions. For more than sixty years, the controversy over it had festered, and the search for a solution presented an ongoing challenge to effective public policy. Time and again, attention had been called to the appalling state of public health in the Crescent City.

As will be seen in the chapters that follow, efforts by city officials to remove slaughtering operations from the city date from 1804. They had virtually no effect, however, because as the city grew, so did the number and political strength of the butchers and stock dealers. By the Civil War era, more than 300,000 animals were slaughtered within New Orleans and adjacent Jefferson City each year. New Orleans lacked a public sewer system; therefore, wastes were either dumped in uninhabited areas of the city, such as the broad levee of the Mississippi River, or simply emptied into open gutters, as was the practice of the large hotels. Similarly, the offal from the slaughterhouses was thrown either into the river or onto city streets. The humidity and swampy environment of New Orleans contributed to these deplorable conditions. Leading physicians branded it the dirtiest and most unhealthy city in the country.

Local studies showed that New Orleans had a staggering death rate. This was partly explained by major epidemics of cholera and yellow fever that repeatedly hit the Crescent City. The yellow fever epidemic of 1853, for example, decimated the population in a single summer. Two years before the statute at issue in *Slaughterhouse* was enacted, a legislative committee received a graphic description of the link between the slaughterhouses and public health. "Barrels filled with entrails, liver, blood, urine, dung, and other refuse portions in an advanced stage of decomposition, are constantly

14. As quoted in Ted Tunnel, review of *No Easy Walk to Freedom: Reconstruction and the Fourteenth Amendment* by Leonard Levy, *American Historical Review* 103 (1998): 1327.

BEEVES—SLAUGHTERHOUSE.

CALVES—SLAUGHTERHOUSE.

HOGS—SLAUGHTERHOUSE.

SHEEP—SLAUGHTERHOUSE.

Slaughterhouse operations. These four woodcuts were used to illustrate a special report on slaughterhouses contained in an 1875 report of the board of health. (John P. Ische Library, LSU Health Sciences Center, New Orleans.)

being thrown into the river . . . poisoning the air with offensive smells and necessarily contaminating the water near the bank for miles."[15]

It is certain, then, that the regulation of slaughterhouses had concerned New Orleans long before 1869, as the following chapters explore in some detail. But the statute at issue must be seen in another context, besides the

15. Testimony of Dr. E. S. Lewis in Louisiana House of Representatives, Special Committee on the Removal of Slaughterhouses, *Minute Book* (1867), Louisiana Collection, LSU Libraries, Louisiana State University.

matter of public health, for it was the controversial product of a controversial legislature. In 1868, under federal protection, a convention created a new constitution for Louisiana. It "was the first major elective body in southern history dominated by a black majority."[16] The new charter contained a remarkable embodiment of Reconstruction goals. It "had provisions for universal desegregated education, a prohibition of racial discrimination in public places, and severe disfranchisement of 'disloyal' voters."[17] The new document outlawed the black codes, and it was the first Louisiana constitution to contain a bill of rights. In certain aspects, later constitutions were modeled after it.

The first Louisiana legislature elected under this new constitution was a truly integrated body. Thirty-five of the 101 members of the house were black, all of them Republicans. Seven of the 36 members of the senate were black and Republican.[18] It enacted several very controversial measures in 1868–1869. The Slaughterhouse Act was one of them. Others included an act that mandated that public schools be open to all races and one that made it a criminal offense to deny African Americans access to certain facilities serving the public, such as hotels, steamboats, and railroad cars. Such enactments from an integrated legislature outraged local white voters, and they were in no mood to distinguish between different statutes with different motives for passage. One newspaper editor was quite candid in his hostility. All laws emanating from this particular legislative body "are of no more binding force than if they bore the stamp and seal of a Haytian [*sic*] Congress of human apes."[19]

In spite of all the controversy caused by the Slaughterhouse Act, the practice of centralizing slaughtering in an urban area was not new. Centralized abattoirs had already been established in European and other American cities, and more than one effort had been made to implement this arrangement in New Orleans, though without success. But the act was the product of a highly conflicted context, and its passage raised a number of issues—all directly applicable to our story. These include concerns about legislative motivation, bribery and corruption, the scope and function of the police

16. Ross, "Justice Miller's Reconstruction," 662, quoting Ted Tunnell, who counted 50 blacks and 48 whites in the legislature.

17. Joe Gray Taylor, *Louisiana Reconstructed 1863–1867* (Baton Rouge: Louisiana State University Press, 1974), 151.

18. Ibid., 174.

19. *New Orleans Bee*, as quoted by Ross, "Justice Miller's Reconstruction," 663. Just before passage of the Slaughterhouse Act, the *Bee* described one of the nonwhite senators as "a coal black Negro with kinky hair, thick lips, and feet the size of a sauce pan." Ibid.

power, the place of public health regulations, the question of monopolies, the actual provisions and implementation of the 1869 statute, the adequacy of the facility it established, the costs to those affected by it, and legitimate doubts concerning the constitutionality of the statute and the role of the courts—both state and federal—in its enforcement.

It will be noted that absent from these concerns is the matter of race. Of course, there can be no doubt that issues of race were involved in Louisiana politics after 1865. But apart from the fact that the act was the product of a legislature that was despised partly because of its racial makeup, it is our contention that race is one of the less important factors in the *Slaughterhouse* story. To argue that the *Slaughterhouse Cases* must be seen primarily in the context of racial Reconstruction is to miss the point that had there been no blacks in the legislature, opposition to the statute still would have been profound. This is not to say, however, that issues of race did not figure indirectly in the *judicial* resolution of the dispute. It was based, after all, on the Fourteenth Amendment, and in 1873, no one could doubt that race had been a factor in bringing about *its* enactment and ratification. How the justices used the issue of race as they wrote the several opinions that make up the case is also explored in later chapters.

Another part of the Whig version of *Slaughterhouse* must be briefly considered: that the statute was the result of a corrupt group of carpetbaggers with no legitimate reason to support the new law, other than their own financial interests. More recently, some scholars have insisted that there was little difference between "lobbying" and "corruption," besides spelling. This assertion, however, needs to be examined carefully. Accusations of misconduct in the passage of the act were widely reported in the conservative New Orleans press and achieved a level of credibility, given the popular antipathy toward the legislature.

Similarly, the claim of legislative collusion in granting the favored butchers a monopoly should be reexamined. There is no doubt that the statute granted one company the exclusive right to build and operate a slaughterhouse in New Orleans. But any butcher who wished to do so could either slaughter his beef at that site or have it slaughtered for him subject to a fee that was stipulated in the statute. Further, as Miller later emphasized in his opinion, the slaughterhouse faced substantial penalties if it denied any butcher access to its facility. In a real sense—and lawyers for the favored group were quick to make this point—far from restricting it, the statute actually facilitated butchering as a profession. "There is no longer any necessity of a butcher providing a slaughter-house for himself. . . . This charter, therefore, is not a monopoly in the sense that it prevents any one from being a butcher; instead of that, it makes it easier to be a butcher than before."[20]

Although the claim of bribery remains unresolved, surely it is reasonable to ask why the legislature granted one company an exclusive right to build and maintain a slaughterhouse. As will be seen, such an approach to slaughterhouse regulation was not new to Louisiana in 1869. There is no doubt, however, that, as was true of other Southern Reconstruction legislatures at the time, what Ross calls "ambitious modernization plans" had been proposed. To bring them to fruition, however, either tax or bond revenues were essential. But by 1869, tax revenues were very scarce, in part because of economic hardship, as well as white taxpayer recalcitrance. State bonds also remained unappealing to investors. This resulting shortage of state revenues may well have pointed legislators toward a policy of granting exclusive privileges to companies that, in return for the "favor," had to meet various public health requirements and conditions of open access.[21] The context in which the 1869 statute was adopted needs to be carefully reexamined.

SPEAKING FOR THE COURT in *Slaughterhouse*, Miller emphasized the limited scope of his decision. "We now propose," he wrote, "to announce the judgments we have formed in the construction of those articles [the Reconstruction amendments], so far as we have found them necessary to the decision of the cases before us, and beyond that we have neither the inclination nor the right to go."[22] This point is important, because Miller may not have intended his opinion to be taken as an "all embracing construction" of the Fourteenth Amendment. Rather, it was a response to the uncomplicated question of whether the Louisiana legislature's exercise of the police power concerning slaughterhouses had been affected by the new amendment. Echoing Chief Justices Marshall and Shaw, as well as Chancellor Kent, Miller had no doubt of the answer.

In referring to recent incidents, including the Civil War, Reconstruction, and enactment of the Southern black codes, events "almost too recent to be

20. Argument of T. J. Durant et al. for defendants in error in the *Slaughterhouse Cases* as reported in 21 L. Ed. 394 (1873), 401.

21. Ross, "Justice Miller's Reconstruction," 660. Ross concludes that it is not unreasonable to view the legislation setting up the slaughterhouse as "a rational response to the city's sanitation needs and the state's shortage of capital." Ibid.

22. *Slaughterhouse Cases*, 16 Wall. (83 U.S.) 36 (1873), 67.

called history," Miller noted that "on the most casual examination of the language of these amendments, no one can fail to be impressed with the one pervading purpose found in them all, lying at the foundation of each, and without which none of them would ever have been suggested; we mean the freedom of the slave race, the security and firm establishment of that freedom, and the protection of the newly-made freeman and citizen."[23] Yet the Fourteenth Amendment's language was broad, and Miller acknowledged that "if other rights are assailed by the States which properly and necessarily fall within the protection of these articles [the three Reconstruction amendments], that protection will apply, even though the party interested may not be of African descent."[24] Miller emphasized, however, that "what we do say, and what we wish to be understood is, that in any fair and just construction of any section or phrase of these amendments, it is necessary to look to the purpose which we have said was the pervading spirit of them all, the evil which they were designed to remedy."[25]

There is no evidence of any reluctance on Miller's part to enforce the new amendment on behalf of the ex-slave, especially since that is not what the Court was called on to do in *Slaughterhouse*. Nor is there any evidence that somehow Miller and his brethren conspired in advance to use the Louisiana statute as a basis for limiting the amendment's scope. He was compelled to confront the claims raised in this controversy as they had reached the Court in briefs and argument. Far from seeking to impose a narrow interpretation on the new enactment, Miller may have had a very different purpose in mind.

It can be argued that Miller's goal, as evidenced by the language he used, was to prevent the Fourteenth Amendment from being diluted and diminished by its application to the issue of localized infighting among white butchers over which group would control the lucrative meat trade in New

23. Ibid., 71.
24. Ibid., 72.
25. Ibid. Nine years after his decision, during oral argument in another case involving the Fourteenth Amendment, Miller emphasized that "I do not know that anybody in this Court—I never heard it said in this Court or by any judge of it—that these articles were supposed to be limited to the Negro race." To which the lawyer replied, "there is a notion out among the people . . . that it was the intention of this Court to give this provision . . . as restricted and limited application as possible." Miller responded that "the purpose of the general discussion in the *Slaughterhouse Cases* on the subject was nothing more than the common declaration that when you come to construe any act of Congress, any statute, any Constitution, any legislative decree you must consider the thing, the evil which was to be remedied in order to understand fully what the purpose of the remedial act was." Julius J. Marke, *Vignettes of Legal History* (South Hackensack, N.J.: Rothman, 1965), 183.

Orleans. Even if one accepted the contention of broad language, as Miller had from the outset, his majority may well have considered this dispute so far beyond the amendment's purview as to warrant rejection.[26]

A similar point can be raised concerning Miller's treatment of the privileges and immunities clause, which apparently remains a viable and—as the high court noted recently—visible part of our living Constitution.[27] Again, there is no evidence of any prior intent on Miller's part, as Amar so eloquently puts it, of "strangling the privileges and immunities clause in its crib."[28] Rather, it can be argued that since Miller based his decision on police power precedents, there was no need to specify in any great detail exactly what the privileges and immunities clause might be interpreted to mean in future litigation. This could be explored later. Whatever "the privileges and immunities of citizens of the United States" were, however, they did not extend to the rights claimed by the bickering butchers. It might be more accurate to view Miller's comments on privileges and immunities as dicta rather than doctrinal holding.[29]

The major criticism levied against Miller is that through his opinion, he sought to hinder—if not to derail entirely—the course of congressional Reconstruction. Once again, not only is there no evidence for such a claim, but its best rebuttal is the opinion itself. Miller did more than accept the well-established presumption of constitutionality doctrine. He upheld as legitimate the action of a biracial reconstructed legislature committed to a program of change, reform, and modernization that—had the legislature persevered—augured well, he believed, for the future. Far from gutting Reconstruction legislation, his opinion endorsed it.

The current view of *Slaughterhouse* ignores these facts, somehow assuming that what happened after 1877 was inevitable in 1873—and this is not so. Miller's Court had no inkling at the time that Reconstruction would wither in the climate of the 1877 compromise, that Congress would lose its sense of commitment, or that an older racial and economic order fundamentally unsympathetic to Louisiana's postwar legislation would regain power. Moreover, Miller never denied the inherent potential in the due process and equal protection clauses. But their very legitimate purpose "was not to pre-

26. Ballard, "Strangled in the Crib?" 14. This, of course, was the crux of the disagreement between the majority and dissent in the case.

27. See *Saenz v. Roe*, 526 U.S. 489 (1999).

28. Amar, *Bill of Rights*, 213.

29. See Ballard, "Strangled in the Crib?" 38–39.

vent states from passing health regulations that had nothing to do with race."[30]

Further, unlike his colleague Stephen Field, Miller simply did not believe that the Fourteenth Amendment gave the Court authority to strike down a police power statute such as that passed in Louisiana in 1869. He would not presume that Congress had intended his brethren to become "a perpetual censor upon all legislation of the States."[31] Such may not have been the intent of the Fourteenth Amendment's framers when they are considered as a whole.[32] Although there are very debatable issues in this closely divided decision, replete with legitimate disagreements, the old Whiggish view of Miller's opinion is no longer tenable.

FINALLY, this overview should mention subsequent judicial commentary on *Slaughterhouse*, beginning most appropriately with Miller himself. Miller served on the high court until his death seventeen years after *Slaughterhouse*, and he remained proud of that decision. Very soon after the case was decided, in April 1873, Miller wrote to his brother-in-law that his two Fourteenth Amendment decisions (*Slaughterhouse* and *Bradwell*) were "undoubtedly the most important opinions delivered in this Court in many

30. Ross, "Justice Miller's Reconstruction," 675. Miller's opinion should be seen in the context of his previous training and career as a physician, his firsthand observations and experiences concerning the spread of cholera, and the terrible results of improper sanitation and inadequate safeguards related to the location and operation of slaughterhouses. See the convincing summary in ibid., 668–70, as well as the extended treatment given police power regulations in this area by Novak in *The People's Welfare*.

31. 16 Wall. 36, 78.

32. Howe, in "Federalism and Civil Rights" (26–27), concluded "that a cautious judiciary was not entirely wrongheaded . . . in seeking restrictive elements in the American tradition which could be used to confine the reach of national power. Had the Court read the Fourteenth Amendment to authorize congressional protection of the lives, liberties, properties, and equalities of all persons" against the type of injuries complained of in *Slaughterhouse*, it would have "given its blessing to a revolution much more radical than even abolitionists had intended." More than thirty years later, Paul Carrington suggested that "had the Fourteenth Amendment been presented to the generation who so reviled *Dred Scott* as a new commission to the Court to impose on suspect legislatures its doubtful wisdom on a wide range of social and economic issues, it would not merely have failed of ratification, but would have been repudiated on almost every side. The Amendment was presented . . . in the only way it could have won approval, as an instrument declaratory of existing rights." Paul D. Carrington, "The Constitutional Scholarship of Thomas McIntyre Cooley," *American Journal of Legal History* 41 (1997): 396–97.

years. I believe they were decided rightly, though no questions have ever given me more trouble in making up my own mind than those therein discussed."[33]

A few months later, Miller wrote to his friend, colleague, and member of the *Slaughterhouse* majority David Davis. Miller noted that he had been mentioned as a possible replacement for the late Chief Justice Salmon Chase but added, "it is said that my, or rather our opinion in the *Slaughterhouse Cases* is to be used with effect against me. If so it will not be the first time that the best and most beneficial public act of a man's life has stood in the way of his political advancement."[34] Eleven years after his decision, Miller spoke for a unanimous Court upholding the right of a new, mostly white Louisiana legislature to repeal the 1869 statute dealing with slaughterhouses. State authority to enact such a law "was the exercise of the police power which remained with the States in the formation of the original Constitution . . . and had not been taken away by the amendments adopted since." A law resulting from such authority "so long as it remains on the statute book as the latest expression of the legislative will, is a valid law, and must be obeyed, *which is all that was decided by this Court* in the *Slaughterhouse Cases*."[35]

Ten years after Miller's death, Justice Rufus Peckham cited *Slaughterhouse* and mentioned the "great ability displayed by the author of the opinion." The views "upon the matters actually involved and maintained by the judgment in the case have never been doubted or overruled by any judgment of this Court."[36] Finally, in 1908, Justice Moody acknowledged that if

33. William Pitt Ballinger Papers, Box 2A201, Folder April, 1873, Eugene C. Barker Texas History Center, Division of Archives and Manuscripts, University of Texas, Austin. Apparently, this letter has never been cited before, as it was not part of the Miller-Ballinger correspondence that Charles Fairman was permitted to examine and later turned over to the Library of Congress. The *Bradwell* case reiterated Miller's conception of the Fourteenth Amendment within a narrow context, although this time, both Bradley and Field concurred. Bradwell, a female attorney, had sought to use the amendment as a basis to compel Illinois to admit her to the practice of law. *Bradwell v. Illinois*, 16 Wall. (83 U.S.) 130 (1873).

34. Miller to David Davis, September 7, 1873, David Davis Family Papers, 1816–1943, Illinois State Historical Library, Springfield, Ill. Actually, Grant did not make his first offer of the chief justice post until November 8, 1873, when he nominated Roscoe Conkling. He did not notify his ultimate choice (his fourth) until January 19, 1874.

35. *Butcher's Union Co. v. Crescent City*, 111 U.S. 746, 747, 750 (1884); emphasis added to illustrate, once again, Miller's belief in the very limited scope of his earlier decision.

36. *Maxwell v. Dow*, 176 U.S. 581, 591 (1900). It is ironic (and this case is replete with irony) that within five years, Peckham would speak for the Court in another five-to four decision—a landmark holding that turned Miller's reasoning on its head.

Miller's views had not prevailed, "it is easy to see how far the authority and independence of the States would have been diminished, by subjecting all their legislative and judicial acts to correction [and] . . . review by the judicial branch of the National Government." But Moody declined to reinterpret *Slaughterhouse*. "The distinction between National and state citizenship and their respective privileges there drawn has come to be firmly established."[37]

Later legal history appears to have rejected Miller's perception of the Fourteenth Amendment. Both congressional and public support for Reconstruction waned, and with it, any hope of multiracial legislatures working to bring reform and economic modernization to the South also faded. Miller's legal positivism had given great deference to legislative discretion. But with the enshrinement of "liberty of contract" came the accompanying view that the Fourteenth Amendment protected, but did not in itself create, such liberty. Any legislation that limited it was suspect, on its face. Thus judicial deference to state legislation became unwarranted and unnecessary.

The great distance the Court had traveled since *Slaughterhouse* can be seen through a brief comparison with *Lochner v. New York* and *United States v. Carolene Products Co.*[38] The ghost of the earlier decision hangs over these cases, and it is most prevalent in the *Lochner* dissents. In noting, for example, that "the word liberty in the Fourteenth Amendment is perverted when it is held to prevent the natural outcome of a dominant opinion," Justice Holmes echoed Miller. So did Justice Harlan when he insisted that "neither the [Fourteenth] Amendment—broad and comprehensive as it is—nor any other amendment was designed to interfere with the power of the State, sometimes termed its police power."[39]

Between 1873 and 1938, when the *Carolene Products* case was decided, liberty of contract reached its apogee. The concept of strict judicial scrutiny concerning legislation had come a long way since 1873. But in *Carolene*

37. *Twining v. New Jersey*, 211 U.S. 78, 96 (1908).

38. 198 U.S. 45 (1905); 303 U.S. 144 (1938).

39. 198 U.S. 76, 65. Actually, Harlan was quoting Justice Stephen Field in *Barbier v. Connolly*, 113 U.S. 27 (1885). Writing for a unanimous Court that still included Miller, and without any citation whatsoever, Field had sustained a San Francisco municipal ordinance regulating the hours during which public laundries could operate. Moreover, "legislation which, in carrying out a public purpose is limited in its application, if within the sphere of its operation it affects alike all persons similarly situated, is not within the [Fourteenth] Amendment." Ibid., 32. Miller had said much the same thing about the statute at issue in *Slaughterhouse*, whereas Field probably had it in mind when he added that "class legislation, discriminating against some and favoring others, is prohibited." Ibid.

Products, once again Miller's descendants—so to speak—argued successfully that it was now acceptable and reasonable to defer to the legislature.
Justice Stone held that the existence of facts supporting the legislative judgment is to be presumed, "for regulatory legislation affecting ordinary commercial transactions is not to be pronounced unconstitutional unless in the
light of the facts made known or generally assumed, it is of such a character
as to preclude the assumption that it rests upon some rational basis."[40]

Miller had made the same point in *Slaughterhouse.* Even Stone's famous
"footnote 4" has a symmetry with the earlier holding. Just as Miller implied
that the Fourteenth Amendment was too important "to waste on political
and commercial infighting" among butchers, so Stone also implied that it
had a more important function, in that "prejudice against discrete and insu-
lar minorities may be a special condition, which tends seriously to curtail
the operation of those political processes ordinarily relied upon to protect
minorities, and which may call for a correspondingly more searching judicial
inquiry."[41]

"For all sad words of tongue or pen," according to John Greenleaf
Whittier, "the saddest are these: 'It might have been!' "[42] Do these words
represent a fair and accurate summary of *Slaughterhouse?* There is no doubt
that things did not turn out as Miller assumed they would in 1873, and it
may be that somehow he and his majority looked back to what had been,
while the dissenters anticipated what was yet to come. Yet Miller endorsed
legislative deference and a healthy respect for federalism—values that, for
better or worse, have continued to influence contemporary constitutional
interpretation.

One source of significance for *Slaughterhouse* may be what it offered for
the future, even though public policy as it evolved after 1877 declined to
follow its direction. Certainly such a course led to tragic results, but that
they followed inexorably from *Slaughterhouse* is neither an accurate nor, we
believe, an acceptable conclusion. What Loren Beth wrote of this landmark
decision in 1963 remains perceptive and persuasive. "Such a case," he observed, "never dies; there is always interest and importance in its reevalua-
tion, and the final word about it is never said."[43] We agree and offer the
following chapters as our contribution to its further understanding—one
based on context, controversy, contents, and consequences.

40. *United States v. Carolene Products Co.,* 304 U.S. 144, 152–53 (1938).
41. Ibid., 153.
42. The line comes from Whittier's 1865 poem *Maud Muller.*
43. Loren P. Beth, "The Slaughterhouse Cases Revisited," *Louisiana Law Review* 23
(1963): 487–88.

2

Private Gain, Public Health, and Public Policy in Antebellum New Orleans

To see the Louisiana slaughterhouse statute of 1869 as merely one example of many that reflected a misguided and ill-managed course of Reconstruction misses the point. In fact, this law should be viewed in the context of New Orleans history, as a result of an extended and often frustrated attempt to bring sanitary reform to a city that desperately needed it. The next several chapters provide such a context and reveal—regardless of the specific provisions of the act—ample justification for its passage.

AT ONE POINT, as it meanders across the marshes and prairies of southern Louisiana, the Mississippi River makes a radical turn southward. It then circumscribes a curve some 5 miles wide before making another sharp turn to resume a southeastern course. Here at this second crescent-shaped bend about halfway between existing French outposts near Mobile and Natchez, Jean Le Moyne de Bienville established a new settlement in 1718 that he named New Orleans. From his perspective, the site may have had a number of advantages. First, it offered ample dockage along its muddy bank, as well as high ground along the river's natural levee and ridges. Moreover, it was only about 110 miles upstream from the point at which "the father of waters" emptied into the Gulf of Mexico: an ideal accommodation for vessels moving either up- or downstream. Further, the location was barely 6 miles from Lake Pontchartrain, a saltwater lake that provided access from the gulf without the problem of strong river currents. Finally, the narrow strip of land that divided the two bodies of water was already traversed by a bayou and could accommodate a future man-made connection.[1]

1. Elements of this description were paraphrased from George W. Cable, "New Orleans: Historical Sketch," in U.S. Census Office, *Tenth Census of the United States, 1880: Report on the Social Statistics of Cities*, Pt. 2, *Southern and Western States*, comp. George W. Waring Jr. (Washington, D.C.: Government Printing Office, 1887), 213–14.

With confidence if not total accuracy, Thomas Jefferson predicted that "New Orleans will forever be . . . the mighty mart of the merchandise brought from more than a thousand rivers. . . . With Boston, Baltimore, New York, and Philadelphia on the left, Mexico on the right, Havana in front, and the immense valley of the Mississippi in the rear, no such position for the accumulation and perpetuity of wealth and power ever existed."[2] And for a time, it seemed as if Jefferson—whose actions as president had made New Orleans part of the United States—might be correct. It appeared that Bienville's outpost would indeed become the key city in a great commercial empire.

After the Battle of New Orleans in 1815 (an engagement that ended the War of 1812, even though the peace treaty had already been signed in Paris), British blockades were removed from eastern ports, and settlement of the Mississippi River valley beyond the Appalachian Mountains expanded. Between 1800 and 1820, settlers moved into the western states and territories along the valleys of the Ohio River and the upper Mississippi above Cairo, Illinois. During the next two decades, they migrated into the lower portion of the Mississippi valley. The movement was of such magnitude that between 1790 and 1860 the U.S. population center shifted westward from a spot near Baltimore, Maryland, to a point southeast of Chillicothe, Ohio.[3] Between 1810 and the Civil War, the population of the western states and territories increased at a faster rate than anywhere else in the country. It doubled from 961,407 to 1,845,863 by 1820, and by 1840, it had quadrupled to nearly 5 million people, or almost one-third of the entire population. Twenty years later it doubled again, embracing 37.8 percent of the American populace.[4]

Still representing and responding to an agrarian-oriented society, the West generated vast surpluses of products in search of a market. The Appalachian Mountains prevented most of this trade from reaching the eastern ports of New York, Philadelphia, and Baltimore. Rather, the route to market followed a southward direction, along the Ohio and Mississippi Rivers and their many tributaries. Thus New Orleans, situated at the base of the great

2. As quoted in Steven Caldwell, *A Banking History of Louisiana* (Baton Rouge: Louisiana State University Press, 1935), 31.

3. Stuart Bruchey, *The Roots of American Economic Growth, 1607–1861* (New York: Harper, 1968), 76.

4. Douglass C. North, *The Economic Growth of the United States, 1790–1860* (Englewood Cliffs, N.J.: Prentice-Hall, 1961), 257, citing data from the U.S. Census Bureau, *A Compendium of the Ninth Census, June 1, 1870*, by Francis Walker, Superintendent of the Census (Washington, D.C.: Government Printing Office, 1872), 8–9.

river system, seemed a natural recipient for this produce, including grain, beef, and other goods. After 1816, the steamboat arrived. This innovation "held out to the merchants of New Orleans, and the newcomers that daily poured into the town, not only present wealth, but the delusion of absolute and unlimited commercial empire inalienably bestowed by the laws of gravitation."[5] For the commercial year that ended in September 1820, 198 steamboats delivered 106,706 tons of produce worth $12,637,079 to New Orleans, and the Crescent City entered a "golden period of its commerce." By 1840, more than half a million tons came to New Orleans, valued at almost $50 million. At least 80 percent of these goods were products of the West.[6]

The city had become a world-class trading center from and through which goods were shipped upriver to ports on the East Coast, to Latin America, or to Europe. But New Orleans attracted people as well as produce. Within a decade, its population increased by 70 percent, from 27,176 to 46,082. By 1840, it had expanded by another 121 percent to 102,193. On the eve of the Civil War, the New Orleans population had increased more than 500 percent since 1820.[7] Only New York, Philadelphia, and Baltimore were more populous. *DeBow's Review* stated categorically that "no city of the world has ever advanced as a mart of commerce with such rapid and gigantic strides as New Orleans."[8] It appeared to be the richest city in America, a growing metropolis that seemed "invulnerable to competition."[9]

But appearances were deceiving. If Yankee ingenuity could design a steamboat, it could also provide more direct and less costly ways of transporting goods to market. The transportation revolution that began in the 1830s utilized canals and railroads, and both proved detrimental to New Orleans as a trade center. Now, trade from the West tended to bypass the Crescent City, and by 1858, the proportion of total receipts coming from the West had declined from a high of almost 80 percent to barely 18 percent. In fact, the flow of western trade reversed itself. One New Orleans newspaper

5. Cable, "New Orleans: Historical Sketch," 251.
6. U.S. Congress, House, *Report on the Internal Commerce of the United States*, by Wm. F. Switzler, 50th Cong., 1st sess., 1888, in *The Growth of the American Economy to 1860*, ed. Douglass C. North and Robert Paul Thomas (Columbia: University of South Carolina Press, 1968), 198, 200; hereafter, *Report on Internal Commerce*. Quotation from Caldwell, *A Banking History*, 31.
7. Donald B. Dodd, comp., *Historical Statistics of the States of the United States* (Westwood, Conn.: Greenwood Press, 1993), 454.
8. As quoted in *Report on Internal Commerce*, 202.
9. Caldwell, *A Banking History*, 32. Quotation from John G. Clark, *New Orleans, 1718–1812: An Economic History* (Baton Rouge: Louisiana State University Press, 1970), 354.

commented on the large number of heavily laden steamboats that were going downstream only as far as the Illinois River, where they turned upstream toward Chicago.[10] *DeBow's Review*, however, best captured the significance of this observation: the economic unit known as the Mississippi Valley had been turned on its head, so that the Mississippi River was flowing north.

> Where is New Orleans now? Where are her dreams of greatness and of glory? Where her untold wealth in embryo? Whilst she slept, an enemy has sowed tares in her most prolific fields. Armed with energy, enterprise, and an indomitable spirit, that enemy, by a system of bold, vigorous and sustained efforts, has succeeded in reversing the very laws of nature and of nature's God—rolled back the mighty tide of the Mississippi and its ten thousand tributary streams, until their mouth, practically and commercially is more at New York and Boston than at New Orleans. Thus have the fates mocked and deceived us in promising rank and greatness.[11]

The forces of economic growth and industrial development turned with even greater vigor against New Orleans as a consequence of the Civil War. But the taste of economic empire the city had once experienced remained. And the mighty Mississippi, its great natural endowment, continued to flow across its doorstep, leaving behind a residue and reminder of past grandeur as well as future potential. Perhaps some tendency toward megalomania also lingered among its wharves, its banks, its brokerage houses and newspaper offices. Within the Crescent City, there were always those who could not shake the notion that somehow they could do it again. Perhaps the beef industry—still rich in possible profits—could play a part in the city's revival.

REFERENCE HAS ALREADY BEEN MADE to the advantages Bienville may have perceived in his new site of New Orleans. But in truth, this location presented a number of disadvantages; these, combined with both an ability to

10. Figures for 1858 receipts are from Alice Theresa Porter, "An Economic View of Ante-Bellum New Orleans: 1845–1860" (master's thesis, Tulane University, 1942), 2. The newspaper reference is from the *New Orleans Daily Crescent*, July 15, 1851, cited by Porter, 6. For another account of New Orleans' shrinking commercial empire, see George D. Green, *Finance and Economic Development in the Old South: Louisiana Banking, 1804–1861* (Stanford, Calif.: Stanford University Press, 1972), 57.

11. Quoted in Mitchell Franklin, "The Foundations and Meaning of the Slaughterhouse Cases, Part I," *Tulane Law Review* 18 (October 1943): 43.

tolerate deplorable sanitary practices and a stubborn refusal to recognize and effectively resolve them, are an important theme in our study. There was, for example, a problem with topography. George Washington Cable, a native son and well-known Southern writer, described the city location as "a fragment of half-made country, comprising something over 1,700 square miles of river shore, swamp and marshland." New Orleans was founded on a site, noted another observer in 1853, "which only the madness of commercial lust could have tempted men to occupy."[12]

This comment may have been based on the fact that the city is in a subtropical zone, where in the nineteenth century the average temperature was 54.4 degrees in the winter months and 79.3 degrees in the summer. The annual rainfall was fifty-two inches, but it could be much more in some years.[13] This warm, humid climate only exacerbated sanitation problems. The highest point in the city was only fifteen feet above sea level, with much of New Orleans below it. Thus, few graves could be dug to full depth without encountering the water table. To make matters worse, the earthen levees intended to keep the river at bay sometimes gave way in periods of unusually high water, and large portions of the city would be inundated. Throughout the nineteenth century, there were complaints about pools of stagnant water standing in low-lying areas, in vacant lots, and under houses.

In such an environment, drainage was a constant problem. Underground drainage did not exist, and the city depended on irregularly graded ditches and canals to carry water away from inhabited areas. But here, the peculiar New Orleans topography contributed to further difficulties. From its high point along the river, the delta sloped gently toward Lake Pontchartrain. The grade, however, was interrupted by cypress swamps situated like so many saucers between the occupied areas of the city and the lake. These low-lying, mosquito-infested swamps constituted drainage problems of their own, creating further sanitation challenges.[14]

12. Cable, "New Orleans: Historical Sketch," 214; *Illustrated London News*, September 10, 1853, as quoted in Flora Bassett Hildreth, "The Howard Association of New Orleans, 1837–1878" (PhD. diss., University of California, Los Angeles, 1975), 6.

13. Edward H. Barton, "Vital Dynamics of New Orleans: A Report to the American Medical Association, May, 1848," in *Selected Publications of Edward H. Barton*, 14, Rudolph Matas Medical Library, Tulane University.

14. The New Orleans drainage system is described in Gordon E. Gillson, *Louisiana State Board of Health*, vol. 1, *The Formative Years* (New Orleans: Louisiana State Board of Health, 1967), 144–45; hereafter, *Formative Years*. A contemporaneous description is provided by city surveyor Thomas S. Hardee, "The Topography and Drainage of New Orleans," *The Sanitarian* 3 (October 1875): 297. Hildreth, "Howard Association," refers to the swamps as "saucers" (21–22).

Moreover, there was neither an operable sewage system nor an effective method of garbage collection. A common practice was simply to dispose of refuse by throwing it into the swamp or dumping it in nearby vacant lots. In dry periods, spasmodic efforts were made to use river water to flush out the contents of the gutters into the swamp, "that great cesspool of the metropolis," but often this policy only pushed the filth from the gutters into canals at the rear of the city, where it accumulated and festered.[15] Some who could afford them hired night-soil companies to service their privies, and the city sought to have this material and other refuse dumped into the river's main stream by means of nuisance wharves or scows. But as often as not, these substances were simply deposited at the edge of the river and were carried away very slowly, if at all. In 1813, Governor C. C. Claiborne complained that "the pollution constantly striking a person walking on the levee, and which arises from the filth of the city thrown into the water's edge, is too offensive for a civilized person to submit to."[16]

The conditions cited by Governor Claiborne persisted for decades. In midcentury, the New Orleans citizenry routinely used the *batture*, the land between the river's edge and the levee, as a dumping ground for sewage, garbage, dead animals, and many other kinds of filth. Although the city required that dead animals and garbage be promptly removed from the streets, in reality, days passed without any action.[17] The contractors employed by the city to collect garbage were subject to little supervision. There were complaints that they retired for the day after collecting only a few pints of material and that during rainy weather they filled potholes in the unpaved streets with the contents of the garbage carts.[18] One butcher defended his practice of throwing the offal from his slaughterhouse into the street by insisting that it represented an effective means of keeping the thoroughfare in good repair!

15. Robert C. Reinders, *End of an Era: New Orleans, 1850–1860* (New Orleans: Pelican Publishing, 1964), 92–93, quoting the *New York Daily Tribune*, April 2, 1861.

16. On the condition of the riverbanks see, e.g., William P. Hort, "Remarks Connected with the Sanatary Condition of the City of New Orleans," *New Orleans Medical and Surgical Journal* 5 (1848–1849): 256–57; Board of Health, "Annual Report of the Board of Health on the Sanatary Condition of the City of New Orleans, for 1848," ibid., 667–68. In this literature, the term "sanitary" is frequently spelled "sanatary." Claiborne's complaint is from John Duffy, ed., *Rudolph Matas History of Medicine in Louisiana*, vol. 1 (Baton Rouge: Louisiana State University Press, 1958), 392. Claiborne had already lost two wives, a daughter, and a secretary to New Orleans' yellow fever epidemics.

17. Edward H. Barton, "Annual Report for the New Orleans Board of Health for 1849," *Southern Medical Reports* 1 (1849): 92.

18. Gillson, *Formative Years*, 28, quoting *Daily Picayune*, April 19, 1848.

Given their nineteenth-century circumstances, many New Orleanians became apathetic about environmental cleanliness. In the 1820s, a visiting French physician reported that "with the exception of the homes of the elite, the condition of the yards is such that you would think that savages lived there."[19] As for the sanitary conditions of the city as a whole, an 1853 "sanitary map" demonstrated the long-standing fact that nuisances such as tanneries, bone-boiling factories, cattle yards, slaughterhouses, and cemeteries—not to mention areas of standing and stagnant water—were scattered throughout the urban incorporated area.[20] Indeed, cemeteries represented an increasingly grave (!) situation. Many could not afford to bury their dead in aboveground tombs. Given the great numbers of corpses sent to the graveyards during epidemics of cholera and yellow fever, along with the area's very high water table, there were times when the best that could be done were shallow, haphazardly located graves, sometimes covered with only a few inches of topsoil. Under such conditions, a good summer rainstorm might effectively disinter a sizable number of a cemetery's residents.

In 1854, Dr. Edward H. Barton, an inveterate antebellum spokesman for sanitary reform, wrote that "New Orleans is one of the dirtiest . . . and consequently the sickliest city in the Union."[21] Barton knew whereof he spoke. A host of diseases continuously plagued this bustling city, in particular, fearful epidemics of cholera and yellow fever. Time and again they struck and exacted terrible tolls.[22] Between 1796 and 1869, New Orleans endured thirty-six epidemics of yellow fever. Eleven epidemics of cholera descended on the Crescent City between 1832 and 1869.[23] In 1851, Dr. Barton had aptly characterized his city as "a great Golgotha."[24]

Not until the 1880s did Dr. Carlos Finley, a Cuban physician, develop

---

19. J. M. Picornell, "Considérations Hygiéniques sur la Nouvelle–Orléans," in P. F. Thomas, *Essai sur la Fievre Jeaune d'Amérique* (New Orleans, 1823), 11, Rudolph Matas Medical Library, Tulane University; translated from the French.

20. See the sanitary map preceding Edward H. Barton, "Report upon the Sanitary Conditions of New Orleans," in New Orleans Sanitary Commission, *Report on the Epidemic Yellow of 1853* (New Orleans: City Council, 1854), 211.

21. Ibid., 220.

22. John Duffy, "Pestilence in New Orleans," in *Past as Prelude: New Orleans 1718–1968*, ed. Hodding Carter (New Orleans: Tulane University, 1968), 88–90.

23. Dr. Stanford E. Chaillé tabulated and classified the seriousness of New Orleans' epidemics in "Vital Statistics of New Orleans from 1769 to 1874," *New Orleans Medical and Surgical Journal* (July 1874): 22–23.

24. Edward H. Barton, "Report on the Meteorology, Vital Statistics and Hygiene of the State of Louisiana: Read before the Medical Society of the State of Louisiana, 7th March, 1851," 23, Rudolph Matas Medical Library, Tulane University.

the hypothesis that the vector of yellow fever was the female member of the *Aedes aegypti* species of mosquito.[25] Prior to his discovery, the medical community had to make do with explanations of disease grounded in both conjecture and common sense. Some held, for example, that disease was transmitted from person to person. Physicians of this persuasion were often called "contagionists," and in New Orleans, they were apt to favor a naval quarantine to protect the city from imported sickness. Another group emphasized the importance of sanitation and argued that disease was of spontaneous origin. A related theory of "miasma" claimed that disease was caused by breathing the gaseous emanations of decaying animal and vegetable matter.

Whatever its other shortcomings, the miasma theory had the effect of focusing attention on the relationship between good health and environmental cleanliness. In 1834, for example, Barton had written that the natural climatic conditions of New Orleans could at times produce "an epidemic constitution of the atmosphere," which, in combination with animal and vegetable decay, created a uniquely noxious mix. He repeatedly called for sound sanitary practices as a way of avoiding pestilence in the Crescent City.[26] "Filth," he claimed, "is the electric spark which fires the other elements."[27] Dr. Erasmus D. Fenner, another antebellum New Orleans physician, agreed. Coeditor of two local medical journals as well as publisher of a short-lived but well-respected journal of his own, Fenner insisted that proper sanitary measures, properly enforced, could remove yellow fever from the city.[28]

Various boards of health organized in New Orleans offered similar remonstrations against the deplorable sanitary practices that were an everyday occurrence in the city. Their annual reports often provided a forum for some of the best-respected advocates of reform. But these boards were political bodies, existing in an atmosphere of conflicting interests. All they had to offer was quarantine, regulations to modify well-established local behav-

25. See Jo Ann Carrigan, *The Saffron Scourge: A History of Yellow Fever in Louisiana, 1796–1905* (Lafayette: Center for Louisiana Studies, University of Southwestern Louisiana, 1994), 97, 134.

26. Edward H. Barton, "Account of the Epidemic Yellow Fever which Prevailed in New Orleans during the Autumn of 1833" (Philadelphia, 1834), referred to in Gillson, *Formative Years*, 5. See also Barton, "Report on the Meteorology," 12.

27. Gillson, *Formative Years*, 6, quoting an 1865 speech by Barton reported in *Boston Medical and Surgical Journal* 55 (1846): 729.

28. Gillson, *Formative Years*, 6, citing *New Orleans Medical News and Hospital Gazette* 2 (1855–1856): 500–1.

ior, and costly proposals to deal with drainage and sewage disposal. They were inevitably established in response to a crisis, such as an epidemic, and when it subsided, support for the board waned, making it easy prey for detractors.

In this fashion, New Orleans saw three separate boards of health come and go between 1800 and 1825. The first was created by city ordinance in 1804, following epidemics of smallpox and yellow fever. Given authority to enter private property and order abatement of certain nuisances, the board apparently "burned itself out in its excess of energy and enthusiasm," and by the end of the next year, it ceased to exist.[29] The second board was created by state statute in 1818, only to be repealed within a year. When it advocated quarantine, it was attacked by Creole physicians who were more interested in sanitation, by commercial interests that viewed quarantine as an intolerable economic nuisance, and by the New Orleans city council, which insisted that the legislature had given away some of its own power. The third attempt came in 1821, and this board was given extensive mandates over both quarantine and sanitation. But despite this enhanced power, epidemics returned, and in 1825, the anti-quarantine faction saw to its abolition.[30]

The question arises why, given the irrefutable evidence of regular epidemics, so little had been done to improve public health in New Orleans. After all, its residents encountered reality every time they went outdoors, inspected the gutters in front of their homes, strolled down by the levee, or tasted the city's water supply. These conditions were not new. Local newspapers seemed to be involved in a "conspiracy of silence" with regard to epidemics. Their reaction followed a typical pattern: (1) denial of an epidemic, (2) quiet admission about a few cases, (3) official silence, and (4) announcement (usually premature) of the epidemic's end.[31]

Several factors, including obtuseness, impeded realistic admissions and movement toward effective reform. One is struck by the consistency with which local observers insisted that their city was a veritable health spa.[32] As the editor of the New Orleans city directory put it in 1838, "no country in the world has suffered more unmerited obloquy than New Orleans, in relation to health." Indeed, he added, "probably there is no portion of America where the mortality is less than with our native and acclimated population."

29. Duffy, *Matas History of Medicine*, 1:389.
30. Ibid., 400–5.
31. Hildreth, "Howard Association," 2; Duffy, *Matas History of Medicine*, 2:125.
32. Duffy, *Matas History of Medicine*, 2:123, 1:404; Carrigan, *Saffron Scourge*, 249.

Whatever their political differences, Creole and American residents were united in their insistence that their Crescent City "was far more salubrious than the great cities to the north."[33]

Many New Orleanians departed the city during the sickly summer months, leaving a population in which newcomers and the poor were over-represented. Thus it was possible to argue that, for the most part, the only people affected were "the ignorant and dissolute poor." Once a newcomer, as opposed to a native, had passed through the "seasoning" or acclimating process, he or she would supposedly be immune from the epidemic diseases.[34] Thus, many could argue that yellow fever in fact represented a "stranger's disease." Although it might claim a few "deeply lamented citizens, it has principally affected the newly arrived immigrants, or those ghastly specimens of humanity that occasionally arrive from California."[35]

A second reason why city officials were loath to concede "the presence of even one case of a major epidemic sickness" concerned the importance of New Orleans as a commercial center. Even "the rumored presence" of an epidemic "was enough to start thousands of panic stricken residents pouring out of the city." Such an event might well trigger "neighboring towns, parishes, and [even] states to erect barricades . . . to safeguard themselves from the danger of infection." It would certainly discourage businessmen from coming to the Crescent City if they could do business elsewhere. The main "business of a commercial port was business, and this could not be carried on when the public was alarmed and frightened."[36]

Finally, there was a resistance generated in part by inertia. Epidemics came and went, and sentiment for reform inevitably seemed to wane as did the virulence of the disease. Also, given the prevalence of a laissez-faire attitude toward governmental authority, it was not clear who was responsible for municipal health. When he stepped down as chair of the Louisiana State Medical Association in 1852, Dr. Barton commented that his group was "compelled to meet opposition of a character peculiar to a republican government, where every man claims the right to follow any occupation or profession most congenial to his own feelings."[37] Moreover, if care for the

33. Duffy, *Matas History of Medicine*, 2:162.

34. John Duffy, *Sword of Pestilence: The New Orleans Yellow Fever Epidemic of 1853* (Baton Rouge: Louisiana State University Press, 1966), 6–7.

35. J. C. Simonds, "On the Sanitary Conditions of New Orleans as Illustrated by Its Mortuary Statistics," *Southern Medical Reports* 2 (1850): 229, quoting *New Orleans Board of Health Report for 1850.*

36. Duffy, "Pestilence in New Orleans," 99.

37. As quoted in Board of Health, *Annual Report of the Board of Health of the State of Louisiana for the Year 1882* (Baton Rouge, 1883), 116, Louisiana Division, Louisiana State

sick was a moral obligation, and many held that it was, such a burden was considered an obligation on an individual, not a municipality.

In short, the path to reform, though seemingly clear, would not be easy. First, there was the task—certain to be "slow and tedious"—of convincing the public that there existed a serious *public* health problem. Second, political decision makers, in spite of various conflicting opinions and viewpoints, would somehow have to be persuaded to use their power to overcome the problem.[38]

By the 1840s, signs began appearing in New Orleans that the status quo was no longer acceptable. Sixteen years passed between the collapse of the last board of health in 1826 and the city council's appointment of another. In that period, New Orleans was visited by epidemics of cholera or yellow fever on an almost annual basis, and pressure for sanitary reform accumulated from the medical profession, the newspapers, and even the general public. When a particularly severe epidemic struck in 1841, the council finally created a new board of health, headed by veteran sanitarian Dr. Edward Barton. His group worked hard to combat the current onslaught, but its ability to fight a disease it did not fully understand was limited, and the epidemic raged on. As a result, the public failed to see a connection between sanitation and good health, and with limited public cooperation, the board collapsed the next year.[39]

But by this time, reform had a more lasting impetus. In 1844, the city council asked the local medical society to serve as a local board of health, and in 1846, it created a new and stronger board—the city's seventh since 1804. The new agency consisted of twelve physicians, headed by Dr. William P. Hort. Unlike previous boards, "in addition to [record keeping,] the new body was supposed to have the entire sanitary condition of the city under its supervision and control."[40]

In his first report on behalf of the board, Hort wrote with a new, hard-hitting frankness. He deplored the unsanitary condition of New Orleans and insisted that the problem required not additional regulation but enforcement

---

Library, Baton Rouge. However, as will be seen later, and as William Novak has brilliantly demonstrated, in antebellum America, laissez-faire was honored more often in the breach than in the observance.

38. Duffy, *Matas History of Medicine*, 1:405.

39. Ibid., 2:169.

40. Gillson, *Formative Years*, 23, citing *New Orleans Medical and Surgical Journal* 3 (1846–1847): 471–72, and *Daily Picayune*, July 17, 1846.

of what had already been enacted years before. "Sanitary codes had been on the books for three decades, but adequate attention had never been given to the problem of enforcement." Despite Hort's efforts, general health conditions in the Crescent City "were indeed deplorable."[41] As if to prove the point, in 1847, a new yellow fever epidemic struck the city. This caused the state legislature to create yet another board of health for New Orleans, the eighth in less than half a century.

Apparently similar in organization to its immediate predecessor, the eighth board of health was given more power over sanitation in New Orleans than all its previous versions had possessed. It had the authority to select health wardens for every ward, with the power to remove nuisances, file suits against stubborn property owners, and enforce the city's contracts with street cleaners.[42] But little was accomplished. As had happened before, an editorial in the *Daily Picayune* noted that "our citizens have just reason to complain of the filthy conditions of our streets, which are apparently growing worse and worse. . . . The offense is rank, [and] smells to heaven." But this time, the *Picayune* went further. It insisted that it was the duty of the board of health and the sanitary commissioners to improve the current system, under which sanitary carts "succeed in gathering about three pints of unpleasant compost within a square, with which they triumphantly retire."[43] The editor of the *New Orleans Medical and Surgical Journal* joined in by criticizing the city drainage system and, in a manner indicative of the growing unity of medical opinion, expressed doubt that the new board had been given sufficient power to regulate the entire hygiene of the city.[44] Yet the most dramatic indication that drastic change was demanded came from Dr. Hort, who stepped out of his official role and, in an article published by the *New Orleans Medical and Surgical Journal,* went public with his complaints concerning the lack of official cooperation.

"Not withstanding the remonstrances of the Board of Health," he wrote, "the Commissaries, in 1847, continued to encumber the bank of the river and fill up the docks with every kind of decaying vegetable and animal matter, the garbage of the city and of the markets." The result was "the most intolerable effluvia, as the river receded, leaving the mass of corruption to be acted on by the sun's rays."[45] Hort now specified in public what many

41. Ibid., 25.
42. Ibid., 27.
43. Ibid., 28, citing *Picayune*, April 19, 1848.
44. Ibid., citing *New Orleans Medical and Surgical Journal* 4 (1847–1848): 797.
45. Hort, "Remarks Connected with the Sanatary Condition of New Orleans," 256–57.

in the medical community had probably discussed in private. Pointing out the fundamental connection between the health of the city and the wealth of its commerce, he argued, "if then, our enterprising citizens really desire that this city should become exempt from that terrible scourge, the yellow fever, they must elect men to the different Councils who will as far as possible carry out those hygienic measures, based on the experience of ages, which have heretofore been repeatedly recommended to the City Authorities."[46]

But Hort did not intend to let his point pass only by implication. "Such measures," he reiterated, "have [been] repeatedly recommended, but without producing any important result. We must suppose that the city authorities have been, and still are, aware of their importance and practicality. Why, then, has so little been done? How is it that we hear every season the same complaints of the filthy conditions of the gutters and streets in many parts of the city—of the offensive garbage thrown on the bank of the river and into the docks. . . . Are the members of the City Council afraid of the expense?"[47]

Hort intimated that the council had been very prompt to ask his board of health "to devise some measure [for] the purpose of effectually preserving the public health and salubrity of the city." But the officials had been equally prompt in ignoring the repeated suggestions that came from the board. Instead, they indulged in what might be called a sanitation waltz of avoidance: several steps sideways, one step forward, and one step backward—always ending up exactly where they had started. "The members of the Board," Hort concluded, "regret that they have met with so little cooperation on the part of the city authorities."[48]

Hort assumed that there already existed sufficient authority to compel sanitary reforms. The 1848 report from the board of health—probably authored by him—emphasized that "wise police regulations have been adopted from time to time by our Councils, and commissaries have been appointed to carry them into effect." Yet the situation had not improved. "Of what avail are solutions and ordinances, if they are not rigidly enforced, and if the officers appointed . . . actually do, or permit to be done, the very things prohibited by the Board, and which have over and over again been

46. Ibid., 260. The difficulty faced by Hort's board was exacerbated by long-term public apathy concerning health and sanitation, as well as by the regularity of epidemics. The perception of the public was that little connection existed between sanitation and public health. Many felt that it made little difference what the city did.

47. Ibid., 261.

48. Ibid., 263, quoting from New Orleans Board of Health to Members of the General Counsel, June 18, 1847.

spoken of as the most fruitful cause of our malignant epidemics."[49] There appeared to be a simple solution. "We say, let *this* nuisance be at once abated; let the commissaries be compelled to do their duty and their whole duty, subject to fine or reform [removal] from office in default thereof."[50]

As long as there were virtually no municipal mortuary records available, those who continually pointed to the apparent beneficence of the Crescent City managed to maintain some credibility. Hort could employ much emphasis, but there was little evidence. His cause, however, soon received major support from Dr. J. C. Simonds, a new entrant in the sanitation battle, who was one of the first to publish medical statistics about New Orleans.

Simonds had attended a meeting in Boston, where he heard many negative comments concerning public health in New Orleans. When he returned home, Simonds was determined to demonstrate beyond any doubt that the Crescent City was on a par with every other major urban center. But what he found proved just the opposite. His remarkable findings were eventually published in Fenner's *Southern Medical Reports,* but first he informed the general public in a series of nine articles that appeared in the *Daily Delta.* Shortly afterward, the Physico-Medical Society arranged a public lecture for him at the city's prestigious Lyceum Hall.[51] In his study, Simonds compared the average annual mortality rates for the major urban centers of Philadelphia, New York, Boston, Baltimore, and Charleston from 1811 to 1849. All, he found, were between 2.4 and 2.9 percent. Based on an eight-year sample, however, Savannah's was 4.16 percent, and in New Orleans, based on only

49. "We allude to the deposit on the banks of the river of so much of the offal of the city, consisting of animal and vegetable remains in a state of putrefaction." Board of Health, "Annual Report on the Sanatory Condition of New Orleans for 1848," 607–8.

50. Ibid. There was more than adequate authority granted by the 1848 statute, including a provision that required the removal of offal and refuse from the streets of New Orleans within two hours. Such a provision "would prove eminently beneficial in promoting the health of the city . . . if rigidly enforced—but it is to be feared that like many other wise regulations and judicial ordinances, it has slumbered on the statute book." Ibid., 615.

51. Simonds, "On the Sanitary Condition of New Orleans," 204–46; *New Orleans Daily Delta,* June 28 and July 2, 3, 4, 9, 12, 13, 18, 1850. See also Simonds, *The Sanitary Condition of New Orleans* (Charleston, S.C., 1851), cited in Gillson, *Formative Years,* 30–31. Simonds had hoped to be "able to convince the world, by an array of unquestionable statistical details and impregnable arguments, that it had done injustice to New Orleans, and that our city was not the Golgotha which it was everywhere represented to be. . . . I found that we were laboring under a delusion. . . . The conclusions to which I have arrived have not been favorable to the opinion here [in New Orleans] entertained, but have justified the worst opinion existing abroad regarding the sanitary condition of our city." Simonds, "On the Sanitary Condition of New Orleans," 205–6.

a four and a half–year sample, the mortality rate was 8.1 percent, "or 1 in every 12, nearly." When Simonds compared New Orleans with Boston, his findings shocked those who claimed the healthful quality of greater New Orleans.[52] Looking at an approximately nine-week period between February and April 1851, Simonds wrote, "We, in New Orleans, consider the past few weeks a period of unexampled health; let us, then compare the weekly statement of deaths here with those in Boston." He found 647 deaths recorded in Boston, with 1,319 in greater New Orleans. "According to the late United States census, the city of Boston contains 8,000 more persons than the cities of New Orleans and Lafayette, in which, during nine weeks of our health season, the deaths are more than double those of Boston."[53]

Simonds emphasized that "an honest statement of the truth with regard to the health of the city, would ultimately promote its true interest and permanent prosperity." Candor was absolutely essential. "At present, the truth is so well known abroad and so studiously concealed at home that the statements of the press are unheeded and disbelieved." As to New Orleans' claims of economic importance, "do these incorrect and dishonest assertions add one iota to her prosperity? Who credits or acts upon them? Go out of the city of New Orleans and find the man who believes them. They deceive nobody but ourselves. The press and people may reiterate the assertions, but unsupported by reliable statistics, and contradicted by private information, they possess no weight abroad." It is time, Simonds insisted, "to adopt a different policy: to direct our attention to an investigation that will determine the truth, regardless of its influence upon opinions abroad, and to commence endeavoring to improve the health of the city."[54]

Simonds's comments are important not only for their calls for reform but also because they reflect the emergence of an organized medical community increasingly prepared to focus attention on significant issues, especially public health. This trend paralleled similar developments on a national scale.

52. Simonds, "On the Sanitary Condition of New Orleans," 214–15.

53. Ibid., 217–18. Simonds claimed that the major cities in England were all healthier than New Orleans. Another New Orleans physician, Dr. Stanford Chaillé, later reached similar conclusions. See Chaillé, "Vital Statistics of New Orleans, Article I," *New Orleans Medical and Surgical Journal* 23 (Jan. 1870): 1–65; and Chaillé, "The Yellow Fever, Sanitary Conditions, and Vital Statistics of New Orleans during Its Military Occupation, the Four Years 1862–5, Article No. II," *New Orleans Medical and Surgical Journal* 23 (July 1870): 563–98. Reflecting the growing interest in public health and sanitary reform, another of Simonds's articles appeared in a national journal. See his "Report of the Hygienic Characteristics of New Orleans," in *Transactions of the American Medical Association* 3 (1850): 267–80.

54. Simonds, "On the Sanitary Conditions of New Orleans," 207.

When, for example, the American Medical Association was organized in 1848, doctors from New Orleans had been in attendance. Indeed, a year later, one physician presented a study titled "Yellow Fever Quarantine at New Orleans" that was duly published in the second volume of AMA proceedings.[55] By 1835, New Orleans had its own medical school, which in 1847 became the medical department of the newly established University of Louisiana.[56] The city was also home to the *New Orleans Medical Journal*, a periodical that continues to be published today, albeit under a different title. At first, the journal accepted the conventional wisdom "that only strangers and visitors sickened and died in New Orleans."[57] By 1851, however, a compilation of urban mortality tables—themselves a reflection of the new trend toward professional medical documentation of the costs of sickness and death—indicated otherwise. Faced with the unpleasant evidence that New Orleans was in fact one of the unhealthiest of American cities, the editors of the *Journal* were among the first to admit their error. Henceforth, with few exceptions, the periodical stoutly supported the cause of sanitation and public health.[58] So did *DeBow's Review*. Its editor confessed that "we have been the last to yield to the proposition that New Orleans is an *unhealthy city*, very unhealthy, and have done as much, perhaps, as anyone circulating the contrary opinion. . . . The facts are, however, against us."[59]

Hort and Simonds were joined by Dr. Edward Barton, who in an 1851 article criticized not only the poor public health in New Orleans but also the apparent lack of official interest in making lasting improvements. Like Simonds, he conceded the poor quality of public health in his city. Indeed, it had "a mortality exceeding any city" in America. Moreover, "the present system of police is a mere mockery, leaving the public here, and those interested in our city abroad, with the impression that its salubrity is unimprovable."[60]

55. Erasmus D. Fenner, "Yellow Fever Quarantine at New Orleans," *Transactions of the American Medical Association* 2 (1849): 625–26.

56. Its first dean was Dr. Thomas Hunt, whose two brothers William and Randell played leading roles as attorneys in the early stages of the *Slaughterhouse Cases*.

57. Duffy, *Matas History of Medicine*, 2:276–77.

58. Ibid.

59. *DeBow's Review*, 9 (1850): 245–46, cited in Gillson, *Formative Years*, 32.

60. By "police," Barton did not mean a conventional force to maintain law and order. Rather, he had in mind a view of the police power commonly held in the mid-nineteenth century. It was the authority "to prescribe regulations to preserve and promote the public safety, health and morals, and to prohibit all things hurtful to the comfort and welfare of society." See Novak, *The People's Welfare*, 13.

Barton emphasized the "two great difficulties" confronting would-be reformers. "First is the great error under which we have long labored in relation to our salubrity; and the second is the procurement of the actual facts to ascertain what that condition has been." Given the apparent refusal to accept reality, Barton conceded that "it requires some moral courage to disabuse a community of a long and deeply cherished error." In truth, "we hug our chains with delight, and stone the man who will attempt to convince us that they are but the chains of sciolism and ignorance, forgetful at the time that we but deceive ourselves, and the world is not to be gulled at this enlightened epoch by our assertion, when unsupported by facts, and our complacency when not based upon the truth."[61]

Simonds also had the police power in mind when he warned his readers not to attribute the high mortality rate to "the want or imprudence of strangers and the unacclimated." Rather, "commence immediately . . . an examination of the causes of the prevalence of disease, and proceed vigorously to remove them." Most important, "revise your sanatory [sic] regulations; compel your Board of Health to do its duty, and . . . institute such new police regulations as may be found necessary, and consider the protection of human life against disease and crime, as paramount in importance to every other question. Until this be done New Orleans will always remain unhealthy."[62] The confluence of Simonds and Barton by the 1850s is important. As medical historian Duffy put it many years later, "although the struggle between the public health reformers and the conservatives was to continue for many years, never again was New Orleans to feel the sense of complacency which had characterized the townspeople in the period prior to 1850."[63]

Evidence was now available, statistics had been gathered, valid explanations for the city's health problems had been published. Yet in themselves, these facts still were not sufficient to bring about needed changes. Between 1853 and 1858, however, New Orleans endured the worst yellow fever epidemics in its history. The 1853 attack killed one-tenth of the population in a single summer. The city came to a virtual standstill during this time while residents cared for the sick and disposed of the dead.[64] The 1853 outbreak was followed by yellow fever epidemics almost as severe in both 1854 and 1855. These were followed by still another onslaught of yellow fever in 1858,

61. Barton, "Report on the Meteorology," 22–23.
62. Simonds, "On the Sanitary Condition of New Orleans," 207–8.
63. Duffy, *Matas History of Medicine*, 2:167.
64. The story is compellingly told by Duffy in *Sword of Pestilence*.

second in its severity only to the epidemic of 1853. Another medical reformer, Dr. Stanford Chaillé, later declared the six years between 1853 and 1858, and especially the three years between 1853 and 1855, "a culminating epoch in the yellow fever and mortality history of this city, from its foundation to the present day; . . . in the entire history of New Orleans, no three successive years can be found at all comparable in fatality with those mentioned."[65]

The city council convoked a sanitary commission to study the 1853 tragedy and named Dr. Edward Barton as chairman. Barton had repeatedly contended that the city's health problems were entirely removable by an effective use of the police power. Now, in the commission's final report, he declared, "The 'let alone' system has been tried long enough. . . . The trial has been full and unsatisfactory. All unite in saying there must be sanitary reform."[66] In 1854, for the first time in its history, Louisiana established a statewide board of health. Yet despite the continued yellow fever epidemics, New Orleans failed to implement changes. Nevertheless, between the medical community's repeated calls for an effective exercise of the police power and public officials' being forced into action by dire circumstances, an assumption had been created that public officials had some responsibility for public health.[67]

In 1859, for example, Dr. A. F. Axson, president of the board of health, denounced the city's condition and lamented the incredible tolerance for "scandalous nuisances" shown by its officials. "Populous hotels poured their ordure from brimming sinks through the chief avenues of the city; gutters sweltered with the blood and drainings of slaughter-pens; sugar refineries opened their sluices and whole streets reeked of their rank odors; and every highway that chanced to be unpaved was broadcast with the rakings of gutters and the refuse filth of private yards and stables." The board's remonstrance against "these palpable outrages was unavailing, nor could it be otherwise, as long as there was the marked 'diversity of opinion upon sanitary measures' among our city fathers, as avowed by the mayor."[68] Even on the eve of the Civil War, the board of health deplored the New Orleans city council's continued refusal to accept the need for sanitary regulations, such

65. Chaillé, "Yellow Fever, Sanitary Conditions, and Vital Statistics," 566.

66. Barton, "Report upon the Sanitary Conditions of New Orleans," 218.

67. From the seriousness of the 1853 epidemic and the response of at least some city officials, Duffy concludes: "Henceforth it was assumed in New Orleans that civic officials should take responsibility for the public welfare." Duffy, *Sword of Pestilence*, 171.

68. A. F. Axson, *Report of the Board of Health to the Legislature, January, 1859* (New Orleans: James M. Taylor, 1859), 35.

as a proposed "nuisance" ordinance in 1855, which the council rejected. The board had consistently failed to convince the city fathers of "the utter destitution of the city in every essential of sanitary regulation necessary to health or even to decency and public self respect."[69]

Dr. Chaillé summarized the sanitary conditions of New Orleans between 1796 and 1869 as "one long, disgusting story of stagnant drainage, foul sewerage, environing swamps, ill and unpaved streets, no sanitary regulations, and filth, endless filth every where."[70] Of course, the unsanitary conditions of the Crescent City had long antedated the Simonds and Barton exposés. Perhaps it was the consistent denial of reality by the politicians and the press that led the two physicians to target them. Simonds and Barton, however, were about to receive aid from a most unlikely source, and change was imminent. This time, however, it would not be implemented by the city fathers; rather, it would be imposed on them by the general commanding Union forces, Benjamin Butler.

New Orleans surrendered to Union naval forces late in April 1862. Admiral Farragut promptly turned control of the city over to General Butler, and on May 1, Butler assumed responsibility, only to be shocked by the sanitary condition of his surroundings. "The streets," he later recalled, "were reeking with putrefying filth."[71] A few days later, he took his wife on a carriage ride to inspect the city. As they approached a basin near Lake Pontchartrain, "the air seemed filled with the most noxious and offensive stenches possible, so noxious as almost to take away the power of breathing. The whole surface of the canal and the pond was covered with a thick growth of green vegetable scum, variegated with dead cats and dogs or the remains of dead mules on the banking."[72]

Previously, Butler had ordered that all existing public health regulations were to be enforced and that city officials would retain responsibility for all municipal services. Upon inquiry to the individual in charge of streets and canals, the general was informed that "the enormous stink . . . was no more than usual."[73] His response was to undertake a major cleanup of the city.

69. *Report of the Board of Health to the Legislature for 1860*, 8.

70. Chaillé, "Yellow Fever, Sanitary Conditions, and Vital Statistics," 567–68.

71. Benjamin F. Butler, "Some Experiences with Yellow Fever and Its Prevention," *North American Review* 147 (1888): 528.

72. Benjamin F. Butler, *Butler's Book* (Boston: A. M. Thayer, 1892), 395.

73. Ibid., 396.

Accordingly, he ordered the city to hire a force of up to 2,000 men to restore the streets, squares, and unoccupied areas to suitable conditions. Moreover, for each day's work, they were to be paid 50¢ by the city. Also, they would receive a day's rations from Butler's own supplies, worth about the same amount. Possibly with a sense of relief, city officials readily agreed and in fact raised the municipal contribution to $1 a day.[74]

Even as the cleanup got under way, Butler learned that prayers were being offered in local churches for the arrival of a robust epidemic of the "saffron scourge." If the South was unable to defeat Union military might, perhaps the disease could decimate mortal Union men. He also learned the identities of prominent local residents who had contributed more than $1 million for the defense of New Orleans against Federal invasion. In response, the general amended his original orders. He raised the daily wage to $1.50, the same amount that workers had been paid to fortify New Orleans against attack. The full amount was to come directly from those individuals who had earlier contributed to the defense of their city. Butler reasoned that the people who had contributed to bringing the Crescent City to its present state of ruin ought to be held chiefly responsible for its relief. Already unpopular for his notorious order that New Orleans women who did not show proper respect to his troops were to be treated as prostitutes, Butler's latest move provoked further outrage.[75] Butler's biographer may have been guilty of understatement when he observed that "the effect produced by a measure so boldly just, upon the minds of the ruling class, can scarcely be imagined."[76] In the meantime, the cleanup continued.

Butler's approach to enhancing public health involved both quarantine and sanitation. First, he established a quarantine station seventy miles below the city and required inspection of every vessel before it could move up into port. Further, no vessel on which sickness had been detected or that had arrived from an infected port could proceed to dock in less than forty days. Second, he ordered a massive cleaning of New Orleans that was long overdue. One of Butler's staff, Colonel T. B. Thorpe, assumed responsibility for the cleanup, and Butler's biographer described his efforts: "He waged incessant and most successful war upon nuisances. He tore away shanties, filled

74. Ibid., 403–4; Gillson, *Formative Years*, 103.

75. According to one distinguished Civil War historian, "Butler had issued this maladroit order after considerable provocation, climaxed by a woman who dumped the contents of a chamber pot from a French-Quarter balcony on Fleet [Commander] David Farragut's head." James M. McPherson, *Battle Cry of Freedom: The Civil War Era* (New York: Oxford University Press, 1988), 552.

76. James Parton, *General Butler in New Orleans* (New York: Mason Brothers, 1864), 312.

up holes, purged the canals, cleaned the streets, repaired the levee, and kept the city in such perfect cleanliness" that even die-hard secessionists admitted that "the federals could clean the streets, if they couldn't do anything else."[77]

Dr. Elisha Harris, a national leader in the drive for better public health, superintendent of the New York Metropolitan Board of Health, and a member of the U.S. Sanitary Commission that was so important during the Civil War, documented the New Orleans experience. He lauded Butler's efforts. Private premises were "kept in a state of unusual cleanliness by an absolute authority. . . . Privies and garbage, stables and butcheries . . . were all brought under police control." Livestock was impounded, and cattle boats were scrubbed before receiving permission to enter the city. The Spanish had provided the French Market with a paved floor for sanitary purposes, but apparently no one had ever cleaned it. At the time Butler launched his cleanup, it was said that accumulations of decaying animal matter reached as high as two feet on some of the stalls. According to Harris, "so clean a city had never before been seen upon the continent."[78]

General Butler moved on to another assignment in December, declaring as he went, "I have demonstrated that the pestilence can be kept from your borders."[79] His successor, Major General Nathaniel Banks, maintained the policy of civic cleanliness, and New Orleans was spared from epidemics throughout Federal occupation. Native son George Washington Cable would one day accuse New Orleans of "an invincible provincialism" for its failure to recognize and remedy important problems in the first half of the nineteenth century.[80] In this instance, change had come about at the insistence of outsiders. After the military returned the city to civilian control on March 19, 1866, however, what would happen? Whether the vigorous sanitary efforts initiated by Butler would continue remained an open question, but not for long.

77. Ibid., 308–9.
78. Elisha Harris, "Hygienic Experiences in New Orleans during the War," *Bulletin of the New York Academy of Medicine* 30 (September 1865): 464, 470.
79. Quoted in Parton, *General Butler*, 605.
80. Cable, "New Orleans: Historical Sketch," 253.

3

Regulation Prior to Slaughterhouse

The idea that slaughterhouses ought to be centralized was new to neither the Crescent City nor—as will be seen—to nineteenth-century urban municipal administration. Early in the century, slaughtering in New Orleans had been confined to a small area located directly across the Mississippi from the city and known as "Slaughterhouse Point."[1] From there, slaughterhouse waste could be dumped into the river, and the powerful current would sweep it downstream toward the Gulf of Mexico. When the population consisted of a few thousand, it was mostly centered in a small expanse of land fronting on the deep curve of the river that gave New Orleans the name Crescent City. Butchers accomplished their slaughtering at night and transported their daily supply of meat across the river to the city markets. By the mid-nineteenth century, however, the New Orleans population had increased by about tenfold.

Wharves, landings, and warehouses were established further and further upstream to deal with the commerce flowing downriver. The expanding population followed, leading to the establishment of suburbs such as Lafayette and Jefferson City. Responding to their growing market, the butchers moved their operations from Slaughterhouse Point across the river into the city and its suburbs, always migrating upstream with the population. The demand for dressed meat increased, as did the numbers of stock dealers and butchers. They became prosperous and politically influential. By mid-nineteenth century, their influence contributed to the city's inability to compel their removal.

In the eighteenth and nineteenth centuries, a slaughterhouse was not always considered a legal nuisance in every jurisdiction. Most courts pre-

---

1. Although the growth of the city shifted in an upstream direction, and Slaughterhouse Point ceased to be the center of such activity, the name stuck. George Washington Cable later recalled the sight of Union navy ships as the city prepared to surrender to David Farragut. "Ah, me! I see them now as they come slowly around Slaughterhouse Point into full view, silent, grim and terrible." Quoted in Allan Nevins, *The War for the Union: War Becomes Revolution 1862–1863* (New York: Charles Scribner's Sons, 1960), 101.

New Orleans from the west bank of the Mississippi in 1851. On the extreme right, Slaughterhouse Point faces the city's famous crescent-shaped riverbank. (The Historic New Orleans Collection, #1939.1.)

sumed that it was at least feasible that a slaughterhouse could be operated
in a way that would not give offense to its neighbors. Whether a legal
nuisance or not, however, the business of slaughtering animals and providing meat to the markets of a growing metropolis through a system of private
slaughterhouses was of necessity a noxious one, attended by a variety of
evils. It required nearby stockyards to receive and hold both hogs and steers
while they were bought or sold and until they could be processed. The
business gave rise to related enterprises such as bone-boiling (tallow) factories and fertilizer plants. Moreover, private slaughterhouses made it virtually
impossible to enforce either rules of cleanliness or an effective system of
inspection aimed at preventing the meat of diseased animals from reaching
the market.[2]

In New Orleans, animals were routinely herded through the streets.[3]
Slaughtering sometimes took place out in the open within sight of the public,
including children. When offal was disposed of "correctly," it was loaded
into open carts (which represented a nuisance themselves) that were driven,
leaking and reeking, through the streets to "nuisances wharves," where it
was supposed to be dumped into the river. But much of it was simply discarded into the streets and gutters or left to rot and fester in butchers'
backyards. Though the practice continued unabated, public perception of its
unfortunate results changed after 1850. Barton's 1850–1851 report on the
"meteorology" of the Crescent City recommended that "all slaughterhouses
. . . be removed to the outskirts."[4] Following the 1853 epidemic, Barton's
sanitary commission insisted that cemeteries and slaughterhouses should be
removed from inhabited areas. Political realities, however, prevented such
action, and on the eve of the Civil War, Dr. Axson listed among the city's
prime nuisances "gutters sweltered with the blood and draining of slaughter-
pens."[5]

These deplorable conditions aside, the ineluctable fact remained that the
butchers were a politically strong, cohesive group that always seemed to
have effective representation on the city council, a point that helps explain

2. The evils of a system of private slaughterhouses are cataloged in Bushrod W. James,
"How Abattoirs Improve the Sanitary Conditions of Cities," *Public Health: Reports and
Papers* 6 (1880): 231–38.

3. "Yesterday at the corner of St. Charles and Jackson, a lady was chased by one of the
wild steers and barely escaped with her life." *Daily Picayune*, March 23, 1870, 3. The next
month, the *Picayune* deemed the arrest of eighty-five head of "wild Texas cattle" on Carondelet Street as "eminently proper." Ibid., April 25, 1870, 3.

4. Barton, "Report on the Meteorology," 38.

5. Axson, *Report of the Board of Health, January, 1859*, 35.

why reform was so elusive. Another factor was the apparent inability to determine exactly how many slaughterhouses were in operation at any one time. The 1838 city directory for Lafayette, for example, listed thirty-nine individual butchers. Since the majority of them likely slaughtered at home, this figure can be used as a rough estimate of the number of slaughterhouses. In 1866, the *New Orleans Times* complained about a "multitude of slaughter-houses." An 1868 estimate placed the total number of slaughterhouses in the New Orleans area at 150, and in 1869, the board of health reported 40 such establishments in the Fourth District alone.[6]

Loopholes impeding effective municipal slaughterhouse regulation were numerous. An ordinance might be enacted calling for slaughterhouses to be kept clean, but it provided no penalties for violators. A statute might be passed requiring council approval before a new slaughterhouse could be established within the city, but such approval could be easily obtained. Still another enactment might forbid the operation of any slaughterhouse on the river upstream from the intake pipes of the city water supply, but it would be so qualified as to make it ineffectual. In truth, more often than not, the city ordinances were not enforced, and they had little effect on limiting the number of slaughterhouses. Yet the would-be reformers remained confident that city or state officials had long possessed the authority to bring about effective and lasting regulation. This authority was based on a governmental power well established by midcentury, and some explanations for both the emergence of the centralized abattoir and the development and scope of this "police power" are appropriate here.

IN ANCIENT ROME, slaughtering became the exclusive privilege of a "guild" of butchers, with a portion of the public marketplace set aside for this purpose.[7] Public slaughterhouses were available in parts of Germany by the mid-thirteenth century, and for a time, some of the butchers were compelled to use them.[8] Common slaughterhouses had appeared in Paris by the twelfth

6. J. Gibson, comp., *Gibson's Directory of the Cities of New Orleans and Lafayette for 1838* (New Orleans: J. Gibson, 1838); *New Orleans Times,* August 22, 1866, 4; *Daily Picayune,* March 15, 1868, 3; Louisiana Board of Health, *Report of the Board of Health* (1869), 27, as cited in Gillson, *Formative Years,* 2:140, n. 23.

7. Gustave Devron, *Abattoirs: Report on the Crescent City Live Stock Landing and Slaughterhouse Company to the Board of Health [1875]* (New Orleans: Peychaud and Garcia, 1876), 1; Oscar Schwarz, *Public Abattoirs and Cattle Markets,* ed. G. T. Harris and Loudon M. Douglas (London: Ice and Cold Storage Publishing Co., 1903), 2.

8. Schwarz, *Public Abattoirs,* 2.

century. In 1807, Napoleon ordered the establishment of five slaughter-houses, all located on the outskirts of Paris; by 1818, private slaughterhouses had been forbidden in the city.[9] In 1867, the year in which the Louisiana legislature first considered compulsory consolidation of the New Orleans slaughterhouses, the five separate Paris abattoirs were consolidated into one "grand" establishment at La Villette.[10] Two years later, when the controversial Louisiana statute was enacted, there were compulsory public slaughterhouses in Germany, Scotland, Spain, Switzerland, Belgium, Austria, and Poland.[11]

But Southern supporters of such a move did not have to look as far away as the Continent for precedent. They could search much closer to home for similar developments. By the 1850s, as discussed in the previous chapter, public health had become a national public issue. Within three years (1857 to 1860), no fewer than four national sanitary conventions were held, attended by leading exponents of public health, including a number from New Orleans.[12] At the 1859 convention, Dr. John Bell presented a report in which he stressed the importance of removing slaughterhouses from cites and urged widespread adoption of the French concept of a centralized abattoir.[13] Related reports presented at the same meeting pointed out the dangers of offal to a city's water supply and proposed a draft for a model sanitary code that singled out slaughterhouses and urged their careful regulation by a board of health.[14]

In his outstanding study *The People's Welfare*, Professor William Novak cites *Commonwealth v. Alger* (1851), a decision by Chief Justice Lemuel Shaw of the Massachusetts Supreme Judicial Court, as the prototype for police power decisions. It was one that occupied a "central place in nineteenth century jurisprudence," a holding that accurately articulated a vigorous and expansive police power doctrine.[15] Shaw stated that "every holder of prop-

9. G. S. Franklin, "Abattoirs," *Columbus Medical Journal* 2 (1883–1884): 447.

10. Schwarz, *Public Abattoirs*, 3.

11. Ibid., 6 ff.

12. John Duffy, *The Sanitarians: A History of American Public Health* (Urbana: University of Illinois Press, 1990) 102–8; Wilson G. Smillie and Edwin D. Kilbourne, *Preventive Medicine and Public Health*, 3rd ed. (New York: Macmillan, 1965), 8; Wilson G. Smillie, *Public Health: Its Promise for the Future* (New York: Macmillan, 1955), 3–6.

13. John Bell, "The Importance and Economy of Sanitary Measures to Cities," in *Proceedings and Debates of the Third National Quarantine and Sanitary Convention* (New York: Board of Education, Edward Jones and Co., 1859), 441–620.

14. John Griscom, "Report on Water Supply and Offal," in ibid., 434–40.

15. Novak, *The People's Welfare*, 20, 21.

erty, however absolute and unqualified may be his title, holds it under the implied liability that his use of it may be so regulated, that it shall not be injurious to the equal enjoyment of others . . . nor injurious to the rights of the community."[16] Novak emphasizes that this decision, coming as New Orleans was poised at the brink of major demands for sanitation reform, was "firmly entrenched in the intellectual, political, and legal traditions of nineteenth-century America."[17]

Indeed it was, as examination of a number of state cases makes clear. In 1849, the Supreme Court of Georgia ruled that "every right, from an absolute ownership in property, down to a mere easement, is purchased and holden [*sic*], subject to the restriction that it shall be so exercised as not to injure others."[18] Seven years later, the same court that had handed down the *Alger* decision again insisted that "the public health, the welfare and safety of the community, are matters of paramount importance, to which all the pursuits, occupations and employments of individuals, inconsistent with their preservation, must yield."[19] In 1867, in a case that involved slaughter-houses, the California Supreme Court emphasized that "the power to regulate or prohibit conferred upon the Board of Supervisors not only includes nuisances, but extends to everything 'expedient for the preservation of the public health and the prevention of contagious diseases.' Now there are many things not coming up to the full measure of a common law or statutory nuisance, that might, both in the light of scientific tests and of general experience, pave the way for the introduction of contagion and its uncontrollable spread thereafter. Slaughterhouses, as ordinarily and perhaps invariably conducted in this country, might, within the limits of reasonable probability, be attended with these consequences."[20]

Yet not all courts were sympathetic toward municipal efforts to deal with slaughterhouses. Even as the California court affirmed such an attempt, the Illinois Supreme Court rejected an award by the city of Chicago to one firm for the exclusive right to operate a slaughterhouse. Indeed, the experiences of both Illinois and New York offer contrasting examples of the interplay among jurisprudence, police power doctrine, and private entrepreneurial activity. They provide a paradigm for the New Orleans *Slaughterhouse* contro-

16. Ibid., 19–20.
17. Ibid., 21.
18. *Green v. The Mayor and Aldermen of Savannah,* 6 Geo. 1, 13 (1849).
19. *Commonwealth v. Upton,* 72 Mass. 473, 476 (1856).
20. *Ex Parte Shrader,* 33 Cal. 279, 284 (1867). "A competent legislative body has passed upon the question of fact involved, and we cannot go behind the finding."

versy, because the statute at issue in Illinois may well have been the model for the Louisiana counterpart.

By the mid-nineteenth century, Chicago was well on its way to becoming the nation's leading livestock market and meatpacking center. After the Civil War, it was disposing of a thousand head of cattle on a daily basis.[21] The resulting expansion of packing and fertilizer plants, tanneries, and glue factories contributed to a pollution problem of historic proportions that—as was seen in Louisiana—defied solution both logistically and politically. Much of the slaughterhouse waste material was dumped into open spaces beyond the city limits, and for years, enormous quantities were discharged into the Chicago River. The time came when certain parts of the river became clogged with a layer of decaying animal matter as much as two feet thick. Although fear of cholera could prompt the adoption of ordinances creating a board of health and banning new slaughterhouses within the city, as it did in 1849 and 1850 (again, as was true in New Orleans), once that possibility had abated, enthusiasm for sanitation reform waned.[22] But the problem persisted in all its magnitude.

Responding once again to the specter of cholera, toward the end of 1865, the Chicago city council undertook to establish the nation's first compulsory municipal slaughterhouse. In an ordinance that ultimately would be struck down in Illinois but later copied in New York, Milwaukee, Boston, and New Orleans, it awarded an exclusive ten-year franchise to a single firm to operate a large slaughterhouse in Chicago. The new facility could charge no fee for its use but could retain for future sale various parts of beef that were slaughtered on its premises. After it opened at Ogden Slip in April 1866, no other slaughterhouses could operate in Chicago, "except that done at the regular packing houses for packing purposes."[23] The statute was promptly denounced by the butchers as a monopoly and an unreasonable restriction of their right to slaughter wherever they wished.[24] By 1867, the matter was before the Illinois Supreme Court.

In a unanimous vote, noteworthy for its total lack of case citation, the court struck down the ordinance, even as it extolled the legitimacy of the police

---

21. James Parton, "Chicago," *Atlantic Monthly* 19 (March 1869): 325, 332.

22. Louise Carroll Wade, *Chicago's Pride: The Stockyards, Packingtown, and Environs in the Nineteenth Century* (Urbana: University of Illinois Press, 1987), 29–30.

23. Joseph E. Gary, comp., *Laws and Ordinances Governing the City of Chicago, Jan 1, 1866* (Chicago, 1866), 519–22, Chicago Historical Society Library. This exception notwithstanding, the statute clearly eliminated the right of small, family-owned, local butchers to slaughter, *except* at the new facility. *City of Chicago v. Rumpff*, 45 Ill. 90, 93 (1867).

24. Wade, *Chicago's Pride*, 68.

power. Justice Pinkney H. Walker denounced the statute as a nonregulatory enactment that was beyond the authority of the city council to pass. The creation of municipal corporations "is convenient, if not essential, for the regulation of the local police; to adopt and enforce all needful sanitary regulations; to establish and control markets . . . and perform the various other duties necessary to promote the comfort and well being of such densely crowded communities as constitute large cities."[25] Without mentioning the term, Walker here recognized the inherent legitimacy of the police power. The council did indeed have the right "to so regulate the business of slaughtering animals, as to prohibit its exercise, except in a particular portion of the city, leaving all persons free to erect slaughtering houses, and to exercise the calling at the place designated."[26]

But "an ordinance confining such a business to a small lot, or even a particular block of ground, is unreasonable, and tends to create a monopoly." Nor was it legitimate "to say that butchering animals is a nuisance." If it is, then why was the favored company permitted to maintain a slaughterhouse? And if its establishment "was not, how can it be said that others on adjoining lots, or even in its vicinity, similarly constructed and kept, would be nuisances?"[27] Walker insisted that "when privileges are granted by an ordinance, they should be open to the enjoyment of all, upon the same terms and conditions." The court did not doubt that the city had authority "to designate the particular quarter of the city within which the business may be conducted, and prohibit it in others . . . but in doing so, all persons should be free to engage in the business within these localities by conforming to the municipal regulations."[28] In some ways, this unanimous decision can be seen as a harbinger of what was to come, but in 1867, the Illinois Supreme Court swam against the current judicial wave of police power decisions.

The distinction of having the first centralized abattoir in North America, some 200 years before *Slaughterhouse,* appears to belong to New York City. Established in 1676 and privately owned but franchised by the city, it had the effect of both confining slaughtering to a single place and facilitating

25. 45 Ill. 95.

26. Ibid., 96–97. "Where privileges are granted by an ordinance, they should be open to the enjoyment of all, upon the same terms and conditions."

27. Ibid., 97, 98.

28. Ibid., 99. It would seem that there was ample precedent available to sustain the statute under attack in this case as a simple police measure. But, possibly because of political factors, the judges, all of whom had to face the exigencies of an electorate, declined to emphasize the police power, opting instead to denounce the alleged nonregulatory nature of the ordinance.

some sort of municipal inspection. As residential neighborhoods grew up around the site, and as the butchers expanded their business, they demanded more space. Inevitably, some began to kill cattle on their own premises, and by 1749, New York City found it necessary to adopt a new ordinance prohibiting slaughtering anywhere in the city except at the public slaughterhouse. After the Revolution and in the midst of continued urban expansion, the system of public inspection faltered. New York's early system of public slaughterhouses similarly declined.

Like so many other municipalities, by the mid-nineteenth century, New York City had a critical public health problem. According to John Duffy, "Municipal regulations, slowed down by Jacksonian democracy and the principle of laissez faire, had simply not kept pace with the city's expansion." And when ordinances were eventually adopted, they often went unenforced.[29] As was true in other municipalities, failure on the local level led to involvement of the state legislature. "New York's City Council could not be expected to discard a system that provided jobs and contracts for the political faithful."[30] Rebutting the usual arguments that urban problems were not a concern of the state as a whole, and that state legislators were not competent to deal with them, "passage of the Metropolitan Health Act of 1866 marked a new era for New York and American public health."[31]

Almost immediately, the newly established Metropolitan Board of Health clashed with local butchers. There were more than 200 slaughterhouses in New York in the mid-1860s, and it would take years of pressure before the last slaughterhouse was finally relocated.[32] The butchers' arguments would become all too familiar as other cities sought to rein in slaughtering through use of the police power in this period when urban expansion tried to accommodate itself to industrialization. A slaughterhouse, they insisted, was not necessarily a nuisance, per se. It could be operated in an inoffensive man-

---

29. John Duffy, *A History of Public Health in New York City, 1625–1866* (New York: Russell Sage Foundation, 1968), 377. "The sanitary problems of New York never arose from a dearth of ordinances—the difficulty as always was in the enforcement." Ibid., 379.

30. Charles E. Rosenberg, *The Cholera Years: The United States in 1832, 1849, and 1866* (Chicago: University of Chicago Press, 1979), 188–89.

31. Duffy, *History of Public Health in New York City*, 563–64, 569.

32. Ibid., 383; E. H. Janes, "Sanitary View of Abattoirs and the Slaughtering Business in New York," *Public Health Reports and Papers* 3 (1877): 1, 29, 30 n. 1. The New York experience is especially well documented in a group of papers and newspaper clippings dating from 1660 to 1866 collected by Thomas F. Devoe, New York butcher and market historian, Devoe Collection, New York Historical Society.

ner.[33] Efforts to centralize butchering were described as "only the beginning of a vast monopoly in which the Board of Health will have an interest."[34] Further, the butchers claimed that given the costs of relocating their establishments, a "sudden expulsion" from the city limits "would so embarrass the business as to seriously interfere with the [city's] supply of meat."[35] Finally, "as butchers were, like other freemen, aware of their rights," they claimed that schemes to force them into consolidated facilities "interfered with peaceable possession of private property."[36] And time and again the butchers went to court. Unlike their cattle, they would not be driven. "Despite its theoretically almost unlimited powers, the orders of the board were nullified again and again by injunction. This was a decade of understanding judges."[37]

But the board of health was not alone in its interest in slaughterhouse reform. Inevitably, other parties saw a potential for private profit in the situation. In August 1866, *Scientific American* reported that "a new abattoir, somewhat on the French plan, is now in the course of construction at the foot of 106th street."[38] Similarly, a group of entrepreneurs from Chicago obtained a charter from the New Jersey legislature for the New Jersey Stockyard and Market Company, located near the New Jersey Central Railway on the Bay of New York. Owned largely by railroad stockholders from New York to Chicago, it was intended to serve the New York market.[39] In still another private effort that closely paralleled the forthcoming New Orleans dispute, a coal dealer with no experience in the livestock industry constructed a set of cheap buildings on 39th Street and 11th Avenue and dubbed them "The New York Abattoir." The scheme failed to achieve council support, however. According to Devoe, the buildings remained as

33. *New York Times*, March 10, 1866 (clipping), Devoe Collection. In January 1850, a committee of the New York Common Council referred to the idea that a slaughterhouse was a nuisance per se as "a principle at war with the experience of mankind in all ages." Quoted in Thomas F. Devoe, "Abattoirs: Paper Read before the Polytechnic Association, June 8, 1865," reprinted in *New York Times*, April 1, 1866, 2.

34. *New York Times*, September 16, 1866 (clipping), Devoe Collection.

35. Henry G. Crowell, "Sanitary Regulations Relating to Abattoirs," *Public Health Reports and Papers* 3 (1877): 19, quoting the 1867 board of health report.

36. Devoe, "Abattoirs."

37. Rosenberg, *Cholera Years*, 207.

38. "An Abattoir for New York," *Scientific American* 15 (August 18, 1866): 120.

39. *New York Evening Post*, June 16, 1866; "New Jersey," *New York Times*, July 10, 1866 (clippings), Devoe Collection; E. H. Janes, "The Management of Slaughterhouses," *The Sanitarian* 2 (October 1874): 289–95.

"a monument of impractical application and of a speculation destined to perform a different service from that first intended."[40]

After making little progress in discussions with the butchers, in 1867, the board of health prohibited all cattle from being driven or slaughtered anywhere in New York City below 40th Street. Predictably, the butchers sued to block implementation of the order and insisted that the real intent of the board was to remove all slaughterhouses from the city. In addition, they argued that the board's action violated a provision of the New York State Constitution holding that "no person shall be deprived of life, liberty or property without due process of law." In 1868, just one year before adoption of the Louisiana slaughterhouse statute, the case reached the New York Court of Appeals. But there is an even more intriguing symmetry between the 1868 decision and the Supreme Court litigation yet to come. The decision in the New York case of *Metropolitan Board of Health v. Heister* is of special interest because it was authored by Chief Justice Ward Hunt. In 1873, he would be appointed by President Grant to the U.S. Supreme Court, where the first major case he participated in was *Slaughterhouse*.

In *Heister*, there was no denial that the butcher had violated the health ordinance that prohibited both the driving and the slaughtering of cattle in the city of New York south of 40th Street. Rather, Heister insisted that the ordinance was unconstitutional. Speaking for a divided court, Hunt upheld the statute and observed that "no one has been deprived of his property or of his liberty by the proceedings in question." The health commissioners had determined that "cattle shall not be driven upon certain streets except at certain hours of the day. They have also provided that the business of slaughtering cattle shall not be carried on in the city of New York south of a designated line." Contrary to Heister's claim, "these regulations take away no man's property."[41]

If, added Chief Justice Hunt, "Mr. Heister owns cattle, his ownership is not interfered with. He may sell, exchange and traffic in the same manner as any other person owning cattle may do. If he owns a slaughterhouse, his property remains intact. He may sell it, mortgage it . . . and may use it just as any other man or all other men in the State combined may do." Simply put, "the health regulations of the district operate upon his cattle and his slaughterhouse in the same manner that they do upon live property owned by all others, and the use of the streets for dangerous purposes of the prose-

40. Devoe, "Abattoirs."
41. *Metropolitan Board of Health v. Heister*, 37 N.Y. 661, 668 (1868.)

cution of a business dangerous to the public health is regulated by the ordinances in question."[42]

Enactment of the regulation had not deprived Heister of his right to pursue his chosen calling. He could not, however, butcher below a certain area, and neither could he run his cattle through a specific part of the city. Moreover, Heister had insisted that the regulation unlawfully conferred on the board of health quasi-judicial power, in violation of the New York Constitution. Again, Hunt rejected the contention and in so doing clarified an important dimension of the police power. Judicial authority was not the issue.

> The power to be exercised by this Board upon the subjects in question is not judicial in its character. It falls more properly under the head [*sic*] of an administrative duty. . . . It is no more judicial than is the action of commissioners of excise [*sic*] in the country, or of the metropolitan police board, who, as commissioners of excise, discuss the question of whether a license shall be granted to an individual to keep an inn or to sell spirituous liquors. . . . But such powers have never been held to be of a judicial character. The power of the metropolitan board to act upon the latter subject has been distinctly sustained in this court.[43]

In dissent, Justice Theodore Miller claimed that the ordinance "was local in its operation, and related to the city of New York." The provisions of the statute establishing the board of health invade "the powers guaranteed by the Constitution to local authorities, and confer them upon officers who hold their offices by appointment from the governor and senate, and who are not chosen by the electors of the city of New York or appointed by any body so elected, and who do not hold from any authority which invest them with the prerogatives of local legislation." As far as Miller was concerned, the board did not possess the authority it had exercised.[44] Even worse, however, was the obvious violation of due process.

"The order of the board pronounced condemnation of the defendant's business without any sort of preliminary notice, and with no opportunity to be heard and to try the question before rendition of judgment."[45] Apparently, "the board of health have authority, without notice to the party to be affected by their proceeding, by partial and hearsay evidence, to declare the

42. Ibid. "This practice is not forbidden by the Constitution, and has been recognized from the organization of the State government."
43. Ibid., 672.
44. Ibid., 678.
45. Ibid., 681.

property of a citizen a nuisance, dangerous to life and health and unless afterward satisfied by the owner that [this] judgment is erroneous and should be reversed, to affirm and ratify the order thus made. Such a proceeding is unknown to the proceedings in any court of justice, and there is no power, in my opinion, to delegate to a board of health the right to define what shall be a nuisance, or to make acts criminal which the law holds innocent."[46] Miller may have had logic on his side, but he did not have the votes, and Hunt's opinion to the contrary reflected the dominant view in mid-nine-teenth-century American law that the police power did indeed apply to the regulation of slaughterhouses.

In short, the famous Louisiana case with which this study is concerned must be seen in the context of these earlier holdings. By the time slaughter-house reform was brought to the Louisiana legislature in 1869, the script for the drama had already been presented in many different theaters. Every scene—recognition of the sanitary problems, initial unsuccessful efforts for reform at the local level, resistance by butchers, resort to the state legisla-ture, and eventual vindication of the state's use of the police power—would be faithfully replayed in New Orleans. However heated, the New Orleans drama was a rerun, not a new production.

In 1873, the twelfth edition of James Kent's *Commentaries*, edited by Oliver Wendell Holmes, was published. Appearing eight months after the *Slaughterhouse Cases* were decided, it represents a fitting summary of the police power doctrine. Included among Kent's comments on property was the claim that property rights, though important, "must be made subservient to the public welfare." Moreover, what Novak describes as "unwholesome trades [and] slaughterhouses" fell under Kent's "general and rational princi-ple, that every person ought so to use his property as not to injure his neighbors, and that private interest must be made subservient to the general interest of the community."[47] Two years after *Slaughterhouse*, another con-temporary treatise, specifically on the law of nuisances, insisted that "no man is at liberty to use his own without any reference to the health, comfort or reasonable enjoyment . . . by others."[48]

46. Ibid., 682.

47. Novak, *The People's Welfare*, 49–50. Novak emphasizes that Kent had invoked "nothing less than the two great principles of the well-regulated society, *sic utero tuo* and *salus populi*." Not only was a property owner barred from using his property in a way that might injure others, but the public safety was of *primary* concern to the legal order.

48. Ibid., 44–45, quoting Horace G. Wood, *A Practical Treatise on the Law of Nuisances*, 2nd ed. (Albany, N.Y., 1883), 21. As will be seen, *Slaughterhouse* may stand as a watershed of major change in police power interpretation. In the future, focus would be less on the limitations and sacrifices that private property owners might have to accept in the name of the police power and more on the rights that various segments of society might insist

*   *   *

IT IS NOT SURPRISING, especially after the travail described in chapter 2, that in 1862 the city council of Jefferson City took up the slaughterhouse issue. There is no way of knowing if the city fathers had any sense of the rich potential inherent in the police power, but it is clear that erstwhile reformers had consistently emphasized the ability of municipal government to take action concerning the problem. In 1862, Jefferson City contained the majority of the slaughterhouses within greater New Orleans. Thus the move to centralize these establishments was significant. Perhaps the decades of indifference, the inexorable progress of the epidemics, and the growing influence of the medical community as a convincing voice for reform had finally begun to make a difference.

On April 7, 1862, the city council of Jefferson City, the stock landing and slaughtering hub of the Crescent City area, took a significant step toward both slaughterhouse reform and the great constitutional litigation with which this study is concerned. It awarded an exclusive franchise to three businessmen, William Hepp, Albin Rochereau, and Raymond Pochelu, plus others "who may join them." They received authority to erect "at their expense" a "general slaughterhouse . . . and to have and enjoy, during twenty-five years from the completion thereof the exclusive privileges of slaughtering animals within the limits of [Jefferson City]." Moreover, once the facility was completed and opened to the public, the city council was required to give public notice for thirty days about the changes that were to take place. "All private slaughterhouses within the incorporated limits of the City of Jefferson shall be closed and . . . it will no longer be permitted to slaughter cattle or swine there; under a $100 penalty for each violation, all animals must be slaughtered in the general slaughterhouse."

The new company would use the existing stock landing but it had the option to expand it at its own expense. Further, the mayor could appoint inspectors who would issue certificates to owners of cattle to be slaughtered, and the city would set the fees to be paid to the inspectors for the account of the city. The ordinance set the tariffs that the company could charge for use of its facilities. Finally, after the expiration of the franchise, the city had an option to purchase the facility from its proprietors.[49]

---

on—including the right to pursue one's occupation free of any police power regulations except those that fell equally on all who pursued it.

49. City of Jefferson, La., Board of Aldermen, *Minutes*, vol. 3 (1861–1868), 73–74, City Archives, Louisiana Division, New Orleans Public Library. In August 1861, the aldermen had formed a three-member committee, with the mayor serving ex officio, to confer with New Orleans authorities about the possibilities of establishing public slaughterhouses under the joint control of both cities. At the same time, the committee protested a proposed New

Several important points about this ordinance should be noted. In the first place, the vote approving it appears to have been unanimous. The official records reveal no evidence of recorded opposition to its ultimate enactment. Moreover, examination of the three local newspapers failed to locate any mention whatsoever of the franchise ordinance. Apparently, it caused little, if any, stir within the community. Nevertheless, the implications of such a statute are noteworthy. It would have given an exclusive franchise for a slaughterhouse to a single company for twenty-five years and designated the area in which it could be constructed. After due notice, all slaughtering in Jefferson City could be undertaken *only* on its premises. In other words, this ordinance—which would have affected most of the butchers in greater New Orleans and was adopted with little debate and no apparent public interest, let alone opposition—was identical in all essentials to what only seven years later would cause bitter opposition and prolonged litigation.

Yet this slaughterhouse was never constructed. There are several possible explanations. One reason may be that other butchers were disinclined to join the venture, given the uncertainty of the times. Quite possibly, there were fears concerning the enormous resentment that would almost certainly arise when the butchers learned that they would have to pay a fee to use the company's facilities and that it was no longer permissible to operate a private slaughterhouse. Perhaps the most important reason, however, is that about three weeks after passage of the ordinance, General Benjamin Butler occupied New Orleans. As Randell Hunt, one of the attorneys in the forthcoming *Slaughterhouse* litigation later explained, the city "was cut off from trade and commerce, and from intercourse and communication with other parts of the Union. General Butler was here; a large number of citizens were expelled; the city was walled in by military rule. Is it a wonder, then, that Hepp and Rochereau could not use the powers and privileges conferred upon them by the ordinance?"[50]

* * *

Orleans ordinance that would have given a fifteen-year monopoly to New Orleans butchers to slaughter all meat offered for sale within the city. The proposal was "unjust and injurious" to a large portion of Jefferson City's citizens. However, one month later, the committee reported that it had learned that any such ordinance passed by the New Orleans city council would be vetoed by the mayor, "making it unnecessary for" any committee action. Ibid., 29–31. Support for any jointly operated slaughterhouse was not evident.

50. William Henry Hunt, ed., *Selected Arguments, Lectures, and Miscellaneous Papers of Randell Hunt* (New Orleans: F. F. Hansell and Brother, 1896), 70.

GENERAL BUTLER came and went. By March 1866, New Orleans had reverted to civilian control, and there followed a scenario all too familiar in the Crescent City. Butler's provost marshal during the occupation later recalled that "it was only by the rigorous exercise of military power in the enforcement of the sanitary regulations that the city was exempt from the yellow fever." The writer, General James Bowen, predicted that "with the usual lax administration of such laws by civil authority, the city will once again be subject to its visitation."[51] Bowen's comments were reiterated by Dr. Edward Fenner, who emphasized that the municipal cleanup during the recent occupation represented "a Herculean task, and in our humble opinion, nothing short of military despotism would have accomplished it. The good work [however] is not yet completed."[52]

Fenner knew whereof he spoke. Only days before the return of civilian control (and the cessation of enforced sanitation rules by the military), the mayor issued a lengthy proclamation warning against a possible epidemic and urging strict adherence to all requirements, including the ordinances regarding the condition of slaughterhouses.[53] Less than two weeks later, the *Picayune* noted that nobody was doing anything to comply with the mayor's request.[54]

The street commissioner urged the city council to take over the job of cleaning the streets because the contractor was not performing that duty, and "our country is threatened by a direful epidemic."[55] In August 1866, the editors of a local medical journal complained, "This city is now filthy in the extreme."[56] The specter of disease in major proportions quickly returned. Cholera struck the Crescent City twice in 1866—first in March, and again even more virulently during the summer. A year later, yellow fever revisited New Orleans.[57]

51. Harris, "Hygienic Experiences in New Orleans during the War," 464, 470.

52. Erasmus D. Fenner, "Remarks on the Sanitary Conditions of the City of New Orleans during the Period of Federal Military Occupation from May, 1862 to March, 1866," *Southern Journal of Medical Sciences* 1 (1866): 23–24.

53. *Daily Picayune*, March 14, 1866, 6.

54. Ibid., March 26, 1866, 3.

55. Street Commissioner to Common Council, New Orleans Board of Assistant Aldermen, *Minutes*, vol. 21 (May 10, 1866), 107, City Archives.

56. "Editorial: On the Health of the City," *Southern Journal of Medical Science* 1 (August 1866): 395.

57. Dr. George A. Avery, the chief medical officer during the occupation, recalled in 1871 that after New Orleans "passed into the keeping of the civil authorities, it soon degenerated back to its old condition—or perhaps worse." George A. Avery, *A Lecture on the Progressive Spirit of the Medical Profession Delivered before the New Orleans Academy of Sciences, April 10, 1871* (New Orleans: Hopkins Press, 1871), 21.

Shortly after the end of occupation, on April 16, 1866, the Louisiana State Board of Public Health was reorganized. It had been created by the legislature in 1855 but had not functioned since the imposition of martial law in 1862. The newly resurrected board created a committee to recommend measures that it deemed "necessary to enforce a thorough sanitary police for the city during the present season," and it urged the city to form a similar committee of its own.[58] In the meantime, a prominent item on the board's agenda was the problem of the slaughterhouses. At its meeting of June 11, for example, the board heard a letter raising anew the complaint that slaughterhouses above the city should be removed because their habits of throwing offal and dead cattle into the river jeopardized "the health of the whole community."[59]

It should be understood that the reconstituted board of health was not a Reconstruction body. That would occur, but not until November 1868, when newly elected Governor Henry C. Warmoth appointed a board consisting entirely of fellow Republicans. Nevertheless, the interests and constituencies represented by the board of health, on the one hand, and the city council, on the other, had always been quite different. Even before Reconstruction, ordinances proposed by the board did not sail through the council to easy adoption. Quite the contrary. Shortly after its reorganization, the board submitted a comprehensive sanitary ordinance, but the city authorities dragged their feet. Although the board had acted in a timely fashion, as the *New Orleans Medical and Surgical Journal* later complained, "the city authorities delayed and protracted their actions . . . until cases of both cholera and yellow fever had occurred."[60] Not until July 12 did the city appoint its committee, and the proposed ordinance did not clear the lower chamber of the council until late July.[61]

Impetus for the ordinance came from a petition presented to the city council on May 29, 1866, signed by about 500 citizens and later supported by spokesmen for the waterworks. It denounced the large number of slaughterhouses located near the municipal waterworks. In turn, the Committee on Police and Health recommended that the council take action "to move

58. Louisiana State Board of Health, *Minutes*, June 4, 1866, Louisiana State Archives, Baton Rouge.

59. Ibid., June 11, 1866.

60. "Health of the City," *New Orleans Medical and Surgical Journal* (November 1866): 421.

61. New Orleans Board of Assistant Aldermen, *Minutes*, vol. 21, July 12, 1866, 202; Ordinance No. 235 approved August 2, 1866, *Health Ordinances of the City of New Orleans*, City Archives.

or cause to be moved all slaughterhouses now established . . . in the First
and Fourth Districts of the city, the same being injurious to the health of
the city."[62] According to the *Picayune*, this led to "considerable discussion,"
but no ordinance.[63] In the same period, however, two entrepreneurial individuals approached the council—unsuccessfully, it turned out—with competing proposals.

Henry Bezou and V. Gaschet Delisle offered bids of $40,000 and
$50,000, respectively, for the privilege of building and operating an exclu-
sive slaughterhouse of "great dimensions," and fireproof as well, in the
city's sparsely settled Third District—below the city. Moreover, the slaughterhouses located above the city (the great majority of such establishments)
would have to close.[64] This was the second such proposal for a centralized
slaughterhouse. The first had been the one put forth by Hepp, Rochereau,
and Pochelu, noted earlier. This time, however, opposition was evident and
recorded. Much of it emanated from one council member, John Kaiser, who
well reflected the fact that the butchers and stock dealers formed an organized, coherent, and politically adept organization.

Kaiser was a faithful and energetic representative of the butchers' interests. Although not involved in the livestock industry himself, he had resided
in the Fourth Municipal District for nearly thirty years. Thus, he was familiar with the many livestock operations both there and in nearby Jefferson
City. He could always be counted on to oppose any effort at regulation or
to testify in favor of a particular butcher whose slaughterhouse had been
singled out as a public health nuisance.[65] In his view, there was nothing
particularly unhealthy or deleterious about slaughterhouses. On the contrary, he insisted that when an epidemic struck New Orleans, there was less
sickness among the butchers than anywhere else in the city. Moreover, and,
from his perspective, probably more important, "there is a very large
amount of capital invested in the slaughterhouses in the 4th district, and in
the Parish of Jefferson, and if they were to move them, it would be the
ruination of those people."[66]

62. New Orleans Board of Assistant Aldermen, *Minutes*, vol. 21, May 29, 1866, 153; June
12, 1866, 204, City Archives.
63. *Daily Picayune*, June 13, 1866, 8.
64. *New Orleans Times*, July 19, 1866, 15.
65. See, e.g., *Times*, January 21, 1866, 10.
66. See Kaiser's testimony in Louisiana House of Representatives, Special Committee on
the Removal of the Slaughterhouses, *Minute Book* (1867), 39, Louisiana Collection, LSU
Libraries, Louisiana State University, Baton Rouge; hereafter, *Minute Book of the Special
Committee*.

A good example of Kaiser's watchfulness and political agility occurred during the Bezou and Deslisle efforts to establish a centralized slaughterhouse in the Third District. The idea of relocating these establishments in a single facility below the city enjoyed popular support; indeed, as will be seen, the concept later became a reality. For reasons that are not clear, the Deslisle proposal went no further, but on May 29, 1866, the board of assistant aldermen granted Bezou permission to establish a single stock landing in the Third District. Kaiser, however, succeeded in gaining reconsideration, and in the end, both the Delisle and the Bezou proposals were rejected. Instead, ordinances were adopted to award contracts for a term of fifteen years to the highest bidders for the construction of two separate slaughterhouses—one in the Third District and the other in the Fourth.[67] Thus, Kaiser ensured rejection of the reformers' primary goal: centralization of the slaughterhouses in one district. His "solution," in fact, was a self-defeating ploy because few would go to the expense of constructing (nor would many butchers utilize) a grand slaughterhouse below the city as long as there was at least one to serve the many butchers whose businesses were located in and around the Fourth District.

Kaiser also took on the 1866 health ordinance. Hopes had been high for this proposal. While it was making its way through the city council, the *Times* had hailed it as being on a par with similar ordinances enacted in New York, Philadelphia, and Baltimore.[68] Kaiser disagreed, denouncing the proposed legislation as "more tyrannical than the military law," and when it reached the board of assistant aldermen, he saw to it that the draft was referred to a special committee of four, with himself as chair.[69] What ultimately became law on August 2, 1866, was far from what its petitioners had sought. It required all slaughterhouses and similar facilities to be kept clean and forbade the throwing of "dead animals . . . or other . . . injurious matter into the river above the waterworks." It also imposed a fine for the establishment of a slaughterhouse on the river above the waterworks, "the offal . . . from which, may, by being discharged [into the river], . . . spoil the water supplied by said waterworks to the city."[70]

67. Article 367, Ordinance No. 232 (n.s.), and Article 368, Ordinance No. 233 (n.s.), *Ordinances of 1866,* 13–14. Board of Assistant Aldermen, *Minutes,* May 15, 1866, 122; May 22, 1866, 144; June 5, 1866, 185; July 25, 1866, 335–36; July 26, 1866, 238, City Archives.

68. "Health of the City," *Times,* July 22, 1866, 2.

69. *Daily Picayune,* July 10, 1866, 8.

70. Articles 490–95, Ordinance No. 235 (n.s.), approved August 2, 1866, *Health Ordinances for the City of New Orleans,* City Archives. Kaiser successfully resisted as impractical one provision that would have required dead animals and offal to be transported to a point

It had been widely expected that this ordinance would prohibit slaughter-houses from operating above the waterworks, thus compelling their removal from the Fourth District once and for all. This is what the popular petition of May 29 had sought, and indeed, the city council was criticized for agree-ing to license two new slaughterhouses in the Fourth District, even as it adopted the 1866 ordinance. Yet there was nothing inconsistent about its actions. A close reading of the new ordinance indicates that it was perfectly legal to maintain a slaughterhouse on the river above the waterworks, as long as its offal was not discharged into the river in such a way as to contaminate the water supplied to the city. Left open were a variety of modes of discharging offal into the river that, arguably, would not do this. Moreover, the ordinance did not provide for the closure of any offending slaughterhouse, but only a fine of between $50 and $100 in the unlikely event that anyone was successfully prosecuted under the new law.

This ordinance of August 2, 1866, might have been considered a failure, just another abortive attempt at reform, except for one provision that proved to be of unexpected significance. It provided for the appointment by the board of health of health officers for each of four sanitary districts, corre-sponding with the existing municipal districts. They were to be physicians "of standing and reputation" who would serve as inspectors in their respec-tive districts for $1,500 a year, a sum sufficient to attract competent medical men. More effectively than the board of health itself, these officers institu-tionalized a revived concern for sanitation and public health throughout New Orleans. Only a week after the ordinance had been adopted, the board of health publicized the location of a complaint book in each district and invited the public to report health nuisances from 9:00 A.M. to 6:00 P.M. daily.[71]

Unlike previous efforts, the health officers now conducted regular dis-trict inspections and reported to the board of health. They did not hesitate to call problems to the attention of either that body or the city council. Moreover, they could even order the abatement of a nuisance and enlist the assistance of the street commissioner or the police to enforce their orders. It is doubtful, however, that their power was effective against large and well-established nuisances such as slaughterhouses. Nevertheless, after the health officers had been on the job for less than a month, the board of health's

---

at least one quarter of a mile below the city before being dumped into the river. "City Council," *Daily Picayune,* July 26, 1866, 8.

71. Article 495, Ordinance No. 235 (n.s.), approved on August 2, 1866, City Archives; *New Orleans Bee,* August 9, 1866, 1.

Committee on Health praised them for their diligence and called the results of their efforts "a decided improvement in the health of the city."[72]

Although it is not clear whether the publicity resulting from the inspectors' efforts contributed to the growing pressure for change, at a minimum, their activities were helpful from the outset in proving both the ineffectiveness of present regulation and the need for further legislation. One inspector voiced concern about the "immense quantities" of tainted beef on the market. When the mayor took no action, he ordered the meat to be seized.[73] A month later, the inspector in the Fourth District reported to the board of health about the "multitudes of slaughterhouses" located within his district, as well as various nuisances associated with them. The now familiar litany of complaints always included inadequate drainage and, of course, "the very filthy condition of the slaughter pens."[74]

Besides the perennial lack of commitment to real health reform in New Orleans, the problems of the Crescent City were compounded because their causes extended beyond both its political will and its geographical boundaries. Although many of the slaughterhouses were located in the city's Fourth District, the major part of the industry was centered in Jefferson City, a separately incorporated urban municipality that fronted the river adjacent to and just upstream from the Fourth District. Even if strong regulatory measures had been taken in New Orleans, they would have had no application in Jefferson City, where they were most needed. Within its limits was the stock landing that served the entire metropolitan area. In fact, this facility was the axis around which all the stockyards and slaughterhouses revolved. Rather than improving it, the city council of Jefferson City was more concerned about ensuring that a new tenant would lease the property for $12,000. Similarly, in April 1866, rather than regulate the existing slaughterhouses, the council granted licenses for three new ones.[75]

Obviously, Jefferson City would have to be included in any plan for sanitary reform. Not surprisingly, proponents of reform turned from the city council and urged—at last—that relief be provided by the Louisiana state legislature. On August 10, 1866, a grand jury sitting in the First District Court formally recommended that the slaughterhouse problem be referred to this body and that it be urged to remove "the greatest of all

72. Board of Health, *Minutes*, August 21, 1866, State Archives.

73. *New Orleans Medical and Surgical Journal* 19 (July 1866): 425.

74. *Times*, August 22, 1866, 4; *Daily Picayune*, August 22, 1866, 8; Gillson, *Formative Years*, 114, citing *Daily Picayune* for August 15, 18, 1866.

75. Jefferson City Board of Aldermen, *Minutes*, April 16, 1866, 422, City Archives.

nuisances."[76] Four days later, the superintendent of the municipal water-works addressed a supporting letter to the grand jury. He complained about the effect of the slaughterhouses on his operation and suggested that "their entire removal would be a public benefit." In response, the grand jury issued a special report on August 21, released the superintendent's letter, reminded the public of its earlier submission, and once again called for remedial action by the state legislature. "We recommend that the city authorities should take this matter into immediate consideration, and besides passing the requisite ordinances they should petition the legislature asking that if it be in their power, they pass an act that there should not be allowed to exist, any slaughterhouses or similar places above the city within a specified number of miles." Such an act was needed because, "should the city authorities cause the removal of such establishments from the upper portions of the city, they could be reestablished barely above the city limits and would be as great nuisances than as now."[77] Now the issue of reform rested in the state legislature.

THE LEGISLATURE that convened in New Orleans in January 1867 was not a radical body. It should not be confused with the lawmakers who would later be elected under congressional Reconstruction. Indeed, the First Reconstruction Act had not yet been passed. To be sure, the new state constitution had been drafted in 1864 during military occupation and by a convention that represented only a portion of the state. But the first elections held under its auspices in November 1865 had been hailed by the *Picayune* as heralding a "new era in Louisiana." According to that paper, the new legislature "will represent and express the will of the real citizens of the state, the *bona fide* people of the state."[78] As such, it gave serious consideration to the issue of slaughterhouse relocation.

Introduced in the house by G. F. Thieneman of Orleans Parish, the measure would have prohibited slaughterhouses on either bank of the river at any point above the waterworks and as far as the upper line of Jefferson Parish. The bill received prompt and favorable endorsement from the appro-

76. This quotation appears in Randell Hunt's argument, cited earlier. Although he does not give a date for the grand jury presentment, he is probably referring to the August 10 report. See *Daily Picayune*, August 11, 1866, 8.

77. Ibid., August 22, 1866, 8; Special Report of the Grand Jury of the Parish of Orleans, August 21, 1866, as provided in *Minute Book of the Special Committee*, 44–45.

78. *Daily Picayune*, November 8, 1865, 6; November 10, 1865, 4.

priate committee, but once it reached the floor, a lengthy and sometimes heated debate ensued, mainly among representatives from New Orleans, and arguments were raised that would become familiar rhetoric in the *Slaughterhouse Cases*.[79] Opponents insisted that Thieneman's proposal was essentially the same measure that had already been rejected by the city council. Why should the legislature substitute its judgment in a local matter? It would be more proper to refer the bill to a committee consisting of the entire New Orleans delegation. Further, they accused Thieneman of having a pecuniary interest in his bill. Critics predicted—possibly with greater prescience than they knew—that the proposal would be the "entering wedge of a vast monopoly," one "to benefit speculators" while at the same time depriving "constituents of the benefits of investments of hundreds of thousands of dollars."[80]

Thieneman defended his bill and denied that his support rested on ulterior motives. Moreover, the health of the city should not be sacrificed for the benefit of a few who were interested in keeping the slaughterhouses where they were. In fact, such a location was "a pesthole[,] poisoning air and water."[81] The interests of a few wealthy butchers, "only about 100, no more," should not be permitted to override the welfare of a city of 200,000.[82] Another house member, Alfred Bourges, supported Thieneman, noting that the only men "interested in opposing the measure were a few cattle dealers, a few cow buyers, a few lasso throwers, and a few grog shops."[83]

After more debate, the house referred the removal bill to a special committee composed of ten members—two from each of the four New Orleans municipal districts, plus one from Jefferson Parish and one from St. Bernard. The committee met four times over a three-week period. The members received statements or heard directly from nine physicians, including all four of the city's health officers, the superintendent of the waterworks, a representative of the board of health, several wharf managers, and a number of individuals with knowledge of or interest in slaughterhouse operations or the condition of the river. Although the facts of political life ensured that

79. *New Orleans Daily Crescent*, January 31, 1867, 2; February 15, 1867, 2; February 16, 1867, 1; *Daily Picayune*, February 15, 1867, 2; February 16, 1867, 2.

80. *Daily Crescent*, February 16, 1867, 1. If, added the opponents, the slaughterhouses were really nuisances, the city would have addressed the problem long ago. But in any case, the question of nuisance was a judicial not a legislative matter. See also *Daily Picayune*, February 15, 1867, 2; February 16, 1867, 2.

81. *Daily Crescent*, February 15, 1867, 2.

82. Ibid., February 16, 1867, 1.

83. Ibid.

various interests would be represented on the special committee, this reality did not prevent it from collecting an impressive and authoritative record in support of the argument that slaughterhouses and stockyards presented an extensive and serious sanitary problem, requiring their removal from their present location above the city.

Most important, the evidence amassed by the committee amounted to far more than an assortment of opinions favoring relocation. It constituted a well-thought-out, comprehensive, and fact-based justification for slaughter-house reform. A close reading of the report reveals that no major points were left unaddressed. In other words, almost two years before enactment of the famous (or infamous) slaughterhouse statute, the Louisiana legislature had for its consideration all available evidence, options, alternatives, proposals, justifications, and rebuttals concerning relocation of the slaughterhouses. Much of the testimony echoed points raised earlier. But what ultimately became law in 1869 was not new, original, or unexpected.

Most of the evidence focused on the relationship of the slaughterhouses to the key essentials of public health—pure air and clean water. The great majority of the slaughterhouses were located in well-populated areas of the city, only about one and a half miles upstream from the two large intake pipes for the city's water supply. Since the accepted way of disposing of offal was to dump it in the river, one could readily imagine the result. For those who could not, the testimony of the health officer for the Third District was clear enough. "The amount of filth thrown into the river above the source from which the city is supplied water, and coming from the slaughterhouses, is incredible. Barrels filled with entrails, livers, blood, urine, dung, and other refuse portions in an advanced stage of decomposition, are being constantly thrown into the River, but a short distance from the banks, poisoning the air with offensive smells and necessarily contaminating the water near the banks for miles."[84]

Additional witnesses focused on the way other nations, such as France and England, had resolved the slaughterhouse problem. Purity of air and water in Paris had been assured by "abolishing slaughterhouses within the city, and establishing one only at the northeast extremity." The health officer for the First District (source of the grand jury activity noted earlier) traced the concept of the centralized abattoir to an 1807 decree of Napoleon concerning Paris and demonstrated how the concept had spread. "Throughout the civilized world," concluded Dr. James Burns, "the danger of slaugh-

84. *Minute Book of the Special Committee,* 13.

terhouses have been recognized and earnest efforts have been made to remove them."[85]

And it was not only medical men who took note of the problem. The presiding judge of the earlier grand jury that had urged removal of the slaughterhouses summarized its findings. Judge Abell, though claiming no sanitary expertise, testified that while standing on the stock-landing wharf in December, he had personally observed "six to ten cart loads of bloody fetid matter dumpt [*sic*] into the river" within half an hour. "I can only say I thought it looked revolting when coupled with the idea of drinking the water taken from the river immediately below it."[86] Other witnesses verified the fact that many cattle shipped from Texas for slaughter in New Orleans died en route. One ship captain admitted that he had disposed of eighty-three head by throwing them overboard at the city stock landing. Some individuals had retrieved these carcasses, skinned them for the hides, and tossed what remained back into the river. "Some people," noted one witness, "drank water directly from the river and when in port, vessels filled their water casks" from the same source.[87]

Testimony received by the special committee made it clear that any attempt either to relocate the slaughterhouses on the other side of the river or to dispose of refuse in midstream would do little good. This would have been unfair to the people who lived across from New Orleans in Gretna or Algiers. In addition, a combination of winds and a current coming off the western bank created conditions that carried offal and debris across the river and disbursed it among the shipping lanes and wharves located on the other side.[88] Similarly, there was minimal support for the suggestion that instead of relocating the slaughterhouses, they be ordered to transport their offal to some point below the city. Dr. James Burns, the health officer for the First District, branded this alternative as "a clumsy, thriftless, ineffectual substitute for the proper remedy."[89]

One might have thought that the board of health, the agency whose revival had rekindled the move toward slaughterhouse reform, would have enthusiastically supported their removal. But throughout all the evidence and testimony received by the special committee, the board remained am-

85. Ibid., 6–8, 22–29. In fact, all four health officers appointed by the board of health supported removal and relocation of the slaughterhouses.

86. Ibid., 4.

87. Ibid., 18.

88. Ibid., 14.

89. Ibid., 23 The superintendent for the city waterworks had made a similar point, noting that the slaughterhouses' "entire removal would be a public benefit." Ibid., 19.

bivalent concerning a final solution. It was, in fact, a political body, replete with limits on what it could accomplish, as well as doubts about what it could or should do when property rights in homes and businesses might be adversely affected. Ultimately, the board concluded that it would be unnecessary to relocate the slaughterhouses, provided that their offal was transported and discarded below the waterworks.

In spite of the ambivalence of the board of health, the special committee voted favorably (eight to four) on the proposal to remove the slaughterhouses. The dissenters on the committee, however, insisted that removal was not needed and offered a substitute that focused not on removal of these establishments but rather on the results of their operations. This substitute measure made it an imperative duty of New Orleans and Jefferson City to prohibit dumping in the river. In mid-March 1867, the house passed the substitute bill by a vote of fifty-three to thirty. After futile efforts to construct its own version of a removal bill, the senate simply acquiesced in the house version, and the governor signed the bill into law on March 23, 1867.[90]

One might observe that for all the struggle to achieve it, the 1867 act was another example of legislative futility, a further indication, if any was needed, of the continued inability to solve the slaughterhouse problem. This latest measure neither forbade existing slaughterhouses to operate above the waterworks nor barred the building of new establishments nor required the consolidation of existing facilities. It simply passed the buck back to the city councils of New Orleans and Jefferson City, where real reform seemed as much a political challenge as ever. This viewpoint, however, fails to consider the significance of the special committee's investigation, as well as another development in Jefferson City that took place in 1868.

In that year, an effort was made to revive the franchise granted to Hepp, Rochereau, and Pochelu in 1862, still in existence but ineffectual. A corporate entity, the Slaughterhouse and Chemical Manufacturing and Warehouse Company, identified itself in the March 15, 1868, issue of the *Daily Picayune*. It had acquired the old franchise and would attempt to capitalize itself by offering stock worth $100,000 to the public at $50 per share. As had been true of the 1862 franchise, once the new company was in operation, all slaughtering in Jefferson City would have to take place in its facilities, in accordance with the existing ordinance. But unlike the 1862 version, the new prospectus—one suspects with the 1867 hearings very much in mind— explained the benefits of a centralized slaughtering system. It gave assur-

90. "Senate," *Daily Picayune*, March 22, 1867, 2; *Journal of the Senate*, March 21, 1867, 129; Act No. 111 of March 23, 1867, La. Acts (1867), 207.

ances that its fees would amount to only about half the present costs for slaughtering. Moreover, the new company promised to salt and deliver the hides and other cattle parts to the butchers, as was common practice in the existing slaughterhouses.

Authors of this prospectus may well have anticipated an objection concerning a monopoly. They pointed out that they were offering first option to buy stock to the "butchers and property holders of Jefferson City. If they do not take the stock, they must not complain if they lose control of it." More important, looking to the future, the prospectus cautioned that "unless this establishment does away with the nuisances complained of, all the slaughterhouses will be driven out of the cities in a very short time, to the great injury and detriment of property holders in Jefferson City."[91] The prospectus concluded with the announcement that the company would hold subscription books open for butchers first, then for local "capitalists."

In another development that differed from the 1862 attempt, this time, the *Daily Picayune* had high praise for the new company and listed several advantages it offered. In addition to stockholder benefits, the new facility would abate the nuisance of 150 establishments, with slaughtering to be concentrated in one central location. Moreover, butchers could retain and remain in their shops. Home owners around Jefferson City would see the value of their property increase by at least 50 percent, and this improvement in their environment would get rid of the "intolerable stenches that smell to heaven." Finally, the centralized slaughtering facility would ensure better inspection of stock and beef.[92]

One suspects that the points raised in both the prospectus and the supporting newspaper commentary reflected a new awareness engendered in large part by the 1867 legislative activity. Nevertheless, it appears that the stock of the new company was undersubscribed, and it never went into operation, possibly for some of the same reasons that had doomed the 1862 effort. But the rhetoric employed, as well as much of the legislative evidence and testimony offered a year earlier, point to the probability—as opposed to the mere possibility—of important changes. There was by now (1868) an inventory of ideas concerning slaughterhouse reform that had been accepted by different groups and from which an ultimate solution might be crafted.

The slaughterhouses, given their location and practices, remained a sanitary nightmare. Offal and refuse had to be transported downriver and

91. *Daily Picayune*, March 15, 1868, 4.
92. Ibid., 3.

deposited below the city. By 1868, the concept of a centralized abattoir—praised by some as a required step toward consolidation, and denounced by others as "the beginning wedge of a vast monopoly"—was now seen by the local livestock industry as a fit subject for a profitable franchise. Therefore, the status quo (virtually unregulated slaughterhouses scattered all over New Orleans) no longer seemed feasible. Judge Abell explained his support for removal of the main stock landing from above the waterworks with this comment: "I think it would be politic to remove it if it can be done justly and without personal injury. . . . I am satisfied it will ultimately be done, and another reason is that the people seem dissatisfied for it to be where it now is."[93]

In sum, as both the Crescent City and Louisiana prepared to function under congressional Reconstruction, the problem of slaughterhouse reform had been discussed, debated, and evaluated from virtually every angle for more than a generation. Major parts of the solution, including relocation, centralized slaughtering, distinguishing between neighborhood butcher shops and slaughterhouses, removal of offal, and proper inspection, had been placed before the legislature in one form or another. Time and again, New Orleans had had its opportunities to reform, either by local action or by legislative initiative, and it had managed to squander every chance.

All that was needed as events in 1868–1869 unfolded was an aggressive group of entrepreneurs willing both to take risk and to seek profit. Those who had ensured a seemingly permanent continuance of the status quo were not in a position to complain if the old problems were now resolved in a new manner, within the context of new political factors. Boss Plunkitt once remarked of his activities as a loyal member of Tammany Hall in New York City that "he [had] seen his opportunities, and he took 'em."[94] The same might well be said of this new association of individuals from varied backgrounds, all united by their eagerness to profit from a long-overdue reform.

93. *Minute Book of the Special Committee*, 4.
94. William L. Riordan, *Plunkitt of Tammany Hall*, ed. Terrence J. McDonald (Boston: Bedford Books, 1994), 51.

4

A Centralized Abattoir for New Orleans

S everal factors should be kept in mind when discussing Reconstruction
and Louisiana. In the first place, Lincoln may well have regarded this
state as a prototype for his Reconstruction policies. He lived long enough
to attempt their implementation and to witness the resulting tensions and
contradictions. These were far from resolved by April 14, 1865, when Lincoln was assassinated. In the second place, Louisiana was one of only three
Confederate states in which blacks formed a majority of the population.
Finally, when General Benjamin Butler occupied New Orleans on May 1,
1862, he took possession of the South's "largest and most distinctive city."[1]
Although whites (many of whom were foreign born or from the Northeast)
had always controlled its administration, New Orleans was home to the
"largest free black community in the deep South."[2] Often light skinned in
complexion, many of the so-called free men of color identified more with
French or foreign culture than with American. They had much in common
with the New Orleans Creoles, who were whites of French and Spanish
ancestry and were apt to consider themselves the aristocrats of the population. Moreover, a number of free blacks were wealthy, and although as a
group they could not vote, they could travel freely, testify in court against
whites, and work in various skilled crafts, which they came to dominate.[3]

Inevitably, a tension existed between the growing numbers of newly
freed blacks and the well-established free black community. The latter group
"thought of themselves as the natural leaders of the Negro race."[4] What
united both groups was the growing attraction of the suffrage, especially by

1. Eric Foner, *Reconstruction: America's Unfinished Revolution: 1863–1877* (New York:
Harper and Row, 1988), 45.

2. Ibid., 47.

3. Ibid. Such trades included cigar making, carpentry, and bricklaying. Foner notes that
one free black owned more than 100 slaves, but he was very unusual.

4. Richard N. Current, *Those Terrible Carpetbaggers* (New York: Oxford University
Press, 1988), 13.

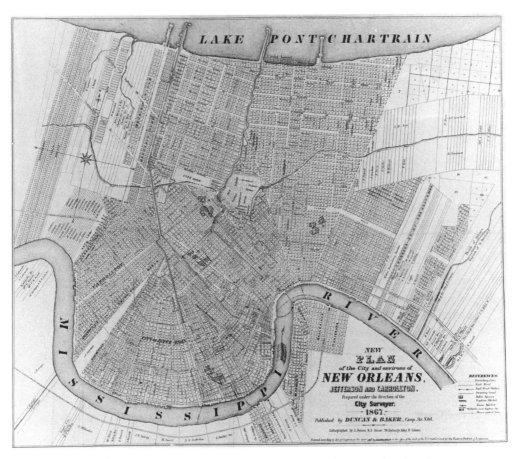

City surveyor's 1867 map of New Orleans. Some areas shown as developed were swamps in 1867. (The Historic New Orleans Collection, #1978.49.)

1864, when there was no doubt that slavery was doomed. But both Lincoln and Congress were unable to move toward black suffrage, although Lincoln had tentatively suggested to Louisiana governor Michael Hahn that "some of the colored people . . . be let in—as for instance the very intelligent."[5] Yet the all-white constitutional convention of 1864, meeting under military occupation and representing only a portion of the state, ignored Lincoln's proposal, and the legislature that convened under the new enactment demonstrated "complete indifference" to black aspirations for both the suffrage

5. Foner, *Reconstruction*, 49.

and education.[6] By 1865–1866, such treatment had solidified the alliance between the former slaves and the so-called freemen of color, again with suffrage as its linchpin.

Such impetus was important for the establishment of a Republican party in Louisiana. According to Richard Current, it could include three disparate elements, and its success depended on the extent to which they could be unified. First was a group of Free State whites, some of whom were "now willing to go beyond [the 1864 constitution] in respect to Negro rights." A second group, and "numerically much the most important," consisted of the African Americans, including both ex-slaves and "thousands who had never been slaves." Unless they could vote, however, calling them Republicans meant nothing. Finally, there was a "growing number of Northerners, many if not most of them" former members of the Union army.[7] Among this last group, commonly known as carpetbaggers, one deserves some attention.[8] At age twenty-six, Henry Clay Warmoth would become the youngest governor in the history of Louisiana, if not the nation. He would also sign the slaughterhouse statute so important to this study. Although ultimately a victim of the intense factionalism that helped destroy the Republican party in Louisiana (he was impeached, but not convicted, before his term ended), Warmoth never renounced his Republicanism. Indeed, he lived until 1931, long enough to see his reputation as a corrupt opportunist compared—whether justly or not—with that of another young Louisiana governor, Huey Long.

A competent but undistinguished Union army officer and a lawyer, Warmoth was attracted to New Orleans by the city's lifestyle. In 1864, he was befriended by its current military commander, General Banks, and for a few months served as a judge of the local provost court. Upon leaving the military in 1865, Warmoth determined to enter politics and soon became a leader in the attempt to establish and maintain the Louisiana Republican party.

From 1865 to 1867, both the Louisiana legislature and the state government were dominated by former Confederates who were intent on returning

6. Ibid., 62. One contemporary noted that the legislature did nothing "except provide for the pay of its members." Ibid.

7. Current, *Those Terrible Carpetbaggers*, 12–13.

8. Foner notes that "in fact, far from the dregs of Northern society, carpetbaggers tended to be well educated and middle class in origin." A number of them "had been lawyers, businessmen, newspaper editors and other pillars of Northern society." Unlike Warmoth, "most carpetbaggers did not move to the South seeking political position." Moreover, he concludes, "their commitment to far-reaching changes in Southern life created a bond of sympathy between carpetbaggers and blacks." Foner, *Reconstruction*, 294, 296.

Louisiana to its prewar status in as many ways as possible. Ultimately, however, their determination to limit the rights of the freedmen alarmed Republicans, radicals, and even the Unionist governor James M. Wells.[9] He supported a plan to reconvene the 1864 constitutional convention "in order to enfranchise blacks, prohibit 'rebels' from voting, and establish a new state government."[10] The first meeting of the convention on July 30, 1866, resulted in a bloody clash between New Orleans policemen, all of them white and most of them ex-Confederate soldiers, and a group of 300 to 400 blacks who had gathered outside the convention hall to show support for black suffrage and other rights. It left at least 37 dead and more than 100 injured, mostly black. General Philip Sheridan wired Washington that it was "an absolute massacre by the police."[11] Louisiana had done its share to bring on congressional Reconstruction.

It took the form of a number of acts that divided the South into five military districts, one of which included Louisiana and Texas. The former Confederate states could seek readmission to the Union only after fulfilling a number of requirements—one of which was to prepare and ratify a new constitution "drawn up by a convention of delegates elected by all adult male citizens except those disenfranchised for rebellion or other crimes."[12] When registration, conducted under military supervision, was complete, the vast majority of Louisiana Republicans were black. For a number of reasons, including apathy, economic hardship, and racial antagonism, many more blacks registered to vote than did whites.[13] They were encouraged by Warmoth and other white Republican supporters, who distinguished themselves from the "radical" Republicans, who were mostly black. Ultimately, the tension between these two groups not only destroyed Warmoth's long-term political future but also hastened the demise of the Republican party in Louisiana.[14] For the moment, however, Republicanism triumphed in the state. The vote to convene the convention was 75,083 in favor, with barely 4,000 votes in opposition. Furthermore, of the ninety-eight delegates, half were black, and only two called themselves Democrats.

9. Typical of legislation enacted during this period was the Louisiana version of the infamous "black codes."

10. Foner, *Reconstruction*, 263. One Northerner observed in 1866 that "a party sustained only by black votes will not grow old." Ibid., 294.

11. Ibid., 263. Warmoth, who witnessed the riot, "wrote in his diary for Monday July 30, 1866: 'A dark day for the city of New Orleans.'" Current, *Those Terrible Carpetbaggers*, 23.

12. Taylor, *Louisiana Reconstructed*, 128.

13. Ibid., 144.

14. Ibid., 145.

Most of the black delegates were literate, former freemen of color, and at least half of them were natives of Louisiana. Many of them had served in the Union army, and most were property owners. As a whole, the blacks at the convention were equal to the whites in terms of education and property.[15] The constitution they wrote included the state's first bill of rights, and it provided for a racially integrated public school system (public schools were virtually nonexistent outside of New Orleans) and for state institutions for people with disabilities. There was little in it that was radical, except, perhaps, that the prospect of universal suffrage seemed to promise that there could be no return to the old Louisiana.

The constitution of 1868 was ratified by a vote of 66,152 for, with 48,739 against. It owed its approval to the black vote. Joe Gray Taylor points out that there were perhaps 2,500 white supporters of radical Reconstruction in the entire state, and 1,500 of these were in New Orleans.[16] In the state canvass, Warmoth won the election, and a decisive majority of Republicans were chosen for both chambers of the state legislature. In the Louisiana house, the party division was sixty-five Republicans, which included thirty-five blacks, and thirty-six Democrats. The division in the state senate was twenty-three Republicans, seven of whom were black, and thirteen Democrats. Although there were black legislators for the first time in Louisiana's history, in no way did they or could they control the legislature. Indeed, any measures they favored required support from their white colleagues.

Members of the legislature were not required to take a loyalty oath either to run for office or to serve in the legislature; General Grant had decided that members need take only the oath of office.[17] As a result, both houses contained many former Confederates. But in the minds of the vast majority of Louisianians, it was a legislature that could do no good, not necessarily because of the particular enactment under consideration but because blacks were involved and their presence represented some effort toward black equality.[18]

15. Charles Vincent, *Black Legislators in Louisiana during Reconstruction* (Baton Rouge: Louisiana State University Press, 1976), 47.

16. Taylor, *Louisiana Reconstructed,* 159–60.

17. U. S. Grant to R. C. Buchanan, Commander Fifth Military District, June 30, 1868 (telegram) in *Official Journal of the . . . Senate of the State of Louisiana at the Session Begun . . . June 29, 1868* (New Orleans: A. L. Lee, State Printer, 1868), 5; hereafter, *Senate Journal 1868.*

18. "What they could not and would not accept was the idea of black men voting and holding office." Taylor, *Louisiana Reconstructed,* 161, 183. Taylor further notes that although "this legislature, and others to follow during the eight years of Radical Reconstruction in

There seems little need to question Warmoth's description of the state and the Crescent City when he became governor in June 1868. "I found," he later recalled, "the State and the city of New Orleans bankrupt." From 1860 to 1867, taxes were in arrears, and the legislature ultimately abandoned all efforts to collect them. "There was no money in either treasury. . . . The slaughterhouses were so located that all of their offal and filth were poured into the Mississippi River, just above the mains that supplied the people with their drinking water. New Orleans was a dirty, impoverished, and hopeless city with a mixed, ignorant, corrupt and bloodthirsty gang in control. . . . Many of the city officials, as well as the police force, were thugs and murderers."[19]

In New Orleans, if not the entire reconstructed South, corruption "cast a shadow over the conduct of public affairs." It preceded Warmoth's tenure and endured long after he had been returned to private life. As Eric Foner notes, "bribery, fraud, and influence peddling have been endemic to American politics. . . . Nor did government in the Reconstruction North—the era of the Tweed and Whiskey Rings—offer a model of probity. Throughout the country, public honor was among the casualties of the Civil War."[20] Thus, an outburst attributed to Warmoth becomes understandable. "I don't pretend to be honest. I only pretend to be as honest as anybody in politics. . . . I tell you [that] these much abused members of the Louisiana legislature are at all events as good as the people they represent. Why damn it, everybody is demoralizing [*sic*] down here. Corruption is the fashion."[21] When a portrait of the young governor appeared in *Harper's Weekly* shortly before Grant's election in 1868, the *New Orleans Times* could not resist a comment. "The reason why Governor Warmoth is depicted in *Harper's Weekly* as looking down is because he has consistently been trying to pick up something ever since he has been in Louisiana."[22]

Louisiana, were vilified and ridiculed[,] . . . they suffer little in comparison with their modern counterparts." Ibid., 174–75.

19. Henry Clay Warmoth, *War, Politics and Reconstruction: Stormy Days in Louisiana* (New York: Macmillan, 1930), 79–80.

20. Foner, *Reconstruction*, 384.

21. Ted Tunnel, *Crucible of Reconstruction: War, Radicalism and Race in Louisiana* (Baton Rouge: Louisiana State University Press, 1984), 175. Tunnel adds that scapegoating Reconstruction as thievery was often used to justify the deeper corruption of violence. "Knights of the White Camelia, the White League and their kin crippled democracy in the state and region for nearly a century. Armies of thieves could not have equaled their damage." Ibid.

22. Francis W. Binning, "Henry Clay Warmoth and Louisiana Reconstruction" (Ph.D. diss., University of North Carolina, 1969), 151–52.

In similar fashion, the adoption of the Slaughterhouse Act was greeted by a storm of protest centering on the charges that the act created a monopoly, that it was the product of bribery, and that far from being a sanitary measure, it was in reality a private measure aimed at the unjust enrichment of a few at the expense of the stock dealers, butchers, and general public of New Orleans. But the ferocious resistance engendered by the Slaughterhouse Act can be thoroughly understood only in terms of the context in which it was enacted and implemented.

Warmoth had greater problems than the accusation of corruption. The "vast majority of the white people of Louisiana never accepted [his government] as legitimate," and although the governor never employed federal troops during his tenure, "the background presence of federal military power was essential to the survival of the Republican state administration."[23] In the antebellum period, New Orleans businessmen and rural planters had dominated the government. Yet Warmoth's government "contained no representatives" of this once-dominant class. Indeed, according to Taylor, a member of that class who joined it "would have forfeited his previous position in the eyes of his neighbors."[24] From their perspective, the state government in 1868 was dominated by men who had served on the enemy side in the late war. As the *Daily Picayune* saw it, it was a time when the "real people" of the state had been deprived of power and "a set of new men, greedy for the rapid acquisition of wealth and utterly unscrupulous as to the means of getting it, have come among us, and joining with the lately emancipated slaves and the meanest portion of the resident white population, have concocted plans for public plunder which they have not found it difficult to put through."[25]

Louisiana's defeat had indeed come home. There could be no more galling reminder to white New Orleans Democrats that they were now being governed by the victors than the fact that the Louisiana legislature of 1869–1871 included blacks for the first time in state history. They constituted about 37 percent of the members of the house and 25 percent of the senate, and for legislation to pass, their support was essential. "This alliance of blacks and carpetbaggers enraged many New Orleans whites." They described the new legislature as a horde of "ignorant negroes cooperating with

23. Taylor, *Louisiana Reconstructed*, 1.
24. Ibid.
25. *Daily Picayune*, March 7, 1869, 4.

a gang of white adventurers."[26] Any and all results from such a body were suspect, regardless of content.[27] During the first three months of 1869, comments to this effect became more frequent. One newspaper editor insisted that laws passed by this legislature "are of no more binding force than if they bore the stamp and seal of a Haytian [*sic*] Congress of human apes instead of the once honored seal of the state."[28] Within this time frame, the legislators passed a statute enforcing open accommodation in public places, including hotels, railroad cars, and barrooms. Another ordinance required integrated public schools in the state. Sandwiched in between these two laws was the slaughterhouse bill.[29]

One suspects that opposition to the Slaughterhouse Act would have been vigorous regardless of race. Unlike other exclusive franchises awarded by the legislature at this time, the Slaughterhouse Act posed a direct threat to the interests of a large and coherent group of tradesmen who knew how to complain. Nonetheless, race was an inseparable element in the opposition. As the *New Orleans Republican* pointed out, the legislature's critics "failed to see any good in the work of those who have been called upon to take part in the state government under the new constitution. . . . Conservatives felt obligated to attack all Republicans in, and acts of, the legislature." Indeed, "everybody has been proclaimed infamous, vile, ignorant and corrupt, that has had anything to do with a state government that recognized the civil and political equality of the colored man."[30] Thus did the issue of slaughterhouse relocation become one with Reconstruction measures in general, and all were unacceptable.

THE ACT THAT PROVIDED the butchers and stock dealers of New Orleans with an opportunity to litigate the provisions of the Fourteenth Amendment for the first time was entitled "An Act to Protect the Health of the City of New Orleans, and to Locate the Stock Landings and Slaughter Houses." It

26. Michael A. Ross, "Justice of Shattered Dreams: Samuel Freeman Miller, the Republican Party and the Supreme Court" (Ph.D. diss., University of North Carolina, 1999), 350, citing *New Orleans Commercial Bulletin*, November 17, 1869.

27. Ibid. "Louisiana newspapers issued a racial call to arms, urging citizens to fight any and all acts passed by this new legislature, and New Orleans papers branded laws passed [by it as] merely a parody of legislation."

28. Ibid., 351.

29. Ibid., 352.

30. Ibid., 353, citing *New Orleans Republican*, March 22, 1870.

incorporated seventeen persons into the Crescent City Live Stock Landing and Slaughter House Company and granted the company "the sole and exclusive privilege" for twenty-five years of conducting the business of landing, keeping, or slaughtering animals for food in the contiguous parishes of Orleans, Jefferson, and St. Bernard. The company was required to erect, by June 1, 1869, "a grand slaughterhouse of sufficient capacity to accommodate all butchers," together with stockyards for all animals received at the port. Thereafter, no stock was to be landed, confined, or slaughtered for the New Orleans market except at the company's facilities. However, the act also provided that if the company refused to allow healthy animals to be slaughtered in its new facility, it was to be fined $250 "in each case." In short, all who sought to slaughter beef had to do it in the new facility, and the company had to permit access to the slaughterhouse to all who wished it. The benefits to the company were ensured by a detailed schedule of fees that it was authorized to charge for the use of its facilities and by provisions allowing it to retain portions of each slaughtered animal for their value as raw material for agricultural fertilizer. An inspector of beef was to be appointed by the governor, and the inspector's certification was required, at set fees, before any animal could be slaughtered. These penalties were collectible by ordinary suit filed by the company and were to be divided equally between it and the auditor of public accounts.[31]

As was noted earlier, although the incorporated suburb of Jefferson City had enacted a similar ordinance in 1862, important differences between it and the 1869 statute indicate that it would be unwise to attach great significance to the earlier measure. In the first place, one was a local ordinance, the other a state statute. Moreover, the Jefferson City ordinance never went into effect. Thus, there is no way of knowing how the butchers would have reacted to it. This fact may well explain why there was no recorded opposition to the ordinance. It could not go into effect unless and until the three favored businessmen raised the necessary capital, which they were unable to do. The passage of and reaction to the 1869 statute was a very different story. The butchers were faced with a statute enacted, approved, and scheduled to go into effect in a matter of a few months. Yet concern about this statute must be seen in a context all its own, one that goes far beyond the internal politics of Reconstruction. When it is examined, one can better understand why it was not unreasonable for a Louisiana legislature in 1869 to focus on a centralized slaughterhouse.

31. Act of March 8, 1869, No. 118, 1869 La. Acts 170.

* * *

ALTHOUGH ADOPTION of the New Orleans Slaughterhouse Act of 1869 was part of a national movement aimed at bringing long-overdue regulation to slaughterhouses, the statute was also part of a more general transformation of the livestock industry that occurred in the years following the Civil War. Even as it passed, and as the judicial drama it provoked was being played out in the courts, several factors were coming together that would modernize the nation's meat industry. As described by Rudolf A. Clemen, one of the chief economic historians of the industry, these factors were "first, the opening and developing of a new source of supply of livestock; second, the extension of railroad transportation to the source of supply; third, refrigeration; fourth, men to organize the distribution of livestock and meat in the most efficient way."[32]

Well before the Civil War, improvements in the transportation network had made it possible for "Chicago to draw its stock not only from the grassy prairies of the nearby states of Iowa and Indiana, but also from the entire beef growing territory of the Northwest."[33] In the years immediately following the Civil War, however, Texas boasted an enormous supply of beef. It was a commodity in great demand everywhere else, and it begged for transportation. Prior to the Civil War, the center of stock raising in the United States had steadily migrated westward with the frontier, in response to the spread of industrialization in the East and a general rise in population. By 1860, it had shifted from Illinois to Texas, and the relatively unknown Texas longhorn overtook short-horned English stock as the country's most plentiful source of beef. Texas offered an environment and land policies highly favorable for cattle raising, and on the eve of the Civil War, 4 million head roamed the vast, unfenced ranges of the Lone Star State.[34]

32. Rudolf A. Clemen, *The American Livestock and Meat Industry* (New York: Ronald Press, 1923), 6–7.

33. Mary Yeager, *Competition and Regulation: The Development of Oligopoly in the Meat Packing Industry* (Greenwich, Conn.: Jai Press, 1981), 13.

34. Edward E. Dale, *The Range Cattle Industry: Ranching on the Great Plains from 1865 to 1925* (Norman: University of Oklahoma Press, 1960), 3, 12. The development of the livestock industry in the United States has been chronicled by a number of works, including Clemen, *American Livestock and Meat Industry;* Joseph G. McCoy, *Cattle Trade of the West and Southwest* (1874; reprint, Ann Arbor, Mich.: University Microfilms, 1966); Ernest S. Osgood, *The Day of the Cattleman* (Minneapolis: University of Minnesota Press, 1929); Jimmy M. Skaggs, *The Cattle Trailing Industry: Between Supply and Demand, 1866–1890* (Lawrence: University Press of Kansas, 1973); Charles W. Towne and Edward N. Wentworth, *Cattle and Men* (Norman: University of Oklahoma Press, 1955).

It had always been difficult to find a market for Texas cattle. The state was relatively isolated from the rest of the country, and the skinny-legged, fierce-looking longhorns were considered uneatable in some places. Their meat had a reputation of being "coarse and stringy," with a taste "almost as wild as the buffalo."[35] Joseph McCoy, a pioneer of the Texas cattle industry, wrote that until postwar shortages sharpened eastern appetites for red meat, longhorns were "as unsaleable in eastern markets as would have been a shipment of prairie wolves."[36]

The Civil War proved disastrous for the Texas cattle industry, as the Lone Star State was cut off from all its major markets. According to McCoy, "then dawned a time in Texas that a man's poverty was estimated by the number of cattle he possessed."[37] Estimates of the number of cattle in Texas in 1860 range from 3.5 million to 4.5 million.[38] During the war, herds multiplied by as much as 25 percent per year, and by 1865, there were between 6 million and 8 million head of cattle in Texas.[39] It had become "a vast reservoir fairly overflowing with cattle."[40]

But beef was in short supply everywhere else. By the end of the war, the number of neat cattle in the country had declined by 7 percent, and they were very unevenly distributed.[41] Even before the war, production had fallen in some areas as the South concentrated on raising cotton and industrialization progressed elsewhere. The supply in both the East and the Midwest was at "a dangerous minimum."[42] Whereas there were between five and eight head of beef per capita in Texas in 1865, as late as 1870, the ratio in New York was still less than half a head (0.46) per capita, and only slightly higher (0.53) in Ohio.[43] These discrepancies between supply and demand were reflected in prices. In 1865, high-grade steers could be had for $3 to $6 a head in Texas; when bought by the herd on the range, they cost as little as $1 a head.[44] The same animals brought ten times as much in northern

35. Osgood, *Day of the Cattlemen*, 27.

36. McCoy, *Cattle Trade*, 53

37. Ibid., 20.

38. Dale, *Range Cattle Industry*, 9; Towne and Wentworth, *Cattle and Men*, 154.

39. Towne and Wentworth, *Cattle and Men*, 163; W. F. Williams and Thomas T. Stoute, *Economics of the Live Stock-Meat Industry* (New York: Macmillan, 1964), 20; Dale, *Range Cattle Industry*, 12.

40. Dale, *Range Cattle Industry*, 76.

41. Clemen, *American Livestock and Meat Industry*, 175; Osgood, *Day of the Cattlemen*, 28.

42. Towne and Wentworth, *Cattle and Men*, 163.

43. Dale, *Range Cattle Industry*, 12.

44. Ibid.; McCoy, *Cattle Trade*, 20, Towne and Wentworth, *Cattle and Men*, 163.

markets. The price in New Orleans in early 1869 was $50 a head.[45] It had been over $60 a head for a brief period in 1867.[46]

New Orleans was a legendary center of trade to which ambitious men had always been attracted. Failure to recognize the economic potential of the tremendous supply of beef just west of the city would have been remarkable. Even as the Slaughterhouse Act was debated and assaulted, New Orleans newspapers were replete with allusions to the importance of the Texas cattle trade. The *Daily Picayune* predicted that "the time is coming when the products of the West will constitute the chief feature of our commerce" and that New Orleans would become "the depot of the trade of the west."[47]

Indeed, New Orleans had been the chief market for Texas cattle before the war, and for some time afterward, hopes were high that prewar patterns of marketing could be maintained. But success was by no means assured, because in the years following the Civil War, there was no way that Texas cattle could be delivered to New Orleans. Prewar drives had typically been small, and none of the existing routes could satisfy postwar demands. Shipments to New Orleans via the Red River from Shreveport or other points in northern Louisiana were impossible for months at a time due to low water. In the southern portion of the state, the eastward route was crisscrossed by innumerable waterways and could be impassable in wet weather. The most promising route to New Orleans was by way of the Gulf of Mexico from Galveston and Indianola aboard steamships owned by Charles Morgan. In 1857, the New Orleans, Opelousas and Great Western Railroad was completed from New Orleans to Berwick Bay at Brashear City (later Morgan City), a distance of eighty miles. It made a railhead available to which Morgan's steamers could deliver cattle for a quick overland run to New Orleans. But the Morgan line had a reputation for high rates and monopolistic practices. Besides, when cattle were shipped by water, they often arrived in a bruised and sickly condition.[48]

There was no rail connection between New Orleans and Texas, and the importance of remedying this problem was widely and vociferously recognized. Cautioned the *Daily Picayune*, "Texas can do without the railroad to New Orleans, but New Orleans cannot do without the railroad to Texas."[49]

45. *Daily Picayune*, January 21, 1869, 3.

46. Byron Price, "The New Orleans Market for Texas Beef, 1821–1867" (paper delivered at the annual meeting of the Western History Association, October 1979), 19.

47. *Daily Picayune*, May 5, 1869, 9; July 17, 1869, 2.

48. Price, "New Orleans Market," 6–7. On this subject, see also McCoy, *Cattle Trade*, 19; Osgood, *Day of the Cattlemen*, 27; Dale, *Range Cattle Industry*, 37.

49. *Daily Picayune*, May 18, 1869, 3.

The press reiterated time and again that a delay in completing a rail connection could cause the Texas trade to find another path to market, and New Orleans would "be forever competing with the Northern states for the Texas trade."[50] In the end, this is precisely what happened.

By late 1865, Texas farmers and men from as far away as Iowa and Illinois were gathering herds and making preparations to drive them north to market.[51] The first of the great cattle drives took place in 1866 when a group of northern drovers and local cattle farmers put together herds totaling approximately 260,000 head and attempted to drive them northward to Sedalia, Missouri, a stop on the Missouri Pacific Railroad. Bad weather, rough terrain, thieves, and irate Kansas and Missouri farmers fearful of Texas cattle fever all combined to turn this first effort into an unprofitable disaster.[52] In Texas, the ranching industry was thrown into a momentary depression, and in New Orleans, cattle fever of another kind soared. But the New Orleans window of opportunity to preempt the cattle trade did not remain open for long. In 1867, only 35,000 head were driven north. In the same year, arrangements were concluded with the Union Pacific Railroad to establish a cattle depot in Abilene. In 1869, 350,000 head were delivered to railheads in Kansas, and the potential of the Texas cattle trade became manifest from New Orleans to Chicago. It was the beginning of the fabled Texas cattle-trailing industry, which, by 1885, would deliver almost 6 million head to railheads in places such as Abilene, Wichita, and Dodge City.[53]

Yet at the time the Slaughterhouse Act was enacted, there was enough speculation about railroads to justify a feverish interest in the Texas trade. Two enterprises actively competed for the state aid and franchises necessary to push westward. One of them, the New Orleans, Opelousas and Great Western, with its eighty-mile leg to Brashear City, was purchased by Charles Morgan in May 1869 with a boast that he would "now show the people of New Orleans how to build a road."[54] The other line was the New Orleans, Mobile and Chattanooga Railroad, which had originally been chartered in Alabama in 1866 by investors from New York and Boston. By the spring of 1869, it had secured from the Louisiana legislature both a charter giving it permission to construct a line westward and a pledge of

50. Ibid. See also November 10, 1869, 1; November 26, 1869, 1; *Republican*, January 29, 1870, 4.

51. Dale, *Range Cattle Industry*, 33; Clemen, *American Livestock and Meat Industry*, 171–75.

52. McCoy, *Cattle Trade*, 37–38; Osgood, *Day of the Cattlemen*, 30–31.

53. Osgood, *Day of the Cattlemen*, 32.

54. *Daily Picayune*, May 26, 1869, 1.

state bonds amounting to $12,500 for every westward mile it constructed.[55] Predictions in the press of the "glorious day" when Texas and New Orleans would be linked by rail ranged from two years to eighteen months.[56] Actually, the connection with Texas would not come about until 1880, but as late as 1871, when 600,000 longhorns were driven to market along the northern trails, New Orleans had not lost hope. "In our railway connection with Texas, which is to mark one of the events of the near future," the *Times* predicted, "New Orleans will become the cattle and beef mart of the continent."[57]

Advances in the science of refrigeration made it possible to reap the full benefits of the vast postwar improvements in the railroad industry. The first American patent for the manufacture of ice was issued in 1851.[58] By 1866, it had become easy enough to manufacture ice that the *Daily Picayune* urged the formation of a company to slaughter beef on the Texas coast and transport it under refrigeration to New Orleans and other markets beyond.[59] In fact, the first shipment of refrigerated beef to New Orleans from Texas arrived by water in the summer of 1869 in the midst of the slaughterhouse dispute.[60] The first American patent for a refrigerated car was issued in 1867. It would take a few years to perfect, but by 1871, experimental shipments were under way, and by 1875, a trade in dressed beef had been established between Kansas City and the East.[61] In addition to a new supply of beef and improvements in transportation and refrigeration, one more element was needed to transform the meatpacking industry from a seasonal and local enterprise to an industry of truly national proportions. This was the energy and ambition of the men who made it all happen.

The livestock industry had always been marked by a tendency toward consolidation. This was reflected in the development of cities such as Boston, New York, Philadelphia, and Chicago as central markets. By the mid-

---

55. On the competition for a westward line, see James C. Baughman, *Charles Morgan and the Development of Southern Transportation* (Nashville: Vanderbilt University Press, 1968); also, Merl E. Reed, *New Orleans and the Railroads: The Struggle for American Commercial Empire, 1830–1860* (Baton Rouge: Louisiana State University Press, 1966).

56. *Daily Picayune*, March 11, 1869, 1; December 9, 1869, 2; *New Orleans Times*, March 19, 1871, 5.

57. *Times*, March 19, 1871, 5.

58. Clemen, *American Livestock and Meat Industry*, 212–13.

59. *Daily Picayune*, December 2, 1866, 2.

60. Ibid., July 13, 1869, 1. The article was headlined: "A Grand Enterprise: The Markets of the World Thrown Open to the Stock Raisers of Texas—Annihilation of the Slaughter-House Monopoly."

61. Clemen, *American Livestock and Meat Industry*, 218–20.

nineteenth century, further developments were occurring within existing markets that suggested a way for individuals in New Orleans to profit from the Texas cattle trade. This was the replacement of the chaotic system of private stockyards in central markets with the more businesslike and profitable consolidated stockyards. The prototype of this improvement was the Union Stockyard and Transit Company, incorporated by the Illinois legislature in 1865 at the behest of a group of railroad men and stock dealers. It opened for business in Chicago on Christmas Day 1865 amid great fanfare.[62] The company acquired nearly a square mile of land just south of the city and immediately erected cattle pens on 345 acres of it. The result was the consolidation of the city's stockyards in a "great bovine city" served by nine railroads. In terms of convenience, efficiency, and improved sanitation, it was a major advance over the former system of having private stockyards distributed throughout the city.[63] The concept was to spread rapidly to other markets.

Among its most important effects, the consolidated stockyard assured a crucial role in the cash livestock market for the livestock commission merchant. The first firm of livestock commission merchants had been established in Chicago only in 1857. These men made it unnecessary for the drovers to find their own buyers. The commission merchants made the market their business, and the drovers could consign their herds to them and go on their way in search of more cattle, relying on the commission merchants' expertise and self-interest to find the best price for their stock. Once the cash livestock market was perfected by the consolidation of stockyards, the role of the commission merchant sprang to the forefront. According to Clemen, he became the "most important factor in a cash livestock market" and "contributed more to the prosperity and progress of the market than any other single cause."[64]

Nineteenth-century New Orleans was a city of middlemen. An enormous amount of money was earned by men who served as brokers, bringing buyer and seller together, or as commission merchants, who performed the same function but often acquired goods for themselves and sold them on

62. On the opening of the Union Stockyard, see ibid., 86. The history of the Chicago stockyards is completely chronicled by Wade, *Chicago's Pride;* on the creation of the Union Stockyard, see 47–60.

63. Parton, "Chicago," 332. Parton attributes the sobriquet the "Great Bovine City of the World" to a Chicago guidebook.

64. Clemen, *American Livestock and Meat Industry,* 87.

their own account.[65] Both these agents tended to specialize in a single commodity such as groceries, liquor, cotton, hogs, and, eventually, beef cattle. The business section of Gardner's city directory for 1869 listed 398 firms of commission merchants (not including cotton brokers), making them easily the most numerous group of businessmen in New Orleans. Another listing of businesses showed about 25 firms of commission merchants clustered around the stock landing in Jefferson City and dealing exclusively in livestock and hogs. Not all commission merchants grew rich, but it was a game that almost anyone could play, and it was *the* game, or some imagined and possibly grandiose variation of it, that attracted the ambitious men who organized the Crescent City Company.[66]

FOR ALL THE CONTROVERSY the slaughterhouse franchise would provoke, even as late as the middle of the nineteenth century, municipalities were still uncertain what functions were proper for them to perform, and it was not uncommon to farm out certain services to private companies. The New Orleans waterworks, for example, had been organized in 1833 as a private company with an exclusive franchise to furnish drinking water to the city.[67] In the postwar years, New Orleans became a bustling city again, and men saw opportunities for personal profit in badly needed internal improvements, particularly if they could be undertaken in partnership with the state in terms of either authority or funding. The first item on a long list of postwar internal improvements (a navigational canal to be privately constructed with state assistance) was approved in January 1865 when the legislature was still in Democratic hands.[68] But as new men arrived and the power of the state passed from traditional elites into the hands of the interests that had won the war (as was indeed the case with the 1869 legislature), a great many sinecures and exclusive franchises for such things as a state lottery, state

65. The various types of marketing agents are discussed in Yeager, *Competition and Regulation*, 15, relying on Glenn Porter and Harold Livesay, *Merchants and Manufacturers* (Baltimore: Johns Hopkins Press, 1971), 3.

66. Chas. Gardner, comp., *Gardner's New Orleans Directory for 1869* (New Orleans, 1868); "Names and Addresses of Business People in the City of Jefferson: 1870" (manuscript), Louisiana Division, New Orleans Public Library.

67. Act of April 1, 1833, 1833 La. Acts 151; Smillie, Public Health, 171; George Rosen, *A History of Public Health* (New York: MD Publications, 1958), 159–60.

68. Taylor, *Louisiana Reconstructed*, 56, citing Acts Passed by the First General Assembly of Louisiana . . . Begun on the 4th of October, 1864 (New Orleans, 1865), 136–40.

printing, hay inspection, and state aid for the construction of navigation and drainage canals were adopted.[69]

"These enactments were not different in kind or overall purpose from many which had been approved before the Civil War."[70] The chief distinction was the increase in both the number of such franchises and the amount of state aid given to them. Nonetheless, they engendered intense resentment because of the widespread belief that they had been obtained dishonestly. The editors of the *Picayune* felt that they knew whereof they spoke when they sympathized with their neighbor to the west over "the making of incorporated companies" as "a pretext for appropriating to the use of individuals the land and other effects of the dead state of Texas."[71]

In time such popular opinion regarding the Slaughterhouse Act would receive a sort of judicial endorsement. About the same time as the *Slaughterhouse Cases* were filed in the New Orleans district courts, a spate of stockholder suits broke out over claims that some of the company's organizers were being denied their rightful number of shares. One of these suits was filed by William Durbridge in Judge William H. Cooley's Sixth District Court in July 1869. Judge Cooley rendered judgment in Durbridge's favor on March 23, 1870, but his decision was reversed by the state supreme court the following year on jurisdictional grounds.[72] On May 19, 1871, Durbridge filed suit a second time in the same court. This time, Cooley assumed jurisdiction and tried the case but refused to grant the plaintiff any relief.[73]

The evidence disclosed, he said, that the court was being asked to distribute an illicit fund. In Judge Cooley's words, the stock over which the litigants were fighting had been allocated to the organizers of the company "in order to bribe the members of the General Assembly and other men who stood in their way in order to obtain the final passage of the bill and its signature by the Governor." The evidence shows, he wrote, "that mem-

69. *Daily Picayune*, February 18, 1869, 1; February 28, 1869, 2; Charles Nordhoff, *The Cotton States in the Spring and Summer of 1875* (New York: n.p., 1876), 60–62.

70. Taylor, *Louisiana Reconstructed*, 189.

71. *Daily Picayune*, February 6, 1869, 3.

72. *La. ex rel. Durbridge v. F. J. Pratt, et al.*, No. 635, Sixth District Court, Orleans Parish, La.; record available at La. Sup. Ct. Docket No. 2832, Louisiana Supreme Court Archives, Earl K. Long Library, University of New Orleans; hereafter, Record, *Durbridge v. Pratt*. The Louisiana Supreme Court's opinion is reported at 23 La. Ann. 730 (1871).

73. *Durbridge v. Crescent City Live Stock Landing and Slaughter House Company, A. J. Oliver, Intervenor*, No. 2532, Sixth District Court, Orleans Parish, La.; record available at La. Sup. Ct. Docket No. 3959, Louisiana Supreme Court Archives; hereafter, Record, *Durbridge v. Crescent City Company*.

bers of the House of Representatives were bribed for their votes and members of the Senate were also bribed for their votes. . . . It further shows that other parties occupying official positions in the City of New Orleans were also bribed, and I think the evidence is irresistable [*sic*] that the Governor's signature to that bill was obtained by the same soft sawder [solder]."[74]

In 1875 on appeal, the Louisiana Supreme Court reached the same conclusion: "On the merits we are satisfied from an examination of the testimony that the ground from which this action springs was a fund created for the purposes of corrupting and improperly influencing members of the Legislature in their action on a matter of legislation then before them. We will have nothing to do with it."[75]

In spite of the courts' emphatic rhetoric, as will be seen in the next chapter, the New Orleans butchers were never given an opportunity to prove their hard-pressed claims of bribery. Historians have been left to debate this charge among themselves. Michael Ross cautions against a reliance on Judge Cooley's conclusions on the grounds that Cooley was a disaffected Republican who had left the party over the radical wing's civil rights agenda. "In fact so pronounced was the outspoken opposition of Judge Cooley to the legislation of the state," according to the *New Orleans Republican*, "that it became necessary for the law making power to relieve him of jurisdiction in matters of injunction and mandamus, because his action threatened at one time to produce great confusion if not positive conflict in matters of local law."[76] Hebert Hovenkamp found, in contrast, that at best, the evidence proves that the organizers were guilty only of aggressive lobbying.[77] And it is entirely plausible that both Cooley and the state supreme court resorted to a finding of bribery as an excuse for dismissing a case

74. "Reasons for Judgment," March 13, 1872, in Record, *Durbridge v. Crescent City Company*, 405–6.

75. 27 La. Ann. 676 (1875).

76. *Republican*, June 3, 1871, as cited by Ross, "Justice of Shattered Dreams," 344. Whatever the state of Cooley's relationship to the party, almost certainly the *Republican* is here either creating or merely repeating political rumor. As will be seen in the next chapter, Cooley was not above bending the law to grant the Crescent City Company temporary relief from a restraining order levied against it. Besides, there were much better reasons for giving exclusive jurisdiction in matters of injunctions and elections to a single judge appointed by Warmoth than any recalcitrance on Cooley's part. Only two days after the Slaughterhouse Act went into effect and the battle of injunctions began in the lower courts, the *Republican* had observed, "The power to issue injunctions needs to be reformed." *Republican*, June 3, 1869, 2.

77. Herbert Hovenkamp, "Technology, Politics and Monopoly," *Texas Law Review* 62 (April 1984): 1263, 1306. See also Hovenkamp, *Enterprise and American Law*, 118–24.

mired in circumstances so unfathomably complex and conflicted that it could not be resolved, but only terminated, by a court.[78]

However, even though the claims of bribery and corruption remain uncertain, a review of the records in the two Durbridge suits (and related stockholder actions) enables us to see why it was feasible for Judge Cooley and the state supreme court to conclude that the act had been obtained by bribery. Moreover, these records, along with the legislative debates and other sources, make it possible to glimpse the Crescent City Live Stock Landing and Slaughter House Company in its formative stages and gain some insight into the motives and methods of the incorporators. The Slaughterhouse Act is an exception to Hovenkamp's observation that "we know very little about how legislatures in nineteenth century America designated the groups of private investors who would receive franchises."[79] Further, the odor of corruption lingers, even though it may be impossible to trace its original source.

First, who were the entrepreneurs behind the Crescent City Company? How did they occupy themselves, and how did they relate to one another? The man who claimed to be the originator of the slaughterhouse project was William Durbridge, a native of London and longtime resident of New Orleans. He was occupied primarily as the proprietor of a popular hat store. "The idea originated in my brain," he claimed.[80] He knew that efforts had been made for years to relocate the slaughterhouses to some point below the city, and he had just bought property in that vicinity. He shared his idea with two business acquaintances, Oliver Mudgett, an employee at the U.S. Custom House, and businessman A. J. Oliver, who in turn discussed it with others. Oliver and Mudgett "took hold and the thing started from that."[81] Before long, Oliver came to Durbridge "and proposed advances of money" and a contract for shares in a slaughterhouse company. In all, Durbridge claimed to have sunk between $13,000 and $14,000 in the enterprise, "which I never got back yet."[82]

The entrepreneurs who were eventually favored by the legislature with an exclusive slaughterhouse franchise, and their associates, were the kind of

78. It might also be noted that throughout Reconstruction, there was no Louisiana statute making bribery a crime, even though Warmoth later claimed that he had sought one, in vain, from the legislature.
79. Hovenkamp, "Technology," 1303.
80. Record, *Durbridge v. Crescent City Company*, 49.
81. Ibid., 50–51.
82. Ibid., 51.

motley group that could always be gathered up in New Orleans. Some of them conformed to the popular image of the carpetbagger as an unscrupulous northern adventurer, but others challenged this stereotypical view. They included natives of both North and South, as well as veterans of both the Union and Confederate armies. City directories show that at least five of the nineteen original organizers had resided in New Orleans since 1860 or earlier. Eight others were newcomers who had arrived after New Orleans fell to Union forces in 1862. Several of the nineteen organizers spent only a short time in New Orleans, but at least six died there.

In terms of occupation, nine of the nineteen were commercial merchants or brokers in 1869 or would soon be occupied in that way.[83] Some of them claimed considerable property holdings in other states. They were all keen to take advantage of the opportunities of postwar New Orleans. Eight of them, including Durbridge, took advantage of the opportunity to purchase plantations around the state at favorable postwar prices.[84] For a number of them, the Slaughterhouse Act was not their only venture into the domain of semipublic enterprise. When the state undertook to clear the Red River of a miles-long accumulation of debris, both Durbridge and Mudgett were there as co-contractors.[85] Edward Wurzburger, another incorporator, was one of the original organizers of the Ship Island Canal Company, which was formed by the legislature to construct a canal linking the Mississippi with the Gulf of Mexico. Still another incorporator, John Lockwood, served on the company's board of directors.[86] In 1869, to the *Picayune*'s chagrin, the legislature awarded Lockwood and others an exclusive contract to furnish

83. These were F. G. Clark, L. H. Crippin, S. P. Griffin, R. T. Packwood, Franklin J. Pratt, Joachim Viosca, E. R. Benton, Jonas Pickles, and Edward S. Wurzburger.

84. Crippin, Griffin, Oliver, Packwood, Viosca, Durbridge, Lockwood, and Pickles.

85. Testimony on Bond, June 19, 1869, in *Butchers Benevolent Ass'n of New Orleans v. Crescent City Live Stock Landing and Slaughter House Company*, No. 466, filed May 26, 1869, Sixth District Court, Orleans Parish, La., available at La. Sup. Ct. Docket No. 2505, Louisiana Supreme Court Archives. In his testimony, Durbridge claimed that he had settled in New Orleans in 1846. His obituaries give 1852 as the year of his arrival; see *Daily Picayune*, December 13, 1905, 6, 12; *New Orleans Times Democrat*, December 13, 1905, 11.

86. The Mississippi and Atlantic Ship Canal Company was created by Act of March 31, 1869, No. 128, 1869 La. Acts 199. George W. Carter, first inspector of beef under the act, was one of the incorporators named in this act. Wurzburger went on to a long career as a deputy sheriff of Orleans Parish. Wurzburger obituary, *Daily Picayune*, August 23, 1887, 4. In an 1870 city directory, both Lockwood and E. B. Benton, another organizer of the Crescent City Company, are listed as directors of the canal company. Richards Edwards, comp., *Edwards Annual Directory for the City of New Orleans . . . 1870* (New Orleans, 1870), 759.

illuminating gas to Jefferson City. In 1872, Lockwood appears in a city directory as the president of the Jefferson City Gas Light Company.[87] In earlier years, he had won a similar contract from the city of Milwaukee, which he quickly assigned to an illuminating company.[88] This practice of obtaining a valuable franchise and then selling it to a more appropriate proprietor at a profit was to be repeated in the slaughterhouse affair.

The organizers appear to have been a devious lot, given to counterletters and side agreements among themselves. Five of the original organizers named in the act divested themselves of their interests as soon as the bill was signed into law.[89] One of these was N. W. Travis, an editor of the *New Orleans Republican;* this paper opposed the act on the grounds that it created a monopoly.[90] The company's first president, Franklin J. Pratt, once denied having any occupation at all. He was a speculator who seemed constantly on the move between New Orleans, New York, and his home in Greenfield, Massachusetts. In 1871, when the U.S. Supreme Court was asked to set aside the company's injunction against the butchers until the case could be decided on its merits, Pratt made arrangements with one of the state's attorneys, Jeremiah Black, to be sent a coded telegram from Washington in case the decision went against him. Evidently, he had no intention of keeping his stock if the price was about to decline.[91]

Even the carpetbaggers among them, however, did not all look so terrible on closer inspection. Captain Samuel P. Griffin, a cotton broker, was a New York native and a graduate of the U.S. Naval Academy at Annapolis. He had once commanded a vessel in a polar expedition. The Crescent City

87. Act of April 1, 1869, No. 96, 1869 La. Acts 117; *Daily Picayune*, February 23, 1869, 1; Richard Edwards, comp., *Edwards Annual Directory for the City of New Orleans . . . 1872* (New Orleans, 1872).

88. *Wisconsin v. Milwaukee Gas Light Co.*, 29 Wis. 454 (1852).

89. Henry V. Barringer to John Lockwood; J. R. Irwin to Jonas Pickles; Wm. McKenna to E. R. Benton; A. J. Oliver to E. R. Benton; and N. W. Travis to Edward Wurzburger; see Articles of Incorporation, March 22, 1869, John W. Shaw, Notary Public, New Orleans Notarial Archives.

90. Sale from Nathaniel W. Travis to Edward S. Wurzburger, March 13, 1869, J. W. Shaw, Notary Public, New Orleans Notarial Archives.

91. *Times*, February 13, 1865, 4; testimony of Franklin Pratt, May 9, 1871, in *McKee v. Griffin*, No. 379, Eighth District Court, Parish of Orleans, Louisiana Division, New Orleans Public Library. Hereafter, Record, *McKee v. Griffin*. About his occupation, Pratt said, "I do not know that I have any." A merchant? "You might as well call it so." Ibid. Pratt to Black, telegram, November 23, 1870, in Jeremiah Black Papers, Manuscript Division, Library of Congress.

Company employed him as its first superintendent.[92] In 1869, Edward B. Benton was a thirty-seven-year-old native of Vermont with a reputation in New Orleans as an aggressive and successful businessman. He had gone south to seek his fortune before the war, and prior to coming to New Orleans in 1867, he had operated a business in Tennessee, practiced law in New York and St. Louis, and served as partner in a successful business in Shreveport. In New Orleans, he became the director of several companies and the president of the Accommodation Bank.[93] James G. Clark, who served as a member of the original board of directors, was a native of Virginia and a Confederate veteran. A cotton broker and dealer in building materials, he was active in public affairs and eventually served as president of New Orleans' prestigious Pickwick Club.[94]

Nor was it entirely true, as the ultraconservative newspaper the *Bee* claimed, that all the organizers were "newcomers here. . . . Not a name among the seventeen is familiar to any old citizen."[95] Joachim Viosca Jr., for example, was the forty-one-year-old son of a prominent local wholesale merchant.[96] Members of the 1869 legislature regarded him as "the only honest man" among the company's organizers. "Viosca's checks were better than anybody's."[97] Neither was it true that none of the incorporators had any experience in the livestock industry. Jonas Pickles owned one of the many slaughterhouses in Jefferson City, as well as a liquor business and real property in New Orleans, Texas, and Mississippi. In city directories for 1872 and 1873, his occupation is given simply as "capitalist." He also served for a time as superintendent of the streets.[98]

92. *Times*, July 6, 1869, 9. Randell Hunt summarized Griffin's career in one of his arguments (ibid.). On the Grinnell expeditions, see Elisha Kent Kane, *The United States Grinnell Expedition* (New York: Harper and Co., 1853), and *The Second Grinnell Expedition*, 2 vols. (Philadelphia: Childs, Peterson, 1856).

93. *Jewell's Crescent City Illustrated* (New Orleans: Edwin L. Jewell, 1873), 62–63.

94. Clement A. Evans, *A Confederate Military History*, vol. 10 (Wilmington, N.C.: Broadfoot, 1899; 1988 reprint), 380.

95. *New Orleans Bee*, June 18, 1869, as quoted in Franklin, "Foundations and Meaning of the Slaughter House Cases, Part I," 21, n. 76.

96. The attorneys used Viosca as proof of the Crescent City Company's respectability; see Randell Hunt's argument, *Times*, July 6, 1869, 9. On the Viosca family, see John S. Kendall, *History of New Orleans*, 3 vols. (Chicago: Lewis Publishing Co., 1922), 3: 940–41. Obituary, *Daily Picayune*, September 27, 1908, 8.

97. Testimony of E. B. Benton, in Record, *Durbridge v. Crescent City Company*, 248.

98. On Pickles, see L. Graham, comp., *Graham's New Orleans Directory for 1867* (New Orleans: L. Graham and Co., 1867); *Edwards Annual Directory for 1872 and 1873;* "Names and Addresses of Business People in the City of Jefferson: 1870;" Chas. Gardner, comp.,

Six men assumed a leading role in the organization of the Crescent City Company and the passage of its enabling act. "The Six," as they came to be known, were S. P. Griffin, Franklin J. Pratt, A. J. Oliver, Joachim Viosca, J. H. Crippin, and Robert T. Packwood.[99] Griffin chaired the committee of six until the bill had been signed into law, but it appears that from the start, Pratt was primus inter pares among the organizers. The Six admitted three other individuals into their privileged subgroup: W. H. Henning, Charles A. Weed, and Robert Bloomer. Henning was a partner in a prominent firm of commission merchants that included both Crippin and Packwood. Bloomer, a longtime resident of New Orleans, was employed to manage the bill in the legislature. In 1865, he had become a partner in a firm of cotton brokers that included S. P. Griffin and John H. McKee, who later became secretary of the Crescent City Company.[100] Several years later, while working with the legislature again, he was implicated in a bribery scheme related to the purchase of land for Audubon Park in New Orleans.[101] No stranger to bankruptcy, he seems at any rate to have been a resourceful lobbyist.

Charles A. Weed deserves special mention as an individual who may well have had a clear idea of the value of a monopoly over the Texas cattle trade. Formerly "an influential Republican citizen of Stamford, Connecticut," Weed had come to New Orleans in 1862 on the heels of General Butler and worked as a commission merchant for a time. It was rumored that in partnership with Butler's brother, Colonel A. O. Butler, Weed had brought Texas cattle into New Orleans at a time when such trade had been interdicted by General Butler himself. It was also said that the general's cooperation with his brother's scheme helped explain why he had been reassigned after only eight months in New Orleans.[102] Perhaps it was Weed's experience with the Texas cattle trade that explains the unusual interest he showed in the Crescent City Company.

Weed was among the dignitaries on hand for the company's grand opening, and at the height of the slaughterhouse furor, he served as a sort of

Gardner's New Orleans Directory for 1860 (New Orleans, 1859); *Times*, December 12, 1863, 3; *Daily Picayune*, December 12, 1863, 1, 2; obituary, *Daily Picayune*, May 8, 1907, 6.

99. On "The Six," see testimony of A. J. Oliver in Record, *Durbridge v. Crescent City Company*, 248; Pickles testimony, ibid., 175–76.

100. Affidavit, January 13, 1871, in Record, *McKee v. Griffin*.

101. *Times*, June 4, 1873, 1. Cf. Nordhoff, *The Cotton States*, 62.

102. *Republican*, April 11, 1869, 1; Parton, *General Butler in New Orleans*, 302–3; Mitchell Franklin, "The Foundations and Meaning of the Slaughterhouse Cases, Part II," *Tulane Law Review* 18 (December 1943): 8, n. 30.

mediator, trying to convince individual butchers to acquiesce in the new franchise. Further, Weed shared a residence with Franklin Pratt, the company's president, and both he and Pratt had frequent discussions about the slaughterhouse venture with Governor Warmoth on the street and in the governor's home and office. In 1869, Weed became proprietor of the *New Orleans Times*, and according to his chief editor, Mark F. Bigney, he and Pratt often conferred about the slaughterhouse matter in the newspaper offices. As early as June 1870, Bigney heard rumors that Weed had become a director of the company.[103] The company's stock book listed him as the owner of 800 shares of stock. His name appears among a list of board members published in 1872, when all the original organizers had divested themselves of their interests in the company.[104] With Weed as publisher, the *Times* served unflinchingly as the company's staunchest apologist.

Indeed, one of the incorporators' chief advantages in pushing for their bill, and perhaps in getting it enacted, was the ready access they enjoyed to Governor Warmoth. In testimony offered later in federal court, the governor readily admitted to being acquainted with Weed and Pratt and other leading slaughterhouse figures, as well as taking action to aid the company at several crucial junctures. But he insisted that they had been taken "not in the interest of the Slaughter House Company nor to the detriment of the butchers, but simply to enforce the law."[105] Warmoth steadfastly maintained that he had no personal interest in the slaughterhouse venture, and no evidence has surfaced to contradict him.[106]

However grand the idea for the new abattoir, the company was never well capitalized. Witnesses in the Durbridge actions readily testified that advances had to be paid in order to have the bill passed. Property needed

---

103. Testimony of Mark F. Bigney in *A. J. Stafford v. C A. Weed and Others* (U.S. District Court, New Orleans), as reported in *Bee*, June 19, 1870, 1. Bigney denied that Weed either wrote his newspaper's frequent defenses of the Crescent City Company or read them before publication.

104. On Weed's shares, see *Bee*, March 20, 1872, as cited in Charles Fairman, *Reconstruction and Reunion, 1864–88* (New York: Macmillan, 1971), 1323, n. 71. On Weed as director, see "The Slaughter House," in *Jewell's Crescent City Illustrated*, 225.

105. Testimony in *Stafford v. Weed*, as reported in the *Bee*, June 19, 1870, 1.

106. Warmoth came away from his slaughterhouse experience with a keen understanding of the criteria for success in the livestock industry. Many years later, he lauded the financial potential of the industry in Louisiana but cautioned that success depended on avoiding "under-capitalization," poor organization, and a selfish indifference to the interest of the investors. "Above all," the venture must be led by men of "high personal character and integrity." Henry Clay Warmoth, *The Louisiana Live Stock Industry from an Investment Standpoint* (New Orleans: Louisiana Company, 1917), 15, 16.

to be purchased, a slaughterhouse outfitted, and a legislature persuaded to sanction their enterprise and no one else's. Some of this initial capital was in the form of cash, and a good deal of it was in promissory notes elicited from various parties for no consideration or for promises to transfer stock— all of which seems to have been used either to attract investors or possibly to buy votes in the legislature. The experience of William Durbridge and one of his colleagues is illustrative of a confusing array of similar transactions.

Despite his claim to be the prime mover, Durbridge was not mentioned in either the act or the articles of incorporation. Rather, his claim to stock stemmed from a series of none-too-clear written agreements with Oliver in which Durbridge acquired Oliver's interest in the company in exchange for Durbridge's note for $3,000 (payable on condition that the slaughterhouse bill passed) and his agreement to pick up certain notes that Oliver had previously given to Robert Bloomer.[107] Jonas Pickles's experience was similar. Though not named in the act, he was one of the signers of the original articles of incorporation. He was recruited into the enterprise during a chance encounter with Robert Bloomer on Canal Street. Apparently, the capitalist in Pickles could not resist the opportunity to acquire for only $10,000 an interest in a new company that Bloomer claimed was worth between $40,000 and $60,000. For this he paid Bloomer $3,000 in cash and promissory notes for the balance. A night or two later, the incorporators elected him to the board of directors.[108]

THE LEGISLATIVE HISTORY of the measure that was to become the Slaughterhouse Act of 1869 began on January 22, 1869, when House Bill 88 was introduced by John McVean. Representative McVean had already guided another controversial monopolistic enterprise, the Ship Island Canal bill, through the house, and since his home in Caddo Parish was located far from New Orleans, his sponsorship emphasized the point that the slaughterhouses were a proper subject for state action and not exclusively a New Orleans affair. Another slaughterhouse bill was already making its way through the house by January 22, and there was talk about the need to consolidate "all the slaughterhouse bills" in a single committee.[109] None of these efforts

107. "Exhibit G: Agreement between A. J. Oliver and William Durbridge," January 29, 1869, in Record, *Durbridge v. Crescent City Company*, 134.

108. Pickles testimony, ibid., 174.

109. *Official Journal of the . . . House of Representatives of the State of Louisiana at the Session Begun . . . January 4, 1869* (New Orleans, 1869), January 22, 1869, 56, hereafter,

succeeded, however, and H.B. 88 seems to have been the only bill that was ordered to be printed.

McVean almost lost control of the bill at the start when opponents succeeded in having it sent to a special committee consisting of ten representatives from the parishes directly affected, namely, Orleans, Jefferson, and St. Bernard.[110] This tactic had also been used to defeat slaughterhouse reform in the 1867 legislature. By the end of the week, however, proponents had managed to bring the bill back before the whole house, where McVean would always be present and, apparently, could command a majority vote.[111]

Even so, the bill had its detractors. When it was first introduced, Representative Mitchell Raymond, a radical and freeman of color from Jefferson Parish, where opposition by the butchers and stock dealers was strongest, promptly suggested that it be referred to the Committee on Immigration.[112] Another opponent proposed an amendment to ensure that the new facility would "admit all cattle, without distinction on account of sex, color or previous condition."[113] Some of the bill's opponents readily admitted the need to relocate the slaughterhouses. James Currell, a white Democrat from Orleans Parish, said that "it would be a benefit to the whole city to remove the slaughterhouses below the city."[114] Said another longtime resident, "I have been here twenty-five years. . . . It is the wish of the people that this slaughter pen should be removed."[115] The principal argument leveled against the bill, however, was that it created a monopoly. "No objection can be made to the removal of the slaughterhouses below the city; but it does not follow that there should be a monopoly of the slaughterhouse business."[116]

In the Committee of the Whole, opponents resorted to frequent roll calls, petty bickering, challenges to the chair, and other dilatory tactics. Time and again the Committee of the Whole adjourned with little progress to report. Complained McVean, "There is too much frivolous discussion in committee for purpose of killing bills."[117] Other proponents complained that

House Journal; Debates of the House of Representatives of Louisiana: Session of 1869 (New Orleans, 1869), January 25, 1869, 38–39; February 3, 1869, 135–36; hereafter, *House Debates*.

110. *House Debates*, January 25, 1869, 38.

111. Ibid., January 30, 1869, 111. Representative William McMillen later pointed out that there was "nothing endorsed on the bill to show how it came into possession of the House." Ibid., February 5, 1869, 165.

112. Ibid., January 21, 1869, 8; February 2, 1869, 129.

113. Ibid., January 30, 1869, 112.

114. Ibid., February 1, 1869, 120.

115. William Murrell, ibid., 123.

116. O. H. Brewster, ibid., 124.

117. Ibid., February 3, 1869, 137.

the house was in "too good humor to discuss a bill relating to the health of the city," and "there is entirely too much levity on this subject."[118]

Indeed, this was not an orderly house. It was largely a legislature of first-time officeholders.[119] But much of the disorder was deliberately dilatory. Besides, the importance of slaughterhouse reform had long been ignored and even derided both by past legislatures and by much of the political leadership of New Orleans. Although the title of the act stated the intentions of the organizers of the Crescent City Company fairly enough, these men were not widely understood to be motivated by an interest in sanitary reform. Few people had been so motivated, and they had always been outmaneuvered. So it is little wonder that the sanitary value of this particular private effort was not taken seriously by most members of the legislature, or that opponents used every stratagem at their disposal to oppose it.

During the crucial week of February 1, the task of articulating the case against House Bill 88 fell to two conservative members in particular: John Page of Jefferson Parish and William Pope Noble of Orleans Parish. Page was a carpenter by trade, and he took pains to point out the cost of the bill to his constituents. Denying the nuisance aspects of the livestock industry, he argued that the bill proposed to take from them property they had accumulated by "years of industry. . . . All they have for their old age is there."[120] Indeed, several classes of people were affected, including the butchers themselves, who "wade in the blood of slaughtered cattle" and who have put down "the poor man's thousand dollars" to begin their businesses and "taken up lands for ten years' credit."[121] And "who are the men composing this company? Who are they? They are not butchers. They are not cattle dealers. . . . We do object that these men should come along to rob our people, to steal away their property, to disturb our firesides."[122]

Noble was a Democrat who had come to New Orleans around 1860 and served as a high school principal. He had served in the Confederate army

118. Faulkner, ibid., January 30, 1869, 111; Reese, ibid., February 1, 1869, 121.

119. Ella Lonn, *Reconstruction in Louisiana* (New York: G. P. Putnam's Sons, 1918), 26, 27, 42, 43. The informalities of the legislature's proceedings produced a famous recollection from one observer: "There was a member of Parliament [who] brought me a letter of introduction, and he asked me if I had any great curiosity to show him. I told him I had— such a curiosity as he would never see in any other civilized country, and I took him to the legislature." Ibid., 26.

120. *House Debates*, February 1, 1869, 123.

121. Ibid., February 3, 1869, 146.

122. Ibid., 147.

for a time.[123] Noble struggled mightily over a two-day period to persuade the house to adopt an amendment striking out the words "sole and exclusive" in the bill's third section, thus depriving the company of any monopolistic claims. His amendment was defeated by a vote of thirty-one to twenty on the afternoon the bill was adopted.[124] It was an indication of the reservations engendered by the monopolistic aspects of the bill that this amendment elicited the highest vote against the measure recorded in the legislature.

After considering each section of the bill individually, the house passed the measure as a whole late in the day on Saturday, February 6, 1869. The final vote was fifty-one for and eighteen against.[125] One-third of the house members either were absent or abstained from voting.[126] It was clearly a victory for the radicals; they had furnished forty-four of the fifty-one favorable votes. Only nine radicals voted against it. Five conservatives voted for the bill and nine against it. The rate of nonvoting was twice as high among conservatives than among radicals—53 percent versus 24 percent. Perhaps the rate of nonvoting can be explained by a lack of interest in a bill addressing a New Orleans problem, or perhaps by the acceptance of its ultimate passage. But among representatives from New Orleans, where the vote was ten for, seven against, and five not voting, those who did not vote may well have reflected a reluctance to oppose a measure, however controversial, that promised to remedy a serious and long-standing municipal problem. For example, Joseph H. Degrange of Orleans Parish actively opposed the bill.

123. Howard J. Jones, "The Members of the Louisiana Legislature of 1868" (Ph.D. diss., Washington State University, 1975), 122. We relied on this work, as well as Vincent's *Black Legislators in Louisiana,* for the party identification, domiciles, and other biographical details of the individuals who constituted the 1869 legislature. Our vote counts on the Slaughterhouse Bill, which were taken directly from the house and senate journals, differ slightly from Jones's.

124. *House Debates,* February 5, 1869, 171–77; February 6, 1869, 181.

125. This count includes the vote of one representative, William McMillen, who abstained from the original roll call but immediately changed his vote to nay, and nine votes (three for and six against) that the house permitted to be recorded the following day. *House Journal,* February 6, 1869, 124; February 8, 1869, 125; *House Debates,* February 6, 1869, 191.

126. The Louisiana Constitution of 1868 called for a 101-member house, but election contests resulted in the seating of additional members. Jones listed the names of 104 members and was able to find at least some voting participation for all but one. It is not clear who, if anyone, among these was ineligible to participate in the vote on the Slaughterhouse Bill. Also, Jones was unable to identify the party affiliation of four of the representatives on his list. Two of these voted for the measure, and two against. See Jones, "Members of the Louisiana Legislature," 76, 172–80.

He supported every effort to mitigate or delay the measure and helped lead the fight against it on the afternoon of February 5, as did L. A. Wiltz, also from Orleans Parish, who rarely voted at all and never for a radical measure. But neither man chose to attend the afternoon session when the bill was finally passed.

That House Bill 88 was a favored measure whose passage was assured was even more evident in the senate. The slaughterhouses were first brought up in the senate in mid-January, when Senator J. D. Beares moved for the appointment of a special committee on the subject, a motion that was promptly tabled.[127] When H.B. 88 passed in the lower chamber, however, the senate was considering another bill, Senate Bill 142, which had been filed as a companion bill to one that had already been swept aside in the house. S.B. 142, a sanitary measure, proposed to incorporate the New Orleans Stock Landing, Slaughterhouse and Chemical Company, and it was reported favorably by the senate's Committee on Parochial Affairs.[128] But when H.B. 88 reached the senate, further consideration of S.B. 142 was quickly tabled. In short order, H.B. 88 was reported favorably by the Committee on Health, and on February 18, 1869, after mustering a four-fifths vote to set aside the constitutional rule requiring bills to undergo three readings on separate days, the bill was read for a third time and adopted as a whole by a vote of twenty-one to five without ever having been printed. The opponents were Senators James C. Egan, Robert W. Futch, John Lynch, Christophe C. Packard, and Samuel M. Todd—two conservatives and three radicals who had consistently argued against the bill. Radicals had provided sixteen of the favorable votes and three against, with five not voting. Among the conservatives, the vote was four in favor, two against, and seven not voting. The heat of the controversy in New Orleans is reflected in the fact that of eleven senators from that area, four (two radicals and two conservatives) voted in favor; two radicals, Packard and Todd, voted against it; and three radicals and two conservatives abstained.[129] All that remained was for the bill to be signed into law.

The first recorded meeting of the men who organized the Crescent City Company was held on the evening of Saturday, February 20, 1869, three days *after* the act had been adopted by the senate. Fourteen men met at the

127. *Daily Picayune*, January 17, 1869, 3.

128. Ibid., February 12, 1869, 2.

129. *Official Journal of . . . the Senate of the State of Louisiana at the Session Begun . . . January 4, 1869* (New Orleans: A. L. Lee, State Printer, 1869), 134–35. In the course of adopting the measure in the senate, M. A. Foute, from Orleans Parish, voted with the proponents of the bill in seven instances. But the senate journal does not record a vote by him on the final passage, and he has been counted as an abstention.

offices of J. H. Henning and Company on Camp Street. Henning himself was present, as was Charles A. Weed.[130] It is evident from the minutes of this meeting that the organizers did not consider the bill to be law yet. The *Picayune* reported the senate passage in a front-page article in which it claimed that the bill meant that "300,000 people are to be heavily taxed upon their necessities for the benefit of a dozen, and this should bring from the Governor his refusal to sign and approve the bill." The chances were excellent, according to the writer, that a veto would be sustained after a debate "showing the outrageous bartering away of birthrights under this bill."[131]

In addition to the possibility of a veto, shortly after the bill passed in the senate, a seemingly technical but potentially serious problem arose. The house returned the bill to the senate on the grounds that it had been rushed through so quickly that it had been improperly engrossed. The organizers formed a committee to accompany Bloomer to the legislature and "to inform themselves on the present state of the bill." Two days later, they resolved that they would all "go to the Senate tomorrow and employ their best efforts in getting the Bill through."[132] They had good reason to be concerned. When the issue was taken up in the senate, the president, Lieutenant Governor Dunn, ruled that the body had already acted on the measure and could not take it up again. The organizers succeeded in having this ruling overturned, however, and the bill was immediately read and passed. The next day, the senate enacted it a second time.[133]

In due course, Governor Warmoth signed the bill into law, making it Act No. 118 of March 8, 1869. Over the next three weeks, the incorporators met nearly a dozen times to perfect the organization of the company and to live up to its legislative mandate to have a grand slaughterhouse ready for the butchers by June 1.[134] As the corporation got under way, it was important to know precisely who owned it. To this effect, they employed Randell Hunt and Christian Roselius to advise them concerning the validity of the maze of transactions among the organizers that had preceded passage of the act and to advise them on the most important issue of all—the very constitu-

130. Minutes of a meeting of the incorporators the Crescent City Company, February 20, 1869, in Record, *Durbridge v. Pratt*, 88–89, 90–92.

131. *Daily Picayune*, February 12, 1869, 1.

132. Minutes of meetings of the incorporators of the Crescent City Company, February 20, 1869, and February 22, 1869, in Record, *Durbridge v. Pratt*, 88–89, 90–92.

133. *Daily Picayune*, February 26, 1869, 9; February 27, 1869, 8.

134. The following account of the early affairs of the Crescent City Company is based on the minutes of meetings held by the organizers between February 20, 1869, and March 23, 1869, in Record, *Durbridge v. Pratt*, 88–120.

tionality of their Slaughterhouse Act. The slaughterhouse men showed good judgment in choosing legal counsel. Hunt and Roselius were two of the most distinguished members of the New Orleans bar and had excellent credentials as lawyers, scholars, and statesmen. They would play a leading role in defending the Slaughterhouse Act in the state courts. At the time, Hunt was president of the University of Louisiana and taught law there, and Roselius served as dean of the law faculty.[135] They had both opposed secession but remained in the state as constitutional unionists.

The organizers also employed Randell Hunt's younger brother, William J. Hunt, a Republican and associate of the governor, to write the articles of incorporation. This instrument was formally executed before a notary public on March 20, 1869, after which, in true Louisiana fashion, the organizers celebrated at the popular Moreau's Restaurant.[136] On the same day, a committee was appointed to select a site for the new, centralized slaughterhouse and suitable quarters for the company's offices. Two days later, S. P. Griffin and Jonas Pickles were appointed as a committee "to confer with the leading butchers on the subject of a locality for the stocklanding and slaughter-houses" and to inquire into the prices of property across the river.[137] Soon they would be levying assessments on the stockholders to gather the funds needed to construct the new facilities and get the business under way. One can only guess at the reaction of the butchers of New Orleans to the Crescent City Company's initiative to confer about a suitable site for the new, consolidated slaughterhouse.

FINALLY, what evidence is there that the Slaughterhouse Act was a product of bribery? The *Picayune* had no doubt. Only a few days after the bill had passed in the senate, it charged that "no sensible man" could deny that bribery was being practiced for "the creation of monopolies designed to enrich a few."[138] According to the paper, the act had cost the incorporators a million dollars, "though only one hundred thousand could be raked up in

135. On Roselius and Hunt see, e.g., *Dictionary of American Biography* (New York: Charles Scribner's Sons, 1935), 164–65; *Times,* August 8, 1869, 4; Hunt, *Selected Arguments.*

136. Articles of Incorporation, dated March 22, 1869, Acts of John H. Shaw, Notary Public, New Orleans Notarial Archives. See also Acts of Concurrence, one by L. P. Sanger, Robert Bloomer, as transferee of William Sanger, Joseph H. Pearson, Andrew J. May, and Joachim Viosca, and a second by William S. Mudgett, both dated March 13, 1869, ibid. The first board consisted of J. Ellison, Franklin J. Pratt, Robert T. Packwood, Joachim Pickles, William Durbridge, E. B. Benton, S. P. Griffin, E. G. Clark, and John Wharton. Minutes of March 19, 1869, in Record, *Durbridge v. Pratt,* 111.

137. Minutes, March 22, 1869, in Record, *Durbridge v. Pratt,* 115.

138. *Daily Picayune,* February 21, 1869, 4.

cash."[139] The *Picayune* believed that even Governor Warmoth was implicated. When he failed to veto the bill after its legislative opponents had allegedly refrained from making amendments in order to present it to him "with its most repulsive features untouched,"[140] the conclusion seemed inescapable that "the Governor holds stock to a very large amount."[141] Presciently, the *Picayune* predicted that "an immense amount of litigation" would follow.[142]

The most fertile sources of information available today on this subject are the records in the suits by William Durbridge and other stockholders mentioned earlier in this chapter. As a whole, the testimony is inconclusive, and some of it is patently suspect. Nonetheless, elements of it ring true and clearly tend to incriminate. According to these records, the six principal organizers "took the lead in the passage of the bill and had charge of it. . . . They were in the room most of the time; took a great deal of interest night and day."[143] It was also generally agreed that The Six "were outside the board. They formed a board themselves."[144] E. B. Benton testified that The Six "had been paying out money to the members of the Legislature to pass the bill," and it was necessary to come to some agreement to compensate these individuals.[145] After some quarrelling among themselves, they agreed on "a grand division of the spoils" (as Judge Cooley put it in his opinion).[146] At their first meeting after the act was passed, the incorporators resolved that the new corporation would issue $2 million of stock. One-half, or $1 million of this stock, was considered to be preferred, fully paid up, and nonassessable, and it was to be divided among the seventeen incorporators as follows: each of The Six was to receive $100,000 worth of stock, or 1,000 shares each at a par value of $100; the remaining four-tenths of this privileged half was to be divided equally among all seventeen organizers, giving 235 shares to each. This explains the distinction made by some witnesses between "trustee stock" allocated to The Six and "incorporator stock" con-

---

139. Ibid., March 14, 1869, 4.

140. Ibid., February 20, 1869, 1.

141. Ibid., June 19, 1869, 1. Later, Warmoth emphasized that "slaughtering of animals was now confined to one place, down river from the city, for reasons of health. Formerly, the slaughtering had been done in the upper part of the city, and the offal was poured into the river, which in consequence, reeked with putridity." Current, *Those Terrible Carpetbaggers*, 244; Warmoth, *War, Politics and Reconstruction*, 80.

142. *Daily Picayune*, March 7, 1869, 4.

143. Jesse Irwin testimony, in Record, *Durbridge v. Crescent City Company*, 159, 161.

144. Pickles testimony, in ibid., 176.

145. Ibid., 201.

146. "Reasons for Judgment," March 16, 1872, in ibid., 401.

sisting of the 4,000 shares divided among all seventeen. The remaining $1 million of stock was to be offered to the public.[147]

It was repeatedly acknowledged that this special allocation of stock was made to The Six to help with passage of the act. It was never expected that they would actually receive this stock. According to Jonas Pickles, a member of the board of directors, "Mr. Pratt had the issuing of that stock and he just took charge of that six thousand shares and gave us our stock 230 shares [sic] and we never paid attention to the rest."[148] The secretary of the company, J. H. McKee, testified to the frequent practice whereby individual incorporators executed written assignments of stock without filling in the name of the assignee. This method had been designed by Pratt so that he could deliver stock to members of the legislature without their names appearing in the stock book.[149]

William Durbridge seems not to have understood that he was supposed to receive only 235 shares of "incorporator stock" and none of the 6,000 shares allocated to The Six. "They came to me with all manner of propositions when I was a director to sign, but I had nothing to do with them. I wanted to do a straight kind of business. I would not connive at any rascality. I threw it up and got out. They would not give me my stock and I have been fighting them ever since."[150]

In any event, under Franklin Pratt's administration, the $600,000 in "trustee stock" was entirely depleted. Just what this stock, or other funds expended in securing the act, was actually used for, however, remains unclear. Most witnesses would not admit to having personal knowledge that money or stock actually found its way into the hands of members of the legislature. They referred instead to "expenses, champagne, sandwiches and such like stuff."[151] The questioning of Jesse R. Irwin is typical:

> Q: Was it not to your knowledge that it was necessary to make expenditures either of stock or funds or something of the kind, for the purpose of facilitating or securing the passage of the law creating the Slaughterhouse Company?
> A: Yes, Sir. It was.

147. Resolution of March 17, 1869, in minutes of a meeting of the incorporators of the Crescent City Live Stock Landing and Slaughterhouse Company, in Record, *Durbridge v. Pratt*, 102–5.

148. Pickles testimony, in Record, *Durbridge v. Crescent City Company*, 181.

149. Ibid., 97–120.

150. Ibid., 52

151. Ibid., 176.

Q: Is it not to your knowledge . . . that a portion of that stock went into the hands of parties connected with the Legislature?
A: No. I never seen any.

By the Court:
Q: Have you not a rather strong suspicion that some did?
A: (Witness laughs.) I have heard a great deal—heard a great deal on the street for two or three years but I never seen it.

Q: Was not that money or some of it to your knowledge used in the Legislature itself?
A: It was used in keeping up these rooms—the expenses.

Q: No. But in the Legislature itself and among the members?
A: No, not to my knowledge.[152]

Jonas Pickles testified that he never saw any member of the legislature with shares of stock or checks in their hands. But, he said, it was customary for members of the legislature to go to the Henning office and "loaf around there."[153]

It was readily admitted that on May 25, 1869, the company had agreed to transfer 1,500 shares of stock to the firm of McQuaid, Mehle and Co. to induce it to move its livestock operations to the new company and "to be disposed of by themselves as they may see fit,"[154] that is, to induce other butchers to follow.

Durbridge himself testified only that money was furnished for "fires, committee rooms, sandwiches, whisky, brandy."[155] But it should be noted that Durbridge was in no position to admit to anything more. His claim to the stock was based on Oliver's alleged transfers to him. The company's defense was that his claim concerned a portion of a fund assembled for the illicit purpose of bribing the legislature. If Durbridge had admitted to anything more than ordinary lobbying activities, he would have admitted himself right out of court, which is indeed where he ended up. It should also be noted that in his second suit, his adversaries were not the company made up of Franklin J. Pratt and his fellow original incorporators. By that time, the Crescent City Company had been sold to a group of New Orleans livestock dealers and butchers. Earlier, these new owners had been among the company's most fierce opponents. They had no interest in defending the mis-

152. Ibid., 162–63, 172.
153. Ibid., 197–98.
154. The written contract is at ibid., 292.
155. Ibid., 58.

deeds of their predecessors and did not hesitate to try to prove that Durbridge had contributed to a fund being gathered for illegal purposes— which is what made it possible for Judge Cooley and the state supreme court above him to dismiss the stockholders' controversy altogether. Once he and his colleagues had divested themselves of their interest in the company, a cooperative E. B. Benton seemed all too anxious to testify about the machinations of The Six:

> A: They were always considered a secret and a matter to be kept confidential. I should hate to state the whole facts unless absolutely necessary.
> Q: It is absolutely necessary.[156]

Benton, who served as an unofficial vice president when Pratt was out of town, was quite explicit in his testimony, as was John McKee, the company's secretary. McKee acknowledged that as secretary of the company he was aware that "a great many hundred shares" of stock were owned by members of the legislature, mentioning, as examples, J. D. Beares, C. C. Antoine, William McMillan, A. L. Lee, and Michael Hahn.[157] Benton acknowledged that The Six had given Robert Bloomer authority to make good on promises to legislators and said that he had actually seen members of the legislature with the stock. He testified, "I think there was some considerable money advanced, and in fact I have seen members of the Legislature have the money and saw them get it. So I am positive there was money paid."[158]

Anyone familiar with the frequent criticism leveled against the bill in the house by the governor's close associate and friend Representative William L. McMillen of Carroll Parish had reason to doubt the governor's support. McMillen was a former general in the Union army, a leading radical, and one of the owners of the *New Orleans Republican*. Both he and his newspaper condemned the monopolistic aspects of the Slaughterhouse Act. Though not a member of the team that had opposed the act, as an individual, he seldom missed an opportunity to criticize it. He had even opposed efforts to ameliorate the bill's worse effects. Playing to the critics, he had insisted that the power of the new company should be "unlimited."[159] He had even urged the house to inquire whether members had been bribed to vote for the bill.[160] He once suggested that the house waive a reading of the bill "in order that gentlemen not be troubled with qualms of conscience."[161] To end the charges

156. Benton, in ibid., 200.

157. Ibid., 100–1; A. J. Oliver and Jonas Pickles testified to the same effect at 81 and 197, respectively.

158. Ibid., 203–6.

159. *House Debates*, February 1, 1869, 120.

160. Ibid., February 2, 1869, 129.

161. Ibid., January 30, 1869, 111.

of monopoly, he liked to argue that every member of the legislature should be included among the incorporators.[162] And he had underscored his opposition by changing his vote from "abstain" to "nay," even after the bill had passed by a substantial majority.[163]

Given his friendship with Governor Warmoth, it may be that McMillen's vociferous opposition was intended as a signal to the bill's proponents that they would have to come to terms with him if the measure was going to become law. If so, there is evidence that the signal was understood; according to Edward Benton, after the bill had passed in both houses, the incorporators "met and it was deemed advisable—good policy for the Company to give Lee, McMillen and Deane some stock—not as a bribe so far as that went."[164] (Lee was another member of the legislature. Deane was the clerk of the Louisiana Supreme Court.) All three were known to be close to Governor Warmoth.

As Benton explained under oath, McMillen, Lee, and Dean "had been bitterly opposed to the bill all through its passage through the legislature and it was thought that it might induce them to use their influence to the final success of the enterprise. It was no bribe. It was entirely unknown to them they were going to get it."

Q: It was a mere gratuity?
A: It was. And entirely unknown to them to my positive knowledge.[165]

Benton said that he and his colleagues had had trouble from an unknown source with "our Ship Island Canal Bill" and wanted to make sure it did not happen again.[166] They later discovered that Governor Warmoth had "nothing whatever" to do with the act after he signed it, "and we felt we had been great asses to make the donation."[167]

With the adoption of the Slaughterhouse Act, an interest in financial speculation and potential profit accomplished what a sense of civic duty had failed to do. However controversial, the act represented an effective means of addressing a persistent public problem in a manner consistent with the

162. Ibid., January 22, 1869, 16; February 1, 1869, 120–21.
163. Ibid., February 6, 1869, 191. Months later, in a personal letter to Governor Warmoth, McMillen asked his friend to send him a copy of the 1869 General Session Laws. "I want to edify and overhaul them for the benefit of future generations." McMillen to Warmoth, November 30, 1869, Warmoth Papers, Southern Historical Collection, University of North Carolina library.
164. Benton, in Record, *Durbridge v. Crescent City Company*, 200–1.
165. Ibid., 203–4.
166. Ibid., 224.
167. Ibid., 270.

mid-nineteenth-century emphasis on minimal government. The contemporary understanding of the act may have been captured best in the words of a district judge in 1871, and it can be contrasted with the views of Judge Cooley discussed earlier. "For years," wrote Judge Henry Dibble,

> the butchers of New Orleans had defied public opinion and the express provisions of laws and ordinances in relation to the locality of the slaughter houses. . . .
>
> The legislature therefore did a wise and practical thing; the corporate defendant was created. . . . Such a corporation with such large interests involved became powerful and strong enough to throttle the butchers. The Company did what the officials of the law had failed to do; they forced all butchering and stock landing below the city and instituted a thorough system of inspection in obedience to other provisions of the law aforesaid.[168]

This is a view of the act that accepts the profit motive as a legitimate incentive to reform precisely because it is likely to be effective. Indeed, the widely perceived linkage between the slaughterhouses and ill health provided the energy to reform, the development of the centralized abattoir elsewhere provided the form, and the public franchise to a private company offered a readily available means of implementation. The accomplishment of public tasks by this means was consistent with the early-nineteenth-century ideological penchant for minimal government and had been frequently used in New Orleans and elsewhere for a variety of purposes, including early sanitary reform.[169] To a great extent, the slaughterhouse bill was a reform measure. But if the organizers of the Crescent City Company obtained their franchise by means that left a good deal to be desired, it was also true, as the *Republican* argued in 1873, that "rings, bargains for patronage, dealings in depreciated public paper and wasteful contracts are no modern invention in New Orleans." As Louisiana historian Joe Gray Taylor wrote many years later, "Louisiana state government was corrupt before Warmoth's administration and was corrupt afterward. It was corrupt when the Republicans were in power and was corrupt when Democrats held the reins."[170]

168. Reasons for Judgment by Henry C. Dibble in *Pratt v. Crescent City Live Stock Landing and Slaughter House Company*, No. 528, Eighth District Court, Parish of Orleans, La., available in record of *Bertin v. Crescent City Live Stock Landing and Slaughter House Company*, La. Sup. Ct. Docket No. 3917, Louisiana Supreme Court Archives. The Dibble opinion is at 230.

169. Smillie, *Public Health*, 171.

170. *Republican*, April 1, 1873, 4; Taylor, *Louisiana Reconstructed*, 251. An earlier version of this conclusion appears in Labbé, "New Light on the Slaughterhouse Monopoly Act," 143–61.

5

The Order of Battle in the Lower Courts

The Slaughterhouse Act became a topic of heated conversation everywhere in New Orleans, from its markets to its houses of worship. News articles, editorials, letters, and formal reports of judicial proceedings in the city's several newspapers kept the public informed about every turn of events. With the exception of the *Times,* all the New Orleans newspapers were critical of the Slaughterhouse Act. But as the spokesman par excellence for popular resentment of the state's Reconstruction government, the *Picayune* served as the measure's chief antagonist. It was just the sort of act it had come to expect from a legislature organized "under the oppressive usurpations of the federal Congress."[1] In true Jacksonian spirit, the *Picayune* had earlier remonstrated against a revenue bill that prohibited physicians, lawyers, and other professional persons from practicing without a license, but here the legislative power of the state had been used to create a uniquely odious monopoly covering a staple item of food. In effect, charged the *Picayune,* the act placed "the whole community under embargo to a few rich men."[2]

When the *Times* attempted to defend the act as a bona fide health measure, the *Picayune* dismissed its arguments as "sophomoric scribbling."[3] The men behind this act "have none but a pecuniary interest in Louisiana and . . . are only desirous of keeping off sickness" to the extent that it results in "the transfer of money from the pockets of our people, into their capacious iron safes, located in colder climes."[4] The measure had been "conceived in iniquity and carried through by the boldest and most unscrupulous of means," and the *Times'* support for it could only be explained by the fact that its publisher, Charles Weed, and some of his employees were financially

1. *Daily Picayune,* June 14, 1869, 4.
2. Ibid., June 22, 1869, 1; on the revenue bill, see ibid., March 18, 1869, 4.
3. Ibid.
4. Ibid., June 20, 1869, 2.

interested in the company.[5] It did not go unnoticed by the *Picayune* that the Fourteenth Amendment (with its protective language about the privileges of citizenship and equality of right) had been adopted by this state government "as its first act." And yet these very men are now "putting obstacles in the way to its fulfillment."[6]

Even the *Republican* (whose owners at one time or another included both Governor Warmoth and his fellow partisan in the house, William L. McMillen) and the *Tribune*, the city's black newspaper, editorialized against the monopolistic aspects of the act.[7] The *Republican* admittedly eschewed a discussion of "the manner in which the charter was obtained." But it noted that the public was sympathetic with the "plea of sanitary reform." And it reiterated the old claim that up to now, the butchers had exercised a sort of monopoly of their own.[8]

But the *Republican* considered the monopoly charge to be "a most formidable position." "The new company sought to monopolize the whole business and deny to all persons the right to pursue the avocation of butchers without the proper consent of the Slaughter House Company. . . . The monopoly charge is well founded."[9] It advised the new company to "lay aside its pretensions to a monopoly of the business and enter the lists boldly as a competitor. . . . The public health will not suffer from three or four small slaughterhouses at proper points."[10]

The individual butchers of New Orleans, as distinguished from the livestock dealers, were often referred to as the "Gascons," because most of

---

5. Ibid., June 22, 1869, 1. The *Times* listed Weed as its "proprietor" beginning with the issue published April 18, 1869, shortly after it had acquired the *New Orleans Crescent*. *New Orleans Times*, April 18, 1869, 8. Its previous owner, W. C. King, had died the previous year. Weed had been mentioned as the "publisher" of the *Times* as early as April 20, 1868. *Times*, April 20, 1868, 4.

6. *Daily Picayune*, June 17, 1870, 4. Lawyers for the butchers had been quick to make the same point. Ibid., June 13, 1869, 1–8.

7. The *Tribune*'s position can be gleaned from the *New Orleans Commercial Bulletin*, June 28, 1869, 1; see also *Daily Picayune*, August 15, 1869, 9. There are no extant issues of the *Tribune* for this period. The *Times* never tired of criticizing the *Republican*; see, e.g., *Times*, June 23, 1869, 2.

8. *New Orleans Republican*, June 4, 1869, 2. "Up to now the business of butchers meat has been entirely in the hands of the Butchers Benevolent Association . . . and drovers and consumers have been at its mercy. . . . The business was unquestionably a monopoly of huge dimensions." Ibid. To the extent that a meat monopoly preexisted the Slaughterhouse Act, it was an informal one that was not controlled by the Butchers Benevolent Association alone; it was shared among individual butchers and especially livestock dealers.

9. Ibid.

10. Ibid.

them were French-speaking immigrants from the Gascony region of France or had ethnic roots there. Taking the level of discourse down a step, the *Times* complained that there was not "an American in the business and the number of Germans may be counted on the fingers of a single hand."[11] These men are "not allied to our people either by nativity or community of interests."[12] The *Times* praised the Slaughterhouse Act as "one of the best provisions ever made for the protection of health and securing cheap meat to the people."[13] The act threatened the Gascon butchers' ability to keep prices artificially high by means of their own informal monopoly, and *that*, charged the *Times*, is what explained their "garlic-scented" cries of "monopoly."[14]

From the earliest stages of the dispute, the butchers were advantaged by the existence of the Butchers Benevolent Association of New Orleans. The association had been formed in 1866 and incorporated in 1867 by a group of French and German butchers to combat the informal monopolies of the large stock dealers and to provide some organizational strength against the frequent municipal efforts to regulate slaughterhouse practices. It pooled small capital and made livestock available to individual butchers at low prices.[15] The very existence of the association was evidence of an occupational, economic, and social divide that existed between most of the butchers on the one hand and the stock dealers on the other. This fissure would eventually have a quite unexpected effect on the course of the litigation. In the spring of 1869, the association could boast about 50 members, but that number grew to perhaps 250 in a year.[16]

The association made it possible for the butchers to respond to the threat of the Slaughterhouse Act with strength and speed. Only days after the effective date of the act, they "placarded the town" with posters inviting the public to attend a protest meeting on June 4 at one of the markets. A throng

11. *Times*, June 23, 1869, 2.

12. Ibid., June 22, 1869, 2.

13. Ibid.

14. Ibid. The *Times* claimed that the Gascons were keeping the retail price of beef at 20¢ a pound and that any thing over 10¢ allowed for an excessive margin of profit.

15. On the organization of the Butchers Benevolent Association, see *Times*, October 26, 1866, 13; November 4, 1866, 17; Articles of Incorporation executed before John French Coffee, Notary Public, January 15, 1867, New Orleans Notarial Archives. The German-language daily reported that about 40 persons attended the organizational meeting. *Tagliche Deutsche Zeitung*, November 3, 1866, 8. Its membership numbered 200 in 1889. *Daily Picayune*, October 28, 1889, 4.

16. Letter to editor from "Many Butchers," *Republican*, June 19, 1870, 5.

of butchers, stock dealers, judges, politicians, and other sympathizers turned out. Whatever their individual interests, at least for the time being, the butchers and stock dealers were united in their opposition to the monopoly. The gathering authorized the association's president, Paul Esteben, to appoint a "Committee of Five" to employ attorneys, solicit funds, and institute necessary actions.[17] Later the *Times* reported that the butchers had raised $40,000 for their lawyers.[18] On June 18, another such gathering nearly a thousand strong held at a saloon on Tchoupitoulas Street led to the appointment of a committee of thirteen leaders to steer the opposition. Indeed, it was this committee that eventually came up with the ultimate strategy to defeat the monopoly.

Opponents of the act insisted that the dispute was not merely a matter of money but that ultimately it involved the inherent rights of the citizen. This transcendent theme became part of the popular outcry. Wrote a *Picayune* reader who signed himself "A Citizen," the dispute had a "higher significance" because it involves "the personal rights of the masses."[19] The *Picayune* gave page-one coverage to the June 18 mass meeting at which the assembled opponents angrily resolved that they held "these truths to be self evident," that "every man in this community has a property in his person and his faculties. That no less sacred than this is his right to the product of those faculties which implies a right to the possession of property, to accumulate property by his labor, and to employ those faculties in any lawful avocation without the control, domination, or direction of any other person or persons in the community for their own emolument."[20] In another resolution, the butchers served notice that they would not "submit patiently to a measure which invades their natural and constitutional rights."[21]

In short, all the makings of a great legal argument were there. As Walton Hamilton described the plaintiffs' position: "American institutions were being flaunted; a monopoly, odious at law and to the people, had been given a legislative blessing; the laborer had been denied his biblical doom and God-given right to work. The enemy was an octopus of a corporation; the cause was the cause of the workingman; the rights at stake were the rights of man."[22] All that was needed was suitable legal representation. That role

17. *Daily Picayune*, June 5, 1869, 1; June 6, 1869, 8.
18. *Times*, June 23, 1869, 2.
19. *Daily Picayune*, June 9, 1869, 1.
20. Ibid., June 19, 1869, 1.
21. Ibid., 8.
22. Walton H. Hamilton, "The Path of Due Process of Law," *Ethics* 48 (April 1938): 274.

was filled by no fewer than three firms of attorneys, but the most prominent legal spokesman was John A. Campbell.[23]

A native of Georgia, Campbell had first been admitted to practice law by a territorial court in Florida at the age of nineteen. In 1830, he was admitted to practice in Alabama and eventually settled in Mobile, where he practiced until 1853, when President Pierce appointed him to the U.S. Supreme Court. Opposed to secession but loyal to the South, he was recruited in 1861 to serve as assistant secretary of war for the Confederacy. So he left the Court and returned south, it was said, with a heavy heart.[24] At the close of the war, he resumed the practice of law in New Orleans as an advocate of legendary reputation. Reportedly, a former slave to whom Campbell had given the money to purchase her family's freedom said of him on her death bed, "Put your trust in God and Mr. Campbell."[25] In the postwar period not

23. Campbell was a member of the firm of Campbell, Spofford, and Campbell (his son). The other firms were Fellows and Mills, and Cotton and Levy. Presumably, Campbell was regarded as head of the legal team, but all three firms participated in the initiation and defense of all the principal actions. Other attorneys appearing for the butchers and stock dealers included Campbell's partner Henry M. Spofford, a New Hampshire native and a graduate of Amherst College in Massachusetts. He had been admitted to the Louisiana bar in 1845 and served on the state supreme court from 1854 to 1858. He was active in Democratic circles. *In Memoriam: Henry M. Spofford* (Nashville: Southern Methodist Publishing House, 1880), Louisiana Collection, Howard-Tilton Memorial Library, Tulane University; *Celebration of the Centenary of the Louisiana Supreme Court, March 1, 1913* (New Orleans, 1913), Louisiana Division, New Orleans Public Library.

Also on hand was J. B. (John Blackstone) Cotton, a native of Georgia who had migrated to Louisiana in 1837 at age thirteen after his father's death. A graduate of Augusta College in Kentucky, he was admitted to law practice in 1848. In association with a brother, he acquired a large Irish and German clientele in New Orleans, and Cotton became well known as a criminal lawyer. An opponent of secession, he had served briefly in the Confederate army until illness forced his resignation. He was active in the Democratic party and served a term as a district judge and as a member of the legislature. In 1869, he was practicing with Lionel B. Levy. Henry E. Chambers, *A History of Louisiana* (Chicago: American Historical Society, 1925), 3:213–14.

John Q. A. Fellows, another principal member of the legal team, was born in Vermont in 1825 and moved to New Orleans in 1850 after graduating from the University of Vermont. He also graduated from the Law Department at the University of Louisiana. He ran for governor as the Conservative Unionist candidate in 1864 and lost to Michael Hahn. In 1869, he was in practice with William R. Mills. Taylor, *Louisiana Reconstructed*, 28; *New Orleans Times-Democrat*, November 19, 1887, 2.

24. Campbell to F. L. Bragg, March 9, 1884, Campbell-Colston Papers, Southern Historical Collection of the University of North Carolina library; "The South" (clipping), dated Louisville, December 5, 1872, ibid.

25. Clipping dated March 1889, Groner Family Papers, Southern Historical Collection.

An 1875 photograph of John Campbell, the former
U.S. Supreme Court justice who served as chief
counsel for the butchers in the *Slaughterhouse Cases*
between 1869 and 1873. (Alabama Department of
Archives and History, Montgomery.)

a few, mostly corporate, clients availed themselves of his services. When he
died in 1889, Justice Joseph P. Bradley wrote to the *Picayune:* "The esteem
in which he was held by the members of the Supreme Court amounted to
reverence. For myself, from the time I first heard him in New Orleans in
the *Slaughter House Case* until his death, he was the *beau* idea of forensic
perfectness."[26]

   As will be seen, Bradley had accepted without question the legal arguments raised by Campbell when the *Slaughterhouse Cases* ultimately reached
the federal courts. Perhaps this explains the encomiums in his tribute. Not
so with Justice Miller, who had praised Campbell in 1870 "as a man of

26. Bradley to Editor, *Daily Picayune*, March 7, 1889, Campbell-Colston Papers.

honor and an unfortunate one" but had harsh words for the former justice seven years later. "I have neither seen nor heard of any action of Judge Campbell's since the rebellion," Miller wrote, "which was aimed at healing the breach he contributed so much to make. He has made himself an active leader of the worst branch of the New Orleans democracy. Writing their pronunciamentos, arguing their cases in our Court, and showing all the evidences of an unsuccessful partizan [*sic*] politician."[27]

IN THE WEEKS FOLLOWING the adoption of the act, the Crescent City Company set out to fulfill its statutory obligation to have "a grand slaughterhouse of sufficient capacity" to accommodate all butchers ready for business by June 1. They purchased riverfront property for $48,000, making a down payment of a quarter of the price and agreeing to pay the balance over the next three years.[28] The property was located opposite the city on the west bank of the river, at Slaughter House Point in Algiers, the very site where the New Orleans slaughterhouses had been confined during the city's colonial period. This location could be defended both on sanitary grounds and by the presence of a railhead belonging to the New Orleans, Opelousas and Great Western Railroad, a line that ran westward for eighty miles and was expected to be part of a line that would eventually connect New Orleans and the beef-rich Texas plains. Two river ferries were located nearby. But, among other inconveniences, the site meant that the butchers would have to commute to their slaughter pens across the river and either pay fees to transport their meat to market or move it themselves. Years later, a principal opponent of the monopoly argued that the "main cause" of the resistance among the butchers and stockmen was the prospect of having to relocate their operations.[29]

An architect was employed to help plan the facilities. A stock landing was constructed, and holding pens and sheds were thrown up in unpainted pine. A building formerly used as a sheet iron warehouse located on the

27. Charles Fairman, *Mr. Justice Miller and the Supreme Court, 1862–1890* (Cambridge: Harvard University Press, 1939), 113, 352.

28. Sales from Joseph Ballister to the Crescent City Company, April 16, 1869; Harriet Sumner et al. to Crescent City Company, June 23, 1869; Minor Children of R. B. Sumner to Crescent City Company, June 23, 1869, Selim Magner Notarial Archives, Orleans Parish Notarial Archives.

29. Testimony of William Fagan in *Bertin et al. v. Crescent City Live Stock Landing and Slaughter House Company*, La. Sup. Ct. Docket No. 3917, 147, Louisiana Supreme Court Archives, Earl K. Long Library, University of New Orleans.

property at the water's edge was outfitted to serve as a slaughterhouse. Its sides were knocked out, and the various accoutrements were installed, including a steam engine to operate water pumps and other mechanical equipment. Carpenters were still at work when the abattoir opened for business. Some of the butchers complained that they had been provided with "trees" rather than hooks for hanging their meat and that they had to outfit the space themselves.[30] Capital was in short supply, and once the facilities were completed, they were criticized for being makeshift and a poor imitation of the European abattoir. "This ridiculous specimen of an abattoir," wrote a veterinarian from France, was unsuited to serve as the *backyard* of any respectable French abattoir.[31] The company's architect was never fully compensated for his services and eventually had to sue for his fee.[32] Several years later, when it served the company's purposes to abandon the Algiers slaughterhouse, the facility was dismantled in a matter of hours.

While work on the slaughterhouse progressed, the Crescent City Company served notice through the newspapers that it would be ready to comply with the conditions of its charter by June 1. The notice included a schedule of charges authorized by the act, and at the same time, the company made an effort to quell the rising tide of opposition. It disavowed any interest in interfering with the smooth operation of business or retaining any parts of the slaughtered animals that were customarily sold in the markets.[33] It even agreed to transfer 1,500 shares of paid-up preferred stock to one of the principal firms of stock dealers associated with the Jefferson City stock landing in return for the firm's agreement to relocate its operations to the new facility "and to use their best efforts to promote the interests of the said Company," that is, to help persuade other firms to follow suit. To facilitate

30. Note of evidence, December 9, 1869, in *Live Stock Dealers and Butchers Ass'n of New Orleans v. Crescent City Live Stock Landing and Slaughter House Co.*, No. 1883, Seventh District Court, Orleans Parish, La.; available at La. Sup. Ct. Docket No. 2506, 44–64, Louisiana Supreme Court Archives. See also Mary L. Dudziak, "The Social History of the Slaughterhouse Cases: The Butchers of New Orleans and the Sacred Right of Labor" (research paper, Yale University, 1983), 15.

31. Dr. R. Delrieu, *Les Abattoirs Public de la Nouvelle-Orléans* (Nouvelle Orléans: Imprimerie de L'Epoque, 1869), 12. "On ne voudrait pas de ce ridicule spécimen d'Abattoirs pour arrière-court de cette classe d'établissements dans n'importe quelle ville secondaire de France."

32. *Benjamin M. Harrod v. Crescent City Live Stock Landing and Slaughter House Co.*, No. 2333, filed March 21, 1871, Sixth District Court, Orleans Parish, La., Louisiana Division, New Orleans Public Library. According to this action, the total cost of constructing the slaughterhouse was $60,000.

33. *Daily Picayune*, April 25, 1869, 5; May 19, 1869, 4.

these initiatives, the agreement made it clear that the stock was being transferred for the stock dealers' "own use and benefit, *and to be disposed of by
them as they may think fit.*"[34] None of this was sufficient to quell the mush-
rooming opposition, however, and before long, the New Orleans courts
were embroiled in a confusing tangle of litigation involving more than 300
suits and many more individual injunctions, the likes of which the American
judiciary probably had never witnessed before. As complicated as the controversy was, however, it is possible to reconstruct the contours of the battle
by focusing mainly on the half dozen actions that were eventually appealed,
initially to the state supreme court and ultimately to the federal tribunals,
where they were consolidated for decision as the *Slaughterhouse Cases.*

When the judicial collision came, it could not have been more head-on.
The judicial system of Orleans Parish in 1869 was made up of seven district
courts. Three of these exercised specialized jurisdiction, but the remaining
four had identical general civil jurisdiction, which they exercised without
regard to the area of the parish in which an action arose or where the parties
resided.[35] The first suit was filed on the morning of May 26, when the
Butchers Benevolent Association, represented by its president, Paul Esteben,
brought a petition to Judge William H. Cooley in the Sixth District Court
seeking an injunction to prevent the Crescent City Company from asserting
any of its rights under the act. Judge Cooley had served as a Republican
delegate to the constitutional conventions of 1866 and 1868; but he was also
a native of Louisiana and a veteran of the Confederate army, and the *Picayune* had given him high marks for taking conservative positions.[36] His han-
dling of the association's suit illustrates how things could be done in the
New Orleans courts during this chaotic period.

In a long and repetitious petition that combined popular criticism with
legal arguments against the Slaughterhouse Act, the association asserted that
its members were engaged in a "lawful and necessary" trade that had been
conducted for more than thirty years in the area covered by the act. Relying
on the absence of any laws preventing them from doing so, a thousand
people, allegedly including 400 members of the association, had invested

34. Contract, Crescent City Live Stock Landing and Slaughter House Company to Mc-
Quaid, Mehle and Co., May 26, 1869, Selim Magner Notarial Archives, Orleans Parish
Notarial Archives; emphasis added. Attorneys later charged that this transfer was made to
enable the firm to bribe fellow tradesmen into compliance.

35. Article 83, La. Const. (1868); Walter B. Hamlin, *A History of the Courts in the Parish
of Orleans* (New Orleans: n.p., 1950), 8–9.

36. *Daily Picayune*, March 2, 1869, 1. "William H. Cooley," in *Jewell's Crescent City
Illustrated*, 288.

"capital and labor" in establishing their businesses, and the members of the association alone now owned property in the affected area valued at more than half a million dollars. In seeking to enforce its exclusive privileges, the company proposed to force the petitioners to abandon the purposes of their organization and destroy important property rights.

Moreover, the petition charged that the Slaughterhouse Act was an absolute nullity. It established "an odious and burdensome monopoly . . . against common right and the common interest," and it had been obtained "by the use of corrupt, fraudulent and illegal applications of bribes"; in fact, both the governor and members of the legislature were stockholders. The provisions of the act indicating that it was a health measure were "mere disguises" designed to conceal its real purpose, which was to create a profitable monopoly at the butchers' and public's expense "for the benefit of a body of adventurers."[37] More specifically, the petition charged that the Slaughterhouse Act violated the "privileges and immunities" clause of the newly adopted Fourteenth Amendment, which "secures to all protection from state legislation that involves the right of property the most valuable of which is to labor freely in an honest avocation." And it alleged that the act violated the power of Congress to regulate interstate commerce, as well as several unnamed provisions of the state constitution that they contended emancipated labor and guaranteed "equality of right."[38]

The ultimate aim of this action was to have the Slaughterhouse Act declared invalid on constitutional grounds, but until that issue could be decided, Judge Cooley imposed a preliminary injunction to prevent the company from asserting any of its rights under the act or from interfering with the business conducted by the association. Within twenty-four hours after the butchers had filed their suit, company president Franklin Pratt was served with the first of many injunctions and with a citation giving the company ten days to reply to the suit.

One of the striking features of the controversy as it played out in the lower courts was the sheer number of efforts made by counsel on both sides—and the energy invested in them—to stymie or defeat the opposition short of arguing the merits of the cases. They seemed to regard every move by their opponents as an attack that had to be repulsed lest the whole cause

37. Plaintiff's petition in *Butchers Benevolent Ass'n of New Orleans v. Crescent City Live Stock Landing and Slaughter House Co.*, No. 466, filed May 26, 1869, Sixth District Court, Orleans Parish, La.; available at La. Sup. Ct. Docket No. 2505, 1–28, Louisiana Supreme Court Archives.
38. Ibid.

might be lost. Efforts that at another time might be dismissed as dilatory were undertaken with the earnestness of an argument on the merits. They filed exceptions (demurrers, in common law) to one another's petitions rather than answer them directly, and they argued these motions heatedly and at length in open court. They challenged the soundness of the sureties offered in support of injunctions. They moved to replace injunctions with monetary bonds. And if their losses in these interlocutory efforts could be appealed, they did so. Like prizefighters, counsel returned blow for blow as though the contest would ultimately be decided by the sheer expenditure of energy.

An example of the earnestness of these preliminary encounters is provided by an exception filed by the company against the association's suit in Judge Cooley's Sixth District Court. The company moved to dismiss the butchers' suit because the plaintiffs had failed to make a valid case against the act and the allegations concerning bribery were "impertinent, scandalous and criminous," too "loose and railing" to admit of proof. Campbell's oral argument in rebuttal spanned nearly two days and took the *Picayune* almost ten columns of its finest print to report. He contended that every man has a natural right of "property in his person and a right to employ that in every lawful trade."[39] He made no effort to deny the regulatory power of the state, but he scorned the contention that this act could be justified as a health measure. "What do they say on their part?" he asked of the incorporators' motivations. "That this monopoly is just? That this monopoly is right? . . . No, sir. They say that the great object of the bill was to secure the health of the city; that the great purpose of this bill was to convey pure air and pure water, nutritive food, wholesome food, to the members of this community."[40] Campbell dismissed this contention as pretense. Quite to the contrary, he contended that the act was a private financial scheme of unprecedented audacity, a "grinding and odious monopoly" obtained by fraud from a legislature all too willing to be corrupted.[41]

As he concluded, the former Confederate official made it quite clear that he was arguing for a greatly expanded role for the courts—for "all the judiciaries of the country"—in the defense of fundamental rights against unreasonable legislative intrusions. The legislative and executive branches had defaulted in their obligation to respect fundamental rights, he argued. "Woe!, woe!, woe! to this country if these tribunals falter in the performance

39. Campbell's argument is reported verbatim in the *Daily Picayune*, June 27, 1869, 10.
40. Ibid.
41. Ibid.

of their duty.''[42] Campbell concluded his long argument by making his expectations of the judges even more explicit. "All modern civilization is de-
rived from the ascendancy which the legal profession acquired. All the
constitutions of Europe emanated from the professional mind and I pray
that the judges of the land may fulfill their high vocation, and defend, and
protect and guard the liberties that are embodied in these constitutions."[43]

Judge Cooley did not rule on the exception until December. Though
similar arguments were held in other courts, the argument of this motion in
Cooley's court before a capacity crowd in late June proved to be the most
celebrated and most prolonged public hearing that any of these cases received in the lower courts.

The second of the six suits to be appealed was initiated only hours after
the Butchers Benevolent Association filed its suit. William H. Hunt, an attorney for the Crescent City Company, was in the New Orleans court building when the attorneys for the butchers applied for their injunction, and he
personally observed the proceedings in Judge Cooley's chambers. Within
hours, he filed a short and hastily prepared petition with Judge Charles
Leaumont in the Fifth District Court asserting the company's exclusive privileges and alleging that the Butchers Benevolent Association had publicly
made known its intentions of thwarting the company in the exercise of its
rights.[44] In response, Judge Leaumont issued an injunction against the association. The butchers replied to this action with an exception and answer in
which they moved that the suit be dismissed on the principal grounds that
the Slaughterhouse Act was invalid for the reasons already given in their
own action and also because it violated the first section of the Civil Rights
Act of 1866, which they claimed protected citizens in all their civil rights.

In Louisiana, as elsewhere, the writ of injunction was an extraordinary
remedy available only if a plaintiff could convince a judge that some action
by the defendant would cause him or her irreparable harm unless the court
intervened immediately to prevent it. In such a case, a preliminary restraining order would be issued ex parte, without waiting to hear from the defendant. Once notified of the action, however, the defendant could move to
have the injunction dissolved upon a showing that the plaintiff was, in fact,
not threatened with irreparable harm. If this motion succeeded, the defen-

42. Ibid.

43. Ibid., 11. For the news article on Campbell's argument, see ibid., June 24, 1869, 8.

44. *Crescent City Live Stock Landing and Slaughter House Co. v. The Butchers Benevolent
Ass'n of New Orleans*, No. 585, filed May 26, 1869, Fifth District Court, Orleans Parish, La.,
record available at La. Sup. Ct. Docket No. 2509, Louisiana Supreme Court Archives.

dant would be permitted to substitute a monetary bond in an amount sufficient to compensate the plaintiff for any damages he or she might suffer in the absence of the injunction, should the case ultimately be decided in the plaintiff's favor.[45] As an extraordinary remedy, an injunction could not be maintained, even as a preliminary order, if the potential damage to the plaintiff was readily ascertainable in dollars and cents.

William Hunt lost no time in seeking permission from Judge Cooley to substitute bonds for the injunction imposed at the behest of the Butchers Benevolent Association. On June 6, Cooley's courtroom "was crowded with representatives of both sides" for their first encounter in open court in an extraordinary Saturday hearing.[46] John Campbell argued strenuously that his clients stood to suffer irreparable harm. The act "would break them up and disperse them." To require the butchers and stock dealers to relocate to the new facilities across the river was tantamount to having an ax "put to the root of a whole community."[47] But Judge Cooley found that immediate compliance with the act by the butchers and stock dealers was merely a matter of dollars and cents. He ordered the dissolution of the injunction, provided that the company furnished a bond of $100,000.

This ruling left the Crescent City Company free to assert its rights under the statute, while the butchers remained enjoined from interfering with them by Judge Leaumont's order. The company's victory seemed only to stiffen the resistance, and that night, at the first of the butchers' mass meetings, resolutions were adopted "with three cheers and a 'tiger'" denouncing the company as "an iniquitous and grinding monopoly," "a nefarious scheme of public plunder," "a willful violation of the Constitution."[48] As if to show its own resolve, the company went back to Judge Leaumont's court on Monday morning and caused the president and three other members of the Butchers Benevolent Association to be fined and briefly jailed for slaughtering outside the company's facilities in violation of its injunction.[49] Rumors of bribery remained rife in this climate. The *Picayune* reported, "We learn that the governor holds stock to a very large amount" and that several legislators are "heavily interested."[50] Warmoth felt compelled to obtain a handwritten statement from the president and secretary of the Crescent City

45. James O. Fuqua, comp., *Code of Practice in Civil Cases for the State of Louisiana* (New Orleans: Bloomfield and Steele, 1867).

46. *Daily Picayune*, June 6, 1869, 6.

47. Ibid.

48. Ibid., 8.

49. Ibid., June 17, 1869, 1.

50. Ibid., June 19, 1869, 1.

Company certifying that "to the best of our knowledge and belief Governor
Henry Clay Warmoth neither is nor has been at any time, directly or indirectly, openly or disguisedly, immediately or prospectively, either a stockholder in the above company or interested in its affairs in any pecuniary
sense whatsoever."[51]

The attorneys for the Butchers Benevolent Association now undertook
a series of moves aimed at restoring their injunctions against the company
so that their clients could conduct their businesses undisturbed, pending the
outcome of the litigation. First, they sought to suspend Judge Cooley's
finding that the butchers did not stand to suffer irreparable injury and his
decision allowing the injunctions to be bonded out, until the issue of irreparable harm could be appealed to the state supreme court, as allowed under
Article 566 of the Code of Practice. Under Article 575, if the appeal were
taken within ten days, the effect of the decision would be suspended until
the appeal had been decided.[52] This motion afforded the opportunity for a
second major confrontation in open court. Once again, John Campbell argued, "My clients tell you their businesses will be broken up, their calcula-
tions for business disturbed and irreparable injury will be caused."[53] Despite
the eloquence, Judge Cooley could not be persuaded to sign the order
allowing the appeal. For the second time, he dumbfounded counsel for the
butchers in his interpretation of the law, this time by holding that Article
566 could not have been intended to apply to a case like this, since it would
have the effect of canceling out Article 304, which allowed the injunctions
to be bonded out in the first place.[54] To reach this decision, Judge Cooley
had to put aside an impressive line of state supreme court decisions that
uniformly supported the practice of allowing suspensive appeals in such
cases. He also rejected one recent decision, deemed illogical by Cooley, in
which the supreme court had specifically justified the suspensive appeal on
the grounds that a lower court judge might misapply the irreparable harm
rule, in which case an aggrieved party would need a suspensive appeal so
that the judge's decision could be reviewed.[55] That, of course, was exactly

51. Certificate signed by Franklin J. Pratt and J. H. McKee, July 7, 1869, Reel 2, Henry
Clay Warmoth Papers, Southern Historical Collection.

52. Fuqua, *Code of Practice*.

53. *Daily Picayune*, June 13, 1869, 8.

54. "Reasons," June 14, 1869, in *Butchers Benevolent Ass'n v. Crescent City Live Stock
Landing and Slaughter House Company*, La. Sup. Ct. Docket No. 2505, 81; *Daily Picayune*,
June 15, 1869, 3.

55. *White and Trufant v. Cazenave*, 14 La. Ann. 57 (1859), in particular. The controlling
precedent, also put aside by Cooley, was *De La Croix v. Villere*, 11 La. Ann. 39 (1856), in
which the court had said, "The test of irreparable injury is not merely whether the damages

the point argued by the butchers' attorneys. In fact, all the decisions cited by Judge Cooley to support his denial of a suspensive appeal actually *acknowledged* the availability of such an appeal.

Failing to win even a temporary suspension of Judge Cooley's decision allowing their injunctions to be bonded out, the butchers now launched a second effort to restore their injunctions. They attacked the bonds given by the Crescent City Company in substitution for the injunction, arguing that the persons who had signed them were not qualified under the law because they neither resided in the parish nor owned property there.[56] This motion called attention to the nature of the slaughterhouse project as a speculative venture. The sureties were shown to be men who had major financial interests in New York and elsewhere and who were used to speculating in real estate. They included Charles Howell, president of the infamous Louisiana Lottery Company. Another man refused to discuss his holdings altogether, and someone had to be found to substitute for him on the bond. But these facts did not rebut the claim that the sureties were good for the bonds, and Cooley had no problem dismissing the motion.[57]

In yet another attack, even before his challenge to the bonds could be decided, Campbell attempted to substitute a bond for the injunction the Crescent City Company had obtained in the Fifth District Court. Judge Leaumont's court was "crowded to suffocation" for the hearing, but the motion was a long shot at best.[58] Only the day before, Campbell had failed in his effort to prevent Leaumont from convicting Paul Esteben and his colleagues of contempt of court. It came as no surprise when this judge refused to permit the company's injunction to be bonded out.

The news of Leaumont's decision caused "angry and indignant excitement" among the crowd attending the July 19 mass meeting at the Tchoupitoulas Street saloon.[59] The butchers were quickly running out of judicial means of keeping the Slaughterhouse Act in abeyance until the merits of the case could be decided—or so it seemed. Judge Cooley had ruled that the Butchers Benevolent Association, an ongoing corporation, did not stand to

---

can be estimated in money but also whether the continuance of the injury will work a more serious injury to the defendant who seeks to bond it out or to the plaintiff who obtained it in the first place." Cooley's other citations were *Jure v. First Municipality of New Orleans*, 2 La. Ann. 321 (1847); *Cobb et al. v. Parham*, 4 La. Ann. 147 (1849); *Stetson v. First Municipality*, 12 Rob. 488 (1846); *Wells v. City of New Orleans*, 20 La. Ann. 300 (1868).

56. Article 3011, Louisiana Civil Code (1825).

57. *Daily Picayune*, June 20, 1869, 2.

58. Ibid., June 18, 1869, 1.

59. Ibid., June 19, 1869, 1.

suffer irreparable damages by having its privileges preempted by a newly formed corporation, and Judge Leaumont had ruled that a recently formed corporation—the Crescent City Company—not yet in the full exercise of its privileges, did indeed stand to suffer irreparable harm by delaying implementation of its franchise. The initial exceptions filed against the company's suit had yet to be tried, but for the time being, the butchers had to either patronize the company's facilities or not slaughter at all. The saloon crowd shouted its support for a resolution calling for a boycott of the markets. Days followed when fresh beef was a scarce commodity in New Orleans, making it impossible for the general public to escape involvement in the dispute.[60] Not long afterward, the butchers denounced the *New Orleans Times* as "an enemy of the people and butchers—the organ of a monopoly," and its proprietor, Charles A Weed, as a "Northern adventurer."[61]

But the butchers now employed more than rhetoric. Paul Esteben emerged from a long, secret session of the leadership to suggest another strategy that would allow practically all the butchers to go on selling meat. Fresh from his confinement in the parish prison, he chose his words carefully to avoid incurring Judge Leaumont's wrath again. But his message was clear: the company's injunction did not bind anyone who was *not* a member of the Butchers Benevolent Association. Therefore, individual butchers could extricate themselves from the injunction simply by resigning from the association.[62] They would then be free to obtain individual injunctions against the company in another court. The New Orleans legal landscape would soon be covered with crisscrossing injunctions.

The first shot in the war of injunctions that followed was fired by Inbau, Aycock and Company, a prominent firm of stock dealers and the owners of a major interest in the stock landing in Jefferson City. Represented by the same team of attorneys who had brought suit on behalf of the Butchers Benevolent Association, Inbau carefully avoided Judge Cooley's court and filed a similar action in the Seventh District Court—whose judge, T. Wharton Collens, had actually appeared at one of the mass meetings in support of the butchers' cause. This action would become the third of the *Slaughterhouse Cases* on appeal.[63]

60. "Now what are the people of New Orleans to do? No meat—nothing to eat." Ibid., June 18, 1869, 1. "The markets were generally deserted yesterday . . . residents of Orleans and Jefferson were this morning deprived of their supply of meat" by a "small body of heartless speculators." Ibid., 4.

61. Ibid., June 22, 1869, 1.

62. Ibid.

63. Ibid., June 6, 1869, 8. *Inbau, Aycock and Co. v. Crescent City Live Stock Landing and Slaughter House Co.*, No. 1537, filed June 18, 1869, Seventh District Court, Orleans Parish,

Inbau made a very strong case for an injunction against the company. As one of the principal lessors of the stock landing in Jefferson City, it had invested thousands of dollars in yards and related facilities and regularly received cattle for sale from customers both in and out of the state. Many butchers depended on Inbau for their supply of beef. Judge Collens responded by ordering Franklin Pratt into court, and on June 21, he enjoined the Crescent City Company from interfering with the conduct of the plaintiff's business.

Predictably, the company moved immediately to dissolve the injunction upon its posting of a bond, and a short time later, it filed an exception to the action similar to the one filed in the butchers' case. The motion to dissolve was extensively argued in early July, but Judge Collens took the matter under advisement and did not rule on it until November, when the controversy was in a much different phase. Meanwhile, Inbau's injunction remained in effect, and the firm continued to do its business undisturbed for the time being.

Other stock dealers and a crowd of angry individual butchers followed Inbau into Judge Collens's friendly Seventh District Court. By the end of June, counsel for the butchers had filed at least 170 new suits to enjoin the company and its functionaries, making a total of approximately 500 injunctions to be issued against the company on bonds of only $500.[64] These actions were lodged by means of printed forms in which each petitioner piously disavowed membership in the Butchers Benevolent Association and attacked the Slaughterhouse Act as a violation of both the state and national constitutions in general and "specially the Fourteenth Amendment."[65]

Meanwhile, from Judge Leaumont's Fifth District Court, the company replied with a volley of its own, consisting of two dozen suits and approximately 200 new injunctions against individual butchers, stock dealers, and

---

La.; record available at La. Sup. Ct. Docket No. 2504, Louisiana Supreme Court Archives. Actually, this was the second action filed by the Inbau firm. It had previously taken an injunction against the company on May 26, 1869, in the Sixth District Court (Docket No. 471), but Judge Cooley had allowed that injunction to be bonded out, along with the one taken by the Butchers Benevolent Association. Yet the company had never taken an injunction against the Inbau firm. Realizing that they had little chance of success before Judge Cooley, they dismissed that action and refiled it in the Seventh District Court. The name of Hortair Inbau is frequently spelled at all levels of this litigation as "Imbau." Except in titles, "Inbau" is used consistently here.

64. Variously titled, the suits bear numbers 1544, 1548–1660, 1667, 1786–1826, 1838–1848, and 1857 of the Seventh District Court, Orleans Parish, La., filed June 21–29, 1869, Louisiana Division, New Orleans Public Library.

65. For a specimen suit, see *Daily Picayune*, June 23, 1869, 1.

steamship operators to force compliance with the act.⁶⁶ One of these actions was filed against the steamboat *B. L. Hodge No. 2* and its owners to collect wharfage fees for 226 head of cattle landed at a place other than the company's wharf. It would become the fourth of the *Slaughterhouse Cases* on appeal.⁶⁷

The most controversial action in this barrage was one filed by the man appointed by Governor Warmoth as the first inspector of stock under the act, George W. Carter. In April, the *Times*, realizing the need to bolster the legitimacy of the new abattoir, had urged the governor to appoint to this important position "an old and experienced butcher, one whose character is well known to the community."⁶⁸ Carter was a native of Virginia and formerly a popular Methodist minister who had served the Confederacy as a colonel in a Texas regiment. At the time of the Slaughterhouse Act, he was traveling in Governor Warmoth's circles, trying, as he once publicly explained, "to bear defeat manfully."⁶⁹ He was one of the original incorporators of the Mississippi and Atlantic Ship Canal Company.⁷⁰ Later, Warmoth would have the legislature create Cameron Parish to make a seat in the house of representatives available to Carter.⁷¹ Shortly after being appointed inspector of beef, Carter had served public notice of his determination to use the police powers given him by the act "to secure the rigid execution of the law."⁷² The fact that he was a far cry from the "experienced butcher" the *Times* had recommended, coupled with the vigor with which he exercised his police power, made him an ideal target for popular resentment of the entire slaughterhouse enterprise.⁷³ The butchers, however, had one small advantage in the war of injunctions. There were a lot of them, and it was practically impossible to locate all of them for purposes of serving the injunctions. Some of the company's injunctions never found their targets. It

66. Ibid., June 24, 1869, 1.

67. *Crescent City Live Stock Landing and Slaughter House Co. v. Steamboat B. L. Hodge, No. 2 and Owners*, No. 720, filed June 26, 1869, Fifth District Court, Orleans Parish, La., record available at La. Sup. Ct. Docket No. 2507, Louisiana Supreme Court Archives.

68. *Times*, April 20, 1869, 1.

69. *Daily Picayune*, December 17, 1869, 2. For a brief Carter biography, see ibid., July 30, 1869, 4; August 18, 1869, 8.

70. *Republican*, April 10, 1869, 3.

71. Warmoth, *War, Politics and Reconstruction*, 266, 109. Carter went on to become speaker of the house, but he and Warmoth eventually found themselves in opposite camps when a major rift developed in Republican ranks. Taylor, *Louisiana Reconstructed*, 213.

72. *Daily Picayune*, June 19, 1869, 4.

73. On Carter and his enforcement actions, see *Daily Picayune*, July 10, 1869, 2; July 15, 1869, 3; July 30, 1869, 4; August 19, 1869, 8; December 17, 1869, 2; April 10, 1870, 8.

was far easier to find Franklin Pratt in his room at the St. Charles Hotel or at his favorite restaurant, where he was reportedly served injunctions "for dessert."[74]

On another front, the city council in Jefferson City complied with the 1867 act demanding that New Orleans and Jefferson City adopt ordinances forbidding offal from being thrown into the river within the city limits and imposing a separate $50 state fine for such behavior.[75] The *Picayune* accused the council of yielding to bribery to the tune of "several thousand dollars." The Inbau firm promptly obtained an injunction against the mayor and city council aimed at protecting its own contractual rights in the Jefferson City stock landing.[76] But before long, individual butchers found themselves attempting to evade $50 fines in actions brought by both Jefferson City and the state attorney general, Simeon Belden.[77]

It became apparent even before the end of June that the merits of the cases would ultimately have to be decided by the state supreme court. When that day arrived, it would be important to make the strongest possible case against the monopoly. From the beginning of the litigation, the butchers and stock dealers had been under enormous pressure to relocate their operations away from the residential areas of the city. The *Picayune* expressed popular sentiment when it reminded the butchers that "public opinion is on their side only so far as it relates to the monopoly";[78] the public was "altogether averse to permitting the stock landings and slaughter houses to remain just above the Water Works."[79] It pointed out that the act did not prevent beef slaughtered outside the three-parish area from being *sold* in New Orleans, and it criticized the butchers for waiting so long to bring the whole dispute to an end by relocating the stockyards and slaughterhouses. A turning point seems to have been reached, however, when Judge Leaumont ruled against the butchers' effort to dissolve the company's injunction. "The court had decided against them," the *Picayune* observed, "and they believed their only remedy was to move out of reach."[80]

In mid-July, after debating various options, the leadership of the butchers and stock dealers revealed their ultimate strategy to defeat the Slaughter-

74. Ibid., June 26, 1869, 8.
75. Act of March 23, 1867, No. 111, 1867 La. Acts 307.
76. *Daily Picayune*, July 6, 1869, 9; August 5, 1869, 10.
77. Ibid., July 14, 1869, 1; August 1, 1869, 11.
78. Ibid., June 19, 1869, 2. On removal, see also ibid., March 9, 1869, 1; March 14, 1869, 4; March 18, 1869, 1; June 11, 1869, 1; June 22, 1869, 1.
79. Ibid., July 24, 1869, 1.
80. Ibid., June 19, 1869, 8.

house Act. A group of thirteen stock dealers and prominent butchers announced the incorporation of a new entity, the Live Stock Dealers and Butchers Association of New Orleans, naming William Fagan as its first president. The new corporation had been formed for the express purpose of purchasing property in St. Bernard Parish, just below New Orleans, from Charles Cavaroc, a prominent banker and merchant, and erecting a huge slaughterhouse capable of accommodating the needs of the whole city.[81] By voluntarily relocating the slaughterhouses, the livestock dealers hoped to make it impossible to rationalize the act as a necessary health measure. The new corporation filed suit immediately in the Seventh District Court, challenging the constitutionality of the Slaughterhouse Act on both state and federal grounds, and Judge Collens dutifully issued an injunction to prevent the Crescent City Company or George Carter from interfering with its plans. This would be the fifth of the cases on appeal.[82]

For once, the company made no immediate effort to dissolve an injunction taken against it. Instead, it chose only to protect itself against a judgment by default by filing a formal answer in which it simply asserted its statutory rights and contended that the Live Stock Dealers and Butchers Association was an illegal corporation. It was now clear to all parties that the dispute was heading for the state supreme court. But before it got there, it was important for the Crescent City Company to mount one final assault.

That attack came a week later when Louisiana's attorney general, Simeon Belden, once again entered the fray on behalf of the company and its legislative mandate, in an action that would become the sixth of the *Slaughterhouse Cases* on appeal. The company was, after all, endeavoring to defend a state legislative act. Why should the state not assume some of the responsibility—and the cost—of the fight? According to the *Picayune*, the attorney general had already "prostituted his office" by joining in the effort to fine individual butchers for violating the 1867 legislative prohibition against dumping offal in the river.[83] Now, in an action filed before Judge Leaumont in the Fifth District Court, the attorney general insisted that the act was a bona fide health measure and that the state had an interest in

81. For the charter, see ibid., July 24, 1869, 5.
82. *Live Stock Dealers and Butchers Ass'n of New Orleans v. Crescent City Live Stock Landing and Slaughter House Co.*, No. 1883, filed July 22, 1869, Seventh District Court, Orleans Parish, La.; record available at La. Sup. Ct. Docket No. 2506, Louisiana Supreme Court Archives. The motives underlying the formation of the Live Stock Dealers and Butchers Association are discussed in *Daily Picayune*, March 14, 1869, 4; March 18, 1869, 1; June 11, 1869, 1; June 20, 1869, 2; July 11, 1869, 2.
83. *Daily Picayune*, August 5, 1869, 1.

seeing it successfully implemented. He obtained an injunction to prevent the Live Stock Dealers and Butchers Association or Charles Cavaroc from attempting to consummate their plans.[84] An effort by the livestock dealers before Judge Leaumont to substitute a bond for this injunction came to nothing, but no matter: Cavaroc promptly obtained an injunction of his own against the attorney general from the Third District Court. At that point, Belden informally agreed to take no action to prevent the construction of the new slaughterhouse, although he predicted—correctly—that the butchers would eventually lose the case in the state supreme court.[85] By mid-September, thus shielded, construction of the new slaughterhouse and wharves began.

Far from makeshift, the new facility would take nearly a year to complete and, including the price of the land, would cost the Live Stock Dealers and Butchers Association around $200,000.[86] On a Sunday in January 1870, only a day or two before the cases were argued in the state supreme court, the livestock dealers staged a grand opening of their new, almost finished slaughterhouse. Through the streets of New Orleans went a brass band and a cavalcade of cattle and butchers dressed in the colorful European costumes of their trade.[87] It was a bit of nineteenth-century public relations: the owners of the rival slaughterhouse were taking no chances that the availability of their new, state-of-the-art facility, safely located below the city, would go unnoticed, especially by members of the judiciary.

Any hope that the Crescent City Company's organizers may have had of easily and swiftly implementing their franchise had been shattered. Its judicial efforts had resulted in a stalemate that allowed the butchers to keep

84. *State ex rel Belden v. Fagan*, No. 809, filed July 27, 1869, Fifth District Court, Orleans Parish, La.; record available at La. Sup. Ct. Docket No. 2508, Louisiana Supreme Court Archives; *Daily Picayune*, July 31, 1869, 1.

85. Cavaroc's action was *Cavaroc v. Belden et al.* Originally filed in the Third District Court, it became No. 120 in Eighth District Court after being transferred. The record is missing from the surviving district court records, but Belden's agreement was reported by Jordan T. Aycock in testimony regarding application for a writ of supersedeas in *The Slaughter House Cases*, 77 U.S. (10 Wall.) 273 (1870). The various sources of the record in the *Slaughterhouse Cases* are provided in the bibliography. On the commencement of work on the livestock dealers' establishment, see *Daily Picayune*, September 16, 1869, 8.

86. Sales from Jules Delery to Charles Cavaroc, March 24, 1869; and Charles Cavaroc to Live Stock Dealers and Butchers Association, March 16, 1870, Joseph Cuvillier Notarial Archives, Orleans Parish Notarial Archives. Construction of the new slaughterhouse was financed by a series of mortgages. See, e.g., Anticresis Agreement, July 26, 1870, Gustave LeGardeur Notarial Archives, Orleans Parish Notarial Archives.

87. *Daily Picayune*, January 16, 1870, 1.

the markets supplied with beef slaughtered in Jefferson City, Algiers, or the new establishment below the city. The company had made several extrajudicial efforts to induce compliance with the act—by offering reduced slaughterhouse rates to any butcher who would patronize the new facility, for example—but these efforts had little result.[88] By the end of June, there were rumors that holders of assessable stock were not willing to meet their installments, that dissension had broken out among the leaders, and that some of the original incorporators were selling out.[89] The company had seen the price of its stock decline from about $40 when it was first offered in early June to less than $30 by the end of the month. In mid-August, it sold for about $18 a share and was about $15 in October.[90] Suits over ownership of stock had broken out among stockholders.[91] In late August, the *Picayune* reported that everything around the company's slaughterhouse had "a sleepy look."[92]

AS SOON AS THE SUPREME COURT reconvened for its regular term on November 1, 1869, the litigants returned to the fray, determined to bring the proceedings in the lower courts to an end and to refer the dispute to the state's highest court. Within a day or two, exceptions that had been carried over from the summer were disposed of, in every instance adverse to the parties raising them. This cleared the way for the defendants to file answers and plead to the merits of the cases if they had not already done so. In a formal agreement executed by Joseph P. Hornor for the Crescent City Company and Fellows and Mills for the Live Stock Dealers and Butchers Association, the parties selected the six principal actions described earlier—three filed by butchers or stock dealers against the company, and three filed on behalf of the company—and agreed to submit them to the district courts for summary decisions on the basis of the documents already on file and a limited amount of additional evidence. The agreement provided that these decisions would then be appealed as a single consolidated action to the state supreme court. Further proceedings in all suits between the company and the other

88. Ibid., September 12, 1869, 8.

89. Ibid., June 19, 1869, 1; June 17, 1869, 12; June 30, 1869, 3; July 10,1869, 1.

90. Ibid., June 6, 1869, 3; June 22, 1869, 2; August 19, 1869, 3; October 6, 1869, 3.

91. Ibid., September 8, 1869, 2.

92. Ibid., August 20, 1869, 1. "So this time property, not adequate to all the necessities of that branch of business, and therefore not [in] compliance with the charter, but vastly too large for the use it is put to, is worse than idle, for it employs many men to stand idle. Its success depe[n]ds upon forcing men to eat its meat, at the end of long lawsuits."

parties to these six actions would be stayed until the supreme court handed down a decision, and when it did, the parties agreed to abide by it.[93]

The answers and last-minute exceptions filed by the parties contained no new arguments. All six cases came up for trial and were submitted for decision in their respective courts on December 9 on the evidence stipulated by the parties in their written agreement. For the butchers, John Campbell introduced a transcript of out-of-court testimony taken from witnesses on both sides concerning the extent to which the slaughterhouse had been ready for business by June 1. The company objected to this testimony on the grounds that this issue could be raised only by the state, and the state had admitted compliance; its objection was noted. Campbell also offered to prove that the incorporators of the company had never had any responsibility for the health of the city or any previous experience in the livestock industry and that the Slaughterhouse Act was a product of bribery.[94] His offer of testimony on these points was refused by the court, and objection to this refusal was noted for purposes of appeal. In addition, it was stipulated that the butchers were engaged in a beneficial trade that they intended to continue practicing unless restrained, and that they owned property worth thousands of dollars, the value of which would be diminished by enforcement of the Slaughterhouse Act. The Crescent City Company admitted that it was asserting certain exclusive privileges, and the Live Stock Dealers and Butchers Association admitted that it had been formed for the purpose of establishing a rival slaughterhouse.

The first decisions were rendered by Judge Collens in the Seventh District Court in the actions filed by the Inbau firm and the newly organized Live Stock Dealers and Butchers Association. Collens had never concealed his sympathy for the butchers' cause and had hinted at how he would decide the cases as early as November 2, when he denied the company's motion made in July to dissolve the Inbau injunction. At that time, he had declared the act unconstitutional, holding that it created a monopoly in violation of the Fourteenth Amendment and Articles 1 and 2 of the Louisiana Constitution, which recognized basic human equality and an equality of civil rights. Now, a month later, and on the same day the cases were submitted to him, he rendered judgments in favor of both Inbau and the Live Stock Dealers and Butchers Association, perpetuating their injunctions against the company.

93. "Agreement K," dated and filed December 9, 1869, in *Live Stock Dealers and Butchers Ass'n v. Crescent City . . . Co.* (see note 82).

94. *Daily Picayune,* December 10, 1869, 9.

The lengthiest opinion was rendered by Judge Cooley in the suit filed by the Butchers Benevolent Association in the Sixth District Court. Cooley had never ruled on the exception taken by the company in that suit, which John Campbell and others had resisted so passionately. But Cooley had also disappointed the butchers earlier by allowing the company to bond out the injunction he had ordered in favor of the butchers and by refusing to suspend this decision until the issue of irreparable injury could be adjudicated on appeal. Now, in an elaborately reasoned opinion that the *Picayune* called "long and able," citing out-of-state legal authorities, the Federalist Papers, and even the writings of Benjamin Franklin, he held that the Slaughterhouse Act was invalid because it had been signed by the governor four days after the legislature had adjourned.[95]

According to Judge Cooley, the governor had violated two articles of the Louisiana Constitution of 1868. Article 39 limited legislative sessions to sixty days and nullified "any legislative action" beyond that period. Thus, in signing the bill when he did, the governor had engaged in prohibited "legislative action." Moreover, Article 66 provided that when a bill was presented to the governor, he could either sign it or veto it by returning it to the legislature. If he did neither, the bill would become law without his signature in five days. However, if the legislature prevented the bill from being returned by adjourning before the lapse of five days, the governor could return the bill on the first day of the next legislative session. Failing that, it would "be a law" without his signature. The effect of this provision, Cooley held, was to prevent the governor from signing a measure into law after adjournment of the legislature.[96] In his view, a bill could become law without the governor's signature on the first day of the next legislative session, but it could not become law *with* his signature sooner.

It was a patently incorrect interpretation that would not pass muster in the state supreme court, but it enabled Judge Cooley to express his disapproval of the radical slaughterhouse measure without embracing that grander radical project, the Fourteenth Amendment. Cooley's interpretation must have offered the butchers' attorneys some vindication for initiating their action in his court, even though, at this point, it made little difference how he decided the cases.

The remaining three actions—the company's suits against the Butchers Benevolent Association and the steamboat *B. L. Hodge*, and Attorney Gen-

95. Ibid., December 13, 1869, 2.
96. "Reasons," filed December 13, 1869, in *Butchers' Benevolent Ass'n v. Crescent City . . . Company* (see note 37).

eral Belden's action against the Live Stock Dealers and Butchers Association—were pending in Judge Leaumont's Fifth District Court, which had been the company's court of choice from the beginning. Like Judge Collens in the Seventh District Court, Judge Leaumont had never made a single decision that was adverse to the interests of the slaughterhouse litigants who had chosen to initiate action in his court. Leaumont offered no cause for disappointment in rendering his final decision. On the day after the cases had been submitted to him for decision, he perpetuated the injunctions against the butchers and stock dealers in all three cases without written reasons.

Shortly after the decisions were rendered, the parties filed formal exceptions in each of the cases on a number of issues as a means of preserving them for appeal, and on December 14, suspensive appeals to the state supreme court were ordered in all cases. The parties lost no time in perfecting their appeal to the state supreme court. The lower court records were filed before Christmas, and the case was argued on January 27 and 28. J. B. Cotton, J. Q. A. Fellows, and John Campbell appeared on behalf of the butchers and stock dealers. The two most eminent members of the opposing legal team, Christian Roselius and Randell Hunt, spoke for the company. By now, both sides had utilized many opportunities to reiterate and refine their arguments. Before turning to the Louisiana Supreme Court decision, however, a summary of the key points presented to the justices is appropriate.

In a printed brief of more than seventy pages, on behalf of the four law firms representing the butchers, Campbell emphasized and embellished a number of points, of which three may be considered essential. In the first place, the statute establishing the Crescent City Company had been enacted through "the bribery of the members of the Legislature, and the purchase of their votes." Any statute, Campbell insisted, "can be set aside for fraud, and the bribery and corruption of the members of the Legislature which passed it."[97] Moreover, the statute violated the Louisiana Constitution (1) because it had been signed by Governor Warmoth after the legislature had adjourned, and (2) because the statute had not been signed within the five-

97. "Brief of the Plaintiffs in the First Three, and of Defendants in the Last Three of These Cases," 5–7, *Louisiana ex rel Belden v. Fagan*, 22 La. Ann. 545 (1870). The titles of the six primary cases and their docket numbers in the state supreme court are provided in notes 37, 44, 63, 67, 82, and 84. The briefs filed in the state supreme court in these cases can no longer be found with the court's records. The "Brief of the Plaintiffs" referred to here is from *Briefs of W. W. King*, Louisiana Collection, Middleton Library, Louisiana State University.

day period mandated by the constitution.[98] Finally, the statute was unconstitutional because in enacting it, the legislature had granted a monopoly, "in every sense of that term." The measure was beyond the scope of legitimate legislative action. Here, Campbell, an ex-Confederate official who had glorified states' rights only five years earlier, now argued that "it is a mistaken idea . . . that the Legislatures of the States have powers of legislation limited only by the express prohibitions of the constitutions of the State or the Union, or by necessary implication."[99] The exercise of legislative power to pass the slaughterhouse statute "is contrary to the fundamental principles and theory of our form of government."[100] Though counsel had resorted to the Fourteenth Amendment in their initial pleadings, it was not until the next-to-last page of his brief that Campbell mentioned the amendment. He insisted that it represented "a new declaration of rights" and "that monopolies cannot be granted by a State Legislature without violating that article."[101]

Extending to barely fourteen pages, Attorney General Belden's brief stands in marked contrast to Campbell's, if only in size. Whereas Campbell had sought to expand constitutional interpretation to new heights, Belden insisted that the Fourteenth Amendment as well as the Louisiana Bill of Rights "have not the remotest application to the solution of the question, presented by the record." The slaughterhouse statute was based on "police regulations, promotive of the health and cleanliness of the city. This is a subject of ordinary legislation, and it seems to us difficult to imagine on what legal ground the Constitutionality of such a law can be assailed."[102] Belden dismissed Campbell's claim of monopoly with similar ease. "That the State itself, might constitutionally, in the exercise of its police power, erect an *abattoir*, where all animals intended for the markets of the city should be killed, . . . and that a reasonable retribution might be levied on those who use it, we suppose will hardly be denied by anyone." But because the state had delegated a corporation to construct at its own cost a central slaughterhouse, "with the right of charging a reasonable toll as a *quid pro*

98. Ibid., 7–33.

99. Ibid., 35, 42–70.

100. Ibid., 70–71.

101. Ibid., 74. As will be seen, Campbell would have much more to say about the Fourteenth Amendment in later slaughterhouse litigation.

102. Brief on behalf of the Crescent City Live Stock Landing and Slaughter House Company and the State of Louisiana, filed by S. Belden, William and Randell Hunt, and C. Roselius, 3–4, *Louisiana ex rel Belden v. Fagan*, 22 La. Ann. 545 (1870), available in the Louisiana Collection, Howard-Tilton Library, Tulane University.

quo, fixed by law for the enjoyment of the facilities thus provided, it constitutes a monstrous monopoly!"[103]

"Is there a single line in the act," asked Belden, "which hinders any one from following the occupation of a butcher?" The right of all who sought to run a meat shop was undisturbed. Only the *locality* where slaughtering of the animals could occur was restricted. All who sought to butcher their own meat *had* to be afforded the right to do so, albeit at the central slaughterhouse facilities. Moreover, Belden reminded the court that "our statute books are full of similar delegations of power."[104] Nor did Belden see any validity in the claim that the slaughterhouse statute had been approved after adjournment. Describing Judge Cooley's "elaborate disquisition" on this point as "rather fanciful than sound," the attorney general insisted that the Louisiana Constitution spoke to "a fatal delay" that limited the time in which the governor could veto a statute. "Not one word is said in any part of the Constitution that he shall approve a law within a given time, or return it to the Legislature after he has approved it."[105]

It fell to Randell Hunt to comment on Campbell's frequent claims of corruption and bribery. First, he described Campbell's argument as "a grave, serious, vituperative, and lengthy address . . . abusive of the character and standing of seventeen citizens against whom there is no evidence in the record, and illegally and acrimoniously denunciatory of a coordinate branch of the government."[106] Hunt summarized at some length and in some detail the past history of the efforts in New Orleans at sanitary reform. If Campbell had implied constitutional limitations, Hunt invigorated constitutional expansion, invoking the rhetoric of Hamilton and Marshall. He insisted that "when a large and consolidated capital is necessary to accomplish works important to the public good, it is quite customary for the States to grant charters of incorporation to private individuals, with special and often exclu-

103. Ibid., 4–5.

104. Ibid., 5. Belden dismissed Judge Collens's decisions in favor of the butchers with the comment that "his proficiency in chemistry no doubt eminently qualifies him to deliver a series of lectures to prove that Slaughter Houses are highly promotive of salubrity instead of being deleterious to public health . . . but we cannot see of what value such speculations can possibly be in judicial decisions; our impression has always been that it was the duty of a Judge to say what the law *is*, not what, in his opinion, it *should* be." Ibid., 5–6; emphasis in original.

105. Ibid., 13.

106. "Argument in the Slaughterhouse Cases," in Hunt, *Selected Arguments*, 65. Concerning Campbell, Hunt stated to the Court, "I should like to know if he ever brings a suit against anyone who is not charged by him with fraud; if fraud is not his monomania; if it is not of that that he speaks whenever he addresses a court of justice."

sive privileges, to effect that end."[107] Further, as had Belden, Hunt emphasized that the slaughterhouse statute "conferred no exclusive privilege on the company to slaughter . . . , but compelled it to furnish whatever is essential to the convenience and accommodation of the butchers for killing their cattle."[108]

However, Hunt saved his most vigorous denunciations for Campbell's oft-repeated statement that the seventeen original incorporators belonged in a penitentiary. "I deny it. There has never been any legal charge made in a form susceptible of legal proof. . . . They pretend that my clients shrank in fear from the investigation. You shrink and you skulk. You skulk behind a generous railing and informal accusation. You say members of the legislature were bribed. Tell us who they are. Name them. Name any one. You say you have witnesses to prove it. Who are the witnesses? Let us have their names. . . . Are you men? Have you the courage of men? Go to the criminal court. . . . You say these men ought to be in the penitentiary. Why not do your duty and put them there?"[109]

The state constitution of 1868, like the constitution of 1864, called for a supreme court composed of five justices appointed by the governor. Governor Warmoth had chosen five active, fellow Republicans for these seats. James K. Taliaferro had run against Governor Warmoth in the gubernatorial election of 1868, nominated by a group of Republicans who feared that Warmoth was more interested in his own agenda than in advancing the ideals of the party. A firm unionist who had been briefly imprisoned by Confederate authorities, Taliaferro later served as president of the 1869 constitutional convention. "He represented," wrote Joe Gray Taylor, "the best of the native white element at the convention."[110] Chief Justice John Ludeling had also opposed secession, and while his two brothers fought for the Confederacy, he refused to aid the Southern cause. A consistent supporter of congressional Reconstruction after the war, Ludeling, along with one John Ray, bought a bankrupt railroad for $50,000 "by means of legal skullduggery and, probably, bribing the agent of purchasers willing to pay a much higher price."[111] In addition, Ray got the Louisiana legislature to pass a bond issue for railroad repair, a piece of legislation that Ludeling, as chief

107. Ibid., 79.
108. Ibid., 81. "When, then, it is said that the act drives one thousand butchers from their business and deprives them of the right to follow their ordinary occupation, the assertion is plainly and palpably untrue."
109. Ibid., 86–87.
110. Taylor, *Louisiana Reconstructed,* 149.
111. Ibid., 197.

justice, later ruled to be valid. In due time, the U.S. Supreme Court voided sale of the railroad to Ludeling and Ray, but not before they had "harvested a considerable profit."[112] Ludeling's extrajudicial business activities should be kept in mind when his opinion for the court in the *Slaughterhouse Cases* is discussed. Taliaferro and Rufus K. Howell were carryovers from the court under the previous constitution. Howell was a pro-slavery Unionist who, with Warmoth's strong support, would later be selected as a federal judge.[113] The remaining justices were William W. Howe and William G. Wyly. The *Picayune* had questioned whether the justices had the "forensic and judicial experience" of some of the justices of the past, but it had applauded some of their decisions and trusted that the justices would not sacrifice state law in their pursuit of Republican goals.[114]

The Crescent City Company's stock traded for about $15 or $16 throughout January, until Randell Hunt concluded his argument and submitted the case for decision; then the price quickly climbed to $25 or more, apparently in anticipation of a quick decision in the company's favor. When this did not come about, the price began to slip. Throughout March and into April, Crescent City Company stock sold at around $21 or lower. Finally, on Saturday, April 9, word leaked out that the court was about to hand down its decision, and in a single day, several thousand shares were traded at prices ranging from $23 to more than $31. On Monday, the court formally handed down its decision, and an additional 2,000 shares changed hands at prices that rose to $34.[115]

In a three-to-one decision, the Louisiana Supreme Court upheld the validity of the Slaughterhouse Act.[116] The court's decision was announced in an opinion by Chief Justice Ludeling in which Justice William W. Howe silently concurred; Taliaferro concurred in a brief separate opinion. Justice William G. Wyly registered a single dissent, and Howell did not participate in deciding the case. The chief justice brushed aside the objections made by the butchers to Attorney General Belden's right to bring suit. The attorney general, he wrote, had ample authority to enter the dispute because the state had a right to enjoin anyone from interfering with the exercise of its laws. Further, added the chief justice, an 1868 statute specifically authorized the attorney general to take action to prevent the usurpation of public offices or

112. Ibid., 197–98.
113. Ibid., 46, 177.
114. *Daily Picayune*, August 1, 1869, 1.
115. Ibid., April 10, 1870, 7; April 12, 1870, 2.
116. *Louisiana ex rel Belden v. Fagan*, 22 La. Ann. 545 (1870).

franchises, referring here to the nullifying effect of the Live Stock Dealers and Butchers Association's charter on the Crescent City Company's exclusive statutory privileges.[117]

The butchers had contended that the act was merely a private measure aimed at enriching its sponsors and hence should be overthrown on grounds of fraud and bribery. Well aware that an argument concerning bribery of legislators might apply to instances besides the slaughterhouse statute, Ludeling, as had the lower courts, rejected this evidence because of the vagueness and indefinite nature of the accusations. Citing none other than John Marshall, Ludeling held that "courts are without warrant . . . to inquire into the motives which may have influenced or actuated the members of the General Assembly in enacting laws." Moreover, the act had all the makings of a public act, since it was addressed to the public at large and aimed at protecting important public interests. Ludeling considered it a well-settled rule that the courts were not entitled to look beyond the face of public acts at the legislature's motives in passing them.[118]

Nor did the chief justice have any difficulty overruling Judge Cooley's decision that the act was invalid because the governor had signed it after the legislature's adjournment and more than sixty days after the commencement of the legislative session. Accepting the point made by Belden, he noted that Article 66 allowed the governor five days in which to veto an act by returning it to the legislature for reconsideration. If the legislature prevented its return by adjourning before the lapse of five days, the governor could return the bill to the legislature at the beginning of the next legislative session, or it would "be a law."[119] That measure had obviously been designed to secure the legislature's right to override the governor's veto and not to restrict his right to approve legislation. Moreover, in limiting legislative sessions to sixty days and prohibiting legislative action beyond that period, Article 39 of the constitution could not possibly have meant to characterize the signing of a bill by the governor as "legislative action." This would have prevented the governor from vetoing legislation after adjournment of the legislature, which he was clearly authorized to do on the first day of the next legislative session.

The attorneys for the butchers had spent a good third of their brief attempting to demonstrate that by creating a monopoly in the Slaughterhouse Act, the legislature had exceeded fundamental boundaries on its

117. Ibid., 547, citing Act No. 58, 1868 La. Acts 71.
118. 22 La. Ann. 547–48.
119. Article 66, La. Const. (1868)

power imposed both by the inherently limited nature of state judicial power—limitations recently confirmed and augmented by adoption of the Fourteenth Amendment—and by specific provisions in the state constitution. For its part, the court preferred to accept the arguments made by Hunt and to abide by well-settled state precedent, which acknowledged "that the legislature, in its sphere, is supreme in all respects, save when restricted by the constitution of the State or of the United States."[120]

But for the first time in the history of the state, its constitution contained a bill of rights, and among its provisions was one guaranteeing to all citizens "the same civil, political, and public rights and privileges."[121] How could an act that robs "one class of citizens of certain rights of property and freedom of action, not for the good of the community, but for the private gain of other individuals in the community," be consistent with such a provision?[122]

Had this been the actual result of the statute, such an enactment might well have violated the Louisiana Bill of Rights. But, reasoned Ludeling, it was simply not true that rights were being limited solely for private gain. The Slaughterhouse Act was defensible as a genuine sanitary measure and was rooted in a long history of sanitary reform, which Randell Hunt had outlined in detail in his oral argument and from which Ludeling now quoted freely. In short, the act was a legitimate exercise of the police power of the state. There was sound precedent, based on the state's power to restrict the sale of oysters to municipally established markets.[123] The court reacted with incredulity to the suggestion that the Slaughterhouse Act infringed on constitutionally protected liberties.

"We think this is a fallacy," Ludeling wrote. "Liberty is the right to do what the law permits." It "presupposes the existence of some legislative provision, the observance of which insures freedom to one, by securing the like observance from the other." Placing his holding squarely within well-established police power case law, Ludeling cited Cooley's already famous *Constitutional Limitations*. "There are, unquestionably, cases in which the State may grant to specified individuals, privileges, without violating any constitutional principle, because, from the very nature of the case, it is impossible that they be possessed and enjoyed by all."[124] Accepting the premise that it was reasonable to restrict slaughtering to one specific area of the city,

120. 22 La. Ann. 550, citing *State v. Volkman*, 9 La. Ann. 411.
121. Article 2, La. Const. (1868).
122. Appellant's Brief, 36, as quoted in 22 La. Ann. 551.
123. Ibid., 555–56.
124. Ibid., 556, quoting Cooley.

it was within legislative discretion to conclude that in exchange for the expenses involved in purchasing the site and building and maintaining such a facility, the grant of exclusive privileges was not an unreasonable step.[125]

In a brief concurring opinion of only two paragraphs, Justice Taliaferro sought to clarify the state constitutional provision that Louisiana citizens "shall enjoy the same civil, political and public rights and privileges, and be subject to the same pains and penalties." As an "abstract general proposition, this is true." In reality, however, equality of right must yield to the will of the people as it seeks to protect the general welfare. "In the public interest and for the public good, legislation which postpones the interests of a few to that of the whole community, is legitimate and proper." And it is not for the courts to gainsay the means selected by the state to pursue its legitimate goals.[126]

In his dissent, Justice Wyly interpreted the act just as Campbell had portrayed it, although he made no reference whatsoever to the claim of bribery and corruption. In requiring a change in the site of livestock operations, the Slaughterhouse Act was a public law, a valid exercise of the police power aimed at protecting the health of the city. But in creating the Crescent City Company, with its exclusive privileges, the act was "clearly a private statute wherein a monopoly is given not necessary to the public health, abridging freedom of trade and labor, for the gain of a private corporation. . . . Whatever legislation is necessary for the public health must be endured by these citizens, however detrimental to their individual interests, but legislation beyond this legitimate purpose, imposing restrictions upon their occupations in favor of a private corporation, violates their civil rights, their liberty, their property, and their pursuit of happiness, to secure which the government was instituted."[127]

It would not do, he added, for the legislature to be left alone to choose

---

125. "It is not an unreasonable presumption that the General Assembly exercised their power wisely. At all events, it was the exercise of a discretion vested in them, and we, as judges, can not arrogate to ourselves the right to correct their errors in matters within their control." Ibid., 555. Ludeling concluded his opinion with a reference to the presumption-of-constitutionality doctrine. "We need hardly add," he noted, "that acts of the General Assembly are not only to be presumed to be constitutional, but that the authority of courts to declare them void will never be resorted to, except in a clear and urgent case, one which requires no nice critical acumen to decide on its character, but which is obvious to the comprehension of any person." Ibid., 557. Was this, perhaps, a reference to Campbell's exhaustive brief?

126. Taliaferro concurring, 22 La. Ann. 558.

127. Ibid., 558–62.

the means with which to exercise the police power, free from interference by the courts. The police power was not unlimited, and it was sufficient for Justice Wyly that, in his opinion, the act could not be squared with the provisions of the Louisiana Bill of Rights guaranteeing freedom and equality. There is no mention in his opinion of the Fourteenth Amendment.[128] He did, however, pay indirect tribute to Campbell. "I think the vast array of authorities . . . presented with such consummate ability by the counsel on behalf of the Butchers Benevolent Association, fully maintains the view I have taken."[129]

The Louisiana Supreme Court had upheld the Slaughterhouse Act as a valid exercise of the state's police power. This decision was supposed to end the case, because the parties had agreed that the cases would be taken to the state supreme court for a final decision on the merits and that both parties "would abide [by] the result" in that court. The agreement had not specifically foreclosed an appeal to the U.S. Supreme Court because, according to the company's attorney William H. Hunt, "no one believed it possible to get the question before that court."[130] Yet once the state's high court handed down its decision, the attorneys for the butchers ignored their agreement and lost no time in initiating an appeal to the U.S. Supreme Court.

128. Wyly's position is reflected in comments on the case by the editor of the *Bee*. He deplored the belief, evident in the majority opinion, "that the power of the legislature is unlimited over all subjects except where there is an express or plainly implied prohibition in the Constitution. With such persons the prohibition must be very clear before they will recognize it." They fail to recognize that "there are certain principles which every man of sense, living in a country constitutionally governed, is supposed to recognize as true." *Bee*, April 13, 1870, 1.

129. 22 La. Ann. 562.

130. *Republican*, June 29, 1870, 1.

6

Appeal, Repeal, and a Compromise

The attorneys for the butchers had made what they could of the various state issues, but none of them ever had much potential as a legal weapon against the Slaughterhouse Act, except in the hands of the most sympathetic state judges. Yet they had also raised federal questions, namely, the precise meaning of the limitations imposed on the states by the provisions of the Fourteenth Amendment. Although these issues had been discarded by the state supreme court for their novelty, they provided the grounds on which the case could be brought to federal court and even appealed to the U.S. Supreme Court. It would take nearly three years of litigation and political maneuvering before the nation's high court would render its historic decision on the merits. The immediate aftermath of the state supreme court's decision was another summer of judicial confusion.

Under existing federal law, whenever a state supreme court upheld a state statute that had been challenged as being inconsistent with the U.S. Constitution, this decision could be appealed to the U.S. Supreme Court by means of a writ of error. Moreover, if the writ were served on the state court within ten days of its decision, it would have the effect of a writ of supersedeas.[1] This meant that the court's decision would be held in abeyance (superseded) until the Supreme Court had disposed of the case. Soon after the Louisiana Supreme Court's decision became final on May 9, a party of the butchers' attorneys and some of their clients traveled to Galveston, Texas, where Justice Joseph P. Bradley was attending to circuit duties. On May 13, Bradley ordered the issuance of a writ of error and approved bonds in the amount of $100,000 in the attorney general's action and $10,000 in each of the other actions. The bonds would serve as security against any damages sustained by the company or the state in the event that the appeal failed.[2]

1. Sections 23 and 25, Judiciary Act of 1787, Act of September 24, 1789, 1 Stat. 73.
2. *Daily Picayune*, May 12, 1870, 6; May 13, 1870, 5; May 14, 1870, 1; *Republican*, May 15, 1870, 1, 4.

The Crescent City Company's first reaction to its victory in the state supreme court had been to file new suits against the Butchers Benevolent Association, the Inbau firm, and the Live Stock Dealers and Butchers Association, seeking damages allegedly suffered by the company as a result of the delay in the implementation of its franchise.[3] The *New Orleans Republican* noted in its financial column that the company would soon boast a full treasury if these actions succeeded, but in fact, these suits were premature and were soon abandoned as the company's attorneys became occupied with the effects of the writ of error.[4] The company had no intention of seeing its advantage put aside, even temporarily, without a fight. Indeed, it had never been in a better position to implement its franchise.

Justice Bradley arrived in New Orleans from Galveston on May 26, and on June 1 he heard arguments concerning the effect of the writ of error. In an ordinary action involving a monetary judgment, the supersedeas effect of a writ of error postponed the losing party's obligation to satisfy the judgment until the dispute was finally resolved on appeal. But could the writ have such an effect in a case involving an injunction? And if so, precisely *what* was superseded—the finality of the state supreme court's judgment, the permanent injunctions rendered (or refused) in the lower courts, the preliminary injunctions initially ordered by the lower courts? An injunction is an equitable remedy granted only when it is necessary to prevent irreparable harm. To hold such an order in abeyance, even for a short time while the merits of the case were being decided, might allow the very harm it sought to prevent to occur. If, for example, an injunction given to prevent trees from being cut down were dissolved, would not the party seeking the injunction have a right to have it reinstated while the merits of the case were decided on appeal?[5]

Two days later, Justice Bradley announced a decision that was not quite satisfactory to either side. Although he had intended the writ to act as a

3. *Daily Picayune*, May 13, 1870, 1, 2.

4. *Republican*, May 1, 1870, 4.

5. In one case relied on by both sides, a landlord obtained an injunction to prevent timber from being felled on his property by his tenant. The injunction was dissolved, and the question arose whether the landlord was entitled to have the injunction reinstated pending a final decision by the House of Lords on the question of ownership of the timber. The chancellor deemed it a wise use of the court's discretionary power to order the continuance of the injunction. The question was, he wrote, "what is the inconvenience and what the danger to the parties which may occur," and whether monetary damages could serve as "a full equivalent" for the rights asserted by the proponents of the injunction." *Earl of Mountcashell v. Viscount O'Neill*, 3 Irish Chancery Reports 619 (1854).

supersedeas at the time he issued it, he had not specifically so ordered. Moreover, his research had convinced him that the effect of the writ of error was to immediately vest jurisdiction over the cases in the U.S. Supreme Court. As a result, all subsequent questions concerning the legal effect of the writ could be answered only by the high court and not by him. On this subject, he said, the "parties must take the law at their peril, as I cannot, sitting here, make any judicial determination which will bind them."[6]

The uncertainty of Justice Bradley's decision caused "wailing and rejoicing" on Carondelet Street, the center of New Orleans' financial district.[7] Crescent City Company stock prices had slipped from nearly $30 a share to just over $20 in the days following the initial announcement of the writ of error. By the time Bradley got to New Orleans, prices were back at the $30 level. But when he was unable to say what effect the writ of error had on the proceedings, prices slipped again to around $25, and the question of the proper effect of a writ of error became a hotly debated topic among the city's financiers.[8]

THE NEW ORLEANS JUDICIAL SYSTEM had undergone an important change during the time the *Slaughterhouse Cases* were pending in the state supreme court. Nothing could have demonstrated more clearly the impracticality of vesting concurrent jurisdiction over injunctions in the several district courts of Orleans Parish than the judicial stalemate and contradictions that resulted from the slaughterhouse melee. The *Daily Picayune* had denounced the "abuse of injunctions," and in a rare instance of consensus, both the *Times* and the *Republican* had joined it in calling for reform.[9] To alleviate the problem, in March, Governor Warmoth persuaded the legislature to create a new district court, the Eighth District Court, giving it *exclusive* jurisdiction in proceedings for injunctions and certain other writs and in all actions to settle election disputes. The latter was a significant power as Warmoth began to prepare for the election of 1870, and indeed, the *Picayune* saw it as a

6. *Butchers' Assn. v. Slaughterhouse Co.*, Fed. Case No. 2234, 1 Woods 50, 4 Fed. Cas. 891, 893 (U.S. Circuit Court, La., 1870); *Republican*, June 4, 1870, 5, 4; Charles Fairman, *Reconstruction and Reunion, 1864–88* (New York: Macmillan, 1971), 1329, citing *New Orleans Times*, June 2, 3, 4, 5, 1870; and *New Orleans Bee*, June 3, 4, 1870.

7. *Republican*, June 4, 1870, 4.

8. *Daily Picayune*, June 15, 1870, 7; May 29, 1870, 6; June 5, 1870, 3.

9. Ibid., January 14, 1870, 4; June 19, 1869, 8; *Republican*, June 3, 1869, 2; *Times*, January 4, 1870, 6.

radical scheme to control elections.[10] The act directed the other district courts to transfer all such cases to the new court.[11]

The new statute departed from the constitutional practice of electing district court judges to the extent that it authorized the governor to appoint an interim judge to serve on the new court until one could be regularly elected in November 1872. For the position, Governor Warmoth chose Henry C. Dibble, a close associate, sometime staff member of the Republican legislature, and the man who had drafted the bill creating the Eighth District Court.[12] Dibble was an Indiana native in his mid-twenties. He had served as a colonel in the Union army and had briefly attended the University of Louisiana before being admitted to the bar in 1865. He confessed to feeling "painfully conscious" of his "inexperience" when he took office.[13]

Although the legislature had acted well within its constitutional powers, this new tribunal was controversial nonetheless. From his seat in the Sixth District Court, Judge Cooley called it "no court at all," and Judges Collens and Leaumont joined him in protesting the statutory mandate to surrender jurisdiction in pending cases to Judge Dibble.[14] It took a decision by the state supreme court in late May to settle the question of the Eighth District Court's legitimacy. By June, all the principal *Slaughterhouse Cases* (and many others) had been transferred to it.[15] At the state level, nothing would happen in any pending slaughterhouse case without the approval of the new jurist who was "painfully conscious" of his "inexperience."

On June 3, Justice Bradley had declared himself unable to say whether the writ of error had a supersedeas effect on the proceedings. But according to the *Republican*, "before the close of the day the slaughter house people, with invincible pluck, were on the war path again."[16] Availing itself of the services of the new "octagon court" and its sympathetic judge, the Crescent

10. Taylor, *Louisiana Reconstructed*, 185; *Daily Picayune*, March 21, 1870, 1.

11. Act of March 19, 1870, No. 2, 1870 La. Acts 4; Hamlin, *History of the Courts*, 10; Ben Robertson Miller, *The Louisiana Judiciary* (Baton Rouge: Louisiana State University Press, 1932; reprint, Baton Rouge: Claitor's, 1981), 52.

12. Francis B. Harris, "Henry C. Warmoth: Reconstruction Governor of Louisiana," *Louisiana Historical Quarterly* 30 (April 1947): 82.

13. *Daily Picayune*, March 26, 1870, 1. On Dibble, see also Fairman, *Reconstruction and Reunion*, 1336, citing *Daily Picayune*, January 21, 1872. On Dibble as attorney for the governor, see *Daily Picayune*, June 26, 1869, 2; *Times*, June 23, 1869, 2.

14. On Cooley's position, see *Daily Picayune*, March 28, 1870, 2; March 30, 1870, 2; April 8, 1870, 4; April 28, 1870, 1.

15. *Louisiana ex rel. Ponchartrain Railroad v. Judge of the Seventh District Court*, 22 La. Ann. 565 (1870); *Daily Picayune*, May 31, 1870, 3.

16. *Republican*, June 4, 1870, 4–5.

City Company, represented solely by its president, Franklin Pratt, filed suit
against the city of New Orleans, the administrators of both police and commerce, and the Board of Metropolitan Police to enforce its franchise without
further delay. These defendants, the company alleged, were in charge of
both the police and the markets of the city, and it was their duty to enforce
the law. Instead, they were "countenancing and permitting" various infrac-
tions of the Slaughterhouse Act by the city's butchers and livestock dealers.
In response, Judge Dibble ordered the issuance of an injunction, not to
enjoin the defendants from taking any action but rather commanding them
to take positive measures "to prevent" anyone from violating the various
terms of the slaughterhouse franchise. The willingness of Charles A. Weed,
the reviled publisher of the *New Orleans Times*, to serve as surety on the
required bond added to the popular ire provoked by Dibble's action.[17]

The Metropolitan Police was a force of nearly 700 men that had been
created by the legislature in 1868 to serve the parishes of Orleans, Jefferson,
and St. Bernard. Appointed and administered by a board of five commissioners headed by the lieutenant governor, in effect, it served as a military force
on behalf of the Republican state government.[18] The deployment of this
force in the service of the Crescent City Company could be seen as another
example of the cooperative relationship that existed between company leaders such as Franklin Pratt and Charles Weed and Governor Warmoth. Although the governor had not actually called out the Metropolitan Police
himself, he admitted to having "instructed" the superintendent of police
and, at the superintendent's request, to have "given him my views of what
constituted his duties under the injunction."[19]

Pursuant to Judge Dibble's injunction, in the predawn hours of Sunday,
June 5, 1870, a posse of police converged on the rival livestock dealers'
slaughterhouse and, without actually closing the establishment, refused to

17. *Crescent City Livestock Landing and Slaughterhouse Co. v. Board of Metropolitan Police
et al.*, No 118, filed June 3, 1870, Eighth District Court, Parish of New Orleans, Louisiana
Division, New Orleans Public Library. Though not appealed to the U.S. Supreme Court, a
copy of the record in this action is available in the record of *The Slaughterhouse Cases*, 77
U.S. (10 Wall.) 273 (1870), on motion for writ of supersedeas, *U. S. Supreme Court Records
and Briefs*, 10 Wall. 204, Library of Congress. See also *Daily Picayune*, June 4, 1870, 1; June
5, 1870, 1; *Bee*, June 5, 1870, 1; *Republican*, June 5, 1870, 8.

18. Act of September 19, 1868, No. 74, 1868 La. Acts 178; Taylor, *Louisiana Reconstructed*,
177–78.

19. Warmoth's testimony before U.S. Commissioner Urban in *J. Stafford v. C. A. Weed,
et al.*, on application before Judge Edward Durell of the U.S. Circuit Court for habeas
corpus on behalf of Weed, as paraphrased in *Bee*, June 18, 1870, 1.

allow between 200 and 300 head of freshly slaughtered beef to leave. Carts laden with beef en route to market were seized and held until the meat spoiled. The police took up positions at the various city markets to prevent the sale of meat slaughtered at the livestock dealers' abattoir and lacking certificates from the inspector of beef. Butchers in large numbers were prevented from unloading carts at the French Market.[20] With only about 150 head being slaughtered daily at the Crescent City Company's abattoir, this new action caused an instant shortage of fresh meat and a sensation in both the press and the public.[21] When Louis Ruch, a butcher, confronted Weed and Pratt about the seizure, Weed told him that he could get justice from Justice Bradley—advice that Weed would later have good reason to regret.[22] On Monday morning, June 6, Attorney General Belden dutifully intervened in this new action in support of the company's efforts at enforcement.[23]

By midweek, disgruntled butchers had filed forty-two new suits against the Crescent City Company seeking a total of $18,000 in damages, but Judge Dibble's injunction continued to be enforced. At yet another mass meeting, this one held at the Henry Clay statue on Canal Street, the butchers echoed the reasoning of the Declaration of Independence and accused the governor and the courts of having "abused the very reason why governments are established."[24] Two leading butchers, Paul Esteben and James Stafford, swore out affidavits before Commissioner D. Urban in the Federal District Court seeking to have Franklin Pratt, Charles A. Weed, members of the Board of Metropolitan Police, and others arrested for allegedly having conspired to violate rights protected under the Civil Rights Act of 1866.[25]

The next morning, all the parties except one appeared before Judge Edward Durell and good-humoredly posted bonds of $1,500 each. The sole exception was Charles Weed, who not only declined to post bond but applied for a writ of habeas corpus. His motion provoked a major argument between both Hunt brothers and Christian Roselius, representing Weed, and John Campbell and John Cotton, representing Stafford. Judge Durell continued the matter until testimony could be taken by the court clerk and

20. For a firsthand account of the incident, see the testimony of William Fagan in *Stafford v. Weed*, as reported in *Bee*, June 19, 1870, 1.

21. *Daily Picayune*, June 4, 1870, 1; June 5, 1870, 1; June 7, 1870, 1; *Bee*, June 5, 1870, 1; *Republican*, June 5, 1870, 1; June 9, 1870, 1.

22. Ruch's testimony in *Stafford v. Weed*, in *Bee*, June 19, 1870, 1.

23. *Daily Picayune*, June 7, 1870, 2.

24. Ibid., June 9, 1870, 2.

25. Ibid., June 12, 1870, 14; June 16, 1870, 1.

Commissioner Urban. This resulted in personal appearances by Governor Warmoth, Lieutenant Governor Oscar Dunn, Judge Dibble, Franklin Pratt, Charles Weed, and other interested parties. Testimony focused on the extent of the monetary damages caused by the meat seizure, the "personal relationship" that apparently existed between the governor and principals in the Crescent City Company, and the lively and continuing interest that Weed took in this enterprise. Campbell sought once again to prove that Weed had conspired to deprive his clients of rights protected by the federal Civil Rights Acts. Durell ultimately discharged Weed, however, and dismissed the matter on the grounds that Stafford could recover any damages from the state courts, if he was entitled to them.[26]

Premature and crass though it may have been, Judge Dibble's enforcement injunction resulted in the opening of a new legal front, and it prompted a new line of argument from Campbell and his colleagues that had immeasurable—if also unknown—potential. On Monday, June 6, J. Q. A. Fellows and John Campbell presented Justice Joseph P. Bradley and Judge W. B. Woods in the U.S. Circuit Court with a lengthy petition in which they reviewed the history of the litigation and charged that the Slaughterhouse Act infringed on federal rights now protected by both the Civil Rights Act of April 9, 1866, and the new Fourteenth Amendment. They sought an injunction requiring the company to suspend all proceedings against them, thus enabling the butchers to construct the facilities they needed and generally to pursue their businesses "subject to no condition more severe than that of any other party." They also asked for an order removing the company's enforcement action from the Eighth District Court and transferring it to the Federal Circuit Court so that the validity of Judge Dibble's injunction could be tested.[27] After a year of litigation, counsel for the butchers had found an unexpected opportunity to explore the potential of their federal arguments before a justice of the U.S. Supreme Court.

Interested spectators jammed the circuit courtroom for the argument two days later. John Campbell spoke for the butchers. He contended that the intent of both the Civil Rights Act of 1866 and the Fourteenth Amendment, which had been proposed by the same Congress in the same year, had been to secure for all citizens an equality of civil rights, which the act defined

26. See ibid., June 16, 1870, 1; June 21, 1870, 1; June 22, 1870, 1; June 24, 1870, 1. The *Bee* reported the testimony at length on page 1 on June 18 and 19, 1870. For Judge Durell's decision, see *Daily Picayune*, June 28, 1870 1; *Republican*, June 26, 1870, 1.

27. For a copy of the petition, see *Bee*, June 5, 1870, 1; *Daily Picayune*, June 7, 1870, 2; in *Reconstruction and Reunion*, Fairman discusses the action at 1330–35.

largely in terms of property rights.[28] He pointed to the all-embracing language used in the documents, the object being "to place every citizen under the protection of the [federal] Government."[29] "Is there," he inquired, "a law of Louisiana in which the rights of citizens are violated? There clearly is. One of the most abominable and outrageous acts that ever was passed." Campbell equated the 1869 slaughterhouse statute with "the vassalage of the Middle Ages." He insisted that the monopoly it granted was unconstitutional, and indeed, "the principles which vitalize our constitution grew out of the struggle against monopolies."[30]

Opposing counsel William Hunt denounced the butchers for reneging on their agreement to abide by the state supreme court decision and insisted that Campbell was resorting to the civil rights law "for a purpose for which it was never intended." Christian Roselius denied that the 1869 statute established a monopoly. All who wished to do so could become butchers, could slaughter their beef at the central slaughtering house, or could have others slaughter it for them. The corporation, he reminded Bradley, "is compelled to prepare and provide the necessary facilities for all butchers. Then where is the monopoly?"[31] Who was not free to pursue his business according to the law of the land?

The irony of the situation was not lost on the *Daily Picayune*. Here was John Campbell, a former justice of the U.S. Supreme Court and a leading supporter of states' rights, now advocating that white butchers were to be protected by a Reconstruction measure. "Few of our people would have dreamed," it observed, "that it would be found necessary to appeal to the Civil Rights Bill to protect the rights of the people in this or any other Southern city from invasion."[32] In the opinion of the editors of the *Bee*, both the Slaughterhouse Act and the Civil Rights Act were equally iniquitous. But there was no chance of defeating the former act in the state courts. The only hope of success lay in applying to the federal courts, and there employing "poison as an antidote for poison."[33]

In June 1870, Joseph Bradley had been on the high court for less than six months. He had built a very successful career as an attorney in New Jersey, and until secession threatened the Union, he considered himself "a

28. *Bee*, June 9, 1870, 1.
29. Handwritten notes of argument on June 8, 1870, 1, Joseph P. Bradley Papers, New Jersey Historical Society, Newark.
30. Ibid., 1–2.
31. Ibid.
32. *Daily Picayune*, June 5, 1870, 4.
33. As quoted in ibid., June 16, 1870, 1.

conservative of conservatives." Shifting from a Whig to a Republican, he had denounced secession and slavery but insisted that "we were always willing to concede to the South all their just rights—the entire control and regulation of their own affairs." Although he had welcomed the Reconstruction amendments, in common with many who had supported the Union, Bradley retained a strongly racist view of society.[34] To what extent it colored his perception of Reconstruction as the process affected Louisiana is uncertain. But it should be remembered that barely concealed in Campbell's rhetoric was a denunciation of Reconstruction in general and the procedures that had established the 1868 interracial Louisiana legislature in particular. Indeed, through the *Slaughterhouse Cases,* Campell refought aspects of the late war all over again. Riding circuit duty in the Deep South, Bradley could not have been unaware of the racial tensions simmering between 1870 and 1877.

At the end of the week, Bradley announced a decision. A controversial holding, it landed like a bombshell in the litigation, although it did not alter the immediate positions of the parties. He described the 1869 statute as "one of a remarkable character," but he declined Campbell's invitation to cite the Civil Rights Act as a basis for its invalidation. That statute "was intended merely to secure to citizens of every race and color the same civil rights and privileges as are enjoyed by white citizens; and not to enlarge or modify the rights or privileges of white citizens themselves."[35] Thus, the white butchers could not claim any new federal protection under its terms. The Fourteenth Amendment, however, was a different matter, one that "must be examined with more attention and care."

In an opinion that touched on all the major issues raised by the case, Bradley declared the Slaughterhouse Act unconstitutional. He noted the very broad language found in the first section of the new amendment. It was possible, he conceded, "that those who framed the article were not themselves aware of the far reaching character of its terms. . . . Yet, if the amendment, as framed and expressed, does in fact bear a broader meaning, and does extend its protecting shield over those who were never thought of when it was conceived and put in form, and does reach social evils which were never before prohibited by constitutional enactment, it is to be pre-

---

34. Jonathan Lurie, "Mr. Justice Bradley: A Reassessment," *Seton Hall Law Review* 16 (1986): 343–75.

35. *Live Stock Dealers' and Butchers' Assn. v. Crescent City Live Stock Landing and Slaughterhouse Company, et al.,* Federal Case No. 8408, 1 Woods 21, 15 Fed. Cas. 649 (C. C., La., 1870), 651.

In 1870, Joseph Bradley was the first Supreme Court
justice to hold Louisiana's 1869 Slaughterhouse Act
unconstitutional, a position he would reaffirm in dissent
in 1873. (Office of the Curator, Supreme Court of the
United States, #1870.29.)

sumed that the American people, in giving it their imprimatur, understood
what they were doing, and meant to decree what has in fact been decreed."[36]
The prohibition in the Fourteenth Amendment that "no state shall make or
enforce any law which shall abridge the privileges or immunities of citizens
of the United States" was more than a guarantee of equality of right among
citizens. That had already been accomplished, wrote Justice Bradley, by the
privileges and immunities clause found in the body of the Constitution,
which required the states to accord to citizens from other states the same

36. Ibid., 652. For another report, see *Chicago Legal News*, October 15, 1870, 1.

rights they accorded their own citizens. The new provision "demands that the privileges and immunities of all citizens shall be absolutely unabridged [and] unimpaired." The case did not require an enumeration of all the privileges that belonged to citizens of the United States.

> Without venturing a complete list of all the privileges of citizenship, we may safely say it is one of the privileges of every American citizen to adopt and follow such lawful industrial pursuit—not injurious to the community—as he may see fit, without unreasonable regulation or molestation, and without being restricted by any of those unjust, oppressive, and odious monopolies or exclusive privileges which have been condemned by all free governments; it is also his privilege to be protected in the possession and enjoyment of his property so long as such possession and enjoyment are not injurious to the community; and not to be deprived thereof without due process of law. It is also his privilege to have with all other citizens, the equal protection of the laws.[37]

A key conclusion followed from these premises. "There is no more sacred right of citizenship than the right to pursue unmolested a lawful employment in a lawful manner. It is nothing more nor less than the sacred right of labor."[38] Bradley recognized that this right was subject to various forms of legitimate regulation, as is implied by the issuance of occupational licenses, patents, or franchises by which a single concern is given the exclusive right to accomplish some task, such as the building of a toll road or bridge. These are things that in their nature cannot be allowed to all members of the public and ordinarily require public indulgence in some form. Admittedly, too, the right is subject to the exercise of a wide police power aimed at protecting the health, safety, or well-being of the community. He noted that certain pursuits or callings "should be regulated and supervised . . . in order to promote the public health, the public order and the general well being." But, Bradley insisted, "they are open to all proper applicants, and none are rejected except those who fail to exhibit the requisite qualifications . . . or who, after proper selections are made, would increase the number beyond what the interests and good order of society would bear."[39]

A few questions arise concerning Bradley's position. In his eagerness to condemn the 1869 statute, he appears not to have considered the implications of permitting all butchers who wanted to maintain a slaughterhouse to do so, even if they maintained their establishments in a limited area. Would

37. 15 Fed. Cas. 652.
38. Ibid.
39. Ibid., 653.

this not result in what Bradley had just called an increase of numbers "beyond what the interests and good order of society would bear"? Was the occupation of butchering, with all its aesthetic and sanitary hazards admittedly dangerous to the public health, a typical occupation? Assuming that not all could be accommodated, how would those chosen be selected? Was it therefore unreasonable for the legislature to decide that one slaughtering facility should be constructed, large enough for all who sought to use it, and that in return for the cost of building and maintaining such a public facility, those individuals willing to invest should have an exclusive franchise for a limited term of years?

Whether Bradley considered any of these issues in arriving at his decision remains unclear. Nevertheless, he denounced the effort to defend the Slaughterhouse Act as an appropriate exercise of the police power as "pretense . . . too bald for a moment's consideration." It conferred on a single corporation "a monopoly of a very odious character." Thus the question, admittedly "one of great delicacy and embarrassment," was whether such an arrangement could be permitted consistent with the Fourteenth Amendment's guarantee of fundamental privileges and immunities.[40] Bradley had no difficulty whatsoever with this question. "It would be difficult to conceive of a more flagrant case of violation of the fundamental rights of labor than the one before us."[41] The plaintiffs were prepared to conform to any and all police regulations governing their businesses. Yet they were required to land, keep, and slaughter their cattle at the defendant's facilities, and pay tolls for the privilege of doing so, because "the ipse dixit of the legislature assigns a lawful and ordinary employment to one set of men, and denies and forbids it to another."[42] Possibly with Reconstruction in mind, Bradley added that "the injustice perpetrated under acts of irresponsible legislation has become a crying evil in our country."[43]

Bradley's holding represented as strong a statement of the act's alleged invalidity as counsel for the plaintiffs could have sought. What followed next must have been a letdown for them. There was one insurmountable technical objection that the company had raised in its answer, and Bradley freely conceded that it would prevent him from affording injunctive relief,

40. Ibid.
41. Ibid.
42. Ibid., 654. Here again, the question can be raised concerning a distinction between slaughtering beef and trimming and selling meat. The statute may have implied such a distinction, but Bradley would have none of it.
43. Ibid.

at least in the precise terms requested. An act of Congress passed in 1793 made it illegal for a federal court to grant an injunction to stay proceedings in a state court.[44] He concluded that, under the circumstances, the parties would have to content themselves with an appeal of the state supreme court's judgment to the U.S. Supreme Court. But the following day, before counsel could respond, Bradley amended his decision.

In his first opinion, he had rejected the relevance of the Civil Rights Act and decided the case solely on the Fourteenth Amendment. He had originally thought that the intention of the act was only to guarantee citizens of every race the same rights enjoyed by white citizens. Considering, however, that the amendment and the act were products of the same committee and the same Congress, he had come to see that the two enactments were related. They were in part "pari materia . . . probably intended to reach the same object." As he now saw it, the act was intended to guarantee to all citizens the same rights protected by the Fourteenth Amendment and to furnish remedies in the federal courts for their infraction; even though it had passed Congress before the Fourteenth Amendment had been enacted. Bradley ordered the issuance of an injunction against the Crescent City Company, the city of New Orleans, and the Board of Metropolitan Police enjoining them from instituting any *new* suits under the act and recognizing the right of the butchers and livestock dealers to carry on all aspects of their businesses on an equal basis with anyone else, subject only to the restrictions as to location and inspection required by the Slaughterhouse Act. Actions already pending in the courts were, however, specifically excepted from the decree.[45]

THE *BEE* HAILED THE OPINION as "luminous," and the *Picayune* called it "one of the ablest that has ever been delivered from the bench."[46] The *Republican* gave first-page coverage to a letter extolling the decision as "sound Republican doctrine." Later, it reported rumors that Bradley had gone too far in declaring the act invalid, when in fact he had no authority to enjoin proceedings in a state court, but the editors agreed that the constitutional issue had been unavoidable.[47] Given Weed's increasingly intimate

44. Act of March 2, 1793, 21 Stat. 333.
45. 15 Fed. Cas. 655.
46. *Bee,* June 11, 1870, 7; *Daily Picayune,* June 11, 1870, 2, 4.
47. *Republican,* June 12, 1870, 1; June 15, 1870, 4.

association with the Crescent City Company, it comes as no surprise that his *Times* bitterly criticized Bradley's holding. In its view, the Fourteenth Amendment had been written "with the sole purpose and intent of abolishing all distinctions of color," and Justice Bradley's interpretation of it would result in "a vast and indefinite extension of the power and authority of the judicial department of the Government." It would "convert our judges into constitution makers and amenders, with full power to lay down and proclaim what are the 'civil rights' of men."[48]

The week had begun with an aggressive use of state judicial power to enforce the company's alleged monopoly and had ended with an equally aggressive use of federal judicial power holding that the Slaughterhouse Act was unconstitutional. Crescent City Company stock had sold for as much as $30 the week before, but it closed at $18 the day Justice Bradley announced his modified decision. Within a few days, it had declined to as little as $15.[49]

Meanwhile, in the Eighth District Court, Judge Henry Dibble regarded both Bradley's opinion on the constitutionality of the act and the ban on any new injunctions as a direct challenge to his enforcement injunction. Actually, Bradley's decision was only the latest in a series of unexpected setbacks to Dibble's efforts at implementation. Shortly after the Metropolitan Police had been activated, butcher attorneys J. Q. A. Fellows and J. B. Cotton had challenged the legality of Dibble's injunction. And before *that* motion could be tried, the city of New Orleans and its administrators of police and commerce had added their own challenge to the same point. They argued that it violated the superseding effect of the writ of error and unlawfully restrained trade, and they pointed out that they had no police force with which to enforce the injunction—that was a job for the Metropolitan Police. Later, they went even further and charged that Dibble's injunction violated the Fourteenth Amendment. To make matters worse, on June 14, the Board of Metropolitan Police entered the fray with a motion of its own protesting the legality of the injunction. The board complained that its efforts to enforce Judge Dibble's injunction had involved it in a "vast amount of litigation," and it was being sued for $50,000 in damages. Besides,

48. *Times*, June 11, 12, 14, 1870, as presented by Fairman, *Reconstruction and Reunion*, 1335–36.

49. *Daily Picayune*, June 11, 1870, 5; June 15, 1870, 3; June 16, 1870, 2. The *Picayune* editorialized on the volatility of the Crescent City Company stock in "The Balloon Bursted," *Daily Picayune*, June 12, 1870, 6.

it claimed, the Slaughterhouse Act provided for its enforcement by the company itself.[50]

The Fellows and Cotton motion came up for trial before Judge Dibble only three days after Justice Bradley had preempted the field by declaring the act unconstitutional and on the same day that the Metropolitan Police filed a motion against the injunction. Under the circumstances, Fellows and Cotton saw no reason to do battle and declined to argue their motion; but Dibble reacted with some irritation. He was determined to try his injunction, he said, and if it held up, he would see it obeyed "even if it were necessary to apply to the troops and navy of the Federal Government." He proclaimed, "let a revolution decide whether or not state lines were to be entirely blotted out and ignored by the simple dictum of a single Federal Judge."[51] Instead, Dibble had to content himself with hearing the arguments of the city officials in opposition to the injunction, after which he took their motion under advisement.

It is important to recall that Judge Dibble's enforcement injunction had not been addressed directly to the livestock dealers' slaughterhouse and did not have the effect of closing it. Therefore, a means had to be found of enforcing the original injunction against the rival slaughterhouse granted by the Fifth District Court at the attorney general's behest and affirmed by the state supreme court. Belden had already seen to the transfer of his action against the butchers from the Fifth to the Eighth District Court. If Justice Bradley's decision had raised doubts whether Judge Dibble was entitled to take further action in his enforcement injunction, there was no question that the attorney general was entitled to pursue the action he had already filed. Now, taking advantage of Bradley's admitted inability to enjoin ongoing proceedings in a state court, Belden did just that. In Dibble's court, he moved for the immediate enforcement of the state supreme court's decree upholding the Fifth District Court's original injunction against the construction of the livestock dealers' rival slaughterhouse. With that, Dibble announced that he would delay making a decision on the motions filed by the city officials and the Metropolitan Police until he had heard the attorney general's motion.

On the same day, inspector of beef George W. Carter was "persuaded" by Governor Warmoth to take parallel action to force the butchers to

50. Variously dated between June 10 and June 18, 1870, these pleadings are part of the record of *Crescent City Live Stock Landing and Slaughterhouse Co. v. Board of Metropolitan Police, et al.* (see note 17).

51. *Daily Picayune,* June 15, 1870, 5; June 16, 1870, 2; *Republican,* June 15, 1870, 1.

knuckle under to the 1869 statute. There was money to be made under the Slaughterhouse Act in the inspection of beef, and indeed, Carter had been inspecting on both sides of the river. "As soon as I saw in the newspapers that Mr. Carter was inspecting there," Governor Warmoth later testified, "I sent for him and gave him my views of the law." "These steps were taken," the governor explained, "not in the interest of the Slaughter House Company nor to the detriment of the butchers, but simply to enforce the law. . . . I came to this decision as to my duty after consultation with Messrs. Weed, Pratt, Beckwith, and others, but such consultation had nothing to do with my coming to that decision."[52] Now, Carter took out newspaper notices and advised the public that in the future, stock would be inspected only at the Crescent City Company's facilities.[53]

When the attorney general's motion to enforce the supreme court's decree came up for trial before Judge Dibble on June 21, Fellows and Cotton replied with a motion to have the case removed to the U.S. Circuit Court under the Civil Rights Acts of 1866 and 1870, asserting that they could not get a fair trial in Dibble's court. This only enraged Judge Dibble and brought counsel $150 fines for contempt of court.[54] Two days later, and again before Judge Dibble, they insisted anew on the supersedeas effect of their writ of error and, as an alternative, added a claim that the Slaughterhouse Act violated their clients' rights under both the Fourteenth Amendment and the Civil Rights Acts. This time, Dibble agreed at least in part and dismissed the attorney general's motion, holding that Judge Bradley's writ of error did indeed operate as a writ of supersedeas, but *only to prevent the enforcement of the final decree rendered by the state supreme court*. This meant that the writ did not suspend the enforceability of the *preliminary injunction* originally issued in the attorney general's favor by the Fifth Dis-

---

52. Warmoth's testimony in *Stafford v. Weed*, in *Bee*, June 18, 1870, 1.

53. *Daily Picayune*, June 15, 1870, 4.

54. The city's German-language daily reported that Dibble "turned white, then yellow in the face from anger, then red as a turkey." Translated from *Tagliche Deutsche Zeitung*, June 22, 1870. The *Zeitung* accused Dibble of acting "like a crazy herring." An application made by counsel for the butchers to federal district court judge Edward H. Durell for a writ of mandamus to compel Dibble to permit the case to be removed was denied on the grounds that Sections 4 and 5 of the Habeas Corpus Act, as amended in 1866, permitted a case whose removal had been refused to be brought directly to the federal court. Counsel chose not to avail themselves of this option. Opinion, dated June 24, 1870, *In the Matter of Paul Esteban et al. praying for an injunction*, No. 6248, U.S. Circuit Court, New Orleans, Record Group 21, Case Files 1837–1911, National Archives, Fort Worth. See also *Daily Picayune*, June 25, 1870, 6; *Republican*, June 28, 1870, 1.

trict Court. "Under this ruling," the *Picayune* pointed out, "the butchers have no recourse until the United States Supreme Court acts."[55]

With that, Attorney General Belden moved swiftly to enforce the *original injunction* rendered in the Fifth District Court against the livestock dealers' abattoir. At Belden's behest, Judge Dibble ordered Paul Esteben and the other organizers of that slaughterhouse into court to show cause on June 27 why they should not be held in contempt of court for having violated the Fifth District Court's injunction by operating the rival slaughterhouse.[56] This rule gave the two sides one final opportunity to argue the question of whether the butchers would be able to go about their business unhindered by the Slaughterhouse Act while the case was pending in the U.S. Supreme Court. Was there, in other words, any validity to the claim that this appeal had stalled or superseded all current attempts to enforce the original injunction obtained by Belden?

Again, Fellows and Cotton insisted that the answer to this question was affirmative, and they attacked the validity of the Slaughterhouse Act. Other arguments were raised—such as the written agreement to abide by the decision of the state supreme court, as well as allegations that the attorney general had informally agreed to take no further action pending a final resolution on appeal—but the chances of blocking the original injunction seemed nil. Dibble had already expressed his view regarding the effects of the writ in connection with Belden's effort to execute the supreme court's permanent injunction, and when he reiterated his interpretation in informal remarks during the course of the argument, Fellows and Cotton abandoned their effort and stormed out of the courtroom. The *Republican* called the event "the closing scene in the great Slaughterhouse controversy," and it had been played to yet another crowded courtroom. "This would seem to end the slaughterhouse controversy at least until it is revived in the Supreme Court of the United States."[57]

At the end of the week, on July 2, Dibble rejected the defendants' arguments and upheld the attorney general's right to enforce the original injunction obtained in the Fifth District Court, at least until the U.S. Supreme

55. "Extract from the Minutes of June 23, 1869," in the record of *Louisiana ex rel. Belden v. William Fagan, et al.*, No. 122, Eighth District Court, Parish of Orleans, La., Louisiana Division, New Orleans Public Library. The record in this action was made part of the record of *The Slaughterhouse Cases* on motion for supersedeas (see note 17). See also *Daily Picayune*, June 24, 1870, 3, 5; *Republican*, June 24, 1870, 5.

56. Order Rule, dated June 23, 1870, in record of *La. ex rel Belden v. Fagan*, No. 122, Eighth District Court.

57. *Republican*, June 29, 1870, 1. See also *Daily Picayune*, June 29, 1870, 4.

Court had decided the case.[58] This meant that, for the time being, the stock dealers and butchers would have to land, keep, and slaughter their cattle at the Crescent City Company's facilities across the river. They appeared to have run out of state legal options. By mid-July, the butchers had relocated their operations to the Crescent City Company's slaughterhouse in Algiers, and at the end of the month, sheriff's deputies took charge of the rival slaughterhouse and padlocked it. Even then, counsel for the butchers continued to urge motions on Justice Bradley, but none of these were granted, and Judge Dibble's enforcement injunction and the preliminary injunction originally obtained by the attorney general in the Fifth District Court remained operative. On October 17, 1870, however, as the U.S. Supreme Court prepared to resume its business after the summer recess, John Campbell was there with yet another motion for a writ of supersedeas.

In arguing for supersedeas, Campbell and his co-counsel, Philip Phillips, sought, in effect, to restore the parties to the positions they had occupied prior to the decision of the supreme court, when all orders to enforce or to prevent the enforcement of the Slaughterhouse Act had been suspended. Arguably, this earlier state of affairs had resulted from mutual agreement of the parties and not from the operation of law, but nothing less would permit the butchers and stock dealers to escape what they claimed to be the inconvenience and costly effects of the act pending the appeal. The respective positions were researched, briefs were prepared, and in mid-November, Campbell and Phillips argued the motion in the high court against Thomas J. Durant and Jeremiah S. Black.

In separate briefs, Campbell and Phillips argued for a suspension of all proceedings in the lower courts pending the outcome of the appeal. They had complied with all the requirements for the issuance of a writ of error imposed by Section 23 of the Judiciary Act of 1789. With Bradley's decision, jurisdiction over the cases had been transferred from the state supreme court to the U.S. Supreme Court. Thus the butchers were now entitled to the "supersedeas effect" of the writ promised by Section 25 of the Judiciary Act.[59] Campbell's argument had a seemingly uncomplicated logic to it. In his view, the preliminary injunction granted to the company in the Fifth District Court to restrain the stock dealers and butchers had remained in effect until it had been converted into a permanent injunction by the district court's final judgment. That judgment, in turn, had been suspended while

58. "Reasons for Judgment," [July 2, 1870], in record of *Louisiana ex rel. Belden v. Fagan; Daily Picayune*, July 3, 1870, 13; *Republican*, July 3, 1870, 8.
59. Act of September 24, 1789, secs. 23, 25; 1 Stat. 73.

the case was appealed to the state supreme court. The decision of the state supreme court affirming the judgment of the district court would have restored the district court's order and permanently enjoined the stock dealers and butchers from violating the Slaughterhouse Act. But the supreme court's judgment had been suspended by Bradley. Even Judge Dibble had admitted as much when he turned down Attorney General Belden's attempt to enforce the supreme court's decision affirming the permanent injunction.[60] But now, Campbell insisted, at Belden's urging, Judge Dibble was attempting to enforce the district court's temporary injunction as though it had been "left flying" in the lower court.[61]

Campbell pleaded that his clients should not be subjected to the expense and inconvenience of having to relocate their operations to the new slaughterhouse even before the case was decided. Campbell added that in the new action brought by the Crescent City Company in the Eighth District Court, in which the attorney general had joined, Judge Dibble had ordered the Metropolitan Police and various municipal officials to prevent anyone from violating the Slaughterhouse Act. Here, Campbell charged, the company and the attorney general were acting in combination to deprive the livestock dealers and butchers of everything they were contending for, even before their rights could be adjudicated on appeal.[62] The court should not permit its authority to be undermined in such a manner.[63] Instead, it should step in and issue writs of supersedeas and injunction suspending further proceedings and enjoining all parties—the state, its attorney general, the city of New Orleans, the Crescent City Company, the Metropolitan Police—from attempting to enforce the Slaughterhouse Act or from interfering with operations at the livestock dealers' slaughterhouse while the case was before the high court.

In reply to these arguments, Durant and Black (joined by Matthew H. Carpenter and Charles Allen) contended that a writ of error did not ordi-

60. Plaintiff's Brief at 5–7, *Slaughterhouse Cases,* on motion for supersedeas.

61. Ibid., 7.

62. Ibid., 12.

63. There was precedent for Campbell's argument that the Court would not permit a lower federal court to do what the New Orleans Eighth District Court was doing. Campbell cited *Washington, Georgetown and Alexandria Railroad Co. v. Bradley,* 74 U.S. (7 Wall.) 575, 19 L. Ed. 274 (1868), in which an injunction given by a lower federal court to prevent the sale of property had been dissolved; then, when it appeared that the property was going to be sold while the case was pending on appeal, the Supreme Court had granted a writ of supersedeas and stayed further proceedings in the lower court until the rights of the parties could be finally adjudicated.

narily have a supersedeas effect in a proceeding involving an injunction. "Supersedeas is a law term, and has no application to a chancery proceeding."[64] It was a point supported by both logic and a number of authorities.[65] A reluctance to stay proceedings could also be discerned in the decisions of the state courts, although the decisions were not uniform on the point.[66]

The U.S. Supreme Court had little difficulty deciding the case, and by a vote of six to one, it denied Campbell's motion.[67] There were no grounds for the issuance of a writ in this case because all the parties had conceded that nothing had been done by the Louisiana Supreme Court to modify, reverse, or execute its judgment. Moreover, the enforcement injunction obtained by the company in the Eighth District Court with the attorney general's concurrence had not been appealed, so the Court had never acquired jurisdiction in the matter. Speaking for the Court, Justice Clifford pointed out that it was precisely such circumstances that Congress had in mind when it passed the act of 1793 prohibiting a federal court from attempting to enjoin proceedings in a state court. Echoing a position he had taken earlier, Justice Bradley appended a short dissenting opinion, admittedly written "with some diffidence." He expressed concern that the Court was disclaiming too much jurisdiction, too quickly, over the state courts.[68] With this decision, the possibility of delaying implementation of the Slaughterhouse Act through judicial intervention came to an end.

CREATED IN THE PERIOD when the *Slaughterhouse Cases* were pending in the state supreme court, the Eighth District Court represented an important institutional change, and it played an active role in promoting the fortunes of the Crescent City Company. But even as the lengthy efforts at a supersedeas proceeded, other important developments came about. However, these were political, not institutional, changes, and in this instance they worked, at least briefly, in favor of the opponents of the Crescent City Company.

Elections held in November 1870, midway through Governor War-

64. "Points of Counsel of Defendants in Error for a Supersedeas and Injunction," 2, in *Slaughterhouse Cases*, on motion for supersedeas.

65. Ibid., 3, citing, inter alia, "General Order of the House of Lords, August 12, 1807," copied in *Huguenin v. Baseley*, 15 Ves. 184; Edmund R. Daniell, *Pleading and Practice of the High Court of Chancery*, 3 vols. (Boston: Little, Brown, 1865), 2:1469.

66. *Hart & Hoyt v. Mayor of Albany*, 3 Paige Chancery Reports 197 (1832).

67. Chief Justice Chase and Nelson were absent. Fairman, *Reconstruction and Reunion*, 1337, n. 111.

68. Bradley dissent, *Slaughterhouse Cases*, 77 U.S. (10 Wall.) 273 (1870).

moth's four-year term, resulted in an enhancement of the Republican party's control of the state and of the legislature in particular. At the same time, however, there were signs that the governor's own power was on the wane. Black Republicans increasingly doubted his commitment to civil rights, and other members of the party had been disappointed by his failure to support their projects. Worse still, a serious rift had developed within the party between politically pragmatic elements represented by Warmoth and his allies and an antagonistic group based in the U.S. Custom House at New Orleans, who regarded themselves as more firmly committed to a radical agenda. Evidence of this fissure surfaced early in the 1871 legislative session when Mortimer Carr, a Warmoth ally, was forced to resign from his position as speaker of the house. He was immediately replaced by the ambitious George W. Carter, whom Warmoth had earlier appointed inspector of beef under the Slaughterhouse Act.[69] Carter owed his position in the legislature to Warmoth. In 1870, the governor had seen to the creation of Cameron Parish, with a mind toward creating a seat for Carter, and he had facilitated Carter's election. But, records a Louisiana historian, "loyalty was not one of Carter's virtues," and with his election as speaker, "the gentleman from Cameron promptly became the leader of the Custom House faction in the House of Representatives."[70] It was an opportune time for a final assault against the Crescent City Company's exclusive privileges, and even before he became speaker, Carter helped lead the charge.

Opposition to the monopoly had never waned among some members of the legislature. As early as February 1870, for example, while the case was being argued in the state supreme court, W. Pope Noble, a representative from Orleans Parish who had passionately opposed the monopolistic aspects of the Slaughterhouse Act, had introduced a bill to deprive the company of its monopoly while at the same time restricting slaughtering to areas downstream from the city.[71] House Bill 187 had been reported favorably out of

69. Taylor, *Louisiana Reconstructed*, 210; *Official Journal of the . . . House of Representatives of the State of Louisiana at the Session Begun . . . January 6, 1871* (New Orleans: A. L. Lee, State Printer, 1871), January 31, 1871, 78–79; hereafter, *House Journal*. Only days before, Carter had bristled over rumors in the house critical of his service as inspector of beef and had obtained the appointment of a three-person committee to investigate his conduct. *House Journal*, January 28, 1871, 74. He was exonerated by the committee a few weeks later. Ibid., March 2, 1871, 215.

70. Taylor, *Louisiana Reconstructed*, 213. "To assure himself an adequate livelihood, he accepted a sinecure as an employee of the Custom House." Ibid.

71. *House Journal*, February 8, 1870, 191. Evidently convinced of the benefits of a wise use of the police power, Noble also sponsored a bill to compel dealers and manufacturers of

committee, but Representative John McVean, successful manager of the 1869 bill, promptly had it sent to the Committee of the Whole, where two weeks later he saw to its defeat by a vote of twenty-four to thirty-five. This was a more narrow victory than the 1869 bill had won (fifty-one to eighteen), and the vote more accurately reflected the sentiments of the house on the issue of monopoly. Much of the difference between this and the 1869 vote can be explained by the fact that of the eighteen conservatives who had *not* voted on the 1869 measure, nine voted on Noble's 1870 bill, and all nine voted in favor of repeal. Radicals who had not participated in the 1869 vote were about equally divided on the second measure.[72]

With Speaker Carter's active cooperation, anti-monopolists were quick to take advantage of the new political dynamics of the 1871 legislature. In January, on the motion of Representative J. B. Matthews, a radical and Carter ally from Tensas Parish, the house had appointed a special three-person committee to investigate the Crescent City Company and specifically "to ascertain whether they have complied with the provisions of their charter."[73] Carter followed suit not long afterward by announcing that he intended to file a bill amending the Slaughterhouse Act.[74] After hearing witnesses and thoroughly studying the matter, the committee reported that the Crescent City Company's slaughterhouse and other facilities were insufficient to meet the needs of all the butchers and stock dealers at the port. Conditions in the abattoir itself were so crowded that butchers had to cart away their beef while it was still warm, which, they complained, was detrimental to both the health of the public and the butchers' financial interest.

The committee concluded that the company had failed to comply with duties imposed on it by the statute, and under the statute, it was no longer entitled to carry on the business of slaughtering "to the exclusion of fair and just competition." As a remedy, the committee proposed House Bill 209 to limit slaughtering to areas below certain defined points on each bank and to strike out the Crescent City Company's exclusive privileges.[75] That evening,

------

coal oil to store it in a special building provided for that purpose. It did not pass. Ibid., February 16, 1870, 227.

72. Ibid., February 28, 1870, 295. These vote counts rely once again on Jones's political classification of the members of the 1868 legislature and do not include the votes of a few legislators not classified by him; see Jones, "Members of the Louisiana Legislature," 122.

73. *House Journal,* January 12, 1871, 31.

74. *Republican,* February 26, 1871, 4.

75. The committee's report is at *House Journal,* February 15, 1871, 136–37. The proposed bill bore the title "An Act to Regulate the Location of Slaughter Houses and the Inspection of Meat in the City of New Orleans and the Parishes of Jefferson, Orleans, and St. Bernard, and the Duty of the Attorney General, the City of New Orleans, and the Board of Metropol-

Speaker Carter allowed another representative to substitute for him in the chair and personally took charge of H.B. 209. Motions to delay were defeated, rules were suspended, and in very short order, the bill was placed on its third reading and adopted by a vote of ninety to six.[76] Word of the house's action spread quickly, and two days later, the senate's lobby was crowded with brokers and other interested parties as the upper chamber prepared to take up H.B. 209. The senate acted as expeditiously as the house and adopted the bill by a vote of thirty-one to one.[77] A legislature dominated by radicals and led in the house by a former Confederate officer had approved a measure to deprive the company of its monopoly. But such action also reflected both the division in Republican ranks and Governor Warmoth's waning influence.

Warmoth promptly vetoed the act, arguing chiefly that in consideration for the exclusive privileges granted to it by the 1869 act, the company had erected a slaughterhouse and had gone to various other expenses, and the state had not reserved the right to alter the grant. In short, a contractual relationship existed between the state and the company, and a state act revoking the company's exclusive privileges would be null and void as an impairment of the obligation of contract, forbidden by Section 10 of Article I of the U.S. Constitution and Article 110 of the state constitution. Moreover, the governor argued, if indeed the company had incurred the penalty of forfeiture by failing to live up to its obligations under the charter, this was a matter for "judicial inquiry alone" and not one for the legislature.[78] Though closely allied with the governor, the *Republican* had always had misgivings about monopolies, and it reported these repeal proceedings with equanimity. But once Warmoth vetoed the measure, the paper found that he had treated the bill with characteristic "perspicaciousness, ability and legal acumen" and predicted that the day would come when everyone would see the Slaughterhouse Act as "an important sanitary measure."[79]

The vote on whether to pass the act notwithstanding the governor's veto

itan Police in Cases Concerning Persons Engaged in Preparing Meats for the Market." For press coverage, see *Republican*, February 16, 1871, 4; February 17, 1871, 2.

76. *House Journal*, February 15, 1871, 138.

77. *Official Journal of the Senate of the State of Louisiana at the Session Begun . . . January 2, 1871* (New Orleans: A. L. Lee, State Printer, 1871), February 17, 1871, 141; *Daily Picayune*, February 18, 1871, 1.

78. Veto message, dated February 25, 1871, *House Journal*, February 25, 1871, 190–91. For the *Daily Picayune*'s report of the veto message and the vote to override, see February 26, 1871, 15.

79. *Republican*, February 26, 1871, 4.

was taken on the same day that the house received it. Once again, Speaker Carter surrendered the chair to a colleague and spoke for half an hour against the veto. He disputed the idea that the company had vested rights to protect in the slaughterhouse arrangement and contended that the issue was only a sanitary one. But the motion to override the veto failed by a vote of fifty-eight to thirty-seven.[80] Under the circumstances, no vote had to be taken in the senate.

The *Daily Picayune* viewed this "whole affair" as being "rooted, steeped, saturated and drowned in chicanery from beginning to end." It accused the legislature of having undertaken the repeal project in order to profit twice more from the interests of the company, supposedly by taking money first to oppose the repeal act and then to support the veto. But, as the *Picayune* saw it, the company had outwitted them. Rather than trying to buy votes in both houses to prevent passage of the repeal act, it had "preferred to trust to a veto"; in this way, it needed to buy the votes of only a third of the house. The result was, the *Picayune* claimed, "the astounding vote of yesterday: thirty-five men who had voted for the repeal of the monopoly turned around and voted to retain it."[81]

It is impossible to accurately discern the motivations of the members of the house who first voted to repeal the monopoly and then failed to vote to override the governor's veto. But several factors come to mind besides venality. One is the utter unpopularity of the monopolistic aspects of the Slaughterhouse Act among both the butchers and opinion leaders, as well as members of the public who associated it with their reconstructed legislature. It must be remembered also that although the radicals held a majority in the legislature in both 1869 and 1871, the membership of the 1871 legislature was not identical to that of 1869. It is entirely possible that new members of the house had doubts about the wisdom of solving a sanitary problem with a monopoly. That issue was the subject of raging controversy. Another factor is the political division in the Republican ranks that, without doubt, gave an appearance of vulnerability to Warmoth-backed projects.

A tally of the vote to override the veto by party, published in 1872, revealed this division. A total of ninety-five house members voted on the motion to override. Of these, twenty-four were Democrats, and all of them

---

80. *House Journal*, February 25, 1871, 190–91; *Daily Picayune*, February 26, 1871, 15; *Republican*, February 26, 1871, 4.

81. *Daily Picayune*, February 26, 1871, 1. In more recent times, Charles Fairman cited the incident as "an episode that reveals the true quality of government in Louisiana." Fairman, *Reconstruction and Reunion*, 1338.

voted in favor of overriding the veto and repealing the monopoly. The remaining seventy-one votes were cast by Republicans, and they were divided almost equally. Thirty-seven Republicans voted to sustain the governor's veto and retain the monopoly, and thirty-four voted to override the governor's veto.[82] The lobbying efforts of the butchers and stock dealers to bring about this result are not recorded but can safely be presumed. For all the record reveals, their methods may have been just as unseemly as those they attributed to the Crescent City Company's supporters.

IN AUGUST 1869, William Fagan, then president of the newly incorporated Live Stock Dealers and Butchers Association, had declared, "there will be no compromise short of an abandonment by the Company of its claims."[83] Now, a year and a half later, a number of butchers and stock dealers agreed to come to terms with the Crescent City Company. This move may have been unexpected, but it was quite understandable. Since losing their appeal to the Louisiana Supreme Court in April 1870, the butchers had tried twice to put aside the Crescent City Company's alleged monopoly, at least temporarily, only to see both efforts come to naught. In December 1870, the U.S. Supreme Court had turned away their motion for supersedeas, and in February 1871, they had won passage of an act repealing the company's exclusive privileges only to see it successfully vetoed by Governor Warmoth. The rival slaughterhouse built by the Live Stock Dealers and Butchers Association on the right bank of the river had been put out of operation by Judge Henry Dibble's injunction in the Eighth District Court.

Most, if not all, of the butchers and stock dealers were now using the Crescent City Company facilities as required by law. And no matter how strong their feelings, it was uncertain whether the company's opponents would be any more successful in the U.S. Supreme Court. The case for the validity of the Slaughterhouse Act as an exercise of the police power was a strong one supported by precedent, similar practices in other cities, and public opinion in New Orleans. And in the end, if the U.S. Supreme Court ruled against them, it was questionable whether they would ever recoup the investment they had made in establishing the rival slaughterhouse. Compromise might well be considered appropriate.

82. "Statement Showing Titles of Bills Killed by Veto of Governor," in O. D. Bragdon, comp., *Facts and Figures, Or Useful and Important Information* (New Orleans, 1872), Special Collections, Tulane University Library.

83. *Daily Picayune*, August 18, 1869, 4.

Conversely, the owners of the Crescent City Company had to ponder some additional factors that may explain why they too turned toward a compromise. Their monopoly had not resulted in the historic financial windfall imagined by some, nor were there signs that it would soon do so. And with the Fourteenth Amendment being played by the butchers as a sort of "wild card" in the game, a victory by the company in the U.S. Supreme Court could not be assumed. After all, Justice Bradley had already indicated that the act was an unconstitutional violation of the new amendment, and his brethren had yet to express any opinion on the subject.

Actually, the first step toward compromise was taken on February 23, 1871, even before the house upheld the governor's veto. The board of directors of the Live Stock Dealers and Butchers Association authorized its president, Paul Esteben, to explore the feasibility of compromise with the Crescent City Company. For reasons that are not clear, the company was represented in these negotiations by Charles Cavaroc, the founding president of the Live Stock Dealers and Butchers Association. Esteben had succeeded Cavaroc as president of the association, but he had never been replaced as president of the older Butchers Benevolent Association, which though inactive was not legally defunct. Thus it was that on March 2, 1871, only a week after the governor's veto had been sustained, the association's board of directors agreed to the terms of a compromise that Esteben laid before them. Subsequently, the proposal was unanimously endorsed by a mass meeting of the stockholders of the Live Stock Dealers and Butchers Association (and anyone else who cared to attend) held in the familiar venue above Fred Bensts's saloon on Tchoupitoulas Street.[84]

In keeping with this agreement, the Crescent City Company transferred 7,500 shares of its stock valued at $25.50 per share, or a total of $191,250, to the livestock dealers. The Crescent City Company's board of directors then resigned, and the stockholders elected a new board to serve until the regular election in March 1872. In this way, members of the board of directors of the Live Stock Dealers and Butchers Association became directors of the Crescent City Company, with Charles Cavaroc as president. The new board consisted of more stock dealers than butchers, but the *Times* declared them all to be "practical butchers."[85]

84. The details of the compromise and related documents are fully set out in the "Motion to Dismiss," filed December 14, 1871, in the record of *The Slaughterhouse Cases*, 16 Wall. (83 U.S.) 36 (1873); hereafter, "Motion to Dismiss."

85. *Republican*, March 11, 1871, 4; March 15, 1871, 4; *Times*, March 15, 1871, 6; March 16, 1871, 6. The *Times* identified the new members of the board of directors as Charles Cavaroc, president, and J. B. Rouede, Louis Ruch, B. Beaubay, W. Mehle, J. T. Aycock, Joseph Gitzinger, William Fagan, and Paul Esteben.

Although there is no reason to believe that all stockholders of the Crescent City Company divested themselves of their interest in the company at the time of the compromise, it does not appear that the original organizers had come to regard the company as a long-term investment. Another election of board members a year later brought several new faces to the board, including the controversial Charles A. Weed.[86] A complete list of the stockholders drawn up in 1873 did not include Weed or any of the other original organizers of the company, except for two: William Durbridge and Jonas Pickles, who were listed as owners of 80 and 100 shares, respectively.[87] To complete the compromise, on March 15, 1871, the newly elected board of the Crescent City Company resolved to purchase the slaughterhouse that the livestock dealers had constructed below the city on the east side of the river for $195,000, with $25,000 to be paid in cash and the remainder in promissory notes.[88] Finally, the Live Stock Dealers and Butchers Association was dissolved and liquidated.

The price of Crescent City Company stock responded very positively to these developments. In February, after the legislature passed the act repealing the monopoly, the stock had declined to only $12 a share. When the governor's veto was sustained, it rose to $24. Now, immediately following news of the compromise, it began selling, according to the *Times,* at between $37 and $45 a share.[89]

A child of controversy since its inception, it was too much to expect that even the newly constituted Crescent City Company would manage to stay out of court for long. For one thing, the company quickly found itself the defendant in a suit brought by Thomas J. Semmes and Robert Mott, two lawyers who had been employed by the company to help draw up the compromise on its behalf. They sued for a $500 fee. The company allowed judgment to be rendered against it by default in this action, but since the legal services had been rendered to the original company, and since the directorship as well as a substantial portion of the ownership of the company had changed hands by this time, it is doubtful whether the disgruntled counsel ever collected.[90]

86. *Jewell's Crescent City Illustrated,* 223, 228.

87. Amendment to Charter dated October 18, 1873, executed before Gustave LeGardeur Jr., Notary Public, New Orleans Notarial Archives.

88. Act of Sale dated April 5, 1871 from Live Stock Dealers . . . Association to Crescent City . . . Company before Joseph Cuvellier, Notary Public, New Orleans Notarial Archives.

89. *Times,* March 17, 1871, 7.

90. *Thomas J. Semmes and Robert Mott v. Crescent City . . . Company,* No. 500, filed April 8, 1871, Eighth District Court, Parish of Orleans, La., Louisiana Division, New Orleans Public Library.

More seriously, the reopening of the new slaughterhouse on the left bank of the river brought fears that the company would close its original, makeshift facility on the right bank. Stock dealer Charles Mehle and Company, for example, had relocated offices and families and had leased property in the vicinity of the original slaughterhouse; now there were signs that the company was preparing to close the facility altogether. Suits were filed in Judge Dibble's Eighth District Court to enjoin both the closure of the original facility and the use of the new one. Even the attorney general filed an action. One of these actions provided Judge Dibble with an opportunity to expound on the appropriateness of using a private corporation to accomplish sanitary reform. But he had no difficulty ruling in every case that the Slaughterhouse Act did not require the company to maintain a facility on the right bank, provided that it maintained at least one facility and that it was located outside the limits proscribed by the statute.[91]

In fact, the newly managed Crescent City Company maintained both its original west-bank slaughterhouse and the newly acquired one on the east bank for only a short time. Once the butchers were given a choice between the company's fairly makeshift original abattoir and the larger, better-equipped one located on the same side of the river as the city, the vast majority quickly abandoned the west-bank facility. With that, the company saw no need to maintain a second slaughterhouse, and on a Sunday morning in July 1871, with police in attendance and with little or no notice to the butchers, the company dismantled its right-bank facility. Jean Bertin, a west-bank butcher, sued. He lost his case before Judge Henry Dibble in the Eighth District Court in September 1871, but four and a half years later, in February 1876 (in the same action), the state supreme court ruled in his favor. The state's high court held that after selecting a location for the new slaughterhouse and "compelling the butchers to repair to it, [the company] will not be permitted to compel them to discontinue their business at this place and follow the corporation to such other locality . . . as caprice may dictate."[92]

91. *C. Mehle and Co. v. Crescent City . . . Company*, No. 478, filed March 22, 1871, Eighth District Court, Orleans Parish, La.; *La. Ex Rel Belden v. Cavaroc, et al.*, No. 508, filed April 13, 1871, Eighth District Court, Orleans Parish, La. For Judge Henry Dibble's view of the Slaughterhouse Act, see "Reasons for Judgment," dated May 25, 1871, in *Samuel B. Pratt v. Crescent City . . . Company*, No. 528, filed April 27, 1871, Eighth District Court, all in Louisiana Division, New Orleans Public Library. A copy of the record in *Pratt v. Crescent City . . . Company* is available in the record of *Bertin v. Crescent City Company*, No. 3917, Louisiana Supreme Court Archives.

92. *Bertin et al. v. Crescent City Livestock Landing and Slaughterhouse Co.*, 28 La. Ann. 210, 215 (1876). While this action was pending, it is very likely that Bertin and the other

Months passed before the company finally complied with the court's mandate to reestablish its abattoir on the right bank. Meanwhile, at least one private slaughterhouse had been established on the right bank for the handful of butchers who remained there. When the company finally protested that this violated the Slaughterhouse Act, Jean Bertin sued to enjoin its interference. Several other actions followed, and it was not until April 1878 that the company won a ruling in the supreme court upholding its exclusive privileges.[93] Even so, it is unclear whether all the west-bank competitors were ever persuaded to patronize the company's abattoir exclusively.

A final matter of conflict, and ultimately the most important, concerned the identity of the parties who had agreed to the compromise. It was generally assumed that the compromise signaled an end to all the *Slaughterhouse Cases.* On March 14, 1871, Paul Esteben, as president of both the Butchers Benevolent Association and the Live Stock Dealers and Butchers Association, and representatives of the William Fagan and Inbau firms agreed in writing "to discontinue, as part of the compromise . . . all suits of *every* kind now pending in the State and Federal courts against" the Crescent City Company "and to dismiss *all* the writs of error concerning said company now pending in the Supreme Court of the United States."[94] Seeing no further need for legal counsel, the directors of the Butchers Benevolent Association authorized fees to be paid to the firms of Campbell, Spofford and Campbell, Cotton and Levy, and Fellows and Mills in the amount of $3,000 each, as agreed on at the beginning of the litigation.[95]

But in the fall of 1871, when J. Q. A. Fellows appeared before the U.S. Supreme Court, he did not move for the dismissal of any of the actions in their entirety. Instead, he moved for the dismissal of the writs of error in three of the *Slaughterhouse Cases:* the two cases brought against the company by the Live Stock Dealers and Butchers Association and the firm of Inbau, Aycock and Company, and the one filed by the Crescent City Company

---

west-side butchers resorted to a private slaughterhouse rather than the centralized abattoir on the east side of the river.

93. *Crescent City Livestock Landing and Slaughterhouse Company v. John Larrieux,* 30 La. Ann. 798 (1878). For another action in this series, with a similarly informative record, see *Larrieux et al. v. Crescent City . . . Company,* 30 La. Ann. 609, record available at La. Sup. Ct. Docket No. 6794, Louisiana Supreme Court Archives. A similar action filed in Jefferson Parish was dismissed as premature. See *Crescent City . . . Company v. Police Jury, Parish of Jefferson,* 32 La. Ann. 192 (1880).

94. "Motion to Dismiss," 5; emphasis added.

95. "Minutes: Butchers Benevolent Association, One Hundred and Ninth Sitting," March 24, 1871, in "Motion to Dismiss," 36–37.

against the steamship *B. L. Hodge*. This left three cases still standing in the high court: the suit filed by the Butchers Benevolent Association against the company in the Sixth District Court, the first of all the cases; the suit filed almost simultaneously by the company against the Butchers Benevolent Association in the Fifth District Court; and the action brought by the attorney general against William Fagan and his fellow stock dealers and butchers in the Fifth District Court. Company attorney Joseph P. Hornor admitted that this action "took the Slaughter-House Company by surprise, as they believed the whole litigation closed and settled." It was not until November 11, 1871, that the company became aware that Campbell and Fellows intended to press on in three of the cases.[96]

As Charles Fairman wrote, "Some of the 'Gascon butchers' still wanted to fight."[97] Later, in a letter to the *Bee*, Sylvain Verges, the new president of the Butchers Benevolent Association, offered some insights as to why. He explained that although the company was under new management, it remained a monopoly, and it was still charging all the fees authorized by the statute. Further, he claimed that only one of the company's directors was a butcher (several others were livestock dealers). "The butchers have no interest in the Company and can have none."[98] His comments might be evidence of an economic and social rift between some of the individual butchers and the stock dealers.

This unexpected turn of events led to an elaborate motion to dismiss filed in the U.S. Supreme Court on behalf of the company and the state by Matthew Carpenter and Thomas J. Durant on December 14, 1871. Company president Charles Cavaroc, a number of major stock dealers, and both Paul Esteben and Franklin J. Pratt all provided affidavits affirming their understanding that the compromise had brought an end to all slaughterhouse litigation. Extracts from the minutes of meetings of the Live Stock Dealers and Butchers Association's board of directors attested to their approval of the compromise. Individual butchers attested to their impression that the compromise had been popularly approved at the mass meeting at the Benst saloon, which had been attended by more than 400 persons. Still others claimed that one of the 1869 mass meetings had empowered Paul Esteben to affect a compromise. In a supplemental brief, Attorney General Belden and counsel for the company provided 1872 reports of a special committee

96. Joseph P. Hornor to Thomas J. Durant, January 11, 1872, in "Motion to Dismiss," 9–10.

97. Fairman, *Reconstruction and Reunion*, 1340.

98. *Bee*, March 24, 1872.

of the house of representatives and of a grand jury, detailing the benefits of the new consolidated system of slaughtering as implemented by the Crescent City Company in its facilities and practices.[99]

In reply, members of the Butchers Benevolent Association, including its current president, Sylvain Verges, and other members of its board, protested that the issue of compromise had never been put before their board or their membership. Esteben had held the office of president of the Butchers Benevolent Association until July 15, 1871, but he had never been authorized by the association to negotiate a compromise. The March public meeting at which the compromise had been approved had been called by the Live Stock Dealers and Butchers Association for its own members, and the Butchers Benevolent Association was not bound by resolutions taken there.

The Supreme Court agreed. It heard the argument on the motion to dismiss along with the arguments on all the other issues, and according to Justice Miller in his opinion for the Court, it was "much pressed by counsel." But Miller pointed out, "there are parties now before the court in each of the three cases . . . who have not consented to their dismissal. . . . They have a right to be heard."[100] With that issue aside, the *Slaughterhouse Cases* were at last in a position to be decided on the merits by the nation's highest court. Claims, counterclaims, multitudinous lawsuits, injunctions too numerous to count—all had finally led to this point. The question now was whether the dispute could be resolved as a simple matter of the police power, without its being transformed by John Campbell's innovative resort to the Fourteenth Amendment into a major constitutional case—one that might launch a new and potent doctrine, a "doctrine headed for parts unknown."[101] As far as he was concerned, in the wake of the Civil War, some battles might be over, but the fighting raged on.

---

99. "Supplemental Brief of Counsel of State of Louisiana and of Crescent City . . . Company" [December 1872], in "Motion to Dismiss." The special committee's report had been taken from the *House Journal* for February 28, 1872.

100. 83 U.S. (16 Wall.) 403 (1873).

101. Hamilton, "Path of Due Process of Law," 270.

7

The Chase Court

In 1872, when John Archibald Campbell appeared before the U.S. Supreme Court for the first of two arguments on the merits in the *Slaughterhouse Cases,* the Court was no longer the Democratic stronghold it had been ten years before. The Judiciary Act of 1862 provided for an important restructuring of the federal judiciary. The act designated five circuits in the North and four in the South, and to a large extent, it redressed a long-standing population imbalance among the circuits that had worked in favor of the selection of Democrats to the Supreme Court. Historian Stanley Kutler described the act as the first of the Republicans' Reconstruction measures because its aim was "to make national institutions more responsive to the needs of the dominant section."[1] Another act, passed the following year, created a tenth circuit on the West Coast. These measures made it possible for Lincoln and Grant to remake the Supreme Court.[2]

The Court that decided the *Slaughterhouse Cases* was nearing the end of the so-called Chase era. The term refers to Salmon P. Chase, who served as chief justice from 1864 to 1873. In 1872, only one of the justices, Nathan Clifford, had been in office since before the Civil War. Five justices, Noah Swayne, Samuel Miller, David Davis, Stephen Field, and Chase himself, had been placed on the Court by President Lincoln between 1862 and 1864. The remaining three justices had been chosen by Ulysses Grant. William Strong and Joseph Bradley took their oaths in 1870. Grant's third selection, Ward Hunt, was seated early in 1873. Only two of the nine justices were Democrats, Clifford and Field; the remainder were Republicans. Once the Chase court was in place, congressional Republicans were apt to regard it as one that could be counted on to legitimate their developing policy agenda.[3]

1. Stanley I. Kutler, *Judicial Power and Reconstruction Politics* (Chicago: University of Chicago Press, 1968).
2. Judiciary Act of 1863; Kutler, *Judicial Power,* 18–20.
3. "Once Lincoln's appointments had altered the Court's sectional and partisan cast, the republicans eagerly anticipated a judicial imprimatur for their policies." Kutler, *Judicial Power,* 162.

Members of the Chase Court shared several traits common among Supreme Court justices: all were male, white, and Protestant and had been active in politics. They were exceptional, however, in the extent to which their political activity continued after appointment to the Court. The chief justice, whose presidential ambitions were as considerable as his legal acumen, had sought the presidency in 1860 and 1864. He even solicited Democratic interest in his availability as a candidate in 1868. Four years later, and in very precarious health, Chase allowed his name to be floated for yet another presidential candidacy. In 1872, Chase's colleague, David Davis, accepted the presidential nomination of the National Labor Union Reform party, although he prudently declined to resign from the Court in advance of his most improbable election. As late as 1884, Stephen Field hoped for favorable consideration as the Democratic presidential nominee, and even Samuel Miller flirted with a possible run in 1880 and 1884.

The justices also shared an important experience. They had all seen the Civil War transform their country. If asked, they might have been unable to articulate exactly how this had happened and to what extent it specifically affected them. But the bloodiest war in American history, a conflict that ended with more than 620,000 dead, 4 million human beings now free, "vast fields, busy cities, quiet villages destroyed, new economic paths charted with unknown costs and consequences ahead," had reshaped the legal environment in which they operated.[4] They did not explicitly refer to this transformation, but some of their opinions reflect it, and one cannot understand the ultimate decision in *Slaughterhouse* without a sense of the transformed context in which the Court operated from 1865 to 1873.

Another distinguishing feature of the Chase Court, and one that also had relevance for the future, was the extent to which the major economic influences operating outside the Court in the postwar period were reflected in the backgrounds and values of individual justices. In a seminal work on the social and political background of Supreme Court justices, John R. Schmidhauser demonstrated the process by which an important change in the recruitment pattern of the justices became discernible after 1862.[5] Until then, Schmidhauser showed, justices had been recruited from families of the landowning aristocracy, and some had fathers with long records of political service. The justices themselves tended to be lawyer-statesmen, lawyers

4. Phillip Paludan, *The Presidency of Abraham Lincoln* (Lawrence: University Press of Kansas, 1994), 304.

5. John R. Schmidhauser, "The Justices of the Supreme Court: A Collective Portrait," *Midwest Journal of Political Science* 3 (1959): 1–57.

whose careers were devoted mainly to politics. This tendency yielded only slightly to the democratizing influence of the Jackson era. After 1862, however, most of the justices were recruited from families of professionals, and the justices had distinguished themselves first as lawyers and only later in political life. They brought to the Court experience and predilections that tended to reflect the economic and sometimes corporate interests they had served in legal practice. The major economic developments that characterized the postwar period produced an "era in which corporate influence was . . . ascendant in the national government."[6] Just as the interests of property were articulated in Congress, they were also articulated in the Supreme Court through the values and predilections of justices such as Field, Bradley, and Swayne. As congressional Republicans in 1862 set out to remake the Court, the ground was shifting beneath them, and patterns of judicial recruitment were being influenced in ways that would eventually result in a new era in constitutional policy.

Some brief biographical information about the justices is important in understanding the decisions they ultimately reached.[7] Nathan Clifford, the ranking member of the Court in terms of seniority, was born in New Hampshire in 1803 and was admitted to the bar before his twenty-fifth birthday. He moved to Maine, where he established both a large family and a successful law practice. By age twenty-seven, he had been elected to the Maine house of representatives as a Jacksonian Democrat, and his fidelity to that party lasted until his death. Clifford consistently opposed, for example, both high tariffs and a national banking system. After three terms in the Maine legislature (one as speaker of the house), he served two terms in Congress.[8] In 1846, President James Polk selected Clifford as his attorney general, but Clifford later resigned from that position to participate in the final peace negotiations with Mexico. In 1858, Clifford's old friend James Buchanan appointed him to the high court, where he did not hesitate to exercise his political predilections.

Clifford can accurately be described as a real doughface, a Northerner with Southern sympathies, and his nomination to the Court was clouded by the ongoing slavery-abolition crises in the Kansas territory. He received

---

6. Ibid., 34.

7. Biographical data have been drawn largely from three sources: Claire Cushman, ed., *The Supreme Court Justices* (Washington, D.C.: Congressional Quarterly, 1983); Melvin Urofsky, ed., *The Supreme Court Justices: A Biographical Dictionary* (New York: Garland, 1994); Kermit L. Hall, ed., *The Oxford Companion to the Supreme Court of the United States* (New York: Oxford University Press, 1992).

8. Hall, *Oxford Companion*, 161.

Senate approval by the narrow margin of twenty-six to twenty-three. His biases were predictable and consistent. He favored strict constitutional construction, objected to the abolitionists, and opposed expanded federal power—even as events moved steadily in that direction. Not unlike many Southerners, Clifford could denounce secession but fault Lincoln's imposition of a naval blockade in the *Prize Cases*.[9] In the postwar period, he agreed with his fellow Democrat Stephen J. Field in rejecting both state and federal imposition of test oaths as a means of reserving public office and the professions for "loyal" citizens.[10] In the *Legal Tender Cases*, he endorsed a ban on the continued use of paper money (greenbacks) as legal tender and angrily dissented when a new majority reversed this holding.[11] In his later years, he demonstrated consistent concern with "extending federal authority" during and beyond the era of Reconstruction.[12]

Noah Swayne was the first of Lincoln's five appointments to the high court. Born in 1804 in Virginia to strict Quaker parents, Swayne was introduced to antislavery views at a very early age. He was admitted to the Virginia bar while still a teenager. Swayne moved to Ohio, where in 1829 he was elected to the state legislature as a Jacksonian Democrat. Indeed, in 1830, Jackson appointed him as a U.S. attorney, a post Swayne retained for the next eleven years. Unlike Clifford, he grew increasingly uncomfortable with the Democratic position on slavery, and by 1854, he had joined the new Republican party. A strong Lincoln supporter, he enjoyed unanimous support from the Ohio congressional delegation in 1862 as he solicited a Supreme Court appointment, even though he had no judicial experience.

Swayne's efforts to lobby on his own behalf included a trip to Washington, and in the end, he proved successful. He possessed what Lincoln understandably looked for in all his Court appointments, a clear and unmistakable commitment to the Union cause. He supported all three constitutional amendments. Indeed, Swayne's efforts to ensure Ohio's ratification of the Fifteenth Amendment were important to that state's ultimate affirmative vote by a very narrow margin—one vote in the senate and two in the house. Yet, as will be seen, his support for the amendment itself could be accompanied by endorsement of a judicial holding that minimized its import.

As a justice, Swayne tended to support business and industrial expansion. In 1864, for example, he upheld the contractual rights of railroad bondhold-

9. 67 U.S. 635 (1863).
10. *Cummings v. Missouri*, 71 U.S. 277 (1867); *Ex Parte Garland*, 71 U.S. 333 (1867).
11. *Hepburn v. Griswold*, 75 U.S. 603 (1870).
12. Cushman, *Supreme Court Justices*, 169.

ers, even in the face of repudiation sanctioned by both the Iowa legislature and state supreme court. Obligations sacred to law, he intoned, cannot be discarded simply because "a state tribunal has erected the altar and decreed the sacrifice."[13] Remaining on the bench until 1881, Swayne eagerly schemed to become chief justice whenever a vacancy occurred, as it did in 1864 and 1873.

Lincoln's second appointment followed the passage of the Judiciary Act of 1862, by which Congress created a new federal judicial circuit consisting only of states west of the Mississippi. It made good political sense that he select a justice from this area and, like Swayne, one who enjoyed overwhelming support from its congressional delegation. Samuel F. Miller was born in 1816 in Richmond, Kentucky. Ironically, he shared a personal characteristic—one that was rare among Supreme Court justices—with Justice Bradley, with whom he often disagreed. Both men were the sons of farmers and the products of families of modest means. Miller had no formal legal training and, again like Swayne, no prior judicial experience. Indeed, in 1838, at age twenty-two, he had received an M.D. degree from Transylvania University. He practiced medicine in Kentucky for almost ten years but taught himself the law; in 1847, having abandoned his medical career, he was admitted to the bar on the motion of his office mate. Two years later, Miller moved to Iowa, where he established a very successful practice and turned to local politics. A staunch Republican and Lincoln supporter with numerous contacts in Congress, Miller became the right man in the right place at the right time with the right credentials once the new western circuit was created.[14] He was confirmed within half an hour after Lincoln submitted his name to the Senate. He was the first justice "born west of the Appalachians, and appointed from west of the Mississippi River."[15]

Possibly because he lacked judicial experience, Miller's opinions reflected a pragmatic approach to problems rather than a strictly logical application of legal doctrine. His legal insights were based more on experience than on formal training. He also had a tendency toward moderation when he rendered his decisions, a trait that his brethren seem to have appreciated. By the time of Miller's death in October 1890, he had spoken for the Court more than 600 times. In this he went far beyond the legendary Chief Justice

13. Hall, *Oxford Companion*, 327, citing *Gelpke v. Dubuque*, 66 U.S. 175 (1864).
14. Michael Ross, "Justice for Iowa: Samuel Freeman Miller's Appointment to the United States Supreme Court during the Civil War," *Annals of Iowa* 60 (2001): 111–38; Cushman, *Supreme Court Justices*, 177–78, Hall, *Oxford Companion*, 547–48.
15. Cushman, *Supreme Court Justices*, 179.

John Marshall.[16] Miller also demonstrated both a consistent reluctance to see his Court act as a censor of legislative policy and a tendency to seek a balance between federal and state lines of authority.

Lincoln's third appointment went to one of two personal acquaintances he named to the high court. David Davis was born in 1815 and was a graduate of Kenyon College in Ohio, which he had entered at age thirteen. By 1840, he had settled in Illinois as a young attorney with an interest in local politics. Indulging a talent for land speculation, which he practiced in Illinois and several other states, Davis developed valuable and lifelong business interests. He ran (unsuccessfully) for the state senate in 1840, but by 1844, he had gained a seat in the Illinois house of representatives. Davis spent the early part of his professional life as an itinerant lawyer, often in the company of another Illinois attorney, self-educated and self-taught Abraham Lincoln. In 1848, Davis was elected to a seat on the state circuit. Over the years, Davis and Lincoln became fast friends. Davis supported Lincoln's losing effort in 1858 to defeat Stephen Douglas as Illinois senator and managed his successful presidential campaign two years later.

Of all Lincoln's high court selections, Davis, appointed in 1862, appears to have enjoyed his tenure least, apparently finding the work tiresome and dull. In common with Lincoln's other appointees, Davis sustained various wartime measures the administration employed between 1861 and 1865, with one notable exception. This exception, however, was one of the landmark cases arising from the Civil War, and it provided Davis with the opportunity to write his most enduring and significant opinion.

Ex Parte Milligan concerned an appeal by a prominent antiwar politician in Indiana who had been arrested by the military for alleged treasonous activities and sentenced to death by a military commission.[17] The Court decided unanimously in Milligan's favor, holding that a military commission was without constitutional authority to try a civilian when and where civil courts were in operation. In a separate concurring opinion, four justices (including Miller and Chase) agreed that in *this* instance, Milligan's trial had been unconstitutional, but they insisted that under appropriate conditions, Congress could authorize the military to try civilian offenders. In *Milligan*,

16. White notes that in his thirty-four-year tenure as chief justice, John Marshall spoke for the Court in 547 opinions. G. Edward White, *The Marshall Court and Cultural Change, 1815–1835* (New York: Oxford University Press, 1991), 191. Miller served on the Court for about twenty-eight years, from 1862 to 1890. During this period, he wrote 626 opinions for the Court. See Paul A. Weidner, "Justices Field and Miller: A Comparative Study in Judicial Attitudes and Values" (Ph.D. diss., University of Michigan, 1958), 302.

17. *Ex Parte Milligan*, 71 U.S. 2 (1866).

among the Lincoln appointees, only Davis and Democrat Stephen Field were of the opinion that Congress lacked this authority under any circumstances (they were joined by Democrat Nathan Clifford). Although the Court announced its decision in early April 1866, it did not release the justices' opinions until December 1866, months after President Johnson had declared the insurrection at an end and shortly after he had criticized the continued substitution of military for civil authority. The time had come, Justice Davis wrote, when existing conditions permitted "that calmness in deliberation and discussion so necessary to a correct conclusion of a purely judicial question."[18] In other words, there was now little likelihood that the Union army might ignore the holding.

Lincoln's fourth appointment to the Court reflected, once again, his dual concerns that the nominee be committed to the Union cause and that he represent a part of the country of major importance in terms of growth— both geographical and legal. A member of the California Supreme Court, Stephen J. Field filled these needs very well. Born in Connecticut in 1816, he was the sixth of nine children and was raised in Massachusetts in a strict Puritan environment by his father, David Dudley Field, a Congregationalist minister. Indeed, portraits of Justice Stephen Field seem to radiate a sense of rigid self-righteousness and certainty. Field spent a number of his teenage years abroad, returning to Massachusetts to enter Williams College at the age of seventeen. He graduated at the top of his class in 1837 and promptly entered the New York law firm of his older brother, David Field Jr., under whom he read law. The elder Field brother was well on his way to becoming one of the outstanding legal practitioners in the eastern United States. But the younger sibling may have found working with his brother a bit confining, because in 1849, he moved to California where he could build a legal career on his own.

Indeed, he did. Field plunged into legal practice and California politics and a series of feuds and personal controversies that seemed to follow the young attorney. Elected to the legislature in 1850, he played a major role in the transformation of a bundle of statutes into a uniform body of civil and criminal law—a code based in part on efforts by his older brother to construct such a piece of legislation for New York State. By 1857, Field had been elected to the California Supreme Court, and he became its chief justice

---

18. Cushman, *Supreme Court Justices,* 185. Davis tended to disassociate himself from the Republicans as the war ran its course. He ultimately left the party over the Johnson impeachment controversy, and when he resigned from the Court in 1877 to accept election as Illinois' senator, he gloried in his stature "as a true independent, unaffiliated with any party." Ibid.

two years later. A close friend of influential Republicans such as Leland Stanford and well versed in land and mining law, Field seemed the right choice for Lincoln as he sought to bind California closer to the Union cause. Moreover, Field was a Democrat, and by selecting him, Lincoln emphasized his desire to place national priorities above partisan political interests.

As a justice, Field's major opinions tended to reflect his values, which included a veneration for property rights and a hostility toward state regulation, whether or not he could find a clear basis for them in either the Constitution or judicial precedent. In his majority opinion in the 1867 *Test Oath Cases,* for example, Field held that "the theory upon which our political institutions rest is, that all men have certain and inalienable rights—that among these are life, liberty, and the pursuit of happiness; and that in the pursuit of happiness all avocations, all honors, all positions, are alike open to everyone, and that in protection of these rights all are equal before the law."[19] Even as Field wrote his opinion, a new constitutional provision, the Fourteenth Amendment, was awaiting state ratification. Later, it would serve Field well as a foundation for his basic assumptions concerning government and society.

Lincoln's final high court appointment, made only a few months before his assassination, was also his most unusual. Salmon P. Chase was born in New Hampshire in 1808. Before he reached the age of twenty-one, he had graduated Phi Beta Kappa from Dartmouth. Apprenticed for a time to Attorney General William Wirt, by the mid-1840s, Chase had established a successful practice in Ohio, where he also became "involved in various reform causes, especially temperance" and abolition.[20] Ernest and eloquent, he found himself drawn to a political career. In 1849, he was elected to the U.S. Senate from Ohio, and upon completion of his term, he served as Ohio's governor from 1855 to 1859. In 1860, he was again elected to the Senate. Known as an experienced politician and able administrator, along with New York senator William Seward, Chase was one of the early favorites to win the Republican presidential nomination. But the convention turned to Abraham Lincoln, who was considered more moderate on the issue of abolition. Political realities required that both Chase and Seward be named to Lincoln's cabinet, as indeed they were.[21]

19. *Cummings v. Missouri,* 71 U.S. 277, 320–22 (1867).

20. Urofsky, *Supreme Court Justices,* 101.

21. Seward served as secretary of state, Chase as secretary of the treasury. Both men considered themselves superior to Lincoln in intellect and ability; both men believed themselves much better suited for the presidency than the incumbent; and both—especially in the early months of his administration—sought to undercut the new president's authority.

But Chase could find no remedy for his presidential fervor. Although he administered the Treasury with skill and successfully financed the vast expenses of the war, he connived against Lincoln on several occasions, seeking to bolster his own political fortunes at the expense of his president. Whenever Lincoln called him on it, Chase would threaten to resign, knowing that Lincoln valued his abilities. By mid-1864, however, the party was unified behind Lincoln in the wake of an ultimately successful campaign for renomination; this, along with increasingly favorable reports from the military front, meant that Lincoln no longer needed to put up with Chase's tactics. So when Chase tendered his resignation over a minor question of patronage concerning his department, Lincoln quickly accepted it. Samuel Miller recalled that Chase's considerable strengths were "warped, perverted and shrivelled by the selfishness generated by ambition."[22] After his reelection, Lincoln began to focus increasingly on the issues of Reconstruction, and when the ailing and aged Chief Justice Roger Taney died, he appointed Chase. It was a shrewd decision, for in one stroke Lincoln raised to the high court an able lawyer, a staunch supporter of the Union, and a perennial political nuisance, albeit one with strong supporters in Lincoln's party. Chase was nominated and confirmed within a few hours by voice vote of the Senate on December 6, 1864. By 1872, he had already suffered a series of strokes, and although he recovered sufficiently to participate in the hearing and adjudication of cases, his speech remained slightly slurred, he could write only with difficulty, and his leadership of the Court—not easy under any conditions with the likes of Justices Miller, Field, and Bradley as colleagues—became virtually nonexistent. He died only a few weeks after the *Slaughterhouse* decision was announced.

For a time, Chase presided over a ten-member Court, as Congress—seeking to ensure that Lincoln would have ample opportunity to appoint pro-Union justices—had added a tenth seat by the 1863 act. This was filled by Stephen Field. By 1867, however, two justices had died, and the struggle between Andrew Johnson and Congress resulted in Johnson's being unable to make any appointments to the high court, a fate shared by only one other full-term president since William Harrison in 1841—Jimmy Carter. With President Ulysses Grant inaugurated in 1869, Congress restored the Court membership to nine, where it has remained ever since.

There, the similarities ended. Seward eventually became one of Lincoln's most trusted and loyal subordinates. The same could not be said of Chase.

22. See G. Edward White, "Salmon Portland Chase and the Judicial Culture of the Supreme Court in the Civil War Era." In *The Supreme Court and the Civil War*, ed. Jennifer M. Lowe (Washington, D.C.: Supreme Court Historical Society, 1996), 38.

Grant had moved promptly to fill the two Court vacancies by nominating his attorney general E. Rockwood Hoar and the former secretary of war Edwin Stanton. But Hoar fell victim to partisan wrangling in the Senate, and Stanton—although appointed and immediately confirmed—died before he could take the oath of office. Again, Grant had two vacancies to fill. He moved to fill them on February 7, 1870, the same day the Court handed down its decision in the first of the *Legal Tender Cases,* in which it held by a four-to-three vote that the continued use of paper money (greenbacks) was unconstitutional.[23] In his opinion for the majority, Chief Justice Chase disavowed as unconstitutional a policy that, as secretary of the treasury, he had earlier endorsed and helped implement. Invariably, the question of a rehearing became linked to the question of where Grant's two nominees might stand on the issue of paper specie.

There was no doubt where one of them stood. William Strong, a native of Connecticut, had enrolled in Yale before he turned sixteen. He later received a master's degree from Yale Law School and was admitted to both the Connecticut and Pennsylvania bars in 1832, at the age of twenty-four. He settled in Reading, Pennsylvania, became fluent in both German and local dialects, and built a very lucrative practice. By 1846, he had been elected to Congress as an antislavery Democrat and served two terms. Having returned to his law practice, and still a Democrat, Strong was elected to the Pennsylvania Supreme Court in 1857 for a fifteen-year term. His antislavery views and strong support of the Union resulted in his shift to the new Republican party. Strong remained on the Pennsylvania bench until 1868.[24]

One of his most important votes as a member of the Pennsylvania Supreme Court came when he joined his colleagues in affirming the constitutionality of the Legal Tender Act of 1862. A number of state courts had already so held, and by 1870, at least sixty state justices had considered this issue, with only one Republican jurist opposing the use of paper money as legal tender.[25] The initial decision of the U.S. Supreme Court on the Legal Tender Act, declaring the measure *un*constitutional, came in February 1870, on the same day that Grant sent Strong's name to the Senate. This led some to accuse the president of seeking to pack the Court in order to gain a rehearing and a reversal of its holding. Although there is no convincing evidence that Grant had so conspired, there is no doubt that Strong's view

23. *Hepburn v. Griswold,* 75 U.S. 603 (1870).
24. Cushman, *Supreme Court Justices,* 196–97.
25. Ibid.

on legal tender was well known. Indeed, within a year, he would write for the new five-member majority in overruling Chase's decision.[26]

Grant's other nominee, Republican Joseph P. Bradley, graduated from Rutgers College in New Jersey and taught himself sufficient law to be admitted to the bar "at the relatively advanced age of twenty six."[27] A voracious reader who was proficient in several languages and also well versed in mathematics, the young attorney built a successful career in Newark. Along the way, he married the daughter of New Jersey Chief Justice William Hornblower. Given Bradley's later hostility to railroads, it is interesting to note that as a lawyer, one of his most important clients was the notoriously corrupt Camden and Perth Amboy Railroad.[28] By 1868, he had become a strong supporter of Grant for the presidency and was one of New Jersey's presidential electors pledged to him, specifically supporting the Legal Tender Act.[29]

As mentioned in an earlier chapter, Bradley was the only justice to have considered and ruled on the merits of the Louisiana slaughterhouse controversy before it reached the Supreme Court. In 1870, while presiding over the circuit court in New Orleans, he had held the Slaughterhouse Act unconstitutional, although he declined on jurisdictional grounds to implement his decision fully. Yet his opinion had revealed a conservative trait in Bradley's thought, even as he focused on the innovative nature of the new Fourteenth Amendment. During the early stages of the Civil War, he had emphasized that the overriding duty was to "put down the rebellion cost what it may. . . . The rebellion must be put down. Nothing else must be thought of."[30] The issue was not slavery. Rather, it was obedience to the Constitution, which should "stand just as it is, word for word and letter for letter." Bradley added that as far as the South was concerned, "the Constitution gives us no power to meddle with them, no more than it gives them

26. *Knox v. Lee*, 79 U.S. 457 (1871).

27. Hall, *Oxford Companion*, 81.

28. Bradley would be the guiding light behind the landmark decision in *Munn v. Illinois*, 94 U.S. 113 (1877), a case in which the Court sustained a regulation adopted in Illinois during the "Granger era."

29. The fact that Grant must have been aware that both Strong and Bradley publicly supported paper specie in no way makes either him or his choices accessories to charges of "Court packing," an accusation often raised in 1871. There is no evidence that he intentionally sought out nominees who favored paper money as legal tender. However, the government moved for reconsideration of Chase's decision *after* Grant's two appointees had taken their seats on the Court; it required little skill in math to determine that three dissenters in the 1870 decision plus Bradley and Strong would make up a new majority.

30. Lurie, "Mr. Justice Bradley," 349.

power to meddle with us."[31] Like many in the North, including Lincoln, by 1865, Bradley had come to the inescapable conclusion that abolition must be joined with saving the Union as the twin goals of the conflict. But his basic racism and conservatism remained unchanged.

Like several of his colleagues, Ward Hunt, Grant's third appointment, had been a Jacksonian Democrat. A native of Utica, New York, he was born in 1810, and for a time he studied law at the famous Tapping Reeve School in Litchfield, Connecticut. By 1832, he had returned to Utica and established a successful law practice. Six years later, he was elected to the state legislature, and in 1844, he became Utica's mayor. Again, like some of his judicial brethren, Hunt found the Democratic party's position on slavery increasingly unacceptable, and in 1856, he joined in establishing the Republican party in New York State. In doing so, Hunt became well acquainted with a leading power in state politics, Roscoe Conkling. This friendship would ultimately lead Hunt to the U.S. Supreme Court.[32]

In the meantime, Hunt had sought state judicial office, running unsuccessfully for a seat on the New York Court of Appeals. In 1853, he tried again and was defeated again. After the war, and now well established as a Republican, Hunt tried for a third time and at last met with success. In 1865, he succeeded his mentor and former partner Hiram Denio on the state high court. In 1868, Hunt became chief justice, and in this capacity he wrote the majority opinion in *Metropolitan Board of Health v. Heister*, discussed in a previous chapter.[33] In this case, Hunt sustained the authority of the legislature to confine slaughtering to one area of New York City. A state constitutional amendment required the reorganization of the court of appeals in 1869, but Hunt managed to stay on as commissioner of appeals.

In November 1872, Supreme Court Justice Samuel Nelson retired. Eighty years old and in poor health, Nelson had missed much of the Court's 1871–1872 term, including the first *Slaughterhouse* argument.[34] That case remained undecided when President Grant—responding to an enthusiastic endorsement from now New York senator Roscoe Conkling—named Hunt to succeed Nelson. Nominated on December 3, 1872, Hunt took his seat early in January 1873, just in time to listen to the re-arguments in *Slaughter-*

---

31. Ibid.

32. Cushman, *Supreme Court Justices*, 207–8.

33. 37 N.Y. 661 (1868).

34. One suspects that the Court found itself split four to four after initial discussion of the case and decided to hold the case over. With Hunt filling the ninth seat, *Slaughterhouse* was scheduled for re-argument in February 1873.

Upon taking his seat on the Court in 1873, Ward
Hunt heard the re-argument of the *Slaughterhouse
Cases* and probably cast the deciding vote to sustain
the statute. (Office of the Curator, Supreme Court
of the United States, #1873.3.)

house barely one month later. The Court's decision came down within three
months.

THE SUPREME COURT was called on to decide a number of constitutional
issues arising out of the Civil War and Reconstruction. Indeed, between
1865 and 1873, it played an important role in the process by which the nation
adjusted to the postwar era, and these decisions affected both its role and its
image. Prior to 1865, the Court had exercised judicial review to pronounce
the unconstitutionality of acts of Congress in only two cases, the famous
Marbury v. Madison in 1804 and the infamous *Dred Scott* case of 1857. Judg-
ing from its frequent exercise of judicial review in the years that followed,
the Court apparently was not chastised by the furor that followed the *Dred*

Scott decision. By 1873, no fewer than twelve acts of Congress had been invalidated by the Court, seven of these since 1869.[35] By the time it handed down the *Slaughterhouse* decision in April 1873, the Court "had regained near equality with the legislative and executive branches, at times aggressively extending its authority to review" state and federal legislation.[36]

Although it is difficult to make generalizations concerning the Chase Court, a few points can be offered. As Lincoln expected, all were united on ensuring the survival of the Union, but this goal had already been assured by the time Chief Justice Chase took his seat on December 15, 1864. Further, it soon became evident that the justices tended to be more conservative than Congress, especially after the radical wing of the Republican party gained dominance between 1866 and 1869. As the era of Reconstruction ran its course, the justices diverged among themselves while they navigated a sort of judicial minefield of explosive issues. Their docket required them to mediate in the struggle between President Andrew Johnson and Congress over Reconstruction, to monitor the "changed nature of federal-state relations," to ensure the "rights of all citizens as promised by the Union victory," to confront if not resolve "constitutional problems posed by the new industrial economy," and, finally, to reach decisions in all these areas within a new judicial context, one that frowned on judicial and legislative instrumentalism and emphasized concern for the limits of legislative authority and for the means of protecting an expanded category of property rights.[37]

In *Ex Parte Milligan*, for example, the entire Court agreed that Milligan's trial by military commission was unconstitutional. But only two of Lincoln's appointees accepted the conclusion that Congress lacked the authority, under any circumstances, to establish tribunals to prosecute civilians who were U.S. citizens. In the *Test Oath Cases* one year later, all four Lincoln Republican justices disagreed with Democrat Field's rejection of loyalty oaths as unconstitutional.[38] As tensions between Congress and President Johnson were exacerbated, and as Congress enacted a number of Reconstruction measures, several pending cases arising from Southern states threatened to play the Court off against Congress. Here, the political instincts of Chief Justice Chase contributed to an avoidance of outright confrontation between Congress and the Court while retaining, to a great extent, its traditional judicial authority.

35. These comments rely heavily on David Bodenhamer's perceptive insights in his essay on Chase in Urofsky, *Supreme Court Justices*, 101–2.

36. Ibid.

37. Ibid.

38. *Cummings v. Missouri*, 71 U.S. 277 (1867); *Ex Parte Garland*, 71 U.S. 333 (1867).

Thus, in cases such as *Georgia v. Stanton* (1868)[39] and *Mississippi v. Johnson* (1867),[40] a unanimous Court declined to get into a judicial evaluation of congressional Reconstruction statutes. Similarly, in the case of *Texas v. White* (1869), Chief Justice Chase described the United States as "an indestructible Union composed of indestructible states."[41] Although the case concerned a dispute over the payment of certain state securities, in fact, it involved serious issues such as the nature of the Union and the legitimacy of federal Reconstruction. By holding that the Union was permanent and indissoluble and that secession had been unlawful, Chase made it clear that Congress possessed plenary authority to deal with Reconstruction as a political process. Finally, in two cases involving the use of habeas corpus, Chase's Court demonstrated what might be described as an exercise in aggressive caution.

Coming at the height of the conflict between Congress and Johnson, the case of *Ex Parte McCardle* involved a Southern editor's challenge to a newly enacted Reconstruction statute based on another recent federal law authorizing "federal courts to issue writs of habeas corpus" when the plaintiff was confined in violation of his constitutional rights.[42] Fearful that the Court might use this habeas corpus appeal to reject congressional Reconstruction, Congress simply revoked the Court's authority to hear such appeals. Although the Court had not yet decided the case, it had already heard oral arguments. Yet by a unanimous vote, the justices acquiesced in this action and dismissed McCardle's appeal for want of jurisdiction.[43] But Chase, sensitive to the claim that the Court was simply "caving in," insisted that the Court's constitutional jurisdiction remained unchanged, as did the authority granted to it by the 1789 Judiciary Act. But the Court's appellate jurisdiction was subject to congressional regulation.

In 1869, the Court reiterated this position in *Ex Parte Yerger*,[44] but neither the government nor Congress was much inclined to press the case. By 1869, congressional Reconstruction was well in hand, the Fourteenth Amendment was now law, and a new Republican president had taken the oath of office. Although the Court claimed jurisdiction in *Yerger*, the justices did not consider its merits, and in 1885, Congress quietly restored the juris-

39. 6 Wall. 50 (1867).
40. 71 U.S. 475 (1867).
41. 74 U.S. 700 (1869); Hall, *Oxford Companion*, 869.
42. 74 U.S. 506 (1869); Hall, *Oxford Companion*, 534–35.
43. Ibid.
44. 8 Wall. 85 (1869).

diction it had removed from the Supreme Court in 1868. Indeed, by 1872, when the justices first considered the constitutional issues in *Slaughterhouse*, they were at the end of an era. The half dozen years between 1866 and 1872 represented a unique period of tension in American legal history, involving all three branches of the federal government, to say nothing of the Southern states undergoing Reconstruction. Certainly the Court had contributed to this situation with its decisions in *Milligan* and the *Test Oath Cases*, its standoff with Congress concerning habeas corpus appeals, and its flip-flop over the validity of paper as legal tender. But by the time it took up *Slaughterhouse*, much of this tension had eased. New issues concerning expansion and regulation of the market were on the docket, and both the Court's jurisdiction and the output of decisions were expanding. The Court was in a period of transition, with an instrumentalist approach to law giving way to a more formalistic emphasis on procedures, precedent (both old and new), and property rights. It was at this juncture that the justices confronted the complex issues of the *Slaughterhouse Cases*. And, as will be seen, its outcome revealed a divided Court, with some justices looking back to what had been and others looking forward to what lay ahead.[45]

45. Harold Hyman and William Wiecek, *Equal Justice under Law: Constitutional Development 1835–1875* (New York: Harper and Row, 1982), 459–60; Fairman, *Reconstruction and Reunion*, 1480–81.

8

The Arguments

B y the time the Supreme Court heard the final arguments in the *Slaugh-terhouse Cases* between February 3 and 5, 1873, the lawyers had had ample time to perfect their positions. They had clashed over this controversy for more than three years—in the Louisiana district courts, the Louisiana Supreme Court, and the federal courts as well. Moreover, the high court had already disposed of the ill-fated supersedeas issue. Indeed, in January 1872, the merits had been debated before eight of the justices, in the absence of the aged and ailing Justice Samuel Nelson. It may well be that these earlier arguments had resulted in a four-to-four division among the eight sitting justices.[1] In any event, the justices carried the argument over to the Court's next term (December 1872), without specifying any new issues on which counsel were to focus. The next step was a re-argument before a full bench, now available with the newly appointed Justice Ward Hunt seated on the Court.

As lead counsel for the butchers, John Campbell appears to have had a dual agenda. Like most in his profession, his first goal was victory for his clients. But the former Supreme Court justice had another subtle, more important objective, one that he concealed within his vigorous opposition to the 1869 statute. It was to employ the new constitutional realities of Reconstruction as a legal weapon to bring about its ultimate demise. Separated from his family while he pursued his law practice in New Orleans, Campbell observed the progress of Reconstruction with dismay. In an 1871 letter to his daughter in Baltimore, he brooded, "the people have ascertained that they have been plundered, but they do not know how to find a remedy. We have the African in place all about us. . . . Corruption is the rule."[2] In

---

1. This may be what Justice Miller meant when, early in his *Slaughterhouse* opinion, he referred to the fact that after the first argument in January 1872, with Nelson absent, "it was found that, on consultation there was a diversity of views among those who were present." 16 Wall. 36, 58 (1873).

2. Campbell to Kate C. Groner, April 9, 1871, Groner Family Papers, Southern Historical Collection, University of North Carolina library.

his racial attitudes and political preferences, Campbell embodied the "old" white South. In spite of his forceful rhetoric on behalf of the butchers of New Orleans, one might ask to what extent he really cared about their ultimate fate. But to use the butchers' cause as part of an effort to gut the work of an integrated and discredited Louisiana legislature and repudiate not only leaders such as Warmoth, who had made it possible, but also the political context in which they operated was another matter indeed. And ultimately, one suspects that this was much more important to Campbell. Thus his briefs and arguments must be considered for their duality of purpose.

Campbell prepared separate briefs for the 1872 and 1873 arguments in the Supreme Court. In the opening pages of his initial brief, Campbell reiterated his basic and often repeated contention that the Louisiana statute of 1869 had been enacted by "legislative caprice, partiality, ignorance or corruption."[3] This was essentially an appeal to righteousness as a measure of constitutionality, and it had always been an element of Campbell's most passionate attacks on the Slaughterhouse Act. This aspect of his argument recalls Justice Samuel Chase's assertion in the 1798 case of *Calder v. Bull* that he was not prepared to uphold the validity of anything a state legislature might do just because there was nothing in the Constitution to prevent it. Chase was arguing—as was Campbell—that the power of a legislature was necessarily limited by "the first great principles of the social contract."[4] Although Chase's reservation had never taken root in constitutional law, there was nothing to prevent fundamental principles from being found in existing constitutional limitations.[5] Thus there was no reason for Campbell

3. Campbell, "Brief for Plaintiffs" in *Slaughterhouse Cases*, 83 U.S. (16 Wall.) 36 (1873), in *Landmark Briefs and Arguments of the Supreme Court of the United States*, vol. 6, ed. Philip B. Kurland and Gerhard Casper (Arlington, Va.: University Publications of America, 1975), 537. The various sources of the briefs are identified in the bibliography. For purposes of this chapter, we have chosen to cite to the readily available Kurland and Casper collection. All the *Slaughterhouse* briefs preserved by the Court are contained in this single volume. Throughout this chapter, our page citations refer to this collection and not to the pages of individual briefs.

4. *Calder v. Bull*, 3 U.S. (3 Wall.) 386, 387–88 (1798).

5. In a treatise published not long after the *Slaughterhouse* decision, Tiedeman observed that "it may now be considered as an established principle of American law that the courts . . . cannot nullify and avoid a law, simply because it conflicts with the judicial notions of natural right or morality, or abstract justice" (citing *Bertholf v. O'Reilly*, 74 N.Y. 509 [1878]). But, he added, "wherever by reasonable construction the constitutional limitation can be made to avoid an unrighteous exercise of police power, that construction will be upheld, notwithstanding the strict letter of the constitution does not prohibit the exercise of

to stop there. New provisions had been added to the Constitution in the form of the recently adopted amendments, and it did not matter that they had been adopted with altogether different purposes in mind. Their terms were expansive, and they had yet to be authoritatively interpreted by the nation's highest court.

Campbell proceeded, then, to the more complex task of demonstrating that the 1869 Slaughterhouse Act subjected his clients to a form of involuntary servitude. He grounded this effort on both the Fourteenth Amendment, with its mention of "privileges and immunities," and on the Thirteenth Amendment's more specific reference to "slavery and involuntary servitude." "The first section of the fourteenth amendment is a corallary [*sic*] to the thirteenth, as was the Civil Rights Act that preceded it, an echo of it."[6]

As an initial step in this argument, Campbell had to demonstrate that the concept of involuntary servitude embraced much more than American Negro chattel slavery and could be applied to protect the rights of white butchers. This was an important first step because it was a given, not challenged by either side, that in the U.S. experience, the concept of slavery had been inseparable from the African American race. "We have never supposed," Campbell insisted, "that these Constitutional Enactments had any particular or limited reference to Negro slavery. The words employed do not describe that form of slavery and that only. They are absolute, universal."[7] In fact, "the prohibition of slavery and involuntary servitude in every form and degree . . . comprises much more than the abolition or prohibition of African slavery. . . . The state of freedom and the state of slavery are contraries, and cannot exist in the same person. In a community where slavery and involuntary servitude are absolutely prohibited, the members must all be free, whether black or white, and whether in relations to a master or in connection with a domain."[8]

Thus, to be a freeman possessing privileges and immunities under the Constitution implied a number of rights:

> 1st. An immunity from compulsory work at the will, or for the profit of another. 2nd. No kind of occupation, employment or trade can be imposed upon him, or prohibited to him, as to avoid all choice or election on his part. 3d. He may engage in any lawful pursuit for which he may have the

---

such a power." Christopher G. Tiedeman, *A Treatise on the Limitations of the Police Power* (St. Louis: H. Thomas Law Book Co., 1886), 7, 10.

6. "Brief for Plaintiffs," 548.

7. Ibid., 539.

8. Ibid., 540

requisite capacity, skill, material or capital. 4th. He is entitled to the full enjoyment of the fruits of his labor or industry without constraint, subject only to legal taxation or contribution.[9]

To these, Campbell added the right to be free of monopolies, so that the course of trade "should be free from unreasonable obstruction." All this was included, he maintained, in the concept of "involuntary servitude." Campbell's passion as well as some of the words employed to express it were inspired partly by classical denunciation of monopolies. In one source available to him, Matthew Bacon had condemned monopolies as "restraining persons from getting an honest livelihood by a lawful employment."[10] Similarly, Edward Coke asserted that "the monopolist that taketh away a man's trade, taketh away his life, and therefore is so much more the odious."[11]

But this lawyer realized that comparing the lot of butchers compelled to slaughter at the Crescent City abattoir with that of African American slaves might be somewhat extravagant. "We do not contend," he admitted, "that . . . plaintiffs . . . have been placed in handcuffs and carried to the houses, pens and yards of this corporation, with violence, to labor for this corporation of seventeen as African slaves might have been." Nor could it be said that they have "been imprisoned or confined to compel them to labor." Campbell insisted, however, that "all of them have been prohibited from doing their usual or customary work, except upon the property and for the compensation and profit of these parties." Further, "they have been compelled to close up the houses and other conveniences of business."[12] Based on these facts, Campbell concluded that "the common rights of men have been taken away and have become the *sole and exclusive privilege* of a single corporation."[13]

Here, Campbell combined a summary of the central terms of the statute with a wild yet powerful distortion of the statute's application to his clients. The 1869 enactment in no way forbade anyone to ply the trade of a butcher by slaughtering animals and selling the meat to the public for a profit. What

---

9. Ibid., 540–41.

10. Matthew Bacon, *A New Abridgment of the Law*, vol. 7 (Philadelphia: T. and J. W. Johnson, 1856), 22.

11. Edward Coke, *The Third Part of the Institutes of the Laws of England* (London: E. and R. Brooke, 1787), 181. In a comment that seems especially apt to Reconstruction New Orleans, Coke also observed that "monopolies in times past were ever without law, but never without Friends." Ibid., 182.

12. "Brief for Plaintiffs," 547.

13. Ibid.; emphasis in original.

it did require was that the slaughtering of animals be done in one central facility. The butchers' trade remained open to anyone who wished to pursue it, and individual butchers remained free either to slaughter their stock themselves in the company's abattoir upon payment of the fees stipulated in the statute or to employ journeymen at the slaughterhouse for this task, a course of action that many of them quickly adopted.[14]

But, as he had done throughout the litigation, Campbell repeatedly asserted that the Slaughterhouse Act barred the butchers from practicing their chosen occupation. "The daily avocation and employment, the means by which, perhaps, a thousand persons have earned their daily bread have been jeoparded [*sic*] and impaired." As Campbell saw it, to defend the statute was to assert the company's "sole and exclusive privilege to conduct and carry on an important business in which hundreds had been engaged." And again, "The butcher is compelled to abandon his trade."[15] But to say that the statute barred a butcher from a chosen occupation was to argue that a butcher could not pursue his calling without owning or operating a slaughterhouse of his own. Clearly this was not the case, as the attorneys for the company often noted. However, as a most partisan advocate, Campbell could not be expected to undercut one of his main arguments.[16] His strenuous and repeated resort to the sacred right of labor gave his argument a unique force, but it was used to disguise a fatal flaw.

The former slave owner emphasized that the basic motive for both the Thirteenth and Fourteenth Amendments "is that as man has a right to labor for himself, and not at the will, or under the constraint of another, [so] he should have the profits of his own industry." Hinting again at his greater objective, Campbell reminded the justices that the Fourteenth Amendment, as well as the Civil Rights Act that preceded it, "guaranteed its protection against sordid interests, selfish aims and ambitious usurpations, or greedy

14. The consolidation of slaughtering in a single abattoir seems to have had a specializing effect on one of the meat industry's key practices in New Orleans. According to one veteran of the trade, in the centralized abattoir, the butchers stopped doing their own slaughtering and began to employ journeymen for this task. "None of the butchers proper do their own slaughtering." Testimony of William Fagan, October 19, 1871, in *Bertin v. Crescent City Livestock Landing and Slaughterhouse Co.*, 28 La. Ann. 210 (1876), available at La. Sup Ct. Docket No. 3917, Louisiana Supreme Court Archives.

15. "Brief for Plaintiffs," 537, 545.

16. Campbell further conceded that his butchers were not "required to labor at the works of this corporation day by day, to be sure, nor have they been arbitrarily commanded to desist from laboring at their trade." Ibid., 546.

appetites."[17] Like them or not, the postwar amendments reflected "a great and weighty significance." Although Campbell would not admit that the amendments had brought about "a radical change in the government of the United States," he held that "they go very far to determine that the Constitution of the United States creates a national government and is not a federal compact."[18] Here, the former Supreme Court justice took a position far from the doctrine of states' rights—in support of which he had followed his state out of the Union a decade before. But he did so not because he criticized its rationale as much as he condemned its results as expressed in the Slaughterhouse Act.

Probably thinking of the effects of Reconstruction and the abolition of slavery, Campbell claimed that "it may have been forseen [*sic*] that disorder would follow from . . . the introduction of a more relaxed system of social life and manners. . . . It was to have been expected," he added, "that there would be more corruption in the state governments, and that the rights of individuals would be insecure. It was to have been expected that in the existing state of society, monopolies would be asked for and easily obtained."[19] The Constitution had always sought to protect certain rights from abuse by Congress. Thus the intent of the new amendments was to guarantee that the citizens' "privileges and immunities shall never be abridged by *State laws,* nor shall the *State* deny them equal protection." The same law that protects freedom of religion, speech, or publication from violation by a state now "protects the personal right to labor."[20] Campbell readily admitted that "the sovereignty of the State government is reduced—and wisely reduced by the Constitution—to a very limited extent." Now, "life, liberty, property, privilege, immunity, civil, political and public rights have been placed upon a foundation that the [state legislatures] cannot subvert or destroy. Their superstruction [*sic*] of law must be made on this foundation, or it will fall of itself."[21]

The fatal constitutional flaw in the Slaughterhouse Act, as Campbell

17. Campbell argued that for those Americans in the Reconstruction era "who were gravely interested in the struggle," the new amendments "have a profound significance." But to those who were "but little concerned either in its chances or changes, and were much interested in the financial opportunities it afforded, and were safe from its perils, these amendments are regarded very much as a party platform, whose value is exhausted at an election." Ibid., 551.

18. Ibid.

19. Ibid., 552.

20. Ibid., 547.

21. Ibid., 557.

viewed it, was its creation of a monopoly. Much of his first brief is devoted
to a detailed account of the abuses caused by monopolies throughout history
and the efforts to alleviate them, beginning with the great sixteenth-century
Case of Monopolies in England.[22] A similar aversion to monopolies was evident in American law. Indeed, Campbell contended that every essential
point in the *Case of Monopolies* was reflected in the provisions of the new
amendments to the Constitution.[23]

In support of his anti-monopoly attack on the statute, Campbell was able
to cite one recent state decision that seemed particularly relevant, if not
decisive. The case deserves some attention because it helps elucidate the
extralegal aspects of Campbell's reasoning and the ultimate weakness of his
position. *City of Chicago v. Rumpff* involved an 1865 municipal ordinance by
which the city, in effect, had entered into a contract granting a single private
firm the exclusive right to have all slaughtering in the city done on its
premises, in return for the company's agreement to erect and maintain the
buildings and stockyards necessary to accommodate the needs of all the
butchers.[24] The ordinance went on to forbid slaughtering to take place elsewhere (packinghouses excepted). The measure had been enacted under the
council's express legislative authority to regulate and direct the location of
slaughtering within the city.

The Illinois Supreme Court declared the ordinance invalid on the
grounds that it was not a regulatory measure but a mere offer to contract.
Unlike a regulatory measure, said the court, the ordinance "did not speak
the language of command," and "it did not declare . . . the business of
slaughtering animals in the city a nuisance."[25] Not even a separate legislative
act confirming the city's authority to enact such an ordinance was sufficient
to dissuade the court from its finding of invalidity.

In stating the legal reasons for its decision, the court made no effort to
conceal the extent to which its reaction was explained by the monopolistic
aspects of the city's arrangements. Municipal bodies, it said, "are never created to enable them . . . to grant monopolies to any portion of [the] community. . . . An ordinance confining such a business to a small lot . . . is
unreasonable. . . . Such action is oppressive, and creates a monopoly that
never could have been contemplated by the general assembly. . . . The
principal of equality of rights . . . is violated."[26] Ever mindful of its political

22. *Darcy v. Allein,* 9 Coke's Reports 84 (1588).
23. "Brief for Plaintiffs," 552–57.
24. 45 Ill. 90 (1867)
25. Ibid., 95.
26. Ibid., 95, 97.

flank, in a related case, the same court later refused to grant damages to a butcher whose slaughterhouse had been shut down by city officials acting pursuant to the ordinance. Since the ordinance was invalid, the court reasoned, the actions of city employees to enforce it were also invalid and could not be used as a basis for suit! The Illinois justices had managed both to side with Chicago's butchers against regulation and to shield the city's taxpayers from any liability for damages.[27]

The *Rumpff* decision was particularly apt for Campbell's purposes. It was a case in which an appellate court had managed to find legal grounds for declaring an unreasonable act invalid. It was also a decision based on notably bogus reasoning in which the justices of the Illinois Supreme Court professed their inability to discern the regulatory aspects of a measure addressing the horrific urban blight caused by Chicago's slaughterhouses and ignored the ample police power available to deal with such problems. In that sense, too, it was precisely the sort of precedent on which Campbell and his fellow counsel needed to rely.

To vindicate his emphasis on the anti-monopoly theme in both European and American history, Campbell quoted and distorted a famous statement from Thomas Jefferson's first inaugural address. The new president had called for "a wise and frugal government which shall . . . not take from the mouth of industry the bread that it has earned." In his brief, however, Campbell went on to attribute to Jefferson a denunciation of monopolies (possibly from John Stuart Mill), which, "at the expense of the interests and rights of the public," had "depressed industry and public prosperity."[28] Having assailed the evils of monopolies, in the last part of his brief, Campbell turned his attention to the Louisiana statute of 1869. Here again, however, his accuracy left something to be desired.

Campbell claimed, falsely, that in the case before the Louisiana Supreme Court, there had been "no question of the health of the city, or the location of the landings for stock."[29] He added, again falsely, that "the waters of the river Mississippi are never mentioned in any connection with . . . [efforts] to spare the waters of that muddy and nasty stream from further pollution."[30] Finally, Campbell argued, "We do not find any material inquiry

27. *Chicago v. Turner*, 80 Ill. 419 (1875).
28. "Brief for Plaintiffs," 559–60. As will be seen shortly, Campbell was guilty of other errors or mistakes of facts in his brief. It was more a product of his advocacy than his accuracy.
29. Ibid., 566. See *La. ex rel. Belden v. Fagan*, 22 La. Ann. 545, 551–52 (1870).
30. "Brief for Plaintiffs," 567; 22 La. Ann. 553–54.

regarding the water supply of New Orleans, nor how the Mississippi waters could be made pure."[31] As previous chapters have indicated, a great deal of evidence concerning the effect of slaughterhouse practices on the city's water supply had been presented to the legislature over a period of about twenty-five years. It would be one thing to confront and rebut such evidence in these three instances, but to dismiss it as nonexistent is questionable. To say the least, Campbell's presentation of the facts was a bit askew.

In his conclusion, Campbell tempered his anger with sarcasm as he offered his interpretation of Reconstruction, which "furnished a broad field of labor for a class of philanthropic adventurers, who desire to do good and grow rich by administering the affairs of the poor." Their number "is legion. State, county and city improvements; the education of the young, the care of the poor; the purification of air and water; the building of roads, canals, railroads; sewerage, drainage, streets, pavements, gas, levees, lotteries, gambling houses, slaughterhouses have severally attracted their benignant observation. . . . Give to any one of them a sufficient fulcrum of State or city bonds, or of sole and exclusive privilege, and they will undertake to move the city to a very extraordinary elevation." Here was Campbell's perception of Reconstruction. "The misfortune is that the issue of the bonds and shares in the companies, find their way in large parcels among those whose official duty it is to protect the public honor and credit." Such had happened in this case; "have we a right to complain to this Court?"[32] To ask the question was to answer it.

In the brief he submitted in support of the 1873 re-argument, Campbell repeated his arguments on monopolies and their inherent evils. In this new version, he further developed his views on the implications of the aftermath of the Civil War, and here the Fourteenth Amendment assumed greater importance in his analysis. Though a Jacksonian Democrat, Campbell the Southerner was no friend of universal suffrage. He was alarmed by the "large and growing population who came to this country without education, under the laws and constitution of the country, and who had begun to exert a perceptible influence over government and administration."[33] Even worse was the fact that emancipation and the franchise had been linked together. Since the war, "nearly four millions of emancipated slaves, without education, capacity, and generally with the habits and ignorance that belonged to a savage condition—'the heathen of the country'— . . . have become free

31. "Brief for Plaintiffs," 568.
32. Ibid., 570.
33. Campbell, "Brief upon the Re-argument," 649.

citizens."[34] The possible enfranchisement of the freedmen disturbed him even more than the alleged abuse of his butcher-clients.

Campbell gave full range to his ideas about the evils of universal suffrage. "The force of universal suffrage in politics is like that of gun powder in war, or steam in industry. In the hands of power, and where the population is incapable or servile power will not fail to control it, it is irresistible. Whatever ambition, avarice, usurpation, servility, licentiousness, or pusillanimity needs a shelter will find it under its protecting influence." To make matters worse in the South, "the flower of the virile population had perished in an inter-states war," and "a large portion of the dominant population had been disfranchised" by the Fourteenth Amendment.[35]

In the South, he lamented, the result "had been a subversion of all the relations in society and a change in social order and conditions." Elsewhere, "there had been a great accumulation of capital and credit; shameful malfeasance had become very common, and there had been an effusion over the whole land of an alert, active, aspiring, overreaching, unscrupulous class, the foulest offspring of the war, who sought money, place and influence in the worst manner and for purposes entirely mischievous. Their associations were formed not for such mutual advantage as is consistent with law, but for the execution of rapines that the laws prohibited."[36] How could order be imposed in such a state of affairs? Campbell had an answer readily available.

"The 14th Amendment embodies all that the statesmanship of the country has ordained for accommodating the Constitution and the institutions of the country, to the vast additions of territory, increase of the population, multiplication of state and territorial governments, the annual influx of aliens, and the mighty changes produced by revolutionary events, and by social, industrial, commercial development."[37] Regardless of the framers' intentions, it is apparent "by the first clause that the national principle has received an indefinite enlargement." The amendment's purpose is "to establish through the whole jurisdiction of the United States one people,

34. Ibid., 665.
35. Ibid., 666.
36. Ibid.
37. Ibid., 667. The fact that congressional debates concerning the new amendment's scope provided little vindication for Campbell's expansive reading troubled him not. "I have assumed," he intoned, "that the 14th Amendment was not adopted as an act of hostility; nor designed to sow discord; nor to answer an ephemeral or unworthy purpose." Further, "those who deprive the first section of its vitality, and demand an interpretation which would leave the State Governments in possession of their powers over persons and property unimpaired, do place a stigma upon the authors of the Article." Ibid., 668.

and that every member of the empire shall understand and appreciate the
constitutional fact that his privileges and immunities cannot be abridged by
state authority." Gathered within its protective shield can be found "the
hope of the laboring man; the confidence and trust of the merchant; the
stability, success and profit of the agriculturist; the leisure and inspiration
of the student; and the peace, the comfort, the enjoyment of the family and
home."[38]

Having described the benefits of the Fourteenth Amendment, Campbell
pointed out that it "is not confined to any race or class. It comprehends all
within the scope of its provisions. The vast number of laborers in mines,
manufactories, commerce, as well as the laborers on the plantations are defended against the unequal legislation of the States. Nor is the amendment
confined in its application to the laboring men. The mandate is universal in
its application to persons of every class and every condition of persons. . . .
Labor under the 14th Amendment is placed under the same protection. The
signs of the time very plainly show that the protection has not been extended
too soon."[39]

In the final section of his brief, Campbell returned to his case for the
butchers. Again he denounced the motives and goals of the Crescent City
proprietors and exaggerated the extent to which they were "without any
knowledge of the business or connections of the people." Again he rebutted the point that public health had any legitimate role in the enactment
of the statute. The real issue, he contended, was "centralization, complained of as destructive of local self government and as tending to the
erection of a despotism." As for the integrated and Republican legislature
that had passed such a statute, "can there be any centralization more complete or any despotism less responsible than that of a State legislature
concerning itself with dominating the avocations, pursuits and modes of
labor of the population; conferring monopolies on some, voting subsidies
to others, restraining the freedom and independence of others, and making
merchandise of the whole?"[40] The ultimate issue at hand for Campbell

38. Ibid., 667–68.
39. Ibid., 670.
40. Ibid., 675–76. "This corporation stalked and strutted through the land as a seignoral
power." Despite such rhetoric, there is merit in Franklin's comment that Campbell's goal
"seems to have been neither the defense nor the overthrow of monopolies in general, but
the undoing of the outcome of the Civil War." With no indication of any inconsistency, he
could insist on a very broad conception of the Fourteenth Amendment, even as he insisted
on a very narrow view of the rights of the ex-slave in Louisiana. The new enactment
protected butchers, as well as, according to Campbell, "the right of a New Orleans theatre
to segregate Negro operagoers, despite a [Louisiana statute] which forbade that form of

appeared to be very simple. "Freedom. Free action, free enterprise—free competition."[41]

JOHN CAMPBELL'S CO-COUNSEL, J. Q. A. Fellows, also submitted a brief for the re-argument on behalf of the butchers. Like Campbell, he did not attempt to resist the effects of the postwar amendments but rather tried to turn them against Louisiana's reconstructed legislature. He noted that after 1789, two political parties arose with opposite interpretations of the Constitution. One contended for a preponderance of power in the national government, and the other regarded the states as the primary governments in the new arrangement. According to Fellows, the "party which contended for a narrowly restricted National Government . . . so prevailed that the judiciary had, to a considerable extent, coincided with these views." Further, "a large majority in one section of the country had imbibed these doctrines and come to consider them as fundamental."[42] Here, Fellows apparently referred to the Taney Court's record on the issues of slavery and national power and conveniently ignored both the nationalist jurisprudence of Chief Justice John Marshall and the debates over slavery between 1820 and 1861. In any event, for him, it was this fundamental disagreement that had led to the Civil War. "Disguise it as we may, present it under whatever forms we choose, advance all the varied reasons the imagination can devise, this difference of opinion, of the interpretation of the Constitution, lays at the bottom of the terrible and bloody struggle which prevailed in the country from 1861 to 1865."[43]

Cleverly and cynically, Fellows related the causes of the war and the intent of the postwar amendments to the alleged rights of his clients as working men. Both the American Revolution and the Civil War had been fought to protect "the unrestricted right of every man to the fruits of his own labor, of the toil of his own hands, of the sweat of his own brow." The proponents of slavery had sought "to appropriate the labor of others . . .

---

racial discrimination." Finally, Franklin notes that even as he attacked the slaughterhouse statute, Campbell had no difficulty defending another Louisiana monopoly granted by the legislature to a New Orleans gas company. Campbell's co-counsel in this case was none other than Randell Hunt! See Franklin, "Foundations and Meaning of the Slaughterhouse Cases, Part II," 228–29.

41. "Brief upon the Re-argument," 682. Here, Campbell used a variant of the Republican party's creed prior to Lincoln's election: free soil, free labor, free men.

42. Fellows, "Brief for Plaintiffs upon Re Argument," 697.

43. Ibid., 698.

and to extend that power." Fellows unabashedly insisted that "this idea lay at the bottom of the doctrine of the sovereignty of the State over that of the Nation."[44] Neither Congress nor the executive nor the courts had succeeded in affording relief, "and the result was the war of the rebellion."[45]

Now that the Union had prevailed on the battlefield, Fellows argued, the question remained whether the concepts of freedom and equality for which the war had been fought would also prevail. This, he wrote, explained the postwar amendments, and Fellows took pains to caution that the interpretation "which this Court may give to the extent and scope of these amendments, will determine whether the statesmen who framed these fundamental provisions accomplished their purpose, whether they have attained the end they most assuredly had in view, or whether new and other amendments will be necessary, enacted, perhaps, after another long and bloody war."[46]

According to Fellows, the postwar amendments had to be read as a piece. The Thirteenth Amendment proclaimed that "slavery and involuntary servitude . . . should cease; that the rights of every man to the fruits of his own labor should be guaranteed."[47] Yet something more was needed, and this was provided by the Fourteenth Amendment. "The same spirit . . . still prevailed which, before the rebellion, had deprived many of the fruits of their industry." Thus the Fourteenth Amendment defined the citizens, and "over them, in all their rights of labor, was thrown the protecting aegis of the national government." Finally, Fellows stated, "that each citizen might have the power to aid in the vindication of his rights, the Fifteenth Amendment was also passed . . . giving to him the right of suffrage."[48]

Fellows did not ask the Court to accept his interpretation of the amendments at face value. Alone among the lawyers who submitted briefs, he explored the intentions of the amendments' framers. He cited Senator Lyman Trumbull, who had emphasized that the 1866 statute "applies to white men as well as black men. It declares that all persons in the United States shall be entitled to the same civil rights; the right to the fruit of their own labor; the right to make contracts; the right to buy and sell, and enjoy liberty and happiness." The reason for the new amendment was to ensure the constitutionality of the new Civil Rights Act. "The leading statesmen . . . determined to put the question beyond dispute . . . and beyond its

44. Ibid., 700.
45. Ibid., 701.
46. Ibid., 699.
47. Ibid., 701.
48. Ibid., 702.

repeal."[49] He quoted Charles Sumner's assertion that the Thirteenth and Fourteenth Amendments had abolished "oligarchy, aristocracy, caste, or monopoly with peculiar privileges or powers."[50]

Fellows also invoked the words of John Bingham, the primary author of the Fourteenth Amendment's first section, who had stated "that the protection given by the laws of the States shall be equal in respect to life, liberty and property to all persons."[51] He further quoted future president and then congressman James Garfield, who argued that the Fourteenth Amendment "proposes to hold over every American citizen, without regard to color, the protecting shield of law."[52] Putting all his citations together, Fellows summarized the intentions of the enactments: "in other words, that the aim, object and intent was to make sure to all men those rights of life, of liberty, and of property, of the right to labor freely, and the enjoyment of the fruit of their own industry."[53]

Although the case was argued before the high court over a two-day period in February 1873, only one of the oral arguments appears to have been recorded—that of John Campbell. There was little original material in it, as he summarized and synthesized what he had presented in the two earlier briefs. Campbell contended anew that the definition of chattel slavery had to be broadened far beyond its traditional American context. Even more important, he emphasized his interpretation of the phrase "involuntary servitude." He stated, "there are many conditions of servitude in the world in which there is no requirement upon the labor of the slave; in which the slave yielded nothing to the master."[54] One could be subject to involuntary servitude and yet not be a slave.

Therefore, "wherever a law of a State . . . makes a discrimination between classes of persons, which deprives the one class of their freedom or their property, or which makes a caste of them, to subserve the power, pride, avarice, vanity or vengeance of others, . . . this constitutes a case of involuntary servitude under the 13th Amendment to the Constitution."[55] To

---

49. Ibid., 705.

50. Ibid., 706, 714. Fellows further quoted Sumner's reference to the United States as "a country which sets its face against all monopolies as unequal and immoral." Ibid., 707.

51. Ibid., 714.

52. Ibid., 713.

53. Ibid., 715. Fellows further intimated that this section was intended to do no more than reiterate what the original provision in Article IV of the Constitution had stipulated, that "the Citizens of each State shall be entitled to all privileges and immunities of Citizens in the several States."

54. Campbell, "[Oral Argument] on behalf of Plaintiffs in Error," 739.

55. Ibid., 740–41.

drive home his point, Campbell exaggerated yet again the effect of the statute on his clients' profession. Insofar as the 1869 statute required of any butcher, "in order to prosecute his industry, that he must do it by force of law in the houses of this Company," such "is a personal servitude affecting the person." When "you tell me that I cannot use a portion of my property at my home; that I cannot protect, preserve, or control it there; that I must for the profit of a company lately incorporated, place it in their possession and under their control, under a tariff of prices fixed, not by me, but by a corporation, I say that it imposes upon me a servitude."[56]

If the Court did not accept his point concerning involuntary servitude— and Campbell was too experienced an advocate not to sense that some of the justices might find it unconvincing—the former Supreme Court justice had a second objection to the 1869 statute, which was that it nurtured a monopoly. "We contend that in this country every man has a right, and no man can be prohibited from exercising the right, of following any lawful avocation on the same terms with his neighbor; that it is free to him to choose his occupation; that it is free to him to pursue that occupation when and where he pleases, provided it does no wrong to the public at large or to any other individual." Further, "he may engage in any lawful pursuit for which he has the requisite capacity, skill, material or capital. He is entitled to the full enjoyment of the fruits of his labor or industry without coercion or constraint."[57]

Finally, Campbell turned back to the Fourteenth Amendment, with which he tried to bind his two previous points. "I contend, that this Constitution . . . has placed every citizen of the United States, within or without a State, equally under the [its] protection . . . ; that this Constitution was designed to make in respect to certain rights one people; one compact body of people, deriving their protection to those rights from the Constitution . . . itself, and that it has taken every citizen of the United States, in respect to their privileges and immunities, immediately under the protecting care of the Federal Government."[58]

Charles Fairman later wrote of Campbell's argument that it was "advocacy with a specific purpose; yet it was the production of a contemplative and resourceful mind."[59] Certainly this advocate had cast a broad net in

56. Ibid., 745, 747–48.
57. Ibid., 756–57. "If an ordinance be unreasonable, if it be unequal, if it be unjust because of its inequality, does it not fall within the exact letter of the 14th Amendment of the Constitution?" Ibid., 755.
58. Ibid., 759.
59. Fairman, *Reconstruction and Reunion*, 1346.

structuring his arguments. He had railed against monopolies and ignored the possibility that in some circumstances a prudent exercise of the police power might justify a resort to exclusive privileges. He had deliberately distorted and oversimplified facts in the record, especially as pertained to the effect of the 1869 statute. His motives may well have sprung from a desire for the South, his section, to reconstruct a return in some instances to the status quo ante. His short-range target was, of course, a specific statute. But his long-range objectives, again, were the conditions and circumstances that had enabled a Louisiana legislature to convene and enact such offensive legislation in the first place. Meanwhile, the lawyers for the state and the Crescent City Company presented their response.

IN HIS FIRST BRIEF on behalf of the company, Thomas Durant relied heavily on leading precedents set by the Court regarding the reserved powers of the states, particularly their power to regulate persons and property for the common good. He cited, for example, *Prigg v. Pennsylvania* to justify his claim that "the police power of the State extends over all subjects within the territorial limits of the State, and has never been conceded to the United States."[60] He drew on the decision in *Gibbons v. Ogden*, in which Chief Justice John Marshall had pointed out that the validity of police power laws "has never been denied," and that they "are considered as flowing from the acknowledged power of a State to protect the health of its citizens."[61] Durant found greater support from the high court in the later case of *City of New York v. Miln*. There, Justice Barbour had set forth a number of what he considered "impregnable positions."

In the first place, a state "has the same undeniable and unlimited jurisdiction over all persons and things within its territorial limits as any foreign nation, where that jurisdiction has not been surrendered or retained by the Constitution." Further, "all these powers which relate to merely municipal legislation, or which may, perhaps, more properly be called *internal police*, are not thus surrendered or restrained, and . . . consequently, in relation to these, the power of a state is complete, unqualified, and exclusive."[62] Finally, Durant referred to *Briscoe v. Bank of Commonwealth of Kentucky* for his

60. 41. U.S. 539 (1842); "Brief for Defendants," 610–11.

61. *Gibbons v. Ogden*, 22 U.S. 1 (1824). Inexplicably, Durant cited the case as *Gibson v. Ogden*. Ibid., 612.

62. *New York v. Miln*, 36 U.S. 102 (1837); Durant, "Brief of Counsel of Defendant in Error," 612–13.

insistence that "a State may grant acts of incorporation for the attainment of those objects which are essential to the interests of society. This power is incident to sovereignty."[63]

Thus Durant placed the 1869 Louisiana statute squarely within what he considered a well-established and well-defined, if not plenary, state police power. What the legislature had enacted obviously involved the "health, comfort, and prosperity of the population." Moreover, "it is manifest that to carry out successfully the policy of the state as displayed in the act . . . no rival establishments could be permitted for such would defeat the very object and design of the act." Taking issue with Campbell, he concluded: "if it can be said with truth that any man has a common law—natural— right to keep a stock landing or a slaughterhouse, so it may be equally said that every man has such a right to build and carry on a railroad, to be a banker, have a ferry, carry letters for pay." Yet "if the sovereign power judges that the interests of society will be better promoted by making such rights the exclusive privilege of a few, or of the State itself, this private right must yield to the public good."[64] Only in the final paragraph of his brief did Durant dismiss Campbell's "erroneous impression that [his clients] are prohibited by the act . . . from carrying on the trade of butchers." "This is not so, their trade is left free. All they are required to do is to have their animals slaughtered at the place provided by the State, and they, the butchers, may slaughter their animals there themselves."[65] Campbell's argument on this point had been made with great vigor, and although it was also one of his weakest, it deserved much more attention than a summary dismissal.

Charles Fairman describes Durant's brief in toto as "undistinguished."[66] It certainly lacked the depth and vigor demonstrated by his opponents, and he had failed to develop some of his strongest positions. Both Durant and his co-counsel, Charles Allen, went much further and reflected a more vigorous tone in the separate briefs they submitted for the re-argument. In the short run, at least, they would be persuasive.

Durant began his second brief with a reference to the title of the 1869 statute, "to protect the health of the city on New Orleans," as well as to "locate the stock landings and slaughter-houses." These objects, he insisted,

63. 36 U.S. 257 (1837); "Brief of Defendant in Error," 613.
64. "Brief of Defendant in Error," 613–14. Durant appears to have weakened his point by citing exactly those professions that were—theoretically, at least—open to all, unlike those of an undertaker, physician, or even attorney, which historically had required some sort of selectivity by the legal order.
65. Ibid., 614.
66. Fairman, *Reconstruction and Reunion*, 1346.

"are all of the highest importance to the welfare of the people of the State; they are, beyond all possibility of dispute, matters entirely within State control . . . such, in short, as are necessary to the very existence of the State." Further, "none of these objects have been surrendered to the United States by the Federal Constitution, and so far as the purposes aimed at are concerned, the Federal judiciary has no more authority to interfere with them than with similar measures adopted in any European State."[67] What of the Fourteenth Amendment, and Campbell's insistence that the statute interfered with the right to labor in the vocation of a butcher? Durant confronted the second issue first. He readily conceded that the plaintiffs were indeed butchers, livestock landing owners, or slaughterhouse keepers, working "in their vocations" after the bill was enacted, just as they had been before it was introduced.

He defined a butcher as one who either "slaughter[s] animals for food" or "sell[s] the flesh of the slaughtered animals." In the latter sense, the statute "does not interfere with the right . . . to labor in their vocation at all, nor does it seek in any way to regulate the exercise of that right." In truth, "every butcher can labor in his vocation of selling meat since the act just as he could before its adoption." As to those who slaughter, "the act does not deny to any citizen or person the right, privilege, or title to labor in such a vocation." Nor was it intended to do so. The statute simply "provides only for regulating the mode in which such vocation shall be exercised." Pointing to the requirements that the animals be inspected prior to slaughtering, Durant added that once approved by this official, the owner of the animal may slaughter "either with his own hands, or by those of his servants." Further, the statute "does not compel the owner of the animal to employ any State agent or corporation servant to slaughter. . . . All the act does is to say where the animal must be slaughtered."[68]

In a real sense, it was the proprietors of the Crescent City Company, more than the butchers, who faced compulsion. If the butchers were compelled to bring their animals to a central point for inspection and ultimate slaughter, the proprietors were compelled to provide at their expense "a grand slaughterhouse of sufficient capacity to accommodate all butchers." Further, the statute imposed a substantial penalty on them if they refused to allow certified animals to be slaughtered there. In short, Durant argued, "every butcher may slaughter his own cattle, and his right to labor in his vocation is not taken away."[69]

67. Durant, "Brief of Counsel . . . of Defendants in Error on Re-argument," 719.
68. Ibid., 720–21.
69. Ibid., 721.

Durant also conceded that the statute did indeed give an exclusive privilege to a chosen set of proprietors. Yet he insisted that English law had long provided for monopolies intended "for the public benefit." Indeed, "there can be nothing better known to the court that the legislative power does constantly, and with undoubted right, grant exclusive privilege to corporations, by which the latter make a profit certainly, but which are intended for the public benefit." The issue of whether such action served the public interest "is not a judiciary question at all, but purely political."[70]

What, then, of the Fourteenth Amendment? The lawyer for the Crescent City Company linked passage of the Civil Rights Act in April 1866 with the submission of the Fourteenth Amendment to the states a few months later. These two acts "explain one another," and they "both have the same object in view." The constitutional amendment "was designed to do nothing more than embody what the [earlier] law had enacted." It was to ensure that the states could not evade or ignore the civil rights statute.[71] Here, Durant took issue not only with Campbell but also with Justice Bradley, who had accepted his argument, employing language "which confers upon this court a jurisdiction over every case there can be imagined in every court of every State in the Union."[72] Since Durant and Campbell obviously disagreed about the "true meaning" of the amendment, Durant suggested consideration of "the reason and spirit of it," or "the occasion and necessity which moved the legislature to enact it."[73]

Here, he insisted, there could be neither doubt nor debate on why the new amendment had been needed. Durant quoted from the now discredited Supreme Court decision in *Dred Scott*, written by Chief Justice Roger Taney and concurred in by then Associate Justice John Campbell. Taney had emphasized the fact that persons of African descent "had no rights which the white man was bound to respect." Hence, "to confer upon the disinherited people the rights, privileges, and immunities they never had possessed [and to place these beyond state interference] was the sole purpose of, as it was the sole necessity for, amending the Constitution." The basic issue was "the constitutional status of the people of African descent, and if there had been no such people in the country, no such amendment would have been pro-

70. Ibid., 722.
71. Ibid., 723–24. "The act and the amendment have no other meaning than to place the blacks on a footing of political and civil equality with the whites." Durant cited Thomas Cooley's famous treatise on constitutional limitations in support of this contention.
72. Ibid., 725.
73. Ibid.

posed. It was adopted for them." Moreover, without any citation, Durant stated that "contemporaneous discussions and debates at the time . . . show that no other object was in view, nor can it be made to embrace any other without sacrificing its spirit."[74]

The all-embracing language of the amendment, he added, was understandable. "When it says that *all* persons born or naturalized in the United States are citizens . . . it can mean by [*all*] only the people of African descent, because all other people were already citizens of the United States." Durant even pointed to several earlier constitutional references to "such persons" or "no person" or "three fifths of all other persons" and insisted that, as used, the term "persons" is "a form of expression usual in the language of the Constitution, where people of African descent are always spoken of in similar terms."[75]

Clearly, the attorney for the company was as adept as Campbell in letting his conclusions gallop far ahead of his premises. Durant emphasized that the privileges and immunities clause of the new amendment "can have no meaning except as to persons of African descent, for in no State were any *citizens* ever subjected to any of the injuries, outrages, and disabilities denounced by the amendment."[76]

Turning back to the 1869 statute, Durant asked, "was it ever held before 1867 that the 'privileges and immunities' of citizens were abridged, or their lives, liberty, or property subject to deprivation . . . by an act to promote the public health of a city, or by an act designating the locality in which a particular pursuit should alone be carried on or by, or which gave a chartered company exclusive privileges? For if so, then the Louisiana act is unconstitutional; but if not, this court can not interfere."[77] He cited again the earlier police power decisions mentioned in his first brief.

Durant also took note of the well-established judicial doctrine that legis-

74. Ibid., 726–27.

75. Ibid., 728.

76. Ibid.; Durant's emphasis. As Michael Curtis has shown, prior to the Fourteenth Amendment, there were some instances of state denial of equal protection not to slaves but to white citizens caught up in disputes involving slavery and abolition. Further, it is beyond debate that a few members of Congress had spoken of the proposed amendment in the broad terms later claimed for it by Campbell. Whether these few individuals echoed the general consensus of their colleagues, however, probably cannot be definitively ascertained, as was noted in chapter 1. See Curtis, *No State Shall Abridge;* also Michael K. Curtis, "Resurrecting the Privileges or Immunities Clause and Revising the Slaughterhouse Cases without Exhuming Lochner: Individual Rights and the Fourteenth Amendment," *Boston College Law Review* 38 (1966): 1–106.

77. Durant, "Brief on Re-argument," 728–29.

lative motive was not a proper subject for judicial inquiry, a position that Chief Justice John Marshall had articulated more than half a century before in *Fletcher v. Peck.*[78] Hence, "it is a matter beyond investigation here" that the 1869 statute "was really adopted in good faith by the Louisiana legislature to enforce its inspection laws, and to promote the health of its capital city. . . . All these are matters beyond controversy." The only possible ground for federal intervention, then, was the new Fourteenth Amendment. If this enactment "forbids such legislation, it annuls all that is past and prohibits all such in [the] future."[79]

Indulging in an early example of "slippery slope" analysis, counsel for the Crescent City Company listed all those legislative grants that would henceforth be barred: "canal charters, turnpike charters, bridge charters, railroad charters, gaslight company charters." Further, he cited regulatory measures for the manufacturing and storage of "nitro-glycerine, gunpowder, petroleum, and other dangerous substances . . . laws imposing licenses and taxes on trades, occupations and professions; laws forbidding labor on the first day of the week." All these and more must be invalid if the amendment "means to constitute individual rights absolutely superior to the public welfare of the States in matters not political." But it was not designed to bring about such a result.[80]

On the contrary, "it is most manifest [that] the design of the amendment was limited to the investiture of blacks with all the rights and immunities of whites, whatever these may be, and to protect them in their lives, liberties and properties just as whites are protected. That is all that was and is necessary." To extend the amendment, as proposed by Campbell, "would break down the whole system of confederated State government, centralize the beautiful and harmonious system we enjoy into a consolidated and unlimited government, and render the Constitution of the United States, now the object of our love and veneration, as odious and insupportable as its enemies would wish to make it."[81]

In addition to Durant's brief, the defendants filed a similar document prepared by co-counsel Charles Allen, who had served as the attorney general of Massachusetts from 1867 to 1872. Later, Allen would sit on the Massachusetts Supreme Judicial Court.[82] His brief both clarified and expanded

78. 10 U.S. 87 (1810).
79. Durant, "Brief on Re-argument," 731.
80. Ibid.
81. Ibid., 732.
82. Fairman, *Reconstruction and Reunion*, 1346.

some of Durant's positions. Taken together, the two arguments offered a clear alternative to Campbell's "expansive mode of thought."[83]

Allen reiterated the applicability of police power precedents to the Louisiana statute and affirmed anew the equally well established practices of awarding exclusive franchises. Moreover, he pointed to the fact that in such instances, these enactments invariably resulted in unequal restrictions on some segments of the citizenry.[84] By 1873, "the validity of such legislation, under similar constitutional provisions, is recognized in the general treatises, and is hardly open to question." Although there is no doubt that the 1869 statute did indeed confer an exclusive franchise on the Crescent City Company, "it was upon the consideration of moneys to be expended and duties to be performed by the corporation for the public benefit."[85] This point was important for Allen, because it undercut the plaintiffs' claim of a monopoly, a foundation on which much of Campbell's brief had been constructed.

It is apparent, he claimed, that "these sums to be expended, and these duties to be performed, furnished a substantial consideration for the granting of the charter."[86] They were, in other words, compulsory obligations imposed on the company by the legislature. This fact distinguished this corporation from a monopoly. According to Allen, a monopoly "is an exclusive privilege, *granted without consideration.*" But the charter granted to the Crescent City Company "was for a consideration." To be sure, "certain persons cannot carry on the business of butchering as advantageously to themselves as they did before." But "other persons can carry on the business more advantageously to themselves than they did before."[87]

Allen emphasized how much easier it now was to become a butcher in New Orleans. "There is no longer any necessity of a butcher providing a slaughterhouse for himself. Any man with capital or credit enough to procure the necessary animals may now be a butcher." Echoing Durant, Allen claimed that far from creating a monopoly, the 1869 statute "makes it easier to be a butcher than it was before." Because it failed the legal test of conferring exclusive privileges without consideration, the Louisiana statute did not fit within the "legal test of a monopoly."[88]

Thus, the only question at issue was whether the Fourteenth Amend-

83. Ibid.
84. "Brief of Charles Allen, Esq.," 590–94.
85. Ibid., 595.
86. Ibid., 596.
87. Ibid., 596–97; emphasis in original.
88. Ibid., 597.

ment "involves the surrender, on the part of all the States, to the general Government, of all rights of legislation of this character." Again, Allen detailed all the existing classes of regulatory legislation that would be invalidated if the answer was positive. He insisted that "it was certainly never intended or contemplated that this amendment should receive such a construction." Congress did not intend "to deprive the legislatures and State courts [of the power] to regulate and settle their internal affairs." It will, "no doubt, be conceded that the [state] legislatures . . . may still regulate all these matters, and that the amendment . . . was not designed to cover them, and does not cover them."[89]

Will this Court, inquired Allen, "sit in judgement to determine whether, as an act of municipal legislation, [the Louisiana statute] is reasonable in all its provisions?" How, he added, shall the Court "judicially know the exigency which will require the granting of such a charter . . . ? How shall the court inform itself judicially of the facts," as may be ascertained through the legislative process?[90] To ask such a question, he implied, was to answer it.

All that remained was for Allen to confront the uncomfortable issue of wording, the broad language employed in the Fourteenth Amendment. Here, he reminded the Court that "the object to be accomplished by the amendment, and the mischief designed to be remedied or guarded against, may also be considered." The amendment must be seen in relation "to the state of things in which it had its origin." Reliance on the actual wording of the enactment outside of such a context would be a mistake. "The letter killeth."[91] Further, Allen cited a number of examples in which actual judicial interpretation departed from "a literal construction of constitutional provisions."

He pointed, for example, to the limiting of ex post facto laws only to crimes, although there is no such limitation in the Constitution. He noted, also, that the constitutional right of a trial by jury had been held not to apply in admiralty proceedings, even though this limitation does not appear in the Constitution. Finally, he observed that the phrase "privileges and immunities of citizens" was already part of this document, and that a number of courts had made it clear that such privileges were those "which are funda-

89. Ibid., 598, 599, 600. "Have Congress and the whole nation been deceived, misled, mistaken? Have they done that which they did not intend to do?" Ibid., 599.

90. Ibid., 600. Allen insisted that the issue of reasonableness, especially as it concerned the police power, was not a matter for the courts. But by 1890, the year of Miller's death, this is exactly what the Court would begin to decide. In terms of judicial philosophy, 1890 was far away from 1873.

91. Ibid., 601–2.

mental." These included travel to and from states, taking up residence in one state from another, or the right of free entrance and exit.[92]

In fact, Allen concluded, what Campbell had sought was to clothe an old term, "privileges and immunities," in a raiment "different from that put upon similar language by this court heretofore; different from that put by State courts upon provisions as comprehensive, and different from that put upon this amendment by Congress or by the people of the nation." There was neither reason nor justification for such a step. "The design in establishing this amendment . . . was simple and well known. It was to assure to all citizens and persons the same rights enjoyed by white citizens and persons. Every citizen should enjoy the same rights as white citizens. Every person should enjoy the same protection of the laws as white persons."[93]

Among them, Campbell, Durant, Fellows, and Allen had placed the momentous issues in the *Slaughterhouse Cases* in every conceivable context before the Supreme Court. Depending on which brief one found most convincing, these attorneys had given that tribunal a clear choice. They might move in the direction discussed by Campbell and later endorsed by Bradley, accepting the proposal that the language in the amendment was universal in its scope and that its presence in the Constitution indicated a new role for the federal government and, of course, the Court. Or they could follow Durant and Allen, agreeing that context was more important than content, that what had changed were the now legitimate expectations of the former slaves, for whom the amendment was clearly intended. Whatever route they took, the results promised to be important and controversial. The arguments were concluded early in February 1873. For a little more than two months, the lawyers and their clients waited. On April 14, the high court handed down its decision, and the Fourteenth Amendment received its first interpretation from the justices. More than a century later, reverberations from this decision continue to affect constitutional law.

92. Ibid., 603. Did the argument of white butchers over where they might slaughter beef within a crowded municipality rise to the level of a "fundamental privilege or immunity"? Although he never stated this query in his brief, one suspects that Allen had no doubt about the answer.
93. Ibid., 603–4.

9

Decision and Dissents

On April 14, 1873, the country observed the eighth anniversary of Lincoln's assassination, President Ulysses Grant had just begun his second term, and in a "practically empty" courtroom, Justice Samuel F. Miller delivered the decision of the Court in the *Slaughterhouse Cases*.[1] Although not the senior justice (that title was held by Justice Clifford), Miller was the logical jurist to speak for the majority. In his eleven years on the bench, he had already served as spokesman of choice in a number of cases involving constitutional issues. He was also at home with issues of public health. In his earlier career as a physician, he had written on the danger of cholera from polluted water. By the time of his appointment to the Court, he had resided for a decade in Keokuk, Iowa, a town on the Mississippi River that had once been the sixth busiest pork-packing center in the nation. Justice Miller was all too familiar with the noxious nature of the slaughtering industry, and he had witnessed a successful regulatory effort in Keokuk.[2]

After a brief summary of the 1869 statute, Miller took note of Campbell's argument that the act had created a monopoly and conferred "odious and exclusive privileges upon a small number of persons at the expense of the great body of the community of New Orleans." Even worse, however, the law deprived "the whole of the butchers of the city of the right to exercise their trade, the business to which they have been trained and on which they depend for the support of themselves and their families." Indeed, Campbell contended that the whole community was affected because "the unrestricted exercise of . . . butchering is necessary to the daily subsistence of the [city] population."[3] Having thus condensed several pages of Campbell's prose into a short paragraph, Miller dismissed his entire thesis in one sentence: "But a critical examination of the act hardly justifies these assertions."[4]

1. Marke, *Vignettes of Legal History*, 177.
2. Ross, "Justice Miller's Reconstruction," 669.
3. *Slaughterhouse Cases*, 83 U.S. (16 Wall.) 36, 60 (1873).
4. Ibid.

A former physician, Samuel F. Miller wrote the land-
mark decision for the Court in the *Slaughterhouse
Cases*. (Office of the Curator, Supreme Court of the
United States, #1862.21.)

No one denied that the statute granted exclusive privileges to a specified
group for twenty-five years. Further, Miller was prepared to discuss
"whether those privileges" had been granted "at the expense of the community in the sense of a curtailment of any of their fundamental rights, or even
in the sense of doing them an injury." But "it is not true," he held, "that it
deprives the butchers of their right to exercise their trade or imposes upon
them any restrictions incompatible with its successful pursuit, [or their ability to furnish] the people of the city with the necessary daily supply of
animal food."[5] Thus, early in his opinion, Miller sustained a key point that
had been asserted in support of the act throughout the litigation and carefully rehearsed by Durant and Allen in their briefs: the act determined the

5. Ibid.

places where stock was to be landed and slaughtered, but it did not prevent anyone from plying the trade of a butcher.

"That the landing of live-stock in large droves, from steamboats on the bank of the river, and from railroad trains, should, for the safety and comfort of the people and the care of the animals, be limited to proper places, and those not numerous, it needs no argument to prove."[6] Similarly, the reliance on a single company to implement the statute's regulatory scheme should not be a matter of concern. "Nor can it be injurious to the general community that while the duty of making ample preparation" for slaughtering within this proper place "is imposed upon a few men, or a corporation, they should, to enable them to do it successfully, have the exclusive right of providing such landing places, and receiving a fair compensation for the service." But Miller recognized that it was the company's exclusive privilege to operate a slaughterhouse (which affected individual butchers), rather than its control of the stock landing and stockyards (which affected mainly livestock dealers), that lay at the heart of the charges of "gross injustice to the public, and invasion of private right."[7]

Miller emphasized that none could deny "the right and the duty of the legislative body . . . to prescribe and determine the localities of where the business of slaughtering for a great city may be conducted." In order to meet such an obligation, "it is indispensable that all persons who slaughter animals for food shall do it in those places *and nowhere else*." All the Louisiana statute did, according to Miller, was to define "these localities and [forbid] slaughtering in any other."[8] Having established this important distinction, he returned to Campbell's main argument.

The 1869 enactment "does not, contrary to [Campbell] prevent the butcher from doing his own slaughtering." In point of fact, "the Slaughterhouse Company is required, under a heavy penalty, to permit any person who wishes to do so, to slaughter in their houses." Further, it is "bound to make ample provision for the convenience of all the slaughtering for the entire city." Thus, the butcher "is still permitted to slaughter, to prepare, and to sell his own meats; but he is required to slaughter at a specified place and to pay a reasonable compensation for the use of the accommodations furnished him at that place." Under such conditions, it was "difficult" for Miller to see how Campbell could insist that his clients "are deprived of the

6. Ibid., 61. As will be seen, however, the dissenting justices did not deny the validity of confining slaughtering to a specific and limited area.

7. Ibid.

8. Ibid.; emphasis in original.

right to labor in their occupation, or the people of their daily service in preparing food, or how this statute, with the duties and guards imposed upon the company, can be said to destroy the business of the butcher" or even "seriously interfere with its pursuit."[9] Having located a legitimate legislative prerogative, Miller had no difficulty identifying its source.

It was, of course, the police power. This power "must be from its very nature, incapable of any very exact definition or limitation." But Miller emphasized that "the regulation of the place and manner of conducting the slaughtering of animals, and the business of butchering within a city . . . are among the most necessary and frequent exercises of this power." In affirming its special relevance for these cases, Miller cited authorities already set forth by Durant and Allen. He invoked the names of famous jurists such as Lemuel Shaw, John Marshall, and James Kent, all of whom had applied or endorsed the police power. The 1869 statute was "aptly framed to remove from the more densely populated parts of the city, the noxious slaughterhouses, and large and offensive collections of animals necessarily incident to the slaughtering business of a large city, and to locate them where the convenience, health, and comfort of the people require" it. And "it must be conceded that the means adopted by the act for this purposes are appropriate, stringent, and effectual."[10]

What if the legislature had placed on the New Orleans municipality "precisely the same duties, accompanied by the same privileges, which it has on the corporation which it created?" The effect on both the public and butchers "would have been the same as it is now." Indeed, "whenever a legislature has the right to accomplish a certain result, and that result is best attained by means of a corporation, [the right of the legislature to create the corporation] and to endow it with the powers necessary to effect the desired and lawful purpose, seems hardly to admit of debate."[11] Thus, unless (as Campbell insisted) the "exclusive privilege" granted to the company "is beyond the power of the legislature . . . there can be no just exception to the validity of the statute. And in this respect we are not able to see that these privileges are especially odious or objectionable. The duty imposed as a consideration for the privilege is well defined, and its enforcement well guarded."[12]

9. Ibid., 61–62.
10. Ibid., 62, 63, 64.
11. Ibid., 64. Here, Miller cited Chief Justice Marshall's reasoning in *McCulloch v. Maryland*.
12. Ibid., 65.

Justice Miller then turned to the question of whether the legislature could ever validly grant exclusive privileges to a citizen or corporation. Although he paid tribute to Campbell's research concerning monopolies and to his eloquence in denouncing them, Miller rejected his argument out of hand.[13] "We think it may be safely affirmed that . . . the legislative bodies of this country have from time immemorial to the present day, continued to grant to persons and corporations exclusive privileges." He conceded that in such instances, the same privileges are "denied to other citizens," and indeed, they "come within any just definition of the word monopoly, as much as those now under consideration." Nevertheless, "the power to do this has never been questioned or denied. Nor can it be truthfully denied that some of the most useful and beneficial enterprises set on foot for the general good, have been made successful by means of these exclusive rights, and could only have [gained] success in that way."[14]

HERE MILLER MIGHT HAVE ENDED his opinion. He had made the case for the Slaughterhouse Act as a valid, even routine exercise of the state's police power by reference to well-established state and federal precedents. The only remaining question was whether the act violated provisions of the Fourteenth Amendment, and this could have been decided without even entering into an exegesis of its provisions. It would have been sufficient to say simply that whatever the amendment meant, it did not mean to prevent the state from passing a sanitary measure like this one. Indeed, counsel for the company had argued strenuously that such a contrary ruling would be at odds with a wide range of licensing and other regulatory measures.

Some sixty years later, in *Ashwander v. Tennessee Valley Authority,* Justice Louis Brandeis would pen a classic dictum in which he cataloged a number of canons ordinarily observed by the Court as a means of limiting its constitutional pronouncements to cases in which they are unavoidable.[15] But these canons were less well recognized in 1873, as was the adage that

13. "The eminent and learned counsel who has twice argued . . . this question has displayed a research into the history of monopolies in England, and the European continent, only equalled by the eloquence with which they are denounced." Ibid.

14. Ibid., 66

15. 297 U.S. 288 (1936). Three of Brandeis's guidelines are of interest here. The Court "will not anticipate a question of constitutional law." The Court "will not pass upon a constitutional question . . . if there is also present some other ground upon which the case may be disposed of." The Court "will first ascertain whether a construction of the statute is fairly possible by which the [constitutional] question can be avoided." Ibid., 346–48.

"hard cases make bad law."[16] Besides, the scope of the case had already been framed by the briefs of counsel. All of them had considered and interpreted the Reconstruction amendments. And Miller was well aware that four of his brethren were prepared to consider and, to a large extent, accept Campbell's constitutional arguments. Moreover, the dissenting justices were readying opinions that would rely heavily on the amendments. These positions could not easily be ignored. Finally, as was noted in chapter 7, by 1873, the Supreme Court had regained a stronger sense of its unique place in the federal government and had demonstrated anew its willingness to address controversial issues of constitutional law. Thus, even though the case may not have been an appropriate context in which to confront Campbell's arguments, one can understand why Miller felt it essential to consider them.

As the Court undertook to interpret the Thirteenth and Fourteenth Amendments for the first time, Miller confessed to an awareness of "the great responsibility which this duty devolves upon us. No questions so far reaching . . . in their consequences . . . and so important in their bearing upon the relations of the United States, and of the several States to each other and to the citizens of the States and of the United States, have been before this court during the official life of any of its present members." Further, he emphasized the lengthy judicial examination these questions had received. "We have given every opportunity for a full hearing at the bar; we have discussed it freely and compared views among ourselves; we have taken ample time for careful consideration, and now we propose to announce the judgments we have formed in the construction of those articles, so far as we have found them necessary to the decision of these cases before us, and beyond that we have neither the inclination nor the right to go."[17]

Miller considered it imperative to begin his analysis with a consideration of the historical events leading up to adoption of the three Reconstruction amendments. "Fortunately, that history is fresh within the memory of us all, and its leading features as they bear upon the matter before us, free from doubt." Issues related either to the curtailment of slavery or to its security

16. See the dissent of Justice Holmes in *Northern Securities Co. v. United States*, 193 U.S. 197 (1904).

17. Miller's opinion, 83 U.S. 67. As the last part of this sentence reveals, Miller made it clear that his holding would be a narrow one. He had already upheld the 1869 statute by a broad reading of the police power. Here, he indicated that he would consider the amendments in as narrow a context as possible, possibly reflecting his conclusion that *this* case might not be the most appropriate vehicle for an original judicial exegesis of the enactments. Yet Miller felt compelled to offer such an exegesis and, as will be seen, with mixed results.

and perpetuation had culminated in an effort by the slave states to leave the Union. "This constituted the war of the rebellion, and whatever auxiliary causes may have contributed to bring about this war, undoubtedly the over-shadowing and efficient cause was African slavery."[18] With the reestablishment of federal authority, it was clear that the "great act of emancipation" could not rest on Lincoln's proclamation or on "the actual results of the contest . . . both of which might have been questioned in after times." Hence, the Thirteenth Amendment was enacted. African slavery had caused the war, and it was the underlying cause of the new enactment.[19]

Here, Miller dismissed Campbell's contention that the Slaughterhouse Act imposed on the butchers a "servitude" in violation of the Thirteenth Amendment. To put aside the obvious purpose of the amendment, Miller wrote, and "with a microscopic search endeavor to find in it a reference to servitudes, which may have been attached to property in certain localities requires an effort, to say the least of it." Miller insisted that all involved in the amendment had understood that, in the American context, involuntary servitude was virtually identical to African slavery. He cited the recent liberation of a Maryland slave by Chief Justice Chase under a writ of habeas corpus as decisive of the issue.[20]

Just as the quest for freedom linked American slaves to the Thirteenth Amendment, so their treatment in freedom's aftermath linked them to the Fourteenth Amendment. Miller described in some detail conditions under the black codes for the ex-slaves. Without further protection from federal authorities, the "condition of the slave race" would "be almost as bad as it was before." By 1866, "something more was necessary in the way of consti-

18. Ibid., 68.
19. Ibid.
20. "The word servitude is of larger meaning than slavery, as the latter is popularly understood in this country, and the obvious purpose was to forbid all shades and conditions of African slavery." Ibid., 69, citing *In Re Turner*, 1 Abb. (U.S.) 84 (1867). The *Turner* case concerned the efforts of a former slave to gain relief from a Maryland statute establishing stringent conditions for black apprentices. See Harold M. Hyman, *The Reconstruction Justice of Salmon P. Chase* (Lawrence: University Press of Kansas, 1997). Miller took the position that in his decision, Chase had implied that slavery and involuntary servitude for blacks in America were one and the same. Hyman points out that Chase may well have had a much broader conception of the Thirteenth Amendment in mind. Nevertheless, Miller simply cited *Turner*, adding that "it is all we deem necessary to say on the application of [the Thirteenth Amendment] to the statute of Louisiana, now under consideration." One can only ponder what the outcome of the *Slaughterhouse Cases* might have been if some of Campbell's clients had been black. Chase, it might be noted, silently concurred with Field's dissent in *Slaughterhouse*.

tutional protection to the unfortunate race who had suffered so much." Not only was the Fourteenth Amendment enacted, but congressional leaders "declined to treat as restored to their full participation in the government . . . the States which had been in insurrection, until they ratified that article by a formal vote of their legislative bodies."[21]

Finally, Miller discussed the Fifteenth Amendment, which he also linked solely to the plight of the former slaves. In the Southern states, the ex-slaves were "denied the right of suffrage. The laws were administered by the white man alone. It was urged that a race of men distinctively marked as was the Negro, living in the midst of another and dominant race, could never be fully secured in their person and their property without the right of suffrage." With the enactment of the Fifteenth Amendment, "the Negro having, by the 14th Amendment, been declared to be a citizen of the United States, is thus made a voter in every State of the Union." Miller thus found common chains of causation for all three Reconstruction amendments, and the importance of this fact became clear in the next paragraph of his opinion:

> We repeat, then, in the light of this recapitulation of events, almost too recent to be called history, but which are familiar to us all; and on the most casual examination of the language of these amendments, no one can fail to be impressed with the one pervading purpose found in them all, lying at the foundation of each, and without which none of them would have been even suggested; we mean the freedom of the slave race, the security and firm establishment of that freedom, and the protection of the newly-made freeman and citizen from the oppressions of those who had formerly exercised unlimited dominion over him.[22]

Miller was careful to explicitly reject the idea that only the ex-slave was entitled to the protection of the amendment. Indeed, "if other rights are assailed by the States which properly and necessarily fall within the protection of these articles, that protection will apply, though the party interested may not be of African descent." Here, Miller is at pains to accept the argument of Durant and Allen that to discern the meaning of the amendment, one had to look beyond its words to the purpose that had inspired it. "What we do say, and what we wish to be understood is, that in any fair and just construction of any section or phrase of these amendments, it is necessary to look to the purpose which we have said was the pervading spirit of them all, the evil which they were designed to remedy."[23]

21. Miller, 83 U.S. 70–71.
22. Ibid., 71.
23. Ibid., 72.

Against this background, Justice Miller launched into the Court's first exegesis of the Fourteenth Amendment, beginning with the definition of citizenship found in Section 1. He noted that "no such definition was previously found in the Constitution" and added, "nor had any attempt been made to define it by act of Congress."[24] The absence of a citizenship clause in the original Constitution had made it possible for the Court to decide in the *Dred Scott* case that a Negro could not become a citizen either of the United States or of a state. This famous (or infamous) decision had never been overruled, and as matters then stood, "all the Negro race who had recently been made freemen, were still, not only not citizens, but were incapable of becoming so by anything short of an amendment to the Constitution." It made good sense, then, for Congress to propose an amendment that would "establish a clear and comprehensive definition of citizenship" both in the United States and in the states.[25] And, Miller added, unlike a statute, the amendment (in theory, at least) would be subject to neither the vagaries of Congress nor the capricious whims of the courts.

The "main purpose" of Section 1, then, according to Miller "was to establish the citizenship of the Negro."[26] This was accomplished by providing that "all persons born or naturalized in the United States and subject to the jurisdiction thereof are citizens of the United States and of the state wherein they reside."[27] To Miller, the wording of the amendment was all-important. In this section, he saw a "distinction between citizenship of the United States and citizenship of a state . . . clearly recognized and established." It is obvious, he wrote, "that there is a citizenship of the United States and a citizenship of a State, which are distinct from each other, and which depend upon different characteristics or circumstances in the individual."[28]

This distinction between citizenship in the United States and citizenship

24. Ibid. This was not accurate. In fact, in the Civil Rights Act of 1866, which was enacted before the Fourteenth Amendment was submitted to the states for ratification, Congress had provided a very similar definition of federal citizenship. "All persons born in the United States, and not subject to any foreign power, excluding Indians not taxed, are hereby declared to be citizens of the United States." *Statutes of the United States*, 39th Cong., 1st sess. (1866), chap. 31, 27–28.
25. Miller, 83 U.S. 72–73.
26. Ibid., 73.
27. Ibid., citing U.S. Const., Amend. 14, sec. 1.
28. Ibid., 73, 74. "He must reside within the State to make him a citizen of it, but it is only necessary that he should be born or naturalized in the United States to be a citizen of the Union."

in a state was a pivotal element in Miller's analysis, because in its next section, the amendment forbids the states to make or enforce "any law which shall abridge the privileges and immunities *of citizens of the United States.*" From this, Miller inferred that the amendment intended to protect only such privileges and immunities possessed by a person in his or her capacity as a citizen of the United States. "It is a little remarkable," wrote Miller, that "if this clause was intended as a protection to the citizen of a State against the legislative power of his own State, that the word[s] 'citizen of the State' should be left out. . . . It is too clear for argument that the change in phraseology was adopted understandingly and with a purpose."[29]

Based on this line of reasoning, Miller concluded for the majority that the amendment applies to only those federal privileges and immunities "which are placed by this clause under the protection of the Federal Constitution and that the latter [meaning privileges and immunities protected by the state constitutions], whatever they may be, are not intended to have any additional protection by this paragraph of the amendment."[30] The privileges and immunities of a state citizen, Miller insisted, "must rest for their security and protection where they have heretofore rested," within the hands of the state.[31] The question, then, was whether the rights being asserted by Campbell on behalf of his butcher-clients were among the privileges and immunities of citizens of the United States. It was not difficult for Miller to conclude that whatever the privileges and immunities of U.S. citizens may be, the rights claimed by the butchers were not among them.

Modern scholars have argued that, ironically, this interpretation of the privileges and immunities clause would later deprive the freedmen of any of its protections—in spite of Miller's earlier insistence that a concern for their freedom had pervaded all the Reconstruction amendments. As Michael Kent Curtis has noted, along with the butchers, the ex-slaves were being left to the "tender mercies" of the state.[32] But there is no evidence to support the claim that such was Miller's intention. He did not attempt an exhaustive definition of "the privileges and immunities of citizens of the United States."

29. Ibid., 74; emphasis added. Here, Miller essentially argued that if *A* refers to one and two, but *B* specifies only one, therefore two is assumed to be excluded from *B*'s frame of reference. *A* sets forth dual citizenship of state and nation, but *B* refers only to privileges and immunities of American citizenship. Therefore, asserted Miller, there must be separate categories of privileges and immunities—some protected only by the federal government under the new amendment, and others protected as they always had been *only* by the states.

30. Ibid.

31. Ibid., 75.

32. Curtis, "Resurrecting the Privileges or Immunities Clause," 77.

He simply assumed that whatever they were, they did not encompass the rights being asserted by the New Orleans butchers. Specifically, he ventured no opinion on the implications for the freed slaves. No such claim was before the Court. He also may have assumed that a future case would permit the Court to explore exactly what the clause meant. Yet, in the remaining seventeen years of Miller's tenure, the justices apparently never reconsidered Miller's doctrines. That the Court failed to do so reflects less on Miller's 1873 holding and more on developments in American law after the end of Reconstruction. Miller is not exempt from criticism, however, because, by his silence, he facilitated subsequent developments.

Miller was able to liken the rights of the New Orleans butchers with the privileges and immunities of state citizens by alluding to previous judicial discussions of the guarantees provided by Article IV of the Constitution. In *Corfield v. Coryell*, decided in 1823 by a circuit court, for example, Justice Bushrod Washington identified "the privileges and immunities of citizens of the several states" as those "which are fundamental; which belong of right to the citizens of all free governments, and which have at all times been enjoyed by citizens of the several states . . . from the time of their becoming free, independent, and sovereign."[33] The Supreme Court itself had previously acknowledged that these privileges and immunities "embraced nearly every civil right for the establishment and protection of which organized government is instituted."[34] Miller added that "they have always been held to be the class of rights which the State governments were created to establish and secure."[35] All this sounded very much like the kind of rights Campbell had pleaded for so passionately on behalf of his clients from the beginning of the litigation.

Miller pressed on with his argument. Before the adoption of the new amendments, neither the federal government nor the Constitution had been looked to as a protector of the fundamental privileges and immunities of the citizen. With the exception of a few limitations imposed on the states directly by the Constitution, such as the prohibitions against ex post facto laws, bills of attainder, and laws impairing the obligation of contracts, "the entire domain of privileges and immunities . . . lay within the constitutional and legislative power of the States, and without that of the Federal government."[36]

33. Miller, 83 U.S. 76, citing *Corfield v. Coryell*, 4 Wash. C. C. 371 (1823).
34. Ibid., quoting *Ward v. Maryland*, 12 Wall. 430 (1870)
35. Ibid.
36. Ibid., 77.

Against that background, Miller forcefully confronted the implications of Campbell's argument and asked, "Was it the purpose of the 14th Amendment, by the simple declaration that no state should make or enforce any law which shall abridge the privileges and immunities of citizens of the United States, to transfer the security and protection of all the civil rights which we have mentioned, from the States to the Federal government?" And since the amendment empowered Congress to enforce the amendment, "was it intended to bring within the power of Congress the entire domain of civil rights heretofore belonging exclusively to the States?" "All this and more must follow, if the proposition of the plaintiffs . . . be sound." Echoing Durant and Allen once again, Miller added that sustaining Campbell's position "would constitute this court a perpetual censor upon all legislation of the States, on the civil rights of their own citizens."[37] He candidly acknowledged that, in its predictions of dire consequences, his "slippery slope" analogy carried certain risks. "The argument we admit is not always the most conclusive which is drawn from the consequences urged against the adoption of a particular construction." In *this* case, however:

> these consequences are so serious, so far-reaching and pervading, so great a departure from the structure and spirit of our institutions; when the effect is to fetter and degrade the State governments by subjecting them to the control of Congress, in the exercise of powers heretofore universally conceded to them of the most ordinary and fundamental character; when in fact it radically changes the whole theory of the relations of the State and Federal governments to each other and of both . . . to the people; the argument has a force that is irresistible, in the absence of language which expresses such a purpose too clearly to admit of doubt.[38]

Without any reference to either the congressional debates or the excerpts cited by Fellows, Miller put the point very simply. "We are convinced that no such results were intended by the Congress which proposed these amendments, nor by the States which ratified them." This single sentence is as close as Miller got to the sticky question of congressional intent. Debate over whether he accurately read or misread such intent, or indeed, whether any clear intention of Congress as a whole concerning the scope of the Fourteenth Amendment can be determined, has raged ever since.[39]

37. Ibid., 77–78.
38. Ibid., 78.
39. Ibid., 79. For citations to the exhaustive if not exhausting literature that this debate has spawned, see the works of Michael Curtis cited above, as well as Michael K. Curtis, "Historical Linguistics, Inkblots, and Life after Death: The Privileges and Immunities of

There is no reason to doubt Miller's sincerity in articulating a limited view of the amendment's scope. The amendment presented him with a serious problem concerning the extent of its impact on the federal system. Further, he found no persuasive evidence that the amendment's framers had intended to make a fundamental change in the federal system, and nothing in its language to require such an interpretation. Speaking for a majority of the justices, Miller had already held that the police power provided a sufficient basis for the Slaughterhouse Act. Therefore, the case did not require the justices to go further and explore ways to reconcile the amendment's guarantee of fundamental rights with the values of the federal system.

Having found that only the privileges and immunities of citizens of the United States were protected against state action by the amendment, and that the rights being claimed by the New Orleans butchers were not among them, Miller concluded that "we may hold ourselves excused from defining the privileges and immunities of Citizens of the United States which no State can abridge, until some case involving those privileges may make it necessary to do so." Nonetheless, it may have occurred to Justice Miller that defining such rights would not only strengthen his opinion but also anticipate the arguments that would certainly be made by the dissenting justices. Hence, he did precisely what he had said it was unnecessary to do. As dicta, he offered some examples of privileges and immunities "which owe their existence to the Federal government, its National character, its Constitution, or its laws."

These included, Miller said, the right of a citizen to travel to the seat of government to seek its assistance or participate in its affairs, the right of access to the nation's seaports and to the state courts, the right to demand the protection of the federal government when abroad, and the right "to use the navigable waters of the United States." He also observed that "the right to peaceably assemble and petition for redress of grievances . . . are rights of the citizen guaranteed by the Federal Constitution."[40] He included the right to become a citizen of any state of one's choosing, guaranteed by the very amendment under consideration, as well as the other provisions of the

---

Citizens of the United States," *North Carolina Law Review* 78 (2000): 1071–151; Bryan H. Wildenthal, "The Lost Compromise: Reassessing the Early Understanding in Courts and Congress on Incorporation of the Bill of Rights in the Fourteenth Amendment," *Ohio State University Law Journal* 61 (2000): 1051–173; Wildenthal, "The Road to Twining: Reassessing the Disincorporation of the Bill of Rights," ibid., 1457–528.

40. Miller, 83 U.S. 78–79. As early as 1833, in *Barron v. Baltimore*, Chief Justice Marshall had held that limitations expressed in the Bill of Rights applied only to the federal government, *not* the states. 32 U.S. 243 (1833).

Fourteenth Amendment and the rights guaranteed by the Thirteenth and Fifteenth Amendments. There was no need to attempt an exhaustive list. The rights listed, he implied, were far above those claimed by the butchers. "We are of the opinion that the rights claimed by these plaintiffs in error, if they have any existence, are not privileges and immunities of citizens of the United States within the meaning of the clause of the 14th Amendment under consideration."[41]

Miller then turned to the arguments that the Slaughterhouse Act deprived the butchers "of their property without due process or law, or that it denies to them the equal protection of the law." The due process clause was destined to become the focus of attention for generations to come, but in its first review by the Court, its relevance was dismissed in a single sentence: "It is sufficient to say that under no construction of that provision that we have ever seen, or any that we deem admissible, can the restraint imposed by the State of Louisiana upon the exercise of their trade by the butchers of New Orleans be held to be a deprivation of property within the meaning of that provision."[42]

Only Campbell's resort to the equal protection clause remained to be dealt with. To do so, Miller returned to what he saw as the "pervading purpose" of the amendment and concluded that "it is not difficult to give a meaning to this clause. The existence of laws in the States where the newly emancipated Negroes resided, which discriminated . . . against them as a class, was the evil to be remedied by this clause, and by it such laws are forbidden."[43]

If, Miller added, the states failed to adjust their laws to conform to the equal protection clause, then under Section 5 of the amendment, Congress was authorized to pass legislation to enforce the amendment. But "we doubt very much whether any action of a State not directed by way of discrimination against the Negroes as a class, or on account of their race, will ever be held to come within the purview of that provision. It is so clearly a provision for that race and that emergency, that a strong case would be necessary for its application to any other."[44] This statement has been considered by many scholars to be particularly regrettable. It unnecessarily limited the broad

41. Miller, 83 U.S. 79–80.
42. Ibid., 80–81.
43. Ibid., 81.
44. Ibid. Durant had argued that in spite of the all-inclusive nature of the amendment's language, the clear thrust of the enactment pointed toward and applied primarily to the ex-slave.

implications of the equal protection clause. Moreover, it could be used to narrow the scope of Congress's enforcement power under the amendment's last section. That the statement was mere dictum, and not a determination required by the facts of the case or for which the decision could be considered binding authority, has done little to exculpate Miller.

Miller concluded his opinion with a brief description of the federal system, as his majority envisaged it. The threat to the Union posed by the Civil War had served as a powerful reminder of the importance of maintaining a strong national government. And undoubtedly, this sentiment had contributed to the adoption of the recent amendments. Nonetheless, he insisted that there was no reason to believe that they had been intended to bring about a fundamental change in the federal system. "We do not see in these amendments any purpose to destroy the main features of the general system. . . . Our statesmen have still believed that the existence of the States with powers for domestic and local government, including the regulation of civil rights—the rights of person and of property—was essential to the perfect working of our complex form of government, though they have thought proper to impose additional limitations on the States, and to confer additional power on that of the Nation."[45] Thus Miller ultimately affirmed Louisiana's Slaughterhouse Act. What started out as a narrow holding endorsing the police power had become—despite the broad and controversial provisions of the Fourteenth Amendment—a commitment to the proposition that, *except* for the ex-slave, the Union is as the Union was. Miller had given; now it was his turn to receive.

ALTHOUGH CHIEF JUSTICE CHASE was the senior justice among the four dissenters, by the middle of April 1873, his health had so deteriorated that he could only indicate his concurrence. Indeed, less than a month after the case was decided, he died. It fell to Stephen Field to speak for his brethren, and if there was any sense of hesitation or tentativeness in Miller's opinion, the same cannot be said of Field's. Now in his tenth year on the Court, he had already fashioned a judicial activism based on both his Jacksonian heritage and his own economic conservatism.[46]

Field reviewed the various complaints that Campbell had leveled against the Slaughterhouse Act on behalf of the butchers and concluded, "No one

45. Ibid., 82.
46. See Paul Kens, *Justice Stephen J. Field: Shaping Liberty from the Gold Rush to the Gilded Age* (Lawrence: University Press of Kansas, 1977), 5–9 and passim.

Stephen Field wrote the lead dissent in the *Slaughterhouse
Cases.* Like his dissent, his portrait radiates a strong sense of
self-confidence in the righteousness of his judicial positions.
(Office of the Curator, Supreme Court of the United States,
#1863.4.)

will deny the abstract justice which lies in the position of the plaintiffs."[47]
He then launched into an opinion aimed at showing that the butchers' position was well grounded in the Constitution.

Just as Miller had summarily rejected a number of points on which
Campbell had expended page after page of argument, so Field made short
work of Miller's efforts to defend the 1869 statute as a valid exercise of the
police power. He readily recognized the power of the state to make regula-

47. Field dissent, 83 U.S. 86.

tions for the health, safety, and well-being of the community. But even the police power had to be exercised in a way that was consistent with constitutionally protected rights. "Under the pretense of prescribing a police regulation, the State cannot be permitted to encroach upon any of the just rights of the citizen, which the Constitution intended to insure against abridgement."

In Field's view, only the provisions of the act requiring the inspection, landing, and slaughtering of animals below the city of New Orleans could properly be called police regulations. He ridiculed the claim that it was legitimate to award to a single company exclusive privileges over all stock landing, yarding, and slaughtering in an area encompassing three Louisiana parishes and 1,154 square miles. He conceded that "the health of the city might require the removal from its limits and suburbs of all buildings for keeping and slaughtering cattle, but no such object could possibly justify legislation removing such buildings from a large part of the State for the benefits of a single corporation."[48]

Nor could Field accept the 1869 statute as an example of an exclusive franchise such as the state might award for the construction and maintenance of a road, ferry, or bridge. Such grants are given for the accomplishment of some purpose falling within the purview of the government, he said. "The grant, with exclusive privileges of a right thus appertaining to the government, is a very different thing from a grant, with exclusive privileges, of a right to pursue one of the ordinary trades or callings of life, which is a right appertaining solely to the individual."[49]

To drive home his point, Field allowed himself to exaggerate and employed some slippery slope reasoning of his own. Disregarding the notorious problems caused in an urban area by a system of distributed stockyards and slaughterhouses, as well as several limitations written into the act, he

48. Ibid., 87–88. Taken together, these three parishes formed the "metropolitan area," and since the purpose of the statute was to isolate slaughtering from the populated districts, it made good sense to include them. Field's citation of the square miles involved ignored the fact that much of St. Bernard Parish consisted of lowland, largely uninhabited. Although his claim that between 200,000 and 300,000 people resided within the three parishes was accurate, the actual total was much closer to 211,000.

49. Ibid., 88. Without question, Field accepted Campbell's linkage of slaughtering beef with the trade of the butcher. In his eyes, the 1869 statute represented "a naked case . . . where a right to pursue a lawful and necessary calling, previously enjoyed by every citizen, and in connection with which a thousand persons were daily employed, is taken away and vested exclusively . . . in a single corporation . . . and there allowed only upon onerous conditions." Ibid., 88–89

argued that if the Louisiana legislature could give exclusive privileges to a seventeen-person corporation, they may

> be equally granted to a single individual. If they may be granted for twenty five years, they may equally be granted for a century, and in perpetuity. If they may be granted for the landing and keeping of animals . . . they may be equally granted for the landing and storage of grain . . . or for any article of commerce. . . . Indeed, upon the theory on which the exclusive privileges granted by the act in question are sustained, there is no monopoly, in the most odious form, which may not be upheld.[50]

Evidently caught up in his argument, Field provided some insight into how he and his fellow dissenters viewed the Fourteenth Amendment. His point is broader than it might first appear to be. "The question presented is, therefore, one of the gravest importance. . . . It is nothing less than the question whether the recent Amendments to the Federal Constitution protect the citizens of the United States against the deprivation of their common rights by state legislation. In my judgment the 14th Amendment does afford such protection, and was so intended by the Congress which framed and the states which adopted it."[51]

Campbell had argued forcefully that the Slaughterhouse Act subjected his clients to a kind of involuntary servitude in violation of the terms of the Thirteenth Amendment. Field admitted that he was so accustomed to thinking of the amendment in terms of Negro slavery that he was not prepared to give it "the extent and force ascribed by counsel." But having said that, he went on to make several observations that seemed to support the very point he had disavowed. He agreed that the amendment "is not confined to African slavery alone. It is general and universal in its application." Moreover, it prohibited not only slavery, strictly defined, but also "involuntary servitude in every form." Although the term "involuntary servitude" had never been judicially defined, in Field's opinion, since the nation was now a nation of free men, all men have "the right to pursue the ordinary avocations of life without other restraint than such as affects all others." Similarly, a person is subjected to a condition of servitude when he or she is "allowed to pursue only one trade or calling, and only in one locality of the country." Indeed, Field pointed out, Campbell's position was also supported by the Civil Rights Act of 1866, which had been adopted to give effect to the amendment. For all that, Field concluded, "it is not necessary . . . for the

50. Ibid., 89.
51. Ibid.

disposition of the present case in favor of the plaintiffs . . . to accept [Campbell's position] as entirely correct."[52]

Field insisted that the Fourteenth Amendment held the key to the case. Without exploring the amendment's history, as Miller had, he rejected Miller's finding that the amendment established a separate citizenship in the United States and in the states, each imbued with its own privileges and immunities. As Field saw it, "A citizen of a State is now only a citizen of the United States residing in that State. The fundamental rights, privileges, and immunities which belong to him as a free man and a free citizen, now belong to him as a citizen of the United States and are not dependent upon his citizenship of any state."[53]

Yet Field asserted that the amendment "does not attempt to confer any new privileges or immunities upon citizens or to enumerate or define those already existing." The amendment assumes that U.S. citizens are endowed as a matter of right with certain privileges and immunities "and ordains that they shall not be abridged by state legislation." Then, taking aim at the narrow definition of the privileges and immunities of U.S. citizens espoused by Miller, Field argued that "if this inhibition . . . only refers . . . to such privileges and immunities as were before its adoption specially designated in the Constitution or necessarily implied . . . it was a vain and idle enactment, which accomplished nothing, and most unnecessarily excited Congress and the people on its passage." It had never been legal for a state to interfere with a citizen's right to seek the protection of the federal government when abroad or to use the nation's navigable waters or to petition for a redress of grievances or any of the other privileges mentioned by Miller as examples of those that belonged to citizens of the United States. With these privileges and immunities "no State could ever have interfered." In short, to accept Miller's interpretation of privileges and immunities would render that portion of the amendment meaningless. However, "if the amendment refers to the natural and inalienable rights which belong to all citizens," as Field insisted it did, then "the inhibition has a profound significance and consequence."[54]

Field observed that the Fourteenth Amendment's phrase "privileges and immunities" was not new to the Constitution. Article IV of the Constitution

52. Ibid., 90–91.
53. Ibid., 95.
54. Ibid., 96. In spite of Field's aggressive rhetoric, it is far from clear to what extent the first section of the Fourteenth Amendment had in fact "excited" either Congress or the people upon its passage.

required each state to accord the same "privileges and immunities" allowed its own citizens to citizens of any other state who might be within its jurisdiction. He noted that these privileges and immunities had been defined in the circuit court case of *Corfield v. Coryell* "as those privileges and immunities which were in their nature fundamental [and] which belong of right to the citizens of all free governments, and which have at all times been enjoyed by the citizens of the several states." Based on this distinction, he found that the "privileges and immunities" of the Fourteenth Amendment "are those which of right belong to the citizens of all free governments. Clearly among these must be placed the right to pursue a lawful employment in a lawful manner, without other restraint than such as equally affects all persons."[55]

At the heart of Justice Field's argument is the idea that the Fourteenth Amendment obligated the states to exercise their power in a way that did not interfere with the equal enjoyment by citizens of the United States of their privileges and immunities. This concept was central to Article IV, which had to do with the equal enjoyment of the privileges and immunities of state citizens. Now, according to Field, "under the 14th Amendment the same equality is secured between citizens of the United States."[56] It was this equality that the Slaughterhouse Act had butchered in 1869 when it gave a monopoly over slaughtering to a single concern.[57] Field discussed the concept and history of monopolies in some detail. He embraced Justice Bradley's 1870 circuit court decision in which he had held that the Slaughterhouse Act was unconstitutional because it subjected a fundamental right to a monopoly. Bradley had declared, "There is no more sacred right of citizenship than the right to pursue unmolested a lawful employment in a lawful manner. It is nothing more nor less than the sacred right of labor."[58] Field, too, insisted that under the amendment, even the police power had to be exercised in a manner consistent with equality of right.

In terms of this analysis, even the Illinois Supreme Court's decision in *Chicago v. Rumpff,* so heavily relied on by counsel for the butchers, took on renewed strength. Field cited it with approval. Counsel for the company had chosen not to attack the decision frontally as a betrayal of Chicago's

55. Ibid., 97.

56. Ibid., 101.

57. Field did not mince words to describe the *Slaughterhouse Cases.* They represented "the most barefaced and flagrant of all" enactments that interfered with the "privilege of the citizen." Ibid., 106.

58. Ibid., 106, quoting *Live-Stock Assoc. v. Crescent City Co.,* 1 Abb. U.S. 388 (La. C.C. 1870).

legislatively granted police power. Instead, they sought to distinguish the case on the spurious grounds that it involved an allegedly unauthorized city ordinance, whereas the Slaughterhouse Act was the product of a fully empowered state legislature. Field summarily dismissed the rebuttal. "A legislative body is no more entitled to destroy the equality of rights of citizens, nor less to fetter the industry of a city, than a municipal government."[59]

Field concluded his dissent with the declaration that "this equality of right, with exemption from all disparaging and partial enactments, in the lawful pursuits of life . . . is the distinguishing privilege of citizens of the United States. To them, everywhere, all pursuits, all professions, all avocations are open without other restrictions than such as are imposed equally upon all others of the same age, sex, and condition." This, he insisted, "is the fundamental idea upon which our institutions rest, and unless adhered to in the legislation of the country our government will be a republic only in name."[60]

Field's heavy reliance on equality of right can be seen as a weakness in his rationale. As a justice of the Supreme Court, he was not in the position of a municipal official in a large city to observe that some pursuits—the privilege of operating a slaughterhouse, for example—could *not* be allowed to all, consistent with public health and good order. As constitutional scholar Thomas Cooley had observed in 1868, "there are unquestionably cases in which the State may grant privileges to specified individuals without violating any constitutional principle, because, from the nature of the case, it is impossible they should be possessed and enjoyed by all."[61]

Justice Bradley supplemented Field's massive dissent with a "few obser-

59. Field dissent, 83 U.S.108.
60. Ibid., 108, 109–10. Field's mention of restrictions should be kept in mind. In the celebrated case of *Bradwell v. Illinois*, decided one day after *Slaughterhouse*, Miller held that the Fourteenth Amendment did not give Myra Bradwell a constitutional right to follow a particular profession, presumably because Illinois law forbade *all* women to practice law. See 83 U.S. 130 (1873). Field joined with Bradley, who wrote a concurring opinion that today could be described only as blatantly sexist. Indeed, even in 1873, according to one contemporary Court observer, "Judge Bradley's opinion seemed to cause no little amusement upon the Bench and on the Bar." See Lurie, "Mr. Justice Bradley," 365.
61. Thomas M. Cooley, *Constitutional Limitations* (Boston: Little, Brown, 1868), 394. Like Miller, who believed that the framers of the Fourteenth Amendment had not intended to change the basic nature of the federal Union, Cooley believed that, for the most part, protection of fundamental rights remained with the states, as that is "where it naturally and properly belongs." See Phillip Paludan, *A Covenant with Death: The Constitution, Law and Equality in the Civil War Era* (Urbana: University of Illinois Press, 1975), 269.

vations" of his own. He was the only member of the Court who had had
some prior experience with the *Slaughterhouse Cases*. New Orleans was part
of his federal circuit, and in 1871, he had expressed the opinion that the
Slaughterhouse Act was unconstitutional. Bradley echoed Field and contended that the act "is onerous, unreasonable, arbitrary and unjust." He
added that "it is one of those arbitrary and unjust laws made in the interest
of a few scheming individuals, by which some of the Southern States have,
within the past few years, been so deplorably oppressed and impoverished.
It seems to me strange that it can be viewed in any other light."[62]

Again echoing Field, he distinguished grants of exclusive privileges for
the "erection of . . . establishments of a public kind" and monopolies "of
ordinary callings or pursuits." But he went further and contended that even
public franchises "are becoming more and more odious, and are getting to
be more and more regarded as wrong in principle." For Miller to cite them
"as proof of the power of legislatures to create more monopolies, such as
no free and enlightened community any longer endures, appears to me, to
say the least, very strange and illogical."[63]

Justice Miller's opinion had been informed from the start by his finding
that the amendment had been written first and foremost on behalf of the
newly freed slaves. Bradley found a serious flaw in this conclusion. "It is
futile, "he emphasized, "to argue that none but persons of the African race
are intended to be benefited by this amendment." They may indeed have
been "the primary cause" for it, but the language "is general, embracing all
citizens, and I think it was purposely so expressed." Alone among his brethren, Bradley argued that far more was involved. "The mischief to be remedied," he said,

> was not merely slavery and its incidents and consequences; but that spirit
> of insubordination and disloyalty to the National government which had
> troubled the country for so many years in some of the States, and that
> intolerance of free speech and free discussion which often rendered life and
> property insecure, and led to much unequal legislation. The amendment
> was an attempt to give voice to the strong National yearning for that time
> and that condition of things . . . in which every citizen of the United States

62. Bradley dissent, 83 U.S. 120.
63. Ibid., 121. Earlier in his dissent, Bradley had commented on what he considered
Miller's strained distinction between federal and state privileges and immunities. "To say
that these rights and immunities attach only to State citizenship, and not to citizenship of the
United States, appears to me to evince a very narrow and insufficient estimate of constitutional history and the rights of men, not so say the rights of the American people." Ibid., 116.

might stand erect on every portion of its soil, in the full enjoyment of every right and privilege belonging to a freeman.[64]

Finally, Bradley confronted Miller's "great fears" that an expansive interpretation of the amendment would lead to interference from Congress, as well as excessive involvement from his own Court. He predicted that "no such practical inconveniences would arise." And if they did? "Even if the business of the National courts should be increased, Congress could easily supply the remedy by increasing their number and efficiency." In focusing on what Bradley believed were simply chimerical fears, Miller missed the point. "The great question is, What is the true construction of the Amendment? . . . The argument from inconvenience ought not to have a very controlling influence in questions of this sort. The National will and National interest are of far greater importance."[65]

In the final dissent, Justice Swayne outdid even Bradley in his hostile reaction to the 1869 statute. "A more flagrant and indefensible invasion of the rights of many for the benefit of a few has not occurred in the legislative history of the country." He further argued that the language of Section 1 meant just what it said. "By the language 'Citizens of the United States' was meant *all* such citizens; and by 'any person' was meant *all* persons within the jurisdiction of the State." There was no intimation of a distinction "on account of race or color," and "this court has no authority to interpolate a limitation that is neither expressed nor implied."[66]

Further, Swayne described Miller's construction as "much too narrow." Although he cited no evidence, he insisted that "it defeats, by a limitation not anticipated, the intent of those by whom the instrument was framed and of those by whom it was adopted." To the extent that this limitation is followed, "it turns, as it were, what was meant for bread into a stone." Swayne was troubled about the implications of the decision for the future, especially in terms of dealing with "wrong and oppression by the States. That want was intended to be supplied by this amendment. . . . I earnestly hope," he concluded, "that the consequences to follow may prove less serious and far-reaching than the minority fear they will be."[67]

* * *

64. Ibid., 123.
65. Ibid., 123–24.
66. Swayne dissent, 83 U.S. 128, 128–29.
67. Ibid., 129–30.

PRESS REACTION TO THE DECISION needs to be understood in the context of a broader reaction to the events of Reconstruction, still unfolding even as the opinions became public. Those that were concerned either by a claim of monopoly or by the course of Reconstruction in the Southern states were critical. The *Cincinnati Enquirer* noted that Miller's majority opinion displayed "the degeneracy of the Court" in a holding based on a statute from a legislature "elected by the bayonet and through the agency of the most degraded and ignorant portion of the population." Truly, this was "the monopolists' decision."[68]

Conversely, those journals that tended to oppose the federal role in Reconstruction were encouraged by Miller's conclusions. Thus, the *Nation* stated that "the Court is recovering from the war fever and is getting ready to abandon sentimental canons of construction."[69] The *Chicago Tribune* argued that although the Court had indirectly sustained a monopoly, its decision "does not turn upon this point."[70] The real issue, according to the *New York World*, was "whether those amendments had changed the previous relations of the States to the Federal Government. The Court very properly decided that they had not."[71]

A similar conclusion appeared in the *New York Times*, which emphasized the great importance of the decision "for several reasons. It is calculated to throw the immense moral force of the Court on the side of rational and careful interpretation" concerning rights both of the states and the federal government. Further, Miller's opinion was intended to maintain and increase "the respect felt for the Court, as being at once scrupulous in its regard for the Constitution, and unambitious of extending its own jurisdiction." Finally, the decision dealt "a severe and, we might almost hope, a fatal blow to that school of constitutional lawyers who have been engaged, ever since the adoption of the Fourteenth Amendment, in inventing impossible consequences for that addition to the Constitution." The writer added that its coverage "was not and could not be that subordination in matters of business and profit which it is not in the province of the National Constitution to regulate, and which the people did not intend to bring within" national jurisdiction.

The editorial conceded that the amendment's provisions were general.

68. Charles A. Warren, *The Supreme Court in United States History*, vol. 2 (Boston: Little, Brown, 1926), 541, 542.

69. Ibid., 543.

70. Ibid., 542 n. 2.

71. Ibid., 543.

But they had been framed for the freedmen, and if the condition of that portion of the American people had not required it, the amendment would never have been passed. There could be little doubt, the editorial concluded, that the amendment "was not a piece of abstract declaration, meant to establish a general definition of rights for Congress to legislate for, and the Supreme Court to adjudicate on." Rather, "it was a piece of practical legislation, meant to remove certain obvious evils, and to establish certain results which were the logical outgrowth of the war."[72]

At least one senator who had participated in the actual framing of the amendment's language claimed that "there is no word in it that was not . . . intended to mean the full and beneficial thing it seemed to mean." Somehow, the Court "radically differed in respect both to the intention of the framers and the construction of the language used by them."[73] In contrast, according to the Washington correspondent for the *Boston Daily Advertiser,* "the opinion of Mr. Justice Miller is held by the Bar to be exceedingly able, while passages in it were regarded as striking examples of judicial eloquence."[74]

In 1926, Charles Warren concluded that Miller's opinion "has been justly regarded as one of the glorious landmarks of American law." In fact, no less a figure than John Campbell himself "admitted that it was 'probably best for the country that the case so turned out.' "[75]

Before placing this retrospective reflection in a broader contemporary context, some brief comments on the conclusion of the slaughterhouse controversy should be noted. By no means did it end with Miller's decision.

72. *New York Times,* April 16, 1873, 6. See also the comments of Paul Carrington cited in chapter 1, note 32.

73. Warren, *Supreme Court,* 541.

74. Ibid., 539.

75. Ibid., 546. Although we argue in this study that, within the context of the police power, Miller's decision was sound law, we cannot concur with Warren's glowing assessment from several generations ago. Unfortunately for Miller, his additional dicta, rather than his actual decision, have often been held against him. Today, we suspect that there are no legal historians or constitutional scholars who would agree with Warren. But as will be seen in the final chapter, our purpose is to explain rather than condemn the holdings.

10

Conclusions

By April 14, 1873, when Justice Samuel Miller announced the Supreme Court's decision in the *Slaughterhouse Cases*, the process of Reconstruction in Louisiana was showing signs of utter disintegration. Bloody race riots in both New Orleans and Colfax in central Louisiana, the latter only days before the Court announced its *Slaughterhouse* decision, made it evident that Louisiana's Republican administration was not in firm control of the state.[1] By the time Warmoth's term as governor sputtered to a close in 1872, he found himself facing impeachment. Divisive campaigns for state offices that year had their effect on Louisiana politics as the Republican party split into pro- and anti-Grant factions, and factions within the Democratic party jockeyed for dominance. Four years later, the Democrats sensed that their return to power in the state was at last within grasp.

Indeed, change was sweeping across the political landscape. National and state elections in November 1876 signaled an end to Reconstruction in Louisiana. The Democratic party quickly regained control of the state, with Francis T. Nicholls as governor. Federal troops were withdrawn from Louisiana in 1877. State elections in 1878 sent Democrats into more than three-quarters of the seats in the state legislature. Divided on some matters, they were united in their determination to effect reform by restoring "white home rule" and taking steps to ensure that "the reign of robbery will never be restored."[2]

As early as the fall of 1877, a number of newspapers called for a constitutional convention to set aside what the *Opelousas Courier* called the "misera-

---

1. On the New Orleans "Liberty Place" and Colfax riots, see Taylor, *Louisiana Reconstructed*, 267–73; and Robert M. Goldman, *Reconstruction and Black Suffrage* (Lawrence: University Press of Kansas, 2001). chap. 3.

2. *Daily Picayune*, February 19, 1879, as quoted in Ronald M. Labbé, "That the Reign of Robbery Will Never Return to Louisiana: The Constitution of 1879," in *In Search of Fundamental Law: Louisiana's Constitutions, 1812–1974*, ed. Warren M. Billings and Edward F. Haas (Lafayette: Center for Louisiana Studies, University of Southwestern Louisiana, 1993), 83.

The 1874 U.S. Supreme Court. With the exception of newly appointed chief justice Morrison R. Waite, all the other justices participated in the *Slaughterhouse* decision. From left to right: Bradley, Field, Miller, Clifford, Waite, Swayne, Davis, Strong, and Hunt. (Office of the Curator, Supreme Court of the United States, #1874.18.)

ble abortion" of 1868.[3] Governor Nicholls initially attempted to stave off the demand for a convention, but by January 1879, he yielded to the inevitability of thoroughgoing constitutional revision. The constitutional convention that met in New Orleans in April 1879 consisted of 134 delegates, only 30 of whom were Republicans. In the new political circumstances, many leading Republicans had left the state, and it was to be expected that they would play only a minor role in the convention. Most of the 104 Democratic delegates were conservatives associated with Governor Nicholls, but the remaining Democrats represented two groups: the highly reactionary and racist "Bourbons," who were bent on revenge and the removal of every vestige of Republican rule, and the New Orleans Ring, which was rooted in the New Orleans Democratic organization and city government and was subservient to the interests of the powerful Louisiana Lottery Company. Though only a minority, these two groups of "strict Democrats" played a dominant role in writing the new constitution.

The constitution of 1879 is a good example of the observation that, historically, "Louisiana's Constitutions have been written" at the climax of major political struggles "to embody the principles and objectives of the victorious party, faction or race."[4] A far cry from the liberal document of 1868, the new constitution defined the "only legitimate end" of government in a decidedly negative way: "to protect the citizen in the enjoyment of life, liberty and property."[5] The new philosophy is reflected throughout the document. Blacks did not fare well in a number of areas of vital concern. Guarantees of equality of rights and a ban against racial discrimination in public schools were omitted.[6] The power of the legislature was limited, and its function was preempted by an unprecedented amount of legislative detail in which various groups enshrined their particular interests in the organic law.

For present purposes, it is sufficient to draw attention to only a few particular instances in which the constitution of 1879 sought to address what the drafters saw as a legacy of legislative irresponsibility. High among these priorities was, of course, the 1869 slaughterhouse statute. With controversies concerning subsidies and franchises that had been lavished on corporations

3. *Opelousas Courier*, September 29, 1877, as quoted in William Ivy Hair, *Bourbonism and Agrarian Protest: Louisiana Politics 1877–1900* (Baton Rouge: Louisiana State University Press, 1969), 64.

4. Mark T. Carlton, "The Louisiana Constitution of 1974," in *Louisiana Politics: Festival in a Labyrinth*, ed. James Bolner (Baton Rouge: Louisiana State University Press, 1982), 16.

5. La. Const. (1879), art. 1.

6. Ibid., arts. 2, 11, 13, 135, 136, 142.

still echoing in the public forum, the new constitution prohibited special legislation "creating corporations" or "granting to any corporation . . . any special or exclusive right, privilege or immunity."[7] Further, in Article 248, it gave exclusive authority to parish and city governments to regulate the slaughtering and keeping of livestock, subject to two provisos: first, that they could not do so by means of a monopoly or exclusive privileges, and second, that their ordinances designating areas in which slaughtering was to take place had to be approved by the board of health.[8] Finally, in Article 258 it abrogated the Crescent City Company's exclusive franchise by providing that "the monopoly features in the charter of any corporation now existing in the State [railroads excepted] are hereby abolished."[9]

These provisions of the new constitution opened the door to the reestablishment of private slaughterhouses within New Orleans city limits, and it was not long before individual butchers began petitioning the city council for permission to do just that. Some of these requests sought to return slaughterhouses to the very area of the city they had been removed from by the 1869 act, and this provoked officials of the waterworks to express strong opposition. More ominously for the interests of both the city and the Crescent City Company was the formation on March 5, 1880, of a new slaughterhouse corporation in New Orleans, the Butchers Union Slaughterhouse and Livestock Landing Company.[10] For its part, the city council began considering an ordinance for the board of health's approval that would regulate slaughtering and designate where it could take place.

The Crescent City Company was quick to recognize that these developments threatened both its exclusive franchise and an investment that was now estimated at half a million dollars, and it wasted no time initiating a series of defensive actions. On February 5, 1880, just two months after the new constitution was ratified, the company filed suit in the Fifth District Court against the city of New Orleans to enjoin it from exercising any

7. Ibid., art. 46.
8. Ibid., art. 248, viz., "The police juries of the several parishes and the constituted authorities of all incorporated municipalities of the State shall alone have the power of regulating the slaughtering of cattle and other live stock within their respective limits; provided, no monopoly or exclusive privilege shall exist in this state, nor such businesses be restricted to the land or houses of any individual or corporation; provided, the ordinances designating the places of slaughtering shall obtain the concurrent approval of the board of health or other sanitary organization."
9. Ibid., art. 258.
10. Charter adopted March 5, 1880, before Edward Robert Hogan, Notary Public, Orleans Parish Notarial Archives.

authority under Article 248. Similar actions were filed against Jefferson Parish and the Butchers Union Company, but these were eventually dismissed on technical grounds.[11]

Entitled *Crescent City Live Stock Landing and Slaughterhouse Company v. New Orleans,* this new action gave the company an opportunity to resort to the U.S. Constitution for protection.[12] The company contended that the Slaughterhouse Act had created a contract between it and the state whereby the company was given an exclusive twenty-five-year franchise to operate a slaughterhouse in return for its agreement to construct and maintain facilities adequate to the needs of the stock dealers and butchers of New Orleans. The company argued that in abrogating this arrangement, Article 258 of the new constitution violated Article I, Section 10 of the U.S. Constitution, which prohibited a state from passing any "law impairing the obligation of contracts."[13] The lower court granted a preliminary injunction but refused to make it permanent, and the company appealed.

The state supreme court rejected the company's argument and upheld the anti-monopoly provisions of the new constitution. The court recognized that the Slaughterhouse Act had been passed in the exercise of the state's police power—its power to legislate for the health, safety, and well-being of the community. It was a power, the court said, that was central to the functions of state government and one that a state could never relinquish or permanently contract away. Consequently, said the court, the nature of the act was not that of a contract but rather a mere *license* authorizing the company to act for the state. In short, what the legislature had formerly granted in the exercise of its police power it could now take away in the exercise of that same power.

Authority for this ruling was not hard to find. Only a year before, in

11. *Crescent City Live Stock Landing and Slaughter House Company v. Police Jury, Parish of Jefferson,* 32 La. Ann. 1192 (1880), dismissed as premature, and *Crescent City Live Stock Landing and Slaughterhouse Company v. Butchers Union Slaughterhouse,* 33 La. Ann. 930 (1881), dismissed because the same issues were pending in the company's action against the city of New Orleans.

12. *Crescent City Live Stock Landing and Slaughterhouse Company v. New Orleans,* 33 La. Ann. 934 (1881); originally No. 10494 in the Fifth District Court, the record is available at Docket No. 7996, Louisiana Supreme Court Archives, Earl K. Long Library, University of New Orleans. The parties stipulated for the record that the assets of the Crescent City Company were then worth $499,745.72. Interestingly, the stipulation also provided that in the ten years of its operation, the company had paid only three dividends of 5 percent each, amounting to $75,000 in all.

13. U.S. Const., Art. I, sec. 10.

Stone v. Mississippi, the U.S. Supreme Court had held that the contract clause was not violated by a provision in the Mississippi Constitution of 1868 that had the effect of abrogating a twenty-five-year charter to conduct a lottery.[14] The Court had explained that the "Legislature cannot bargain away the police power of a State. Irrevocable grants of property and franchises may be made, if they do not impair the supreme authorit[y's power] to make laws for the right government of the State but no legislature can curtail the power of its successors to make such laws as they deem proper in matters of police."[15]

Never one to take no for an answer, the Crescent City Company returned to court in the person of Stoddard Howell, a butcher and ally. With the construction of a new Butchers Union abattoir well advanced, Howell sued the new company in his capacity as a private citizen, allegedly seeking to abate a nuisance. He argued that the privilege of setting up a slaughterhouse belonged exclusively to the Crescent City Company. The defendants complained that the action was a ruse sponsored and funded by the Crescent City Company to prevent the Butchers Union from going into business. The state supreme court ruled against Howell, but an angry Butchers Union Company retaliated by suing the Crescent City Company for damages as a result of a malicious prosecution. The trial court rendered a monetary judgment in favor of the Butchers Union, but this decision was also reversed by the state supreme court.[16]

In its initial effort to have Article 258 declared invalid on grounds of the contract clause of the U.S. Constitution, the Crescent City Company had resorted to the state courts in an action against the city of New Orleans, and it had lost. But the issue had never been litigated in a federal court, nor had the company itself ever filed suit against its latest opponent, the Butchers Union Company. On November 28, 1891, the Crescent City Company called the Butchers Union Company to account in the U.S. Circuit Court in New Orleans in still another effort to defeat Article 258. The result there was the opposite of the one reached by the Louisiana Supreme Court. In the view of the judges of the circuit court, Article 258 could *not* be upheld as an

14. 101 U.S. 814 (1880).

15. *Stone v. Mississippi*, as quoted in *Crescent City Live Stock Landing and Slaughterhouse Company v. City of New Orleans*, 33 La. Ann. 939.

16. *Stoddard Howell v. Butchers' Union Slaughterhouse and Live Stock Landing Co.*, 36 La. Ann. 63 (1884); *Butchers Union Slaughterhouse and Live Stock Landing Co. v. Stoddard Howell*, 37 La. Ann. 280 (1885).

exercise of the police power when in fact the Crescent City Company's operations were already so located that they could not endanger the health of the city.[17]

On appeal, however, the U.S. Supreme Court reversed this decision in *Butchers Union Slaughterhouse and Live Stock Landing Co. v. Crescent City Live Stock Landing and Slaughterhouse Co.*[18] Here the Court was presented with a rare second opportunity to adjudicate the validity of the Crescent City Company's slaughterhouse monopoly, albeit in this instance in terms of the contract clause. Writing once again for the majority, Justice Miller restated the first and central point of his first *Slaughterhouse* opinion, but in doing so, he took pains to emphasize the limited scope of his original opinion. He conceded that as a result of the Slaughterhouse Act, a contract existed between the state and the Crescent City Company, and that the provisions of the constitution of 1879 and the recent city ordinances did indeed abrogate this contract. But he rejected the idea that the state's contract was irrepealable. In creating a corporation and providing it with the exclusive privilege to operate a slaughterhouse, the legislature had acted in the exercise of its *police power*. As such, Miller wrote, it *"is a valid law, and must be obeyed, which is all that was decided by this court in the Slaughter-House Cases."*[19]

This sentence offers an intriguing insight into Miller's position. Now, ten years after the original *Slaughterhouse* opinion, he appeared to have relegated his earlier pronouncements concerning the Fourteenth Amendment to the realm of dicta. It is significant that he saw no need to repeat any of his previous points concerning the meaning of the amendment's various provisions. This is an unmistakable suggestion that Miller considered the Fourteenth Amendment to be, ultimately, irrelevant to the decision in the *Slaughterhouse Cases*. It may be, said Justice Miller, that a state could enter into an irrepealable contract with regard to some aspects of the police power. But "a wise policy forbids the legislative body to divest itself of the power to enact laws for the preservation of health and the repression of crime."[20]

The Court's decision in the *Butchers Union* case was unanimous, but both Field and Bradley chose to write separate concurring opinions. Their

17. *Crescent City Live Stock Landing and Slaughter House Co. v. Butchers' Union Live Stock Landing and Slaughter-House Co.*, 9 F. 743 (1881), preliminary injunction; 12 F. 225 (1882), permanent injunction.

18. 111 U.S. 746 (1884).

19. Ibid., 750.

20. Ibid., 751.

desire to see an end to the slaughterhouse monopoly had been vindicated, yet they still felt a need to elaborate on the volatile ideas they had expressed earlier in dissent about fundamental rights and their protection by the Fourteenth Amendment.

Field began by agreeing that the legislature could not permanently contract away its authority to provide for the health and morals of the public. But he went on to deny that health conditions could ever justify the creation of "a monopoly of an ordinary employment and business."[21] He likened the slaughterhouse monopoly to one over "the ordinary trades and callings of life," such as bread baking and the raising of vegetables.[22] He held that monopolies are against common right. "They are void because they interfere with the liberty of the individual to pursue a lawful trade or employment."[23] As he had in his original dissent, Field's argument combined an appeal to higher law with a reliance on the Constitution's new textual guarantee of equality. He noted that the maintenance of "free institutions" required the recognition of "certain inherent rights." These were the rights referred to by the Declaration of Independence when it spoke of "inalienable rights." Among these rights is the right of men "to pursue any lawful business or vocation, in any manner not inconsistent with the equal rights of others."[24] If textual support were needed for this right of labor, it could be found in the first section of the Fourteenth Amendment, which was, he said, "designed to prevent all discriminating legislation for the benefit of some to the disparagement of others."[25] Field recognized that congressional efforts to enforce the terms of the amendment were controversial, but no one could complain if the amendment was used to support a resort to the *courts* in the defense of truly fundamental rights. He concluded "that the act, in creating the monopoly in an ordinary employment and business, was to that extent against common right and void."[26]

In spite of his rhetoric, Field was less a foe of monopoly than his opinion indicated. Apparently, it depended on *what* the monopoly affected. He was indignant over the supposed restraint on an individual's trade or calling. But barely four years later, when Florida granted a monopoly to a local telegraph company, Field had no objection; and upon the Court's rejection of

21. Ibid., 755.
22. Ibid., 756.
23. Ibid.
24. Ibid., 756–57.
25. Ibid., 758.
26. Ibid., 760.

such a legislative grant, he dissented. Given his position in *Slaughterhouse,* his comments are of interest. "There can be no serious question that . . . Florida possessed the absolute right to confer upon a corporation created by it the exclusive privilege for a limited period." Indeed, Field added, "the exclusiveness of a privilege often constitutes the only inducement for undertakings holding out little prospect of immediate returns."[27] This, of course, was the exact position taken by Miller in 1873.[28]

In the second concurring opinion, Justice Bradley (joined by Justices Harlan and Woods) began by rejecting again the idea that the Slaughterhouse Act had been an exercise of the state's police power. In his view, "the police regulations proper were hitched on to the charter as a pretext."[29] The creation of a monopoly was not within the police power. "I hold it to be an incontrovertible proposition of both English and American public law, that all *mere* monopolies are odious and against common right."[30]

Like Field, he resorted to principles enshrined in the Declaration of Independence. "The right to follow any of the common occupations of life is an inalienable right; it was formulated as such under the phrase 'pursuit of happiness' in the Declaration of Independence, which commenced with the fundamental proposition that 'all men are created equal, that they are endowed by their Creator with certain inalienable rights; that among those are life, liberty and the *pursuit of happiness.*' This right is a large ingredient in the civil liberty of the citizen."[31]

Not content to rely on constitutional theory for authority, Bradley turned specifically to the Fourteenth Amendment. "But why is such a grant beyond the legislative power, and contrary to the Constitution?" The answer, he said, lies in the prohibitive terms of the amendment's first section. "I hold that a legislative grant, such as that given to the appellees in this case is an infringement of each of these prohibitions. It abridges the privileges of citizens of the United States; it deprives them of a portion of their liberty

27. *Pensacola Telegraph Co. v. Western Union Telegraph Co.,* 96 U.S. 1, 15–18 (1887). See the informative analysis by Manuel Cachan, "Justice Stephen Field and 'Free Soil, Free Labor Constitutionalism': Reconsidering Revisionism," *Law and History Review* 20 (2002): 541, 571–72.

28. Once again, in 1884, Field failed to confront the fact that no one had been prevented from earning his living by the Slaughterhouse Act. As shown in chapter 8, the act required only that the butchers perform their slaughtering in facilities provided by the company.

29. 111 U.S. 761.

30. Ibid.

31. Ibid., 762.

and property without due process of law; and it denies to them the equal protection of the laws."[32]

Thus did the U.S. Supreme Court uphold the provisions of the 1879 Louisiana Constitution abrogating the exclusive privileges conferred on the Crescent City Company by the 1869 Slaughterhouse Act and turn down the company's effort to prevent the Butchers Union Company from establishing itself as a competitor. It left its previous pronouncements concerning the privileges and immunities clause intact. With its right to do business confirmed at last by the highest court in the land, the Butchers Union Company returned to court to recover damages from the Crescent City Company for malicious prosecution, just as it had done after the Stoddard Howell decision, and with equally little effect. It argued that once the state supreme court had upheld the validity of the anti-monopoly provisions in the 1879 constitution in 1881, the company had been authoritatively informed of its rights and consequently had no standing to bring up the matter anew in the federal courts. The recent decision of the U.S. Supreme Court in favor of the Butchers Union Company amounted to only a reiteration of the earlier decision of the state supreme court and was proof enough of the worthlessness of the Crescent City Company's claim.

In this action for wrongful prosecution, a jury in the lower court awarded the Butchers Union Company monetary damages amounting to $19,000 and an additional $2,500 in attorneys' fees. The state supreme court affirmed. It ruled that by taking an injunction in the federal courts *after* the state supreme court had ruled against it on virtually the same set of facts, the Crescent City Company had acted without probable cause to believe that it could succeed.[33] In the opinion of the state supreme court, this was the definition of malicious prosecution. On appeal, however, the U.S. Supreme Court reversed this ruling. It pointed out that the Crescent City Company's rights vis-à-vis those of the Butchers Union Company had never been formally adjudicated. Consequently, the Crescent City Company was entitled on the advice of counsel to test its rights in the federal courts.[34]

In fact, the Butchers Union Company did not remain in business for

32. Ibid., 764.

33. *Butchers' Union Livestock Landing and Slaughterhouse Co. v. Crescent City Livestock Landing and Slaughter House Co.*, 37 La. Ann. 874 (1885); factual details from the record, available at Docket No. 9461, Louisiana Supreme Court Archives.

34. *Crescent City Livestock Landing and Slaughterhouse Company v. Butchers' Union Slaughterhouse and Livestock Landing Co.*, 120 U. S. 141 (1887). The Court's opinion provides a useful summary of the series of Butchers Union cases that culminated in this opinion.

very long. In 1891, the New Orleans newspapers were again speaking of only one slaughterhouse in the city, and they were quick to voice opposition to any effort to establish another one. But the New Orleans livestock industry continued to attract the attention of speculators, and the old ways of winning the support of political bodies, though sometimes bitterly criticized, proved to have a staying power of their own. In 1891, for example, a three-person "syndicate" won city council approval of an ordinance permitting it to construct a new slaughterhouse in the city.[35] The *New Orleans Item* dubbed the scheme "one of the periodic speculative moves for the erection of a new slaughterhouse" and opposed the venture on the grounds that "one slaughterhouse is nuisance enough."[36] The mayor vetoed the ordinance for sanitation reasons, but the city council overrode the veto.[37] The board of health ratified the ordinance and then, in the face of growing furor, withdrew its approval, allegedly because a legal defect has been discovered in it.

The dispute quickly widened into a major scandal that was reminiscent of the process that had led to passage of the Slaughterhouse Act in 1869. Long investigative articles appeared in the press. It was reported that the incorporators had made three-eighths of the stock of the proposed company and a sum of money available to B. B. Pringle, a broker, for his use in guaranteeing approval by the council and the board.[38] Claims were made that members of the board of health had been bribed to support the ordinance and had profited from sales of stock in the old slaughterhouse, "to the intense disgust of the public." Three members of the board resigned.[39]

The attorney general was called in, and a grand jury investigated, but no charges were pressed against anyone. The scandal raged until mid-July 1891, when the matter was returned to the hands of the city council.[40] In October, the board of health unexpectedly reversed itself. On the motion of one of the new members of the board, "suddenly without notice to opponents," the board voted to ratify the city ordinance and license an additional slaughterhouse after all.[41]

Perhaps as a result of its long experience with the ways of New Orleans, the *Daily Picayune* seemed to view the affair with a degree of resignation.

35. *Times Democrat*, July 11, 1891, 3.
36. *New Orleans Item*, April 7, 1891, 1.
37. Veto letter of March 31, 1891, *New Orleans Item*, April 1, 1891, 3.
38. *Times Democrat*, May 17, 1891, 6; May 20, 1891, 3; July 11, 1891, 3; *Daily States*, May 19, 1891, 4.
39. *Times Democrat*, October 10, 1891, 4.
40. *Daily States*, May 30, 1891, 1; *Times Democrat*, July 10, 1891, 3.
41. *Times Democrat*, October 10, 1891, 4.

"There is talk of bribery just as there was the same sort of talk in the case of the Board of Health, but nothing will be proved. There was some speculating in slaughterhouse stock; but it appears to be a common thing for officials to speculate in stocks when they have official knowledge which can affect their value, but there is nothing unlawful in that. But the report of the investigation makes good reading."[42]

In 1893, a year before the Crescent City Company's twenty-five-year charter expired, its stockholders rechartered themselves as the Crescent City Livestock Yard and Slaughter House Company, and as such, they purchased all the property belonging to the Crescent City Company.[43] In one corporate form or another, the company continued in operation in the same location until about the 1920s. On June 6, 1963, the *New Orleans Times Picayune* reported the closing of the New Orleans Butchers Cooperative Abattoir, as a result of "labor difficulties and a dwindling supply of cattle due to residential expansion into former pasture area."[44] In operation for sixty years, it was the last slaughterhouse in the New Orleans area.

IN MAY 2002, the authors of this study visited the original site of the Crescent City Company's slaughterhouse and stockyards, located a short drive east of downtown New Orleans and not far from the site of the Battle of New Orleans in 1815. Most of the vast slaughterhouse tract is now occupied by solid middle-class neighborhoods, but near the Mississippi River, evidence of the slaughterhouse plant proper can still be found. Among dilapidated warehouses and vacant lots heavy with weeds, we found remnants of a very old railroad track, an abandoned loading ramp, and the ruins of what appeared to have been a large storage facility. A young workman we talked to recalled that he had once found some discarded meat hooks on a shelf in the nearby warehouse. Street signs in the neighborhood still bear the names of some of the butchers and stock dealers who initiated the *Slaughterhouse Cases*—Esteben, Aycock, Mehle. While wandering in the area, it was not difficult to imagine what it must have been like in 1873, when the stock

42. *Daily Picayune*, July 10, 1891, 4.
43. Charter, dated February 15, 1893, Gustave LeGardeur Jr. Notarial Archives, New Orleans Notarial Archives; sale, dated April 11, 1893, before Gustave LeGardeur Jr. (vol. 14, no. 358), New Orleans Notarial Archives. An elaborate surveyors' plat attached to this instrument shows that the slaughterhouse tract, less a number of small lots sold to individual tradesmen, then measured 4 arpents, 10 toise, and 4 feet (about 800 feet) on the river by a depth of 100 arpents (more than 3.5 miles), taking it well beyond Claiborne Avenue.
44. *Times Picayune*, June 6, 1963, sec. 5, 24.

landing and stockyards were active, buyers and sellers went about their business, and the slaughterhouse itself carried on its noxious task more or less according to nineteenth-century sanitary and environmental standards.

Justice Felix Frankfurter once commented that Supreme Court decisions are like "windows on the world." Peering through the frame of the *Slaughterhouse* decision, we encounter a scene of nineteenth-century politics, greed, and gain; concerns for public health and private property; debate over the values involved in the case, who was right and who was wrong, and how the case should have been decided, in contrast to what actually occurred. As our study concludes, it is appropriate to place the controversy in some sort of historical perspective.

The *Slaughterhouse Cases* involved the grant of an exclusive franchise to a private company for the operation of a centralized slaughterhouse in an urban area. The act can be defended as a routine exercise of the regulatory power of the state. Addressing the sanitary needs of a rapidly growing urban area, it required consolidation of the most noxious aspect of the meat industry (slaughtering) in a single facility located in a designated district. The centralization of slaughtering was a sanitary reform that had already been implemented in other metropolitan areas—though seldom without a political or legal fight from the butchers and stock dealers affected. In New Orleans, however, the struggle was more intense because the franchise had been awarded in the era of Reconstruction, and to a hastily gathered group of investors who were predominantly (though not exclusively) newcomers. The same goal could have been achieved with less controversy by granting the franchise to a consortium of butchers or to an agency of the state, but the Louisiana legislature of 1869 chose to do otherwise.

Attorneys for the New Orleans butchers and stock dealers could find nothing in the original constitution to prevent Louisiana from adopting the Slaughterhouse Act, and indeed, state precedents supported the measure as an exercise of the police power. Consequently, they resorted to the recently adopted amendments to the U.S. Constitution for relief. Most notably, they relied on the Fourteenth Amendment's guarantees of "privileges and immunities" of citizenship, "due process of law," and the "equal protection of the law."

The case they crafted presented the Supreme Court with a uniquely delicate task. John Campbell had asked the Court to hold that the right to earn one's living at a chosen calling was a fundamental right now protected by the Fourteenth Amendment. The Court could agree with this contention only with unpredictable results, particularly with respect to centralized slaughterhouses already existing elsewhere or to other applications of the police power in circumstances yet to arise. Moreover, using the amendment to protect this "right to labor" could lead to a call for the Court to discover other fundamental rights in the amendment. In short, the Court had to resolve the dispute without revolutionizing the federal system in a single decision and at the same time without damaging the potency of the new constitutional provisions guaranteeing the rights of blacks.

As a factual matter, the case brought by white New Orleans butchers did not readily lend itself to an exploration, let alone the resolution, of the questions raised by the Fourteenth Amendment. Indeed, it was an especially inappropriate and unfortunate controversy in which to attempt a resolution. Seldom has the Supreme Court been presented with a case so rich in irony. A Reconstruction amendment intended to secure the civil rights of black Americans had been used to secure the property rights of white butchers. The statute they sought to defeat by the amendment had been enacted by a reconstructed, racially integrated legislature. Counsel for the butchers, John Campbell, had a well-earned reputation as an advocate of states' rights. Yet now he called for an expansive interpretation of the rights, privileges, and immunities to be protected as never before by the federal courts.

Campbell's opponents—including Matthew Carpenter, who had participated in the congressional deliberations leading to the Fourteenth Amendment, and Thomas Durant, whose efforts to help the liberated blacks in Louisiana had resulted in a self-imposed exile from that state—found themselves in a similarly ironic position. To win their case, they had to argue for a narrow interpretation of an amendment cast in very broad language. They had to deny its application to all except blacks, who were in no way party to the case. Thus Campbell—no Reconstructionist—argued for a truly expansive application of the amendment, while Durant called for a restrictive reading of its terms. The former Confederate pleaded for a liberal interpretation of privileges and immunities, while counsel for the Reconstruction government in Louisiana argued the opposite.

These new constitutional provisions under scrutiny in the *Slaughterhouse Cases,* as well as the Civil Rights Act and the several Reconstruction acts that preceded their adoption, were all intended to ensure that newly freed black Americans enjoyed all the civil and political rights long claimed by white Americans. Yet there was nothing in these measures to limit their application to blacks. They all avoided specific identification of the ex-slave as a privileged recipient of special protection. They were drafted to apply to all "Americans equally."[45] Conversely, there was no reason to suppose that these measures were intended to bring about a fundamental change in the federal system as it had traditionally been understood. The thrust of the new legislative and constitutional provisions was to provide for federal intervention when the states either failed to do so or were guilty of such infringement themselves. As Michael Les Benedict put it, the "primary responsibility for . . . protecting their rights from infringement would remain with the states."[46]

In deciding the case, the Court readily found that the police power of the state was ample to support the statute. But in reply to the constitutional arguments, Justice Samuel Miller's majority opinion embraced an interpretation of the privileges and immunities clause of the Fourteenth Amendment whereby it protected only the rights of national citizenship, which he found to be few indeed. Further, it defined the due process clause as exclusively a guarantee of fundamentally fair procedure, and it held that the equal protection clause had relevance only for blacks and not for the white butchers of New Orleans. In a supreme irony, Justice Miller, who had specifically singled out the ex-slave as the primary cause for the new amendment, apparently left his privileges and immunities, for the most part, at the mercy of the state. And arguably, this was done not because the black man "was hated, but because constitutionally established federalism was loved."[47]

There was no reason to doubt Miller's credentials as a Republican who consistently supported the goals of the war and of Reconstruction. It should be remembered that in sustaining the 1869 statute, he affirmed the work of a Reconstruction legislature, elected in part by black votes. It may be that Miller did not intend the 1873 decision to be a broad and definitive exegesis of the Fourteenth Amendment's full scope. He had suggested as much in his opinion in the *Butchers Union* case, the 1884 sequel to *Slaughterhouse*, when he seemed to relegate his interpretation of the Fourteenth Amendment to the realm of dicta. But by choosing not to couch his decision exclusively in terms of the police power, he undercut his intention. He could have found the statute within the police power and gone no further. Such a course would have left the gist of Campbell's expansive vision of the amendment,

45. Michael Les Benedict, in Hall, *Oxford Companion*, s.v. "Slaughterhouse Cases," 790. According to the words actually employed in the amendment, presumably women were also included.

46. Ibid.

47. Paludan, *Covenant with Death*, 13. Paludan well describes the strong hold that the traditions of federalism held for the Civil War generation.

as well as the vigorous comments of the dissenters, unanswered. This, Miller was unable to confront. Although he left no papers that might explain how he came to decide as he did, there is one extant letter in which he commented on both the *Slaughterhouse* and the *Bradwell* cases. He wrote to his brother-in-law that few cases had caused him more difficulty in making up his mind, but that he strongly believed that these two cases had been rightly decided.[48]

Remarks by Justice Oliver Wendell Holmes are perhaps apt in understanding the Supreme Court's decision as Justice Miller crafted it. Very early in his Court career, Holmes observed: "Great cases, like hard cases, make bad law. For great cases are called great, not by reason of their real importance in shaping the law of the future, but because of some accident of immediate overwhelming interest which appeals to the feelings and distorts the judgment. These immediate interests exercise a kind of hydraulic pressure which makes what previously was clear seem doubtful, and before which even well settled principles of law will bend."[49]

Was Miller's opinion the result of what Justice Holmes called an "accident of immediate overwhelming interest which appeals to the feelings and distorts the judgment"? Did Miller's attraction to federalism as he knew it "exercise a kind of hydraulic pressure" that resulted in a distortion of the Fourteenth Amendment? Whatever the answer to these questions may be, there is no doubt that Miller, though he remained on the bench for seventeen years, never expanded on the scope of the Fourteenth Amendment's privileges and immunities clause.

In one sense, the Court's decision in favor of the Crescent City Company was short-lived. Within three years, the company saw the Louisiana legislature returned to Democratic control. One year later, Reconstruction ended, and by 1879, the 1869 statute was a thing of the past. Yet in a different sense, *Slaughterhouse* has had a transforming effect on modern constitutional law. In interpreting the privileges and immunities clause in a way that seemed consistent with American federalism as he knew it, Justice Miller rendered the clause ineffectual—or so it is widely assumed. There is no doubt, however, that in the years after *Slaughterhouse*, other portions of the amendment received much greater emphasis.

The Civil War had been followed by great industrial expansion and a consequent demand for use of the police power to impose regulations on

48. Ballinger Papers, Box 2A201, Folder April 1873, Department of Archives and Manuscripts, Barker Texas History Center, University of Texas.
49. Holmes in dissent, *Northern Securities Company v. U.S.*, 193 U.S. 197, 400–401 (1904).

various aspects of the burgeoning market economy. John Campbell's idea of property as a fundamental right entitled to protection under the provisions of the first section of the Fourteenth Amendment, although put aside in *Slaughterhouse,* had never been defeated. Justices Field and Bradley had trumpeted it anew in their dissents in the *Butchers Union* case. Now, in their search for legal weapons against various regulations in the postwar period, corporate lawyers made it their own, and they found a basis for it in the due process clause. In *Slaughterhouse,* due process had been defined as strictly a guarantee of fair procedure. But now it took on a substantive meaning. It became a measure of the legality of not only *how* the government exercised its powers but also *what* actions the government took.[50]

It took until the end of the century to perfect this theory of substantive due process, but one of the first steps was taken only four years after *Slaughterhouse* when, in *Munn v. Illinois,* the Court upheld an act regulating storage rates at grain elevators against a challenge based on the due process clause. In his opinion for the majority, Chief Justice Morrison Waite accepted the due process argument, but he reasoned that the private property involved in this case had been dedicated to "the public interest." To that extent, it was subject to regulation.[51] In dissent, Justice Field, joined by Strong, took a hard substantive due process stand and disputed the distinction based on property vested with a public interest.[52]

It is not clear whether all the justices were aware that a new doctrine was forming. Yet despite his strong support for *Munn,* Justice Miller bristled at this development. The next year, writing for the majority in *Davidson v. New Orleans,* he took counsel to task for their novel use of due process. He found in the growing body of due process litigation "abundant evidence that there exists some strong misconception of the scope of this provision"

50. For an excellent history of these developments, see William M. Wiecek's *The Lost World of Classical Legal Thought: Law and Ideology in America, 1886–1937* (Oxford: Oxford University Press, 1998). Wiecek's early chapters place *Slaughterhouse* in an important historical context.

51. 94 U.S. 113 (1877). Both Miller and Bradley concurred silently with Waite's opinion. Indeed, Bradley apparently contributed heavily to its preparation. If Miller realized how far the Court had moved from his narrow holding in *Slaughterhouse,* he did not indicate it. He did, however, write to Waite, "approv[ing] unreservedly of all [Waite had] said and [think-ing] it well said and equal to the occasion which [was] a very great one." See Lurie, "Mr. Justice Bradley," 360–61.

52. For aid in summarizing the rise of substantive due process, we relied on the classic account of Walton H. Hamilton, "The Path of Due Process of Law," *Ethics* 48 (April 1938): 269–96.

and lamented its use to test "the merits" of legislation.[53] But Miller's protest notwithstanding, substantive due process continued to evolve as a potent weapon against the regulation of business. Indeed, in 1890, in an opinion authored within ten months of his death, Justice Miller concurred in a decision that saw his brethren doing exactly what he had warned against in 1873 — deciding that the reasonableness of a state police power regulation was a matter within judicial purview.[54] It was another twist of *Slaughterhouse* irony.

The pinnacle in the development of substantive due process was reached in 1897 in the case of *Allgeyer v. Louisiana*.[55] In his opinion for a unanimous court, Justice Rufus W. Peckam, in an apparent effort to write the economic theory of laissez-faire into the law, resorted to the arguments of Field, Bradley, and Campbell in the *Slaughterhouse Cases* to find that the due process clause protected a fundamental freedom to contract. It followed that restraint needed to be justified. Thus the *Allgeyer* decision gave employers a way to challenge legislation regulating various aspects of the employer-employee relationship, and not a few used this line of attack successfully.

With the arrival of laissez-faire thinking, the justices' predilections concerning the reasonableness of regulation came into full play. In 1898, the Court approved a Utah statute limiting the workdays of miners.[56] Less than ten years after the *Allgeyer* decision, in *Lochner v. New York,* a majority of the Court, in another opinion authored by Justice Peckham, rejected a New York statute regulating working hours in bakeries, claiming that it interfered with the laborer's freedom of contract.[57] Unlike the legislature, the Court found no reasonable grounds to justify the law. As was noted at the outset of our study, the shadow of *Slaughterhouse* hovered over this case. The arguments advanced by Field and Bradley formed the basis for Justice Peckham's majority opinion; Miller's earlier holding, forcefully expanded by Holmes, shaped the dissent. The majority and dissenting opinions in *Lochner* stand today as landmarks in the literature of judicial activism and restraint. For the next thirty years, the Court turned Miller's fear that the justices would make themselves the overseer of all kinds of state regulatory legislation into reality.[58]

53. 96 U.S. 97, 103–4 (1878).
54. See *Chicago, Milwaukee & St. Paul Railway Co. v. Minnesota*, 134 U.S. 418 (1890).
55. 165 U.S. 578 (1897).
56. *Holden v. Hardy*, 169 U.S. 366 (1898).
57. 198 U.S. 45 (1905).
58. Hall, *Oxford Companion*, s.v. "Lochner v. New York" (by Paul Kens), 508–11.

The Supreme Court was much slower to employ the due process clause as protection against state infringement on the great substantive rights enshrined in the First Amendment or the procedural rights guaranteed in other amendments of the Bill of Rights. But this began to change even as the Court handed down the *Allgeyer* decision. In 1897, the justices ruled that the Fifth Amendment's guarantee of just compensation applied to the states through the due process clause of the Fourteenth Amendment.[59] In 1925, in *Gitlow v. New York,* the justices read the First Amendment guarantee of free speech into the due process clause, and with that, they began a long process of applying the Bill of Rights to the states.[60]

By the late 1960s, the justices had read virtually all the elements of the Bill of Rights into the due process clause, thereby making them applicable to the states. From 1873 to the present, a majority of the Court steadfastly refused to accept the doctrine of total incorporation, which was the idea that the Bill of Rights had been made applicable to the states, ipso facto, by the Fourteenth Amendment. Instead, the revolution that Miller had resisted in *Slaughterhouse* was brought about on a case-by-case, amendment-by-amendment basis over the course of nearly a century. Today, the Bill of Rights limits the exercise of power by both the national government and the states.

It remains only to note that Justice Miller's declaration in *Slaughterhouse* that the equal protection clause had relevance only to the black man proved shortsighted. The clause was first applied, in 1886, on behalf of a Chinese American's right to operate a laundry business.[61] And the Court was not quick to utilize the amendment on behalf of blacks. But beginning in the twentieth century especially, this provision has been employed with historic significance to remove racial barriers to the political, economic, and social advancement of Americans, including but by no means limited to blacks. The equal protection clause has been successfully applied to cases involving criminal justice, legislative apportionment, and issues of gender relationships within the law.

Today, as a result of its response to a century of litigation in all these areas of the Fourteenth Amendment, the Court has achieved for itself and the other federal courts an all-important role in the system of checks and balances and in the formulation of important national policies as well. In case after case, it has identified fundamental rights and placed them under constitutional protection. In doing so, it has vindicated John Campbell's

59. *Chicago, Burlington and Quincy Railroad Co. v. Chicago,* 166 U.S. 226 (1897).
60. *Gitlow v. New York,* 268 U.S. 652 (1925).
61. *Yick Wo v. Hopkins,* 118 U.S. 356 (1886).

expansive view of the Fourteenth Amendment far beyond his original conception and with far more positive benefits.

The Fourteenth Amendment is still among the most frequently litigated amendments in the Constitution. Throughout it all, the 1873 *Slaughterhouse* holding has survived—now more often than not ignored, but never overruled, not even *sub silentio*. It will not do to emphasize the confining nature of stare decisis as an explanation for the Court's inability to rethink Miller's opinion. Miller himself enthusiastically participated as the Court reversed itself in the *Legal Tender Cases*, and this occurred less than two years after its initial decision. Nor will it do to say that Miller's analysis permanently gutted the effectiveness of the privileges and immunities clause. Rather, cultural and constitutional predilections have caused its desuetude. But expressions of anguish over its supposed demise are premature. Like its sister the contracts clause, the privileges and immunities clause of the Fourteenth Amendment remains part of the living Constitution, readily available whenever the Court wishes to employ it. And indeed, there are a number of cases in which the justices have done just that.[62] More than a century later, blaming Miller for current judicial disinclination to apply the clause is unwarranted. When the Court desires to utilize it, the clause is there.

A variety of factors, some obvious and others much more subtle, come into play when the Supreme Court decides to change its mind. If and when it decides to reexamine *Slaughterhouse*, the Court will only be acting on a basic tenet of our legal history: that the process of accommodating law to change "is never signed, sealed and delivered; it is always incomplete, always inchoate, always a work in progress, a work that is never done."[63]

62. See, e.g., *Hicklin v. Orbeck*, 437 U.S. 518 (1978); *Supreme Court of New Hampshire v. Piper*, 470 U.S. 274 (1985); and *Supreme Court of Virginia v. Friedman*, 487 U.S. 59 (1988). For a recent example in which, by a seven-to-two vote, the Court employed the privileges and immunities clause again, see *Saenz v. Roe*, 526 U.S. 489 (1999). According to Justice Thomas, the majority "appears to breathe new life into the clause today."

63. Lawrence M. Friedman, *American Law in the Twentieth Century* (New Haven, Conn.: Yale University Press, 2002), 689.

APPENDIX

The Slaughterhouse Act

No. 118

AN ACT

To Protect the Health of the City of New Orleans, to Locate the Stock Landings and Slaughter Houses, and to Incorporate "The Crescent City Live Stock Landing and Slaughter House Company."

SECTION 1. *Be it enacted by the Senate and House of Representatives of the State of Louisiana in General Assembly convened,* That from and after the first day of June, A.D. (1869) eighteen hundred and sixty-nine, it shall not be lawful to land, keep or slaughter any cattle, beeves, calves, sheep, swine or other animals, or to have, keep or establish any stock landing, yards, pens, slaughter houses or abattoirs at any point or place within the city of New Orleans or the parishes of Orleans, Jefferson and St. Bernard, or at any point or place on the east bank of the Mississippi river within the corporate limits of the city of New Orleans, or at any point on the west bank of the Mississippi river, above the present depot of the New Orleans, Opelousas and Great Western Railroad Company, except that the "Crescent City Stock Landing and Slaughter House Company" may establish themselves at any point or place as hereinafter provided. Any person or persons, or corporation or company carrying on any business or doing any act in contravention of this act, or landing, slaughtering or keeping any animal or animals in violation of this act shall be liable to a fine of two hundred and fifty dollars ($250) for each and every violation, the same to be recoverable, with costs of suit, before any court of competent jurisdiction.

SECTION 2. *Be it further enacted, etc.,* That Wm. D. Sanger, Joseph H. Pearson, J. R. Irwin, John Wharton, Franklin J. Pratt, R. T. Packwood, N. W. Travis, Henry V. Barringer, L. P. Sanger, W. S. Mudgett, Oliver D. Russell, J. Viosca, S. P. Griffin, L. H. Crippen, Wm. McKenna, A. J. Oliver, F. G. Clark and their successors be and are hereby created a body politic and corporate to be known and designated as the "Crescent City Live Stock Landing and Slaughter House Company," and by that name and style shall sue and be sued, purchase, hold, sell, contract, lease and release, grant and transfer, and may do all things necessary for the purposes hereinafter mentioned and perform all other acts, and exercise and enjoy all other rights and privileges, incident to corporations; adopt and use a common seal, make, publish and alter at pleasure by-laws, rules and regulations for the government of the company or corporation and the carrying on of its business; shall determine and appoint their officers, and fix their compensation and term of office, and shall fix the amount of the capital stock of the said company or corporation and the number of shares thereof.

The domicile of the company or corporation shall be in the city of New Orleans, and the president shall be the proper officer on whom to serve citations, notices and other legal process wherein this company or corporation may be interested.

SECTION 3. *Be it further enacted, etc.,* That said company or corporation is hereby authorized to establish and erect at its own expense, at any point or place on the east bank of the Mississippi river within the parish of St. Bernard, or in the corporate limits of the city of New Orleans, below the United States Barracks, or at any point or place on the west bank of the Mississippi river, below the present depot of the New Orleans, Opelousas and Great Western Railroad Company, wharves, stables, sheds, yards, and buildings necessary to land, stable, shelter, protect, and preserve all kinds of horses, mules, cattle and other animals, from and after the time such buildings, yards, etc., are ready and complete for business, and notice thereof is given in the official journal of the State; and the said Crescent City Live Stock Landing and Slaughter House Company shall have the sole and exclusive privilege of conducting and carrying on the live stock landing and slaughter house business within the limits and privileges granted by the provisions of this act, and cattle and other animals destined for sale or slaughter in the city of New Orleans, or its environs, shall be landed at the live stock landings and yards of said company, and shall be yarded, sheltered and protected, if necessary, by said company or corporation; and said company or corporation shall be entitled to have and receive for each steamship landing at the wharves of the said company or corporation ten (10) dollars; for each steamboat or other water craft, five (5) dollars; and for each horse, mule, bull, ox or cow landed at their wharves, for each and every day kept, ten (10) cents; for each and every hog, calf, sheep or goat, for each and every day kept, five (5) cents, all without including the feed; and said company or corporation shall be entitled to keep and detain each and all of said animals until said charges are fully paid. But if the charges of landing, keeping and feeding any of the aforesaid animals shall not be paid by the owners thereof after fifteen days of their being landed and placed in the custody of the said company or corporation, then the said company or corporation, in order to reimburse themselves for charges and expenses incurred, shall have power, by resorting to judicial proceedings, to advertise said animals for sale by auction in any two newspapers, published in the city of New Orleans for five days; and after the expiration of said five days the said company or corporation may proceed to sell by auction, as advertised, the said animals, and the proceeds of such sales shall be taken by the said company or corporation and applied to the payment of the charges and expenses aforesaid, and other additional costs, and the balance, if any remaining from such sales shall be held to the credit of and paid to the order or receipt of the owner of said animals. Any person or persons, firm or corporation violating any of the provisions of this act, or interfering with the privileges herein granted, or landing, yarding or keeping any animals in violation of the provisions of this act, or to the injury of said company or corporation, shall be liable to a fine or penalty of two hundred and fifty (250) dollars, to be recovered with costs of suit before any court of competent jurisdiction.

The company shall, before the first of June (1869), eighteen hundred and sixty-nine, build and complete a grand slaughter house of sufficient capacity to accommodate all butchers, and in which to slaughter five hundred animals per day; also that a sufficient number of sheds, and stables shall be erected before the date aforementioned, to accommodate all the stock received at this port, all of which to be accomplished before the date fixed for the removal of the stock landing, as provided in the first section of this act, under penalty of a forfeiture of their charter.

SECTION 4. *Be it further enacted, etc.* That the said company or corporation is hereby authorized to erect at its own expense one or more landing places for live stock, as aforesaid at any points or places, consistent with the provisions of this act, and to have and enjoy from the completion thereof, and after the first day of June, A.D. (1869) eighteen hundred and sixty-nine, the exclusive privilege of having landed at their wharves or landing places all animals intended for sale or slaughter, in the parishes of Orleans and Jefferson; and are hereby also authorized (in connection) to erect at its own expense one or more slaughter houses, at any points or places consistent with the provisions of this act, and to have and enjoy from the completion thereof, and after the first day of June, A.D. (1869) eighteen hundred and sixty-nine, the exclusive privilege of having slaughtered therein all animals, the meat of which is destined for sale in the parishes of Orleans and Jefferson.

SECTION 5. *Be it further enacted, etc.,* That whenever said slaughterhouses and accessory buildings shall be completed and thrown open for the use of the public, said company or corporation shall immediately give public notice for thirty days, in the official journal of the state, and within said thirty days notice . . . from and after the first day of June, A.D. (1869) eighteen hundred and sixty-nine, all other stock landings and slaughter houses within the parishes of Orleans, Jefferson, and St. Bernard shall be closed, and it will not longer be lawful to slaughter cattle, hogs, calves, sheep or goats, the meat of which is determined for sale within the parishes aforesaid, under a penalty of one hundred (100) dollars for each and every offense, recoverable, with costs of suit, before any court of competent jurisdiction. That all animals to be slaughtered, the meat whereof is determined for sale in the parishes of Orleans or Jefferson, must be slaughtered in the slaughterhouses erected by the said company or corporation, and upon a refusal of said company or corporation to allow any animal or animals to be slaughtered, after the same has been certified by the inspector, as hereinafter provided, to be fit for human food, the said company or corporation shall be subject to a fine in each case of two hundred and fifty dollars, recoverable, with costs of suit, before any court of competent jurisdiction; said fines and penalties to be paid over to the auditor of public accounts, which sum or sums shall be credited to the educational fund.

SECTION 6. *Be it further enacted, etc.,* That the Governor of the State of Louisiana shall appoint a competent person, clothed with police powers, to act as inspector of all stock that is to be slaughtered and whose duty it will be to examine closely all animals intended to be slaughtered, to ascertain whether they are sound and fit for human food or not, and if sound and fit for human food, to furnish a certificate stating that fact to the owners of the animals inspected, and without said certificate no animals can be slaughtered for sale in the slaughter houses of said company or corporation. The owner of said animals so inspected to pay the inspector ten (10) cents for each and every animal so inspected, one-half of which fee the said inspector shall retain for his services, and the other half of said fee shall be paid over to the Auditor of Public Accounts, said payment to be made quarterly. Said inspector shall give a good and sufficient bond to the State, in the sum of five thousand dollars, with sureties subject to the approval of the Governor of the State of Louisiana, for the faithful performance of his duties. Said inspector shall be fined for dereliction of duty fifty (50) dollars for each neglect. That said inspector may appoint as many deputies as may be necessary. The half of the fees collected as provided above, and paid over to the Auditor of Public Accounts, shall be placed to the credit of the educational fund.

SECTION 7. *Be it further enacted, etc.,* That all persons slaughtering or causing to be slaughtered, cattle or other animals in said slaughter houses, shall pay to the said company or corporation the following rates or perquisites, viz: For all beeves, one (1) dollars each; for all hogs and calves, fifty (50) cents each; for all sheep, goats and lambs, thirty (30) cents each; and the said company or corporation shall be entitled to the head, feet, gore and entrails of all animals, excepting hogs, entering the slaughterhouses and killed therein, it being understood that the heart and liver is not considered as a part of the gore and entrails, and that the said heart and liver of all animals slaughtered in the slaughterhouses of the said company or corporation shall belong, in all cases, to the owners of the animals slaughtered.

SECTION 8. *Be it further enacted, etc.,* That all the fines and penalties incurred for violations of this act shall be recoverable in a civil suit before any court of competent jurisdiction, said suit to be brought and prosecuted by said company or corporation in all cases where the privileges granted to the said company or corporation by the provisions of this act are violated or interfered with; that one-half of all the fines and penalties recovered by the said company or corporation in consideration of their prosecuting the violation of this act, and the other half shall be paid over to the Auditor of Public Accounts, to the credit of the educational fund.

SECTION 9. *Be it further enacted, etc.,* That said Crescent City Live Stock Landing and Slaughter House Company shall have the right to construct a railroad from their buildings to the limits of the city of New Orleans and shall have the right to run cars thereon, drawn by horses or other locomotive power, as they may see fit, said railroad to be built on either of the public roads running along the levee on each side of the Mississippi river. The said company or corporation shall also have the right to establish such steam ferries as they may see fit to run on the Mississippi river between their buildings and any points or places on either side of said river.

SECTION 10. *Be it further enacted, etc.,* That at the expiration of twenty-five years from and after the passage of this act the privileges herein granted shall expire.

SECTION 11. *Be it further enacted, etc.,* That all laws or parts of laws contrary to or inconsistent with the provisions of this act, be and the same are hereby repealed.

SECTION 12. *Be it further enacted, etc.,* That this act shall take effect from and after the first day of June A.D. (1869) eighteen hundred and sixty-nine.

(Signed)   CHAS. W. LOWELL
Speaker of the House of Representatives
(Signed)   OSCAR J. DUNN
Lieutenant Governor and President of the Senate

Approved March 8, 1869

(Signed)   H. C. WARMOTH
Governor of the State of Louisiana

BIBLIOGRAPHY

Judicial Decisions and Records

THE SLAUGHTERHOUSE CASES

Louisiana ex rel. Belden v. William Fagan, 22 La. Ann. 545 (1870).

Inbau, Aycock and Co. v. Crescent City Live Stock Landing and Slaughter House Co., filed June 18, 1869, No. 1537, Seventh District Court, Orleans Parish, La.; La. Sup. Ct. Docket No. 2504, Louisiana Supreme Court Archives.

Butchers Benevolent Association of New Orleans v. Crescent City Live Stock Landing and Slaughter House Company, filed May 26, 1869, No. 466, Sixth District Court, Orleans Parish, La.; La. Sup. Ct. Docket No. 2505, Louisiana Supreme Court Archives.

Campbell, John M. "Slaughterhouse Matter: Speech of Judge Campbell" [oral argument on exception in *Butchers Benevolent Association v. Crescent City . . . Company*, No. 466, Sixth District Court], *Daily Picayune*, June 27, 1869, 10–11.

Live Stock Dealers and Butchers Association of New Orleans v. Crescent City . . . Company, filed July 22, 1869, No. 1883, Seventh District Court, Orleans Parish, La.; La. Sup. Ct. Docket No. 2506, Louisiana Supreme Court Archives.

Crescent City . . . Company v. Steamboat B. L. Hodge, No. 2 and Owners, filed June 26, 1869, No. 720, Fifth District Court, Orleans Parish, La.; La. Sup. Ct. Docket No. 2507, Louisiana Supreme Court Archives.

Louisiana ex rel. Belden v. Fagan, filed July 27, 1869, No. 809, Fifth District Court, Orleans Parish, La.; La. Sup. Ct. Docket No. 2508, Louisiana Supreme Court Archives.

Crescent City . . . Company v. The Butchers Benevolent Association of New Orleans, filed May 26, 1869, No. 585, Fifth District Court, Orleans Parish, La.; La. Sup. Ct. Docket No. 2509, Louisiana Supreme Court Archives.

"Brief of the Plaintiffs in the First Three, and of Defendants in the Last Three of These Cases" [La. Sup. Ct. brief by John Archibald Campbell et al.], available at Brief No. 67, *Briefs of W. W. King*, Louisiana Collection, Middleton Library, Louisiana State University, Baton Rouge.

"Brief on behalf of the Crescent City . . . Company and the State of Louisiana" [by S. Belden, William H. Hunt, Randell Hunt, and C. Roselius], available in Louisiana Collection, Howard-Tilton Library, Tulane University.

Hunt, Randell. "Argument in the Slaughter-House Cases before the Supreme Court of Louisiana." In William Henry Hunt, ed. *Selected Arguments, Lectures and Miscellaneous Papers of Randell Hunt.* New Orleans: F. F. Hansell and Bro., 1896.

Butchers' Ass'n. v. Slaughter House Co., Fed. Case No. 2234, 1 Woods 50, 4 Fed. Cas. 891 (U.S. C.C., La., 1870) (on motion for writ of supersedeas).

Live-Stock Dealers' and Butchers' Ass'n. v. Crescent City . . . Company, et al., Fed. Case No. 8408, 1 Woods 21, 15 Fed. Cas. 649 (C. C., La., 1870) (on motion for injunction).

Slaughter-House Cases, 77 U.S. (10 Wall.) 273 (1870) (on motion for writ of supersedeas).

Slaughter-House Cases, 83 U.S. (16 Wall.) 36 (1873).

For the records and briefs of cases in the U.S. Supreme Court, see the following:

United States Supreme Court Records and Briefs, Legal Division, Library of Congress.

Scholarly Resources Microfilm Edition of the Records and Briefs of the United States Supreme Court. Wilmington, Del.: Scholarly Resources, 1975.

Kurland, Phillip B., and Gerhard Casper, eds. *Landmark Briefs and Arguments of the Supreme Court of the United States: Constitutional Law.* Vol. 6. Arlington, Va.: University Publications of America, 1975.

U.S. Supreme Court Appellate Case File Nos. 5598–5602, Record Group 267, Boxes 708–709, National Archives, Washington, D.C.

RELATED CASES

Butchers Union Slaughter-House and Live-Stock Landing Co. v. Crescent City Live Stock Landing and Slaughter House Company, 111 U.S. 746 (1884).

Butchers Union Slaughter-House and Live-Stock Landing Co. v. Crescent City . . . Company, 37 La. Ann. 874 (1885).

Butchers' Union Slaughterhouse and Live Stock Landing Co. v. Stoddard Howell, 37 La. Ann. 280 (1885).

Crescent City . . . Co. v. Board of Metropolitan Police et al., filed June 3, 1870, No. 118, Eighth District Court, Parish of New Orleans, La.; record available in *The Slaughter House Cases,* 77 U.S. (10 Wall.) 273 (1870).

Crescent City . . . Company v. Butchers Union Slaughterhouse, 33 La. Ann. 930 (1881).

Crescent City . . . Company v. Butchers Union Slaughter-House and Live-Stock Landing Co., 9 F. 743 (C.C., La. 1881) (preliminary injunction).

Crescent City . . . Company v. Butchers Union Slaughter-House and Live-Stock Landing Co., 12 F. 225 (C.C., La. 1882) (permanent injunction).

Crescent City . . . Company v. Butchers Union Slaughter-House and Live-Stock Landing Co., 120 U.S. 141 (1887).

Crescent City . . . Company v. City of New Orleans (Martin Wolf, Intervenor), 33 La. Ann. 934 (1881).

Crescent City . . . Company v. Police Jury, Parish of Jefferson, 32 La. Ann. 1192 (1880).

Durbridge v. Crescent City . . . Co. (A. J. Oliver, Intervenor), 27 La. Ann. 676 (1875); record available at La. Sup. Ct. Docket No. 3959, Louisiana Supreme Court Archives.

Harrod v. Crescent City . . . Co., filed March 21, 1871, No. 2333, Sixth District Court, Orleans Parish, La.

In the Matter of Paul Esteban et al. praying for an injunction, No. 6248, U.S. Circuit Court, New Orleans, Record Group 21, Case Files 1837–1911, National Archives, Fort Worth.

La. ex rel. Belden v. Cavaroc, et al., filed April 13, 1871, No. 508, Eighth District Court, Orleans Parish, La.

La. ex rel. Durbridge v. F. J. Pratt, et al., 23 La. Ann. 730 (1871); record available at La. Sup. Ct. Docket No. 2832, Louisiana Supreme Court Archives.

Live Stock Dealers' and Butchers' Assn. v. Crescent City . . . Company, et al., Fed. Case No. 8408, 1 Woods 21, 15 Fed. Cas. 649 (C. C., La., 1870).

Louisiana ex rel. Ponchartrain Railroad v. Judge of the Seventh District Court, 22 La. Ann. 565 (1870).

Mehle and Co. v. Crescent City . . . Company, filed March 22, 1871, No. 478, Eighth District Court, Orleans Parish, La.

New Orleans Gas Light Co. v. Louisiana Light and Heat Producing Co., 115 U.S. 650 (1885).

New Orleans Waterworks Co. v. St. Tammany Waterworks Co., 14 F. 194 (C. C., La. 1882).

Samuel B. Pratt v. Crescent City . . . Company, filed April 27, 1871, No. 528, Eighth District Court, Orleans Parish, La.; record available in *Bertin v. Crescent City . . . Company*, La. Sup. Ct. Docket No. 3917, Louisiana Supreme Court Archives.

Stoddard Howell v. Butchers' Union Slaughterhouse and Live Stock Landing Co., 36 La. Ann. 63 (1884).

Thomas J. Semmes and Robert Mott v. Crescent City . . . Company, filed April 8, 1871, Docket No. 500, Eighth District Court, Parish of Orleans, La.

OTHER CASES AND RECORDS

Ashwander v. Tennessee Valley Authority, 297 U.S. 288 (1936).

Barron v. Baltimore, 7 Peters (32 U.S.) 243 (1833).

Bradwell v. Illinois, 16 Wall. (83 U.S.) 130 (1873).

Briscoe v. Bank of Commonwealth of Kentucky, 11 Peters (36 U.S.) 257 (1837).

Chicago, Burlington and Quincy Railroad Co. v. Chicago, 166 U.S. 226 (1897).

Chicago, Milwaukee & St. Paul Railway Co. v. Minnesota, 134 U.S. 418 (1890).

City of Chicago v. Rumpff, 45 Ill. 90 (1867).

Commonwealth v. Upton, 72 Mass. 473 (1856).

Corfield v. Coryell, 4 Wash. Cir. Ct. 371 (1823).

Cummings v. Missouri, 71 U.S. 277 (1867).

Darcy v. Allein (Case of Monopolies), 72 Eng. Rep. 769, 9 Coke 84 (K.B. 1599).

De La Croix v. Villere, 11 La. Ann. 39 (1856).

Earl of Mountcashell v. Viscount O'Neill, 3 Irish Chancery Reports 619 (1854).

Ex Parte Garland, 71 U.S. 333 (1867).

Gelpcke v. Dubuque, 66 U.S. 175 (1864).

Georgia v. Stanton, 6 Wall. 50 (1767).

Gibbons v. Ogden, 9 Wheat. (22 U.S.) 1 (1824)

Gitlow v. New York, 268 U.S. 652 (1925).

Green v. The Mayor and Aldermen of Savannah, 6 Geo. 1 (1849).

Hart & Hoyt v. Mayor of Albany, 3 Paige Chancery Reports 197 (1832).

Hepburn v. Griswold, 75 U.S. 603 (1870).

Hicklin v. Orbeck, 437 U.S. 518 (1978).

Huguenin v. Baseley, 15 Vesey's Chancery Rep. 179 (1808).

Knox v. Lee, 79 U.S. 457 (1871).

Lochner v. New York, 198 U.S. 45 (1905).

Maxwell v. Dow, 176 U.S. 581 (1900).

Ex Parte McCardle, 74 U.S. 506 (1869).

Metropolitan Board of Health v. Heister, 37 N.Y. 661 (1868).

Ex Parte Milligan, 71 U.S. 2 (1866).

Mississippi v. Johnson, 71 U.S. 475 (1867).

Munn v. Illinois, 94 U. S. 113 (1877).

New York v. Miln, 11 Peters (36 U.S.) 102 (1837).

Northern Securities Co. v. U.S., 193 U.S. 197 (1904).

Pensacola Telegraph Co. v. Western Union Telegraph Co., 96 U.S. 1 (1887).

Prize Cases, 67 U.S. 635 (1863).

Saenz v. Roe, 356 U.S. 489 (1999).

Ex Parte Shrader, 33 Cal. 279 (1867).

Stone v. Mississippi, 101 U.S. 814 (1880).

Supreme Court of New Hampshire v. Piper, 470 U.S. 274 (1985).

Supreme Court of Virginia v. Friedman, 487 U.S. 59 (1988).

Texas v. White, 74 U.S. 700 (1869).

Twining v. New Jersey, 211 U.S. 78 (1908).

United States v. Carolene Products, 303 U.S. 144 (1938).

Ward v. Maryland, 12 Wall. 430 (1870).

White and Trufant v. Cazenave, 14 La. Ann. 57 (1859).

Wisconsin v. Milwaukee Gas Light Co., 29 Wis. 454 (1852).

Ex Parte Yerger, 8 Wall. 85 (1869).

Yick Wo v. Hopkins, 118 U.S. 356 (1886).

Primary/Contemporary Sources

"An Abattoir for New York." *Scientific American* 15 (August 18, 1866): 120.

Avery, George A. *A Lecture on the Progressive Spirit of the Medical Profession*

Delivered before the New Orleans Academy of Sciences, April 10, 1871. New Orleans: Hopkins Press, 1871.

Axson, A. F. *Report of the Board of Health to the Legislature, January, 1859.* New Orleans: John M. Taylor, 1859.

Bacon, Matthew. *A New Abridgment of the Law.* Vol. 7. Philadelphia: T. J. W. Johnson, 1856.

Barton, Edward H. "Annual Report for the New Orleans Board of Health for 1849." *Southern Medical Reports* 1 (1849): 77–106.

———. *Report on the Meteorology, Vital Statistics and Hygiene of the State of Louisiana: Read before the Medical Society of the State of Louisiana, 7th March, 1851.* New Orleans, 1851. Rudolph Matas Medical Library, Tulane University.

———. "Report upon the Sanitary Conditions of New Orleans." In New Orleans Sanitary Commission, *Report on the Epidemic Yellow of 1853.* New Orleans: City Council, 1854.

———. "Vital Dynamics of New Orleans: A Report to the American Medical Association, May, 1849." In *Selected Publications of Edward H. Barton: 1832–1857.* Rudolph Matas Medical Library, Tulane University.

Bell, John. "The Importance and Economy of Sanitary Measures to Cities." In *Proceedings and Debates of the Third National Quarantine and Sanitary Convention.* New York: Board of Education, Edward Jones and Co., 1859.

Board of Health. *Annual Report of the Board of Health of the State of Louisiana for the Year 1882.* Baton Rouge, 1883. Louisiana Division, Louisiana State Library, Baton Rouge.

———. "Annual Report of the Board of Health on the Sanatory Condition of the City of New Orleans, for 1848." *New Orleans Medical and Surgical Journal* 5 (1848–1849): 607–23.

Bragdon, O. D., comp. "Statement Showing Titles of Bills Killed by Veto of Governor." *Facts and Figures, Or Useful and Important Information.* New Orleans, 1872. Louisiana Collection, Tulane University Library.

Butler, Benjamin F. *Butler's Book.* Boston: A. M. Thayer, 1892.

———. "Some Experiences with Yellow Fever and Its Prevention," *North American Review* 147 (1888): 525–41.

Chaillé, Stanford E. "The Vital Statistics of New Orleans, Article No. I." *New Orleans Medical and Surgical Journal* 23 (January 1870): 1–65.

———. "Vital Statistics of New Orleans from 1769 to 1874." *New Orleans Medical and Surgical Journal* (July 1874): 1–29.

———. "The Yellow Fever, Sanitary Conditions, and Vital Statistics of New Orleans during Its Military Occupation, the Four Years 1862–5, Article No. II." *New Orleans Medical and Surgical Journal* 23 (July 1870): 563–98.

Coke, Edward. *The Third Part of the Institutes of the Laws of England.* London: E. and R. Brooke, 1797.

Cooley, Thomas M. *Constitutional Limitations.* Boston: Little, Brown, 1868.

Crowell, Henry G. "Sanitary Regulations Relating to Abattoirs." *Public Health Reports and Papers* 3 (1877): 16–23.

Daniell, Edmund R. *Pleading and Practice of the High Court of Chancery.* 3 vols. Boston: Little, Brown, 1865.

DeBow's Review: Devoted to the Restoration of the Southern States and the Development of the Wealth and Resources of the Country. After the War Series, 1866–1870.

Delrieu, Dr. R. *Les Abattoirs Public de la Nouvelle-Orléans.* Nouvelle Orléans: Imprimerie de L'Epoque, 1869.

Devoe, Thomas F. "Abattoirs: Paper Read before the Polytechnic Association, June 8, 1865." Reprint, *New York Times,* April 1, 1866, 2.

Devron, Gustave. *Abattoirs: Report on the Crescent City Live Stock Landing and Slaughterhouse Company to the Board of Health* [1875]. New Orleans: Peychaud and Garcia, 1876.

Edwards, Richard, comp. *Edwards Annual Directory for the City of New Orleans . . . 1870.* New Orleans, 1870.

———. *Edwards Annual Directory for the City of New Orleans . . . 1872.* New Orleans, 1872.

———. *Edwards Annual Directory for the City of New Orleans . . . 1873.* New Orleans, 1873.

Fenner, Erasmus D. "Remarks on the Sanitary Condition of the City of New Orleans during the Period of Federal Military Occupation from 1862 to March, 1866." *Southern Journal of Medical Sciences* 1 (1866): 22–43.

———. "Yellow Fever Quarantine at New Orleans." *Transactions of the American Medical Association* 2 (1849): 623–34.

Franklin, G. S. "Abattoirs." *Columbus Medical Journal* 2 (1883–1884): 447–50.

Fuqua, James O., comp. *Code of Practice in Civil Cases for the State of Louisiana.* New Orleans: Bloomfield and Steele, 1867.

Gardner, Chas., comp. *Gardner's New Orleans Directory for 1860.* New Orleans, 1859.

———. *Gardner's New Orleans Directory for 1869.* New Orleans, 1868.

Gary, Joseph E., comp. *Laws and Ordinances Governing the City of Chicago, Jan. 1, 1866.* Chicago, 1866. Chicago Historical Society Library.

Gibson, J., comp. *Gibson's Directory of the Cities of New Orleans and Lafayette for 1838.* New Orleans: J. Gibson, 1838.

Graham, L., comp. *Graham's New Orleans Directory for 1867.* New Orleans: L. Graham and Co., 1867.

Griscom, John. "Report on Water Supply and Offal." In *Proceedings and Debates of the Third National Quarantine and Sanitary Convention.* New York: Board of Education, Edward Jones and Co., 1859.

Hardee, Thomas S. "The Topography and Drainage of New Orleans." *The Sanitarian* 3 (October 1875): 297–301.

Harris, Elisha. "Hygienic Experiences in New Orleans during the War." *Bulletin of the New York Academy of Medicine* 30 (September 1865): 463–79.

Hort, William P. "Remarks Connected with the Sanatary Condition of the City of New Orleans." *New Orleans Medical and Surgical Journal* 5 (1848–1849): 256–66.

Hunt, William Henry, ed. *Selected Arguments, Lectures, and Miscellaneous Papers of Randell Hunt.* New Orleans: F. F. Hansell and Brother, 1896.

In Memoriam: Henry M. Spofford. Nashville: Southern Methodist Publishing House, 1880. Louisiana Collection, Howard-Tilton Memorial Library, Tulane University.

James, Bushrod W. "How Abattoirs Improve the Sanitary Conditions of Cities." *Public Health: Reports and Papers* 6 (1880): 231–38.

Janes, E. H. "The Management of Slaughterhouses." *The Sanitarian* 2 (October 1874): 289–95.

———. "Sanitary View of Abattoirs and the Slaughtering Business in New York" *Public Health Reports and Papers* 3 (1877): 1–31.

Jewell's Crescent City Illustrated. New Orleans: Edwin L. Jewell, 1873.

Kane, Elisha Kent. *The United States Grinnell Expedition.* New York: Harper and Co., 1853.

Lincoln, Abraham. *Collected Works.* Edited by Roy P. Basler. Vol. 5. New Brunswick, N.J.: Rutgers University Press, 1953–1955.

Nordhoff, Charles. *The Cotton States in the Spring and Summer of 1875.* New York: n.p., 1876.

Parton, James. "Chicago." *Atlantic Monthly* 19 (March 1867): 325–45.

———. *General Butler in New Orleans.* New York: Mason Brothers, 1864.

Picornell, J. M. "Considérations Hygiéniques sur la Nouvelle-Orléans." In P. F. Thomas, *Essai sur la Fievre Jeaune d'Amérique.* New Orleans, 1823. Rudolph Matas Medical Library, Tulane University.

"Report of the Medical Community of Louisiana Regarding Measures to Be Taken to Insure the Salubrity of New Orleans." New Orleans, June 4, 1816. Louisiana State Museum Library, New Orleans.

Simonds, J. C. "On the Sanitary Condition of New Orleans as Illustrated by Its Mortuary Statistics." *Southern Medical Reports* 2 (1850): 204–46.

———. "Report of the Hygienic Characteristics of New Orleans." *Transactions of the American Medical Association* 3 (1850): 267–80.

Tiedeman, Christopher G. *A Treatise on the Limitations of the Police Power.* St. Louis: H. Thomas Law Book Co., 1886.

NEW ORLEANS NEWSPAPERS
Bee (L'Abeille)
Commercial Bulletin
Crescent
Daily Crescent
Daily Picayune
Daily States
Item
Price-Current and Commercial Intelligencer
Republican

States-Item
Tagliche Deutsche Zeitung
Times
Times-Democrat

MANUSCRIPTS AND ARCHIVAL MATERIAL
Department of Archives and Manuscripts, Earl K. Long Library, University of New
    Orleans
    Louisiana Supreme Court Archives
Eugene C. Barker Texas History Center, University of Texas, Austin
    William Pitt Ballinger Papers, Box 2A201, Folder April, 1873
Louisiana Division, City Archives, New Orleans Public Library
    Journal of the Minutes and Proceedings of the Board of Assistant Aldermen,
        1852–1869, 1870–1897
    New Orleans Board of Assistant Aldermen, *Minutes*, vol. 21 (1866)
    City Council. Calendar of Petitions, Protests and Ordinances, vol. 3 (1854–1866)
    "Names and Addresses of Business People in the City of Jefferson: 1870" (manu-
        script)
    City of Jefferson, Louisiana, Board of Aldermen, *Minutes*, vol. 3 (1861–1868)
    Judiciary Collection (District Court Records, Orleans Parish)
Louisiana State Archives, Baton Rouge.
    Louisiana State Board of Health, *Minutes*, 1866–1870
Southern Historical Collection of the University of North Carolina Library
    Groner Family Papers
    Henry Clay Warmoth Papers
    Campbell-Colston Papers
    Henry Groves Connor Collection
Illinois State Historical Library, Springfield
    David Davis Family Papers, 1816–1943
New Jersey Historical Society, Newark
    Joseph P. Bradley Papers
Library of Congress, Manuscript Division
    Jeremiah S. Black Papers
    John A. Campbell Papers
    Felix Limongi Collection
    Phillip Phillips Family Papers
Orleans Parish Notarial Archives, New Orleans
    Joseph Cuvillier Notarial Archives
    Edward Robert Hogan Notarial Archives
    Gustave LeGardeur Notarial Archives
    Selim Magner Notarial Archives
New York Historical Society
    Thomas F. Devoe Collection
    Thomas J. Durant Papers

GOVERNMENT PUBLICATIONS AND DOCUMENTS

Act of March 2, 1793, 21 Stat. 333.

Act of April 1, 1833, No. 96, 1833 La. Acts 117.

Act of March 23, 1867, No. 111, 1867 La. Acts 307.

Act of September 19, 1868, No. 74, 1868 La. Acts 178.

Act of March 8, 1869, No. 118, "An Act to Protect the Health of the City of New Orleans, to Locate the Stock Landings and Slaughterhouses . . . ," La. Acts (1869), 170; as amended by Act of May 16, 1877, No. 144, La. Acts (1877), 239.

Act of March 31, 1869, No. 128, 1869 La. Acts 199.

Act of March 19, 1870, No. 2, 1870 La. Acts 4.

Cable, George W. "New Orleans: Historical Sketch." In U.S. Census Office, *Tenth Census of the United States, 1880: Report on the Social Statistics of Cities*. Pt. 2, *Southern and Western States*. Comp. George W. Waring Jr. Washington, D.C.: Government Printing Office, 1887.

Debates of the House of Representatives of the State of Louisiana: Session of 1869. New Orleans, 1869.

Judiciary Act of 1787, Act of September 24, 1789, 1 Stat. 73.

Louisiana Civil Code, 1825.

Louisiana Constitution, 1868, 1879.

Louisiana House of Representatives. *Minute Book: Special Committee on the Removal of the Slaughterhouses, 1867*. Louisiana Collection, Louisiana State University Library, Baton Rouge.

New Orleans City Council. *Reports of Various Departments, April 1866–Sept. 1869*. City Archives, Louisiana Division, New Orleans Public Library.

New Orleans Common Council. *The Laws and General Ordinances of the City of New Orleans*. Comp. Henry J. Leovy. New Orleans, 1857.

———. *The Laws and General Ordinances of the City of New Orleans*. Comp. Henry J. Leovy. New Orleans, 1866.

———. *The Laws and General Ordinances of the City of New Orleans*. Comp. Henry J. Leovy and C. H. Luzenberg. New Orleans, 1870.

Official Journal of the . . . House of Representatives of the State of Louisiana at the Session Begun . . . June 29, 1868. New Orleans, 1868.

Official Journal of the . . . House of Representatives of the State of Louisiana at the Session Begun . . . January 4, 1869. New Orleans, 1869.

Official Journal of the . . . House of Representatives of the State of Louisiana at the Session Begun . . . January 6, 1871. New Orleans: A. L. Lee, State Printer, 1871.

Official Journal of the . . . Senate of the State of Louisiana at the Session Begun . . . March 21, 1867. New Orleans: A. L. Lee, State Printer, 1867.

Official Journal of the . . . Senate of the State of Louisiana at the Session Begun . . . June 29, 1868. New Orleans: A. L. Lee, State Printer, 1868.

Official Journal of . . . the Senate of the State of Louisiana at the Session Begun . . . January 4, 1869. New Orleans: A. L. Lee, State Printer, 1869.

Official Journal of the . . . Senate of the State of Louisiana at the Session Begun . . . January 2, 1871. New Orleans: A. L. Lee, State Printer, 1871.

U.S. Census Bureau, *A Compendium of the Ninth Census, June 1, 1870*. By Francis Walker, Superintendent of the Census. Washington, D.C.: Government Printing Office, 1872.

Secondary Sources

BOOKS

Amar, Akhil Reed. *The Bill of Rights: Creation and Reconstruction*. New Haven, Conn.: Yale University Press, 1998.

Baughman, James C. *Charles Morgan and the Development of Southern Transportation*. Nashville: Vanderbilt University Press, 1968.

Benedict, Michael Les. *A Compromise of Principle: Congressional Republicans and Reconstruction*. New York: W. W. Norton, 1974.

Bruchey, Stuart. *The Roots of American Economic Growth, 1607–1861*. New York: Harper, 1968.

Butterfield, Herbert. *The Whig Interpretation of History*. London: G. Bell and Sons, 1951.

Caldwell, Steven. *A Banking History of Louisiana*. Baton Rouge: Louisiana State University Press, 1935.

Carrigan, Jo Ann. *The Saffron Scourge: A History of Yellow Fever in Louisiana, 1796–1905*. Lafayette: University of Southwestern Louisiana, 1994.

Celebration of the Centenary of the Louisiana Supreme Court, March 1, 1913. New Orleans, 1913. Louisiana Division, New Orleans Public Library.

Chambers, Henry E. *A History of Louisiana*. Vol. 3. Chicago: American Historical Society, 1925.

Clark, John G. *New Orleans, 1718–1812: An Economic History*. Baton Rouge: Louisiana State University Press, 1970.

Clemen, Rudolf A. *The American Livestock and Meat Industry*. New York: Ronald Press, 1923.

Current, Richard N. *Those Terrible Carpetbaggers*. New York: Oxford University Press, 1988.

Curtis, Michael K. *No State Shall Abridge: The Fourteenth Amendment and the Bill of Rights*. Durham, N.C.: Duke University Press, 1986.

Cushman, Claire, ed. *The Supreme Court Justices*. Washington, D.C.: Congressional Quarterly, 1983.

Dale, Edward E. *The Range Cattle Industry: Ranching on the Great Plains from 1865 to 1925*. Norman: University of Oklahoma Press, 1960.

Dictionary of American Biography. New York: Charles Scribner's Sons, 1935.

Dodd, Donald B., comp. *Historical Statistics of the States of the United States*. Westwood, Conn.: Greenwood Press, 1993.

Duffy, John. *A History of Public Health in New York City, 1625–1866*. New York: Russell Sage Foundation, 1968.

————. *The Sanitarians: A History of American Public Health*. Urbana: University of Illinois Press, 1990.

————. *Sword of Pestilence: The New Orleans Yellow Fever Epidemic of 1853*. Baton Rouge: Louisiana State University Press, 1966.

————, ed. *Rudolph Matas History of Medicine in Louisiana*. 2 vols. Baton Rouge: Louisiana State University Press, 1958.

Evans, Clement A. *Confederate Military History*. Vol. 10. Wilmington, N.C.: Broadfoot, 1899; reprint, 1988.

Fairman, Charles. *Mr. Justice Miller and the Supreme Court, 1862–1890*. Cambridge: Harvard University Press, 1939.

————. *Reconstruction and Reunion, 1864–88*. New York: Macmillan, 1971.

Foner, Eric. *Reconstruction: America's Unfinished Revolution: 1863–1877*. New York: Harper and Row, 1988.

Friedman, Lawrence M. *American Law in the Twentieth Century*. New Haven, Conn.: Yale University Press, 2002.

Gillson, Gordon E. *Louisiana State Board of Health*. Vol. 1, *The Formative Years*. Vol. 2, *The Progressive Years*. New Orleans: Louisiana State Board of Health, 1967.

Goldman, Robert M. *Reconstruction and Black Suffrage*. Lawrence: University Press of Kansas, 2001.

Green, George D. *Finance and Economic Development in the Old South: Louisiana Banking, 1804–1861*. Stanford, Calif.: Stanford University Press, 1972.

Hair, William Ivy. *Bourbonism and Agrarian Protest: Louisiana Politics 1877–1900*. Baton Rouge: Louisiana State University Press, 1969.

Hall, Kermit L., ed. *The Oxford Companion to the Supreme Court of the United States*. New York: Oxford University Press, 1992.

Hamlin, Walter B. *A History of the Courts in the Parish of Orleans*. New Orleans: n.p., 1950.

Hovenkamp, Herbert. *Enterprise and American Law: 1836–1937*. Cambridge: Harvard University Press, 1991.

Hyman, Harold M. *The Reconstruction Justice of Salmon P. Chase*. Lawrence: University Press of Kansas, 1997.

Hyman, Harold, and William Wiecek. *Equal Justice under Law: Constitutional Development 1835–1875*. New York: Harper and Row, 1982.

Kane, Elisha Kent. *The Second Grinnell Expedition*. Philadelphia: Childs, Peterson, 1856.

Kendall, John S. *History of New Orleans*. 3 vols. Chicago: Lewis Publishing Co., 1922.

Kens, Paul. *Justice Stephen J. Field: Shaping Liberty from the Gold Rush to the Gilded Age*. Lawrence: University Press of Kansas, 1977.

Kutler, Stanley I. *Judicial Power and Reconstruction Politics*. Chicago: University of Chicago Press, 1968.

Lonn, Ella. *Reconstruction in Louisiana*. New York: G. P. Putnam's Sons, 1918.

Lurie, Jonathan. *Law and the Nation.* New York: Alfred A. Knopf, 1983.

Marke, Julius J. *Vignettes of Legal History.* South Hackensack, N.J.: Rothman, 1965.

McCoy, Joseph G. *Cattle Trade of the West and Southwest.* 1874. Reprint, Ann Arbor, Mich.: University Microfilms, 1966.

McPherson, James M. *Battle Cry of Freedom: The Civil War Era.* New York: Oxford University Press, 1988.

Miller, Ben Robertson. *The Louisiana Judiciary.* Baton Rouge: Louisiana State University Press, 1932. Reprint, Baton Rouge: Claitor's, 1981.

Nelson, William. *The Fourteenth Amendment: From Political Principle to Judicial Doctrine.* Cambridge: Harvard University Press, 1988.

Nevins, Allan. *The War for the Union: War Becomes Revolution 1862–1863.* New York: Charles Scribner's Sons, 1960.

North, Douglass C. *The Economic Growth of the United States, 1790–1860.* Englewood Cliffs, N.J.: Prentice-Hall, 1961.

North, Douglass C., and Robert Paul Thomas, eds. *The Growth of the American Economy to 1860.* Columbia: University of South Carolina Press, 1968.

Novak, William J. *The People's Welfare: Law and Regulation in Nineteenth Century America.* Chapel Hill: University of North Carolina Press, 1996.

Osgood, Ernest S. *The Day of the Cattleman.* Minneapolis: University of Minnesota Press, 1929.

Paludan, Phillip. *A Covenant with Death: The Constitution, Law and Equality in the Civil War Era.* Urbana: University of Illinois Press, 1975.

———. *The Presidency of Abraham Lincoln.* Lawrence: University Press of Kansas, 1994.

Reed, Merl E. *New Orleans and the Railroads: The Struggle for American Commercial Empire, 1830–1860.* Baton Rouge: Louisiana State University Press, 1966.

Reinders, Robert C. *End of an Era: New Orleans, 1850–1860.* New Orleans: Pelican Publishing Co., 1964.

Riordan, William L. *Plunkitt of Tammany Hall.* Edited by Terrence J. McDonald. Boston: Bedford Books, 1994.

Rosen, George. *A History of Public Health.* New York: MD Publications, 1958.

Rosenberg, Charles E. *The Cholera Years: The United States in 1832, 1849, and 1866.* Chicago: University of Chicago Press, 1979.

Schwarz, Oscar. *Public Abattoirs and Cattle Markets.* Edited by G. T. Harris and Loudon M. Douglas. London: Ice and Cold Storage Publishing Co., 1903.

Skaggs, Jimmy M. *The Cattle Trailing Industry: Between Supply and Demand, 1866–1890.* Lawrence: University Press of Kansas, 1973.

Smillie, Wilson G. *Public Health: Its Promise for the Future.* New York: Macmillan, 1955.

Smillie, Wilson G., and Edwin D. Kilbourne. *Preventive Medicine and Public Health,* 3rd ed. New York: Macmillan, 1965.

Taylor, Joe Gray. *Louisiana Reconstructed, 1863–1877.* Baton Rouge: Louisiana State University Press, 1974.

Towne, Charles W., and Edward N. Wentworth, *Cattle and Men.* Norman: University of Oklahoma Press, 1955.

Tunnel, Ted. *Crucible of Reconstruction: War, Radicalism and Race in Louisiana.* Baton Rouge: Louisiana State University Press, 1984.

Urofsky, Melvin, ed. *The Supreme Court Justices: A Biographical Dictionary.* New York: Garland, 1994.

Vandal, Gilles. *The New Orleans Riot of 1866: Anatomy of a Tragedy.* Lafayette: University of Southwestern Louisiana, 1983.

Vincent, Charles. *Black Legislators in Louisiana during Reconstruction.* Baton Rouge: Louisiana State University Press, 1976.

Wade, Louise Carroll. *Chicago's Pride: The Stockyards, Packingtown and Environs in the Nineteenth Century.* Urbana: University of Illinois Press, 1987.

Warmoth, Henry Clay. *The Louisiana Live Stock Industry from an Investment Standpoint.* New Orleans: Louisiana Company, 1917.

―――. *War, Politics and Reconstruction: Stormy Days in Louisiana.* New York: Macmillan, 1930.

Warren, Charles A. *The Supreme Court in United States History.* Vol. 2. Boston: Little, Brown, 1926.

White, G. Edward. *The Marshall Court and Cultural Change, 1815–1835.* New York: Oxford University Press, 1991.

Wiecek, William M. *The Lost World of Classical Legal Thought: Law and Ideology in America, 1886–1937.* Oxford: Oxford University Press, 1998.

Williams, W. F., and Thomas T. Stoute. *Economics of the Live Stock-Meat Industry.* New York: Macmillan, 1964.

Yeager, Mary. *Competition and Regulation: The Development of Oligopoly in the Meat Packing Industry.* Greenwich, Conn.: Jai Press, 1981.

ARTICLES

Beth, Loren P. "The Slaughterhouse Cases Revisited." *Louisiana Law Review* 23 (1963): 487–505.

Cachan, Manuel. "Justice Stephen Field and 'Free Soil, Free Labor Constitutionalism': Reconsidering Revisionism." *Law and History Review* 20 (2002): 541–76.

Carlton, Mark T. "The Louisiana Constitution of 1974." In *Louisiana Politics: Festival in a Labyrinth,* ed. James Bolner. Baton Rouge: Louisiana State University Press, 1982.

Carrington, Paul D. "The Constitutional Scholarship of Thomas McIntyre Cooley." *American Journal of Legal History* 41 (1997): 368–99.

Curtis, Michael K. "Historical Linguistics, Inkblots, and Life after Death: The Privileges and Immunities of Citizens of the United States." *North Carolina Law Review* 78 (2000): 1071–151.

―――. "Resurrecting the Privileges and Immunities Clause and Revising the Slaughterhouse Cases without Exhuming Lochner: Individual Rights and the Fourteenth Amendment." *Boston College Law Review* 38 (1996): 1–106.

Duffy, John. "Pestilence in New Orleans." In *Past as Prelude: New Orleans 1718–1968*, ed. Hodding Carter. New Orleans: Tulane University, 1968.

Franklin, Mitchell. "The Foundations and Meaning of the Slaughterhouse Cases, Part I." *Tulane Law Review* 18 (October 1943): 1–88.

———. "The Foundations and Meaning of the Slaughterhouse Cases, Part II." *Tulane Law Review* 18 (December 1943): 218–62.

Hamilton, Walton H. "The Path of Due Process of Law." *Ethics* 48 (April 1938): 269–96.

Harris, Francis B. "Henry Clay Warmoth: Reconstruction Governor of Louisiana." *Louisiana Historical Quarterly* 30 (April 1947): 1–133.

Hovenkamp, Herbert. "Technology, Politics and Monopoly." *Texas Law Review* 62 (April 1984): 1263–311.

Howe, Mark DeWolfe. "Federalism and Civil Rights." Pamphlet of lecture delivered November 19, 1965. Massachusetts Historical Society, 1965.

Labbé, Ronald M. "New Light on the Slaughterhouse Monopoly Act of 1869." In *Louisiana's Legal Heritage*, ed. Edward F. Haas. New Orleans: Louisiana State Museum, 1983.

———. "That the Reign of Robbery Will Never Return to Louisiana: The Constitution of 1879." In *In Search of Fundamental Law: Louisiana's Constitutions, 1812–1974*, ed. Warren M. Billings and Edward F. Haas. Lafayette: Center for Louisiana Studies, University of Southwestern Louisiana, 1993.

Lurie, Jonathan. "Mr. Justice Bradley: A Reassessment." *Seton Hall Law Review* 16 (1986): 343–75.

———. "One Hundred and Twenty Five Years after *Slaughterhouse:* Where's the Beef? *Journal of Supreme Court History* 24 (1999): 269–81.

Parmet, Wendy E. "From Slaughterhouse to Lochner: The Rise and Fall of the Constitutionalization of Public Health. " *American Journal of Legal History* 40 (1996): 476–505.

Ross, Michael. "Justice for Iowa: Samuel Freeman Miller's Appointment to the United States Supreme Court during the Civil War." *Annals of Iowa* 60 (2001): 111–38.

———. "Justice Miller's Reconstruction: The Slaughterhouse Cases, Health Codes, and Civil Rights in New Orleans, 1861–1873." *Journal of Southern History* 64 (1998): 649–76.

Schmidhauser, John R. "The Justices of the Supreme Court: A Collective Portrait." *Midwest Journal of Political Science* 3 (1959): 1–57.

Tribe, Lawrence. "Pursuing the Pursuit of Happiness." Review of *A New Birth of Freedom: Human Rights, Named and Unnamed*, by Charles L. Black, Jr. *New York Review of Books*, September 24, 1998, 30–35.

Tunnel, Ted. Review of *No Easy Walk to Freedom: Reconstruction and the Fourteenth Amendment*, by Leonard Levy. *American Historical Review* 103 (1998): 1326–27.

White, G. Edward. "Salmon Portland Chase and the Judicial Culture of the Supreme Court in the Civil War Era." In *The Supreme Court and the Civil War*, ed. Jennifer M. Lowe. Washington, D.C.: Supreme Court Historical Society, 1996.

Wildenthal, Bryan H. "The Lost Compromise: Reassessing the Early Understanding in Courts and Congress on Incorporation of the Bill of Rights in the Fourteenth Amendment." *Ohio State University Law Journal* 61 (2000): 1051–173.

————. "The Road to Twining: Reassessing the Incorporation of the Bill of Rights." *Ohio State University Law Journal* 61 (2000): 1457–528.

UNPUBLISHED THESES AND PAPERS

Ballard, Patrick. "Strangled in the Crib? Or Proper Limitations? Another Look at the Slaughterhouse Cases." Research paper, Samford University Law School, 1995.

Binning, Francis W. "Henry Clay Warmoth and Louisiana Reconstruction." Ph.D. diss., University of North Carolina, 1969.

Dudziak, Mary L. "The Social History of the Slaughterhouse Cases: The Butchers of New Orleans and the Sacred Right of Labor." Research paper, Yale University, 1983.

Hildreth, Flora Bassett. "The Howard Association of New Orleans, 1837–1878." Ph.D. diss., University of California, Los Angeles, 1975.

Jones, Howard J. "The Members of the Louisiana Legislature of 1868." Ph.D. diss., Washington State University, 1975.

Porter, Alice Theresa. "An Economic View of Ante-Bellum New Orleans: 1845–1860." Master's thesis, Tulane University, 1942.

Price, Byron. "The New Orleans Market for Texas Beef, 1821–1867." Paper delivered at the annual meeting of the Western History Association, October 1979. Mimeo.

Ross, Michael A. "Justice of Shattered Dreams: Samuel Freeman Miller, the Republican Party and the Supreme Court." Ph.D. diss., University of North Carolina, 1999.

Weidner, Paul A. "Justices Field and Miller: A Comparative Study in Judicial Attitudes and Values." Ph.D. diss., University of Michigan, 1958.

INDEX

Page references in italics denote illustrations.

slaughterhouses as, 46–47, 47 n.33,
60 n.80

Oaths, loyalty, 174, 180, 182
Offal
  correct disposal of, 40
  dumping, 6–7, 38, 44
  1866 health ordinance on, 6–7, 22,
    56–57
  fines for, 121
  Jefferson City ordinances on, 121
  Louisiana State Board of Public
    Health on, 54
  transporting, 62, 63
  water supply and, 42, 61, 63
Ogde. See Gibbons v.
Ogden Slip, 44
Oliver, A. J., 84–85, 88, 90, 99
Opelousas Courier, 232, 234
Orbeck. See Hicklin v.
O'Reilly. See Berthof v.

Packard, Christophe C., 94
Packwood, Robert T., 85 n.83, 88
Page, John, 92
Parmet, Wendy, 3 n.5
Peck. See Fletcher v.
Peckham, Rufus, 14, 14 n.36, 249
Pennsylvania. See Prigg v.
*Pensacola Telegraph Co. v. Western
  Union Telegraph Co.*, 239–40
People's Welfare, The (Novak), 42–43
Philips, Philip, 153
Physico-Medical Society, 30
Picayune. See Daily Picayune
Pickles, Jonas, 85 n.83, 87, 90, 96, 98,
  162
Pickwick Club, 87
Pochelu, Raymond, 51–52, 55, 63–64
Police, Metropolitan (New Orleans),
  140–41, 148, 149–50
Police power
  Allen on, 204, 205 n.90

Belden on, 128
Bradley on, 146, 147, 240
Carter on, 120
  in *Chicago v. Rumpff*, 44 n.23, 45, 45
    n.28
Commonwealth v. Alger on, 42–43
constitutional limits on, 184–85 n.5
definition of, 32 n.60
Durant on, 198–99, 202
Field on, 222–23, 226, 227
Fourteenth Amendment and, 4, 5 n.9,
  10, 13, 13 n.32, 15
  vs. judicial authority, 49
Ludeling on, 133
Marshall on, 10, 198
*Metropolitan Board of Health v.
  Heister* on, 49, 50
Miller on, 10, 12, 210–11, 231 n.75,
  246, 249
post civil war usage of, 247–48
property rights and, 42–43, 50–51
  n.48
public health and, 32, 33, 37
scope of, 41
state precedents for, 244
Polk, James, 169
Pope, William, 92
Population
  of Louisiana, 66
  of New Orleans, 19
  of the United States, 18
Pratt, Franklin J.
  arrest of, 141–42
  Butchers Benevolent Association suit
    and, 112
  Civil Rights Act of 1866 violations
    and, 142
  Crescent City Company
    incorporation and, 85 n.83, 88–89
  Inbau, Aycock and Co. and, 119
  injunctions against, 121
  motion to dismiss and, 165
  occupation of, 86, 86 n.91
  stock received by, 98